Magnus C. Granath

Searching for the Promised Land

Basildon and the Pursuit of Happiness

GoldStar Books

Searching for the Promised Land

First published in Great Britain in 2004
by
GoldStar Books, Bexleyheath, Kent DA7 6QB, England
www.goldstarbooks.co.uk

British Library Cataloguing in Publication Data
A CIP catalogue record for this title is available from the British Library

ISBN 1-904976-00-X

Printed by Palladian Press Ltd, Colchester, Essex, England

To my father. Greatly missed

I wrote this book with the intention of amusing myself. If it amuses others then I am happy.

To dream of vast horizons of the soul
Through dreams made whole,
Unfettered, free ... help me!
All you who are dreamers too,
Help me to make
Our world anew.
Langston Hughes.

Go East, young man.
After Horace Greeley.

The cover picture features the Mother and Child Statue that was erected in 1962 and was adopted as the official symbol of Basildon New Town in 1984.

Contents

Preface

I am convinced that every person, if they think hard enough and know how to relate their experiences to the outside world, has at least one book within them.

On my fiftieth birthday in 2002, I decided to write a book as a birthday present to myself. I gave myself exactly one year and settled for the idea that what could not be written down within a year was not worth writing. I finished writing on the day of my fifty-first birthday in 2003.

Although I met my target, I would argue that this book has actually taken me fifty years to write. I could not have written it when I was thirty; I could not have written it when I was forty, and I doubt if I could have written it when I was forty five.

The usual problem with historians and political commentators is that they are handicapped by the fetish of scholarship and the belief in objective truth. They tend to write books and articles on very narrow subjects that are only read by a proof reader and a doting mother.

I had no intention of writing a book that would not be read. I wanted to write an unruly book that has, to use the words of John Locke, *'been spun out of my own coarse thoughts'*. Whether or not it is unruly enough depends on the judgment of others. It would be even more unruly if I was not constrained by the boundaries of decency and fairness, the fear of causing offence to my friends, and the tyrannical laws of libel. Underlying the narrative may be seen the fears of Chidioc Tichborne that; *'I saw the world, and yet I was not seen.'*

As John Milton wrote, three hundred and fifty years ago, in Areopagitica: "Books are not absolutely dead things, but do contain a potency of life in them to be as active as that soul whose progeny they are…"

Introduction

What is written without effort is, in general, read without pleasure.
Samuel Johnson

In 1776, Thomas Jefferson, the author of the American Declaration of Independence, told us that all of mankind have an inalienable right to the pursuit of happiness. Jefferson, in turn, was building upon the ideas of Englishman, John Locke who, a hundred years previously, had first argued the existence of a natural law that gave inalienable rights to men, amongst which were life and liberty.

Uncomfortably, Jefferson owned somewhere in the region of two hundred black slaves upon whose labours he depended for his gentlemanly existence. Although he was aware of the contradictions of his position, it did not prevent him buying and selling slaves for profit on his Monticello estate.

James Hubbard, one of Jefferson's more awkward slaves, discovered that the pursuit of happiness was little more than a distant fantasy. When he was captured after running away, Jefferson had him 'severely flogged' and then sold him.

Jefferson also fathered at least one child by another slave, Sally Heming, a fact that should cause us to sit up and take notice of the contrast between 'what great men say' and 'what great men do'. Such facts illustrate not only the complexity of human character but also demonstrate there is no straight line between the outpourings of a great and original mind and the way society develops. On the whole, it is probably most useful to look upon Jefferson as a shameless, opportunistic scoundrel rather than an elevated liberal intellectual.

Despite this minor, but rather awkward, diversion it is undeniable that Jefferson was chief among those who, in the second half of the eighteenth century, watered the tree of liberty and infected Western Europe and the Americas with the idea that we all have an inalienable right to fulfilment in our lives.

Although Jefferson may have put this great and overwhelming objective into words, there has existed, in every generation and in every society through the whole of human history, a group of people who are not content with the status quo. However, they did not have the eloquence of the third American president.

In an authoritarian or totalitarian state such people learn to internalise their discontent and somehow live a different life through the richness of their imagination. In an open liberal democracy where people can, by and large, do what they want if they observe the law, then they are free to try to build another life for themselves outside the mainstream orthodoxy.

Britain, with its liberal tradition of relative openness, tolerance and pluralism, provides a rich list of those who have attempted, through their own efforts, free from the influence of the state, to create a better world for themselves. The two key impulses for this movement were the religious and political upheavals and persecutions of the 16th and 17th centuries, and the industrialisation and urbanisation of the 19th century.

The religious motive led to the formation of such groups as the Scrooby Separatists – extreme Puritans from remote Lincolnshire who, in the early 17th Century, set sail for a new life in Holland. The same impulse led to the formation of separatist communities such as the Amish and the Hutterites in the rural parts of North America. The political imperative of the English Civil War led to the formation of the Diggers with their espousal of a primitive agrarian communism.

Industrialisation and the increasingly impersonal nature of society accelerated the desire to find alternative ways of living. At New Lanark, Robert Owen tried to demonstrate that industrialisation and the factory system did not always need to be a brutish and dehumanising process.

The Agapemonites, the free love cult of the second half of the nineteenth century based in Clapton, on the cusp of East and North London were a reaction to the increasing rigidity of the nuclear family. The 'back to the land' aspirations of the Chartists in the mid-nineteenth century, the William Morris-inspired arts and crafts colonies of the late-nineteenth century, and the Garden City Movement, as exemplified by Letchworth at the beginning of the twentieth century, were all manifestations of that pure desire to find a better way of life.

Significantly, in varying degrees, they all signalled a belief that government had little role in the process beyond allowing people to shape their own lives. All are a testament to the endless struggle of the human spirit.

Beneath the authoritarianism that even the most benign of governments exhibit, there lies a hidden world of individuals and groups who refuse to accept the conventional mores of society and are determined to live life on their own terms.

The Pioneers sprung out of this tradition. They were a group of mainly working class men and women who moved to Basildon New Town between 1949 (when the town was founded) and 1957. They were not a formal political party, more a loose grouping of ethical socialists who, in the light of austerity and post-war housing shortages, made the collective decision to move to the new Essex town, thirty miles east of London.

They were socialists in an old-fashioned mutualist sense although in some ways it would be easier to leave the 'S' word out. It reflected the immediate post-war optimism, the spirit of the age, rather than a statement of practical intent. It is important not to confuse socialism with an active collectivist state. One of the tragedies of the past hundred years is that socialism has become equated with an overarching, regimented and intrusive government. The Pioneers lay outside that tradition. Most of them would view a Labour government as simply another variety of state collectivism little different from the Conservative government it probably succeeded.

A small advertisement in a 1948 edition of Tribune was enough to bring the original Pioneers together. They came from disparate backgrounds but they were united by a belief that, through their own efforts and by applying the principles of mutual aid, they could make a better life for themselves. In Basildon, they reasoned, there would be houses and jobs and, above all, the chance to form a community of their own.

They were not overtly political although most, if not all of them, would have accepted the label 'socialist' in its broadest sense as a reasonable description of their outlook. Most of them came from backgrounds of the Communist Party, the Labour Party and the Independent Labour Party which, up to the 1930s, remained a significant political force. A few of them had been in the Socialist League, some had been part of the Social Credit Movement and at least one of them had been with Wal Hannington's Unemployed Workers Movement.

One of the couples remembered the ruthless application of the means tests in the 1930s, which had driven their mother to subsist in a dirty lodging house torn from the family home. Another had fought as a young man in the Spanish Civil War and retained vivid memories. All had powerful residual memories of the poverty and hardship of the 1930s and the inability and unwillingness of governments, both Labour and Conservative, to address the needs of ordinary people.

The Pioneers settled in the older eastern side of Basildon town on the Fryerns Estate, most arriving in the two years following 1949. They comprised no more than fifty families, all living within a three quarter mile radius of each other in the respectable solid red brick houses that were constructed in the early 1950s. They held normal jobs and pursued reasonably normal lives within the confines of their beliefs. They were not exclusive and neither were they highly political in a conventional sense. They were bound together by memories of the 1930s privations and then the war years. They believed the election of a Labour Government in 1945 would bring about the building of a New Jerusalem. In a very real and practical way, Basildon was to be their New Jerusalem.

In most ways the Pioneers were normal members of the industrial working class. They had jobs, they took a week's holiday every year at Clacton, or a similar resort, they lived in nuclear families in their council houses, they watched Sunday Night at the London Palladium, they did the football pools, they had toast and dripping for Sunday afternoon tea and they subscribed to a Co-op funeral plan.

They did not live together communally, they did not wear dark blue Mao suits, they had no leader and they did not have any overwhelming ideological commitment. They did, however, nurture a sense of working class destiny and solidarity that told them living in close proximity, supporting each other and exercising a healthy degree of contempt for all the manifestations of state authority, could improve the circumstances of their lives.

Chapter 1: Just what is Socialism?

Socialism is what the Labour Party does.
Herbert Morrison.

This party is a moral crusade or it is nothing.
Harold Wilson. 1962. The year before he became Labour Party leader.

Until almost a hundred years ago, this was a question that only demanded the vaguest of answers concerning such abstract ideals as social equality and universal brotherhood. To socialists, it meant the fight against injustice and an end to the tyrannies of poverty, disease, squalor, war and ignorance. Exact definitions were not a problem as long as the dreamers remained at the margins of power.

During the first half of the last century, the question was being asked more seriously because the people who had been the utopian idealists now found themselves in power. In Russia it was the result of a violent revolution while in most of Western Europe the march of the people was facilitated by the ballot box.

Whether it was the Russian Bolsheviks in 1917 or Clement Attlee's Fabian-inspired post-1945 Labour government, all had to ask themselves the same very basic question: what was socialism and how would they implement it? Unfortunately they came to some very different conclusions.

*

If you aspire to the socialist ideal of a better way of life for ordinary people, then there are three possible courses of action.

Firstly, you can participate in a revolution that will probably be bloody, will proclaim a dictatorship of the proletariat and then, twenty years later will almost certainly be worse than the system it replaced. This is known as scientific socialism and the experiences of the past eighty years suggest that it will always result in mass human suffering. My very modest experience of the consequences came in 1977 when I stayed in Warsaw for a few weeks. A few doors away from the city centre hotel where I was staying, was a shop packed full of western luxury goods. Curtains in the front windows prevented ordinary Poles seeing what they were being denied. This was a dollar shop, so called because dollars were the only currency it accepted. In typically communist fashion, it was only open to western businessmen and diplomats, and to elite members of the Communist party – the nomenclature.

I observed those sleek communist party officials, and their squat peasant wives plastered in garish make up, clasping cartons of Marlboro cigarettes. I looked to my host for explanation of this injustice in a socialist society. He replied with a shrug and a knowing smile that said: "This is the way of the world no matter how it is organised. There will always be rich and poor, privileged and the dispossessed. Do not worry about it."

The trouble is I did – and I still do.

Around the corner was a shop for ordinary Poles where, in the good times, they could buy hard bread that was almost impenetrable to ordinary teeth, together with dried sausage and masses of jarred pickled vegetables. More often than not, the shelves were simply empty. This was what the noble ideal had sunk to. I went back to Poland last year, ten years after the start of its capitalist experiment. Again there were shops full of western goods that were only open to the elite but now it was an elite based upon wealth and criminal connections rather than membership of a political party. For ordinary Poles, it is still pickled cabbage and dried sausage followed by Sobieskie cigarettes rather than Marlboro.

As the saying goes, at least these shops are open to anybody, just like the Ritz Hotel. In the communist era, they had the decency to hide from view what the poor were being denied. Now it is part of the nature of capitalism to rub the faces of the dispossessed in what they cannot have. The idea is that it infects them with aspiration.

A little further east to the Russia of the Brezhnev era in the late 1970s, a small number of top party functionaries and elite Kremlin officials had cars that sported a licence plate which effectively gave them freedom from all traffic regulations. The rest of the population either walked or they drove battered Moskovichs for which petrol was sometimes available. Today, after thirteen years of something like capitalism, the situation is much worse. Moscow's Kutzovosky Prospect is now a speedway for luxury western cars cruising down a reserved lane. The users are the wealthy businessmen and mafia crime bosses who can afford ten thousand dollars to buy one of the new 0-00 plates that gives the freedom of the road to a small and privileged elite. The roads are full of the cars of Duma Deputies, Kremlin officials and lowly functionaries who have gained access to the licence plates denied to the rest of Russia. Ordinary Muscovites still driving ancient battered Ladas and Moskovichs, are consigned to the unreserved slow lanes.

The Mercedes of the new elite are, in many cases, heading for the gated communities of Zukovka and Barvicha that have become the secure hangouts for the new rich worried at the lawlessness and insecurity that unbridled capitalism has released. The depressing conclusion, for ordinary Russians, is that it makes little difference what sort of government is in power.

Not that double standards was the sole prerogative of the old Soviet-style socialism or the brave new Russia. In late 1986, I boarded a British Rail train from Ipswich to Liverpool Street. The standard class carriage (what does it say about our society that we divide people into first class and standard class?) was extremely full and almost all the standing room was taken as well. The adjacent first class carriage was empty except for the veteran left-wing Labour MP, Eric Heffer, accompanied by his wife Doris. He was reading the Times as he ate his sandwiches and drank his coffee. Heffer was one of those unreconstructed socialist left-wingers who have now almost disappeared from the Labour Party. He was a John Prescott for the 1970s but without the charm, intellect and public speaking abilities.

Mr Heffer was a bullying bruiser, a champion of the working class, and a defender of Militant Tendency at the 1986 Labour Party Conference. Yet he did not seem unduly concerned that his comrades on the railways were crammed into standard class while he lounged in first class. This was in the days when first class was sacrosanct and it was not possible to buy a supplement to the standard class ticket. A few bolder members of the standard class carriage, including myself, moved into first class to the obvious irritation of Comrade Eric who tutted and rustled his newspaper at our loud complaints about British Rail. It may be that my travelling companions recognised Mr Heffer from his performance when he had stormed out of the Labour Party Conference a few months earlier in protest at Neil Kinnock's rather flatulent speech attacking Militant Tendency.

Unfortunately, one of our party had had too much to drink and recognised the left-wing firebrand. He was not subtle or restrained in his criticism. "Oi Heffer you socialist ****. What are you doing in first class?" Here was drunken, lager-swilling John Bull, Sun-reading England juxtaposed with a brand of doctrinaire ideological socialism that we have never really been comfortable with. It was not a pleasant sight. Mr Heffer did not enter into an ideological debate along the lines that "as I have been issued with a free first-class House of Commons rail pass it is my socialist duty to travel in a first class carriage in order to make the accommodation in proletarian standard class less crowded." Instead he went in search of protection. A few minutes later he returned with a ticket inspector and pointed in the direction of our group.

It is difficult to imagine what the conversation was like.

"He called me a socialist ****. I don't travel first class in order to be called a socialist ****. I'm a Member of Parliament, you know."

"Perhaps it falls into the category of fair comment, sir," the inspector might have replied.

For the rest of the journey we argued good-naturedly against the inspector's demand that we all buy first-class tickets. Eventually, as the train approached Liverpool Street, we went back into standard class and left Comrade Heffer to get on with his Times.

The second road to socialism is that you can support and vote for a party that claims to represent the interests of ordinary people and will pass legislation to make life for ordinary people fairer. This is called parliamentary socialism. All it requires is that you vote every four or five years and give them some money. If you say that you want to be involved and that, through political campaigning, you want to help bring about a more just society, then you will be firmly rebuffed. These sorts of socialists, or perhaps more accurately, social democrats, (if we are feeling generous towards them), will tell you that capitalism is a good thing but that it just has to be tamed and controlled to ameliorate its worst effects.

Some of them – Peter Mandelson, for example – will tell you that they are 'intensely relaxed' about people becoming 'seriously rich' provided that not too many people become 'seriously poor'. His friends tell us that there is such a thing as the social market where the forces of the free market can be harnessed for the good of everybody.

For the last thirty years we have been arguing about whether such a modest aspiration merits the name socialism. Is it just one of a number of political variants for allowing the rich to keep their money and remain in that happy state while pretending we are pursuing a fair and just society? It is part of the lexicon of these people who are to be found mainly, but not exclusively, on the right of the Labour Party that left-wingers (i.e. socialists) are really the new conservatives because they hanker after a past when governments really did try to create a fairer society, in the days when Labour was not quite so terrified of the Daily Mail. In this world, conservative has become an all-purpose world used to describe anything that does not concur with their views. It is all very confusing.

In pursuit of the truth of these matters, I have developed a minor masochistic hobby of going to hear Tony Blair speak (four times in the past two years). In response to a question posed, he claimed, without blushing, halting or obvious embarrassment, that he was a socialist. On other occasions I have heard him say that he believes in socialist values.

Perhaps Mr Blair has answered the question that George Orwell wrestled with more than sixty years ago when writing about the excesses committed in the Soviet Union in the name of socialism. "Can you have socialism without liberty, without equality and without internationalism?" It would appear that the answer in this new ABC of socialism to each of those three fundamental questions is 'yes'.

Watching Mr Blair speak, and listening to what he had to say, I was struck by the sense that here was a man who was burdened down by his own sense of righteousness and destiny. Beneath the smiles and the charm, there lies a deeply authoritarian character who is intolerant of the views of others when they are not identical to his own. If he had been born into another country and another age, he would have had the capacity to be a terrifying zealot; one of those appalling figures from the European Reformation, a fanatic clothed in the language of reason. He could equally have been a Savonarola, burnt at the stake in late fifteenth century Florence for criticising papal excesses; an Ignatius Loyola, the founder of the Jesuits endowed with a fierce and destructive piety, or a Thomas More, Henry VIII's Chancellor, a credible but dangerous fanatic prepared to go to the block and sacrifice his own life with the same alacrity as he sacrificed the lives of others.

I find Mr Blair particularly alarming when he dresses himself in the garments of reason to explain his case but his eyes burn with the conviction of the zealot. Human nature does not change and there is little reason to think that our political leaders, if they were transported five hundred years back into the past, would not have been burnt and beheaded with the best of them.

However, for all my suspicions of Mr Blair, I feel forced to defend him against the charge that he has betrayed the socialist cause. If we examine the core values that comprise democratic socialism then the record is quite reasonable. The nod in the direction of communitarianism reflects an interest in fraternity while the use of child tax credit and child benefit signals a very significant redistribution of wealth towards the working poor. There is also an admirable determination to tackle the problems of the NHS and a dysfunctional state education system that can only benefit the vast majority of the population. The New Deal for the unemployed represents a revival of the old socialist ideal of the dignity of labour. The introduction of the minimum wage has not lead to the collapse of the British takeaway pizza industry in the way that the Conservatives and the CBI predicted.

The traditional socialist faith in the capacity of the state to solve deep-seated human problems remains. But somehow it does not seem enough. Where is the inspiration to create the New Jerusalem? Where are the socialist dreamers in the government or are we always destined to be ruled by grim-faced, market-led, pragmatists?

New Labour is struggling against the grain. The rampant consumerism of the last twenty years presages an intensely individualistic philosophy that no government of the future will be able to counter. Once the twin forces of aspiration and the free market had been released from Margaret's Box, it was always inevitable that it would not be possible to put them back again.

The third socialist alternative is that you can live your life free from political parties and pseudo-scientific ideas pretending to be political philosophy. Through developing yourself as an individual, it is possible to achieve self-realisation through self-education which in turn will benefit those around you. You can try, through your daily actions and the way that you structure your life, to create a freer and more just society within your community. This is called ethical socialism.

A belief in the sovereignty of the individual is not incompatible with a commitment towards the ideals of community and fraternity. Such a viewpoint and ideal has a long and honourable history. There is a continuous thread going back nearly seven hundred years of ways in which the Common People, as the historian G.D.H. Cole termed them, have struggled to be the masters and mistresses of their own destiny. More than 600 years ago, John Ball, the radical priest, told the peasants on the outskirts of London:

> When Adam delved and Eve span
> Who then was the gentleman?

What must once have been a pleasant spot in the countryside surrounding the city is now the Balls Pond Road in Hackney. It is an area of poverty and deprivation interspersed with pockets of wealth. Only a few miles away, in Islington, Hampstead and the City, there is almost unimaginable wealth and yet, on the spot where John Ball preached, the question that he asked is now more relevant than ever. Why are some high and some low? Why do some have more wealth and material goods than they can ever spend in a lifetime, while others survive the day-to-day ordeal of grinding poverty? Why do one third of children live in poverty when we are one of the richest countries in the world? The fact that little has changed can either be interpreted as meaning that inequality and unfairness is an integral part of the human condition, or that government-inspired collectivism has failed. But this supposes that governments hold the solution to such problems.

An alternative is to look upon it as a means of structuring, enriching and ordering one's life in order to create a sea change of attitudes that will give individuals the confidence to address their problems.

Peering back over the past four hundred years at the intellectual and emotional roots of the Socialist Pioneers, it is the Diggers of the period of the English Civil War who stand out. Reading about Gerrard Winstanley and William Everard, and all those who aspired to a fairer life, it is clear that, if any of the Socialist Pioneers could have transported themselves back from 1960s Basildon to the year 1650, they would have felt entirely at home with their new companions and their aspirations. During the ferment of the English Civil War, Winstanley, Everard, and about forty companions took over the uncultivated common land at St George's Hill in Surrey and proclaimed that the land was rightfully theirs by virtue of their use of it.

Winstanley posed the fundamental question: "Was the earth made to preserve a few covetous, proud men to live at ease, and for them to bag and barn up the treasures of the earth from others, that those may beg and starve in fruitful land; or was it made to preserve all her children?"

Today we are struggling to answer the same question and are no closer to providing an answer. We live in a society in which, no matter what the government, the few are encouraged to 'bag and barn up the treasures of the earth' to the exclusion of the general good. The Diggers were extreme religious pacifists and agrarian communists. Like the Pioneers they did not have an overt political programme. To use the phrase of the historian, R.H. Tawney, theirs was the 'doctrineless communism of the open field'.

Their experiment met with hostility from the landowners and the Commonwealth and, by 1651, they had been driven away from St George's Hill and the area around Cobham. Their small community was broken up, although it is significant that many of their number, including Winstanley, went on to found the Quakers. Winstanley was a driven man, tormented by fears of what he would, or would not, achieve in his lifetime. He agonised over whether those who he led would follow him in creating a new world, or whether their timidity would master them.

> All men have stood for freedom…and now the common enemy has gone you are all like men in a mist, seeking for freedom and know not where nor what it is: and those of the richer sort of you that see it are ashamed and afraid to own it, because it comes clothed in a clownish garment…. For freedom is the man that will turn the world upside down, therefore no wonder he hath enemies.

There is perhaps a tendency to romanticise the radical past and to ascribe modern day materialist motives. It is just possible though to see in the Diggers the beginnings of a social and world outlook that is beginning to reflect a modern mindset. Peering through the glass we start to see the stirrings of an inchoate sense that within each of us lies the divine spark of the individual.

It is deeply ironic that St George's Hill now lies in the middle of the very exclusive and very private, Wentworth Estate. Living behind high gates, protected by private security guards, driving down private roads and playing on their private golf courses, the wealthy inhabitants worry about their fellow citizens. They worry that the rabble outside the closeted kingdom will invade St George's Hill just as Winstanley and his

Diggers did three hundred and fifty years ago.

This is a strange un-English kingdom of the Pringle-sweater-wearing classes where the security guards have security guards. It is a Bermuda Triangle into which the very rich discreetly disappear and hide amongst the groves and thickets of sandy coniferous Surrey.

It is a land of elderly game show hosts who wear brightly-coloured slacks and terrible wigs; a place where Prince Andrew finds that he is amongst his own kind. It is a land of the sort of comedians that you will not find at the Edinburgh Fringe; a place where you might expect Ronnie Corbett to emerge from a hidden driveway in a golf buggy. This is the England of pro-am golf tournaments where Jimmy Tarbuck might tee off with Peter Allis and where, in a few year's time, Sir Mick Jagger will be wafting his driver. Following him down the fairway will be a threesome of anonymously wealthy Americans.

To the north there is a polo ground and to the south a military golf course. To the east, on the wrong side of the M25, lies Thorpe Park, that monument to containing the masses. Meanwhile the elderly gentlefolk of Wentworth roll their putts over manicured greens, free from the fear that a taxi driver will stub his cigarette out on the green while shouting "Fuck it!" when he misses a putt. It does not feel like England at all.

In 1999, the good folk of Wentworth experienced another rather more welcome invasion. They provided hospitality for the odious General Pinochet and his entourage during the ex-dictator's recent enforced stay in England. They even welcomed Mrs Thatcher to Wentworth when she came to express her gratitude to the former dictator of Chile and mass murderer. A fondness for grisly dictators always seemed to be the Iron Lady's worst weakness.

In 1999, I sent ten pounds to the Digger Fund to help pay for a memorial that was to be erected on the spot where, three hundred and fifty years before, Winstanley and his followers first broke the ground.

The rich and privileged folk of the Wentworth Estate objected and the spot remains unmarked. It is acceptable in those parts to give succour and comfort to a torturer and murderer, but it is unacceptable to acknowledge the role of forefathers who gave comfort and hope to the poor and the dispossessed. The world may be starting to turn upside down but it will not be happening on the Wentworth Estate.

I want to dislike the houses on the Wentworth Estate but I cannot. The architecture has a homogeneity and an integrity that is sadly lacking in

Hadley Wood, an area of similar wealth near to Barnet where I live. Most of this is due to the efforts of Walter Tarrant, a speculative Byfleet builder with some business acumen who, in 1911, purchased 964 acres of land from the Egerton family. It became the St George's Estate.

The First World War intervened but, in the 1920s and 30s, the heath and conifer were gradually replaced by the manicured residential semi-countryside of the rich. With his own brick factory, cement and ash works, a timber mill, and a joinery workshop in Byfleet, Tarrant was able to produce houses in the Surrey vernacular style of a quality that eludes modern builders with their modern-day addiction to stud partition and breeze block. Even the normally sniffy Pevsner concedes that they are 'completely delightful'.

Despite the tendency to ascribe the Surrey ideal to Edwin Lutyens, it is Tarrant who more accurately reflects the twin Surrey characteristics of money and a desire for something that looks like the countryside without all the muck and inconvenience. Tarrant's mistake was to endow each of his beautifully-crafted houses with generous grounds.

Lacking conservation orders, they are constantly under the eye of greedy builders and rapacious estate agents ever eager to offer a development that is 'the last word in sophisticated modern living'. Of the four hundred or so houses on the St George's Estate, only one hundred are Tarrant originals while most of the rest are the result of some rather vulgar infilling: Tuscan villas and American colonial mansions rub shoulders with the more traditional Surrey idylls as new money tries to muscle in on one version of understated Old England

There is something about Surrey that hangs heavy on the heart. It is a county that has been taken over by London money and it has lost any distinctive soul that it ever had. To run through that list of London dormitories – Woking, Walton-on-Thames, Cobham, Leatherhead, Dorking, Reigate and Epsom – is to witness the victory of London over the countryside. The inhabitants of the council estates of Guildford may not agree, but there is something that reeks of unearned privilege about Surrey. It has allowed itself to become the embodiment of stockbroker England and golf club fascism.

John Betjeman was right;

> Miss J. Hunter Dunn, Miss J. Hunter Dunn,
> Furnish'd and burnish'd by Aldershot sun.
> What strenuous singles we played after tea,

We in the tournament - you against me.

The scent of the conifers, sound of the bath,
The view from my bedroom of moss-dappled path,
As I struggle with double-end evening tie,
For we dance at the golf club, my victor and I.

The Hillmans, Austins and Rovers may have been replaced in the golf club car park by Mercedes and BMWs but Surrey today remains the same sort of county that it was sixty years ago.

Nearly two hundred years ago that journalist of undiluted genius and defender of Old England, William Cobbett, expressed the fear that Surrey, the county of his birth, would succumb to the Great Wen in London, the incubus that drains and weakens all around it. Cobbett was right to be fearful. The victory of the city over the country is now complete. Surrey has become a husk.

With the creation of London County Council in 1888, London sliced away its northern reaches along the Thames. It then threw a net on small dormitory towns that lie within the shadow of London to the south and west, before girding it with a lattice of motorways and dual carriageways upon which run the BMWs and Mercedes of the Surrey class of person.

Conifer County of Surrey approached
Through remarkable wrought-iron gates.

It is the wrought iron gates of the private estates that stick in the mind's eye. They are a denial of the ideal of equal citizenship, a visible symbol that in the twenty-first century we have become afraid of each other. Having been forcibly ejected by security guards from the Wentworth Estate and, as one who was born in Surrey, I feel qualified to make these assertions.

One of the more delightful pleasures of reading H.G. Wells' 1898 novel, *The War of the Worlds*, is that it involves the destruction of Surrey. Who could not thrill to the news that Leatherhead had disappeared in a ball of fire and ash and that desperate battles with the invading Martian forces were being fought across the towns that nestle in the North Downs within the shadow of London?

I cannot accept that it was coincidence that the battery fire that brought down the Martian machines was launched by the men of St George's Hill, hidden in the pine woods. Once again it was a beacon of hope to the people of England. Wells was a man of Kent, a county equally deserving of the Martian X-ray treatment. A basic loyalty prevented him from conjuring up Martian machines striding across the Kentish Weald destroying Sevenoaks, Maidstone and Tunbridge Wells. I suspect there was something in his vaguely socialist nature that compelled him to decree the destruction of the enclave of unrefined privilege that Surrey represented. He could have chosen anywhere in England, but he chose Surrey.

Close to my home there lies in Friern Barnet the brooding symbol of the containment of London madness – the old Colney Hatch Lunatic Asylum. It has now become one of those vaunted, gated communities built for twin-income, thirty-something couples complete with manicured parklands and leisure health centre. In some parts of Britain we are only one step away from American style corporate management communities where life is regimented to the extent that residents are fined for parking an 'unbecoming vehicle' for 'hanging curtains of an unapproved colour' or the 'asymmetrical placement' of a dustbin.

In Friern Barnet the half life of the madhouse has been substituted for the half life of 'the community of the future (with secure parking)'. The building is a mid-Victorian mock gothic wonder. Built one hundred and fifty years ago on the very edge of London, it is a vast complex that must have housed many hundreds of people. It was the receptacle into which the great city to the south decanted its broken and damaged.

And where have all the mad people gone now? They have been decanted out into the community. Are they now wandering the streets in their pyjamas and dressing gowns or have we all become sane?

The old madhouse has been renamed Princess Manor Park by Comer Homes. It sounds like an East London arterial suburb. I cycle in on a warm autumn morning. The security guards, cosy in their little hut wearing yellow day glow jackets, eye me suspiciously. This is unauthorised physical activity. The health and leisure centre is the decreed area. There is something written in the deeds that we have to ingress and egress the property in a small sporty Peugeot or an Audi Coupe. My dilapidated bicycle with a missing front mudguard does not fit the identikit occupant profile.

The young woman at the sales office is charming, small, dark, petite and vivacious. I would have bought an apartment from her but I suppose that is the intention. She promises me a lifestyle revolution, the chance to experience gracious living in the London suburbs if I choose to become a resident of Princess Manor Park.

As I leave the office I notice that she has caught sight of the bicycle clip on my right leg. I hide my finger nails that are still full of grease from when the chain came off. Cycling back out through the gates with the glossy brochure strapped to the rear rack, the security guards stare at me quizzically.

Returning to the events in Surrey three hundred and fifty years ago, the prescient Winstanley observed of their efforts: "And now I must wait to see the Spirit do his own work in the hearts of others…" Granted the gift of immortality, he would still find himself waiting today.

I cannot say with any confidence that any more than a few of the Pioneers would have been aware of the Diggers. It is only during the last thirty years that the new-agers and eco-warriors have claimed them for their own. Their fate before that was to suffer the condescension of posterity. The fact that I see so much of the Pioneers in their Digger ancestors reminds me of what William Morris wrote in *A Dream of John Ball*.

> …I pondered all these things, and how men fight and lose
> the battle, and the
> Thing
> That they fought for comes about in spite of their defeat,
> and when it comes turns
> Out not to be what they meant, and other men have to fight
> for what they meant
> Under another name…

There lies within all of us the need to create that shimmering city in the distance that we call a better life. We will never achieve it, of course, because we define and alter it as we go along. The important point is that we continue to aspire. Some see it just for themselves while others want to create it for those around them. They know that the struggle will never be won for it is part of the human condition to be always looking for what lies just beyond the horizon.

The original Diggers certainly were less than fifty in number and, given the way population increases through the generations, there must be tens of thousands of people in this country and, indeed, scattered all around the world who are the direct descendants of the original Diggers.

Average persons, however, can only trace their ancestry back three generations while less than five per cent of the population can trace back more than five generations. Typically, the Diggers lie thirteen generations back. In the intervening years, the winds of history have blown over and buried the roots that all of us have in the past.

There is a tendency to talk of the Diggers and Levellers as if they were the same thing. They were not, of course, but such is the looseness of our thought and language, probably because contemporaries referred to the Diggers as True Levellers to indicate the extreme nature of their communist views.

The Levellers emerged during the tumult of the mid-1640s when the world was truly turned upside down and men and women no longer knew their place in the world. Unlike the Diggers, who were weak and few in number, the Levellers, at their peak, were a formidable force, given their influence within the ranks of that remarkable organisation, the New Model Army.

By 1645 the King had been defeated and some of the radicals were beginning to suggest that the new order should be truly representative of the people. As the great and irrepressible Leveller leader, John Lilburne, wrote: "The poorest that lives hath as true a right to give a vote as well as the richest and the greatest."

The gentry, those who had risen as a result of the war, were unimpressed. They had not deposed a king only to pass their new won power over to the unlettered masses. Lilburne and his supporters were convinced they were the victims of the war. "All you intended when you set us a'fighting," Lilburne told the Lords, "was merely to unhorse and dismount our old riders and tyrants that you might get up and ride in their stead."

It is difficult not to draw the same conclusion with the Labour government that came to power in 1997. The voters were exhorted to unseat the old riders and now they find that those who ride in their stead are not so different. It would seem that, within the framework of the conventional nation state and the way that it is governed, this will always be the fate of the 'Common People'. Competing elites will seek the legitimacy of popular election but they will, with a few minor variations of emphasis, pursue the same policies as their predecessors.

Leveller influence within the New Model Army grew to the extent that the fate of England and the direction of the Civil War now rested upon a power struggle within the army. At the Putney Debates, the Leveller, Colonel Rainborough, uttered the famous words: "The poorest he that is in England has a life to live as the greatest he; and therefore truly sir, I think it clear that every man that is to live under a government, and I do think that the poorest man in England is not at all bound in a strict sense to that government that he had not a voice to put himself under." These words echo down the centuries.

We have now had universal suffrage for the past seventy years yet it appears that the radical Colonel Rainborough was mistaken. He forgot about human nature. Our society remains as divided and unequal as ever. Even more dispiriting, people are disengaged from the political process in a way that would have staggered even the Levellers.

A survey in 2002 indicates that only one person in ten can name five members of the cabinet while nearly half can name the finalists in *Big Brother*. It should be a matter of the deepest concern that the public have become disengaged from the political process.

The reasons are complex but that is not a reason to neglect attempts to discover them. No society can remain a proper democracy on current levels of involvement. A high degree of apathy and indifference suits government which, on the whole, can then get on with its business without feeling any obvious obligation of accountability.

This government seems to think that allowing citizens to cast their votes in supermarkets will solve the problem. People vote when they think it will make a difference. If we think back to the first post-apartheid election in South Africa in 1994, we get a vision of what the process would be like in an ideal society. People queued excitedly for twenty-four hours to vote because they thought it would improve their lives. Five years later in 1999 there were no queues. Despite the absence of white rulers, ordinary black South Africans realised that poverty and hardship were their inherited lot whichever way they voted. In the gap between the first and second post-apartheid elections, voter turnout fell from 86 per cent to 63 per cent. The purpose of democracy is to empower people but the reality is that it emasculates them. I suspect that most politicians would prefer indifference and apathy to a new generation of Levellers demanding that the world be turned upside down.

When Lilburne prophesied that "posterity ... shall reap the benefit of our endeavours, whatever shall become of us" we understand what he is saying but it is difficult to believe, with any certainty, that the sort of society we have today is the one that John Lilburne and his fellow Levellers envisaged.

The staggering thing about the Levellers is that they existed for less than three years as an organised political force and they had to start from scratch. There were no pre-existing organisations on which to model their programme yet they seemed very modern with their use of lobbying petitions, mass demonstrations, and their own propaganda newspaper, *The Moderate*. Their leaders – Lilburne, Richard Overton, William Walwyn and Agitator Sexby – were men of high intellect, drive and ability but, in an illiterate society dominated by the parson and the squire, they were doomed to failure.

Each day I feel obliged to wear a tie for work and most days I make a point that goes unnoticed so you might judge it to be worthless. Despite my socialistic leanings, I never wear a red tie. Instead I wear a variety of sea green ties – sea green being the colour of the Levellers.

Even the brewers are inspired. I attended a minor beer festival recently with the intention of sampling McMullen's Gladstone bitter, as the great man remains one of my political heroes. I was intrigued to see a micro-brewery offering Leveller Ale and I felt obliged to have a pint. It was thick, dark and malty and, I suspect, it would have levelled me had I not exercised some moderation.

Historians argue about how democratic and egalitarian the Levellers really were, and debate about whether they really wanted to extend the vote to the lowest in society. This is somehow to miss the point that they gave hope and expression to the poor, the dispossessed and the excluded, whatever may have been their precise intentions. They also struck fear into the new establishment. As Cromwell cynically put it: "If a Commonwealth must needs suffer, it should rather suffer from rich men than from poor men."

I would argue that it has been suffering thus ever since. Unfortunately the examples of countries suffering the government of 'poor men' do little to inspire the belief that life would be any better under their rule. The Levellers have retained their power to inspire both hope and fear in equal measure.

Tony Benn, in his diaries, records how, in 1971, he arranged for a newly-elected Labour MP, who had been a university history lecturer, to give him a private tutorial on the Levellers. That must have been nice. It was a moment of personal revelation for him. He had no idea of the radicalism of the Leveller demands for annual elections, a peoples' parliament, universal suffrage, and the right to a full and fruitful life for all. Four years later, Benn attended a Digger anniversary celebration at Burford in Oxfordshire and the rest, as they say, is history.

That was the moment the scales fell from his eyes and he saw, for the first time, the sense of historical continuity that his political struggle embodied. It was a significant step on the road from being Minister for Technology, and the man who brought us Concorde, to emerging from the chrysalis as the moral conscience of the idealistic left.

History teaches us some dangerous and powerful lessons. During the late 1980s, when the Conservative government of Mrs Thatcher was agonising over what sort of history should be taught in the National Curriculum, a series of letters appeared in the Times advocating the sort of history that can be summed up as Elizabeth I, Waterloo and Trafalgar.

"Otherwise," one correspondent warned, "we shall have a generation of school children who have been taught no more than the Peasants' Revolt, the Levellers, and Human Rights."

Chapter 2: Not for the first time, I died in Basildon

Hold fast to dreams,
For if dreams die
Life is a broken winged bird
That cannot fly.
Langston Hughes.

JG: Magnus do you have many friends in Basildon?
MCG: Everybody in Basildon is my friend.

In the poem, *Zima Junction*, the Russian poet, Yevgeny Yevtushenko, says: "Breaking the earth in our new found land, we were dizzy with joy and dreams." Yevtushenko is referring to the Virgin Lands experiment in the Soviet Union of the early 1960s when groups of eager young communist pioneers were sent to open up the vastness of the Russian lands to the east of the Ural Mountains.

It was like that when we moved, in 1958, to Basildon in the flatlands of south Essex. Instead of the vast tractor plant at Magnitogorsk, we had Ford Tractors at Cranes Farm. For the harvester plant at Chelyabinsk, we had York Shipley in Nevendon. The SovCom workers housing project was substituted by the Basildon Development Corporation. We were part of a vast scheme in social engineering on a scale that Britain had never previously seen. However, instead of tilling the virgin earth we sweated on the light industrial estates making cigarettes for Carreras, perfume for Yardleys, and television valves for Marconi.

The official version has it that the Cockney population were bombed out of the East End by the Luftwaffe during the war and that it was an act of kindness to move them out. This, combined with ruling class guilt over the privations suffered during the depression of the 1930s, began the impulse to create a New Jerusalem for the working class once hostilities ended.

The Beveridge Report of 1942 had created the blueprint for this new and better society. Sir William spoke of slaying the five giants of ignorance, want, sickness, idleness and squalor in the creation of this new society. With the election of Clement Attlee's Labour Government in 1945, the opportunity came to create the New Jerusalem along Soviet planning lines. At this time it was still not realised just how inefficient centralised systems of socialist state planning were.

The real reason for the move east was that, for the Great and the Good of 1945, the East End was an infestation to be ignored; a moral sewer, hopelessly beyond any form of redemption. It was a symbol of a working class that was both degraded and beyond the control of the state.

The answer, according to Sir Patrick Abercrombie's Report of 1948, was to build new towns on the thinly populated lands around London. The impulse was to wipe the slate clean and start again in the belief that a morally improving environment would create a morally improved person.

Visit any new town, high-rise tower block, the old Birmingham Bull Ring or Edmonton Green Shopping Centre to see the truth of this belief. See if the politicians, the planners and the architects who made the crucial decisions lived anywhere near their creations.

It is now too late to travel to Portsmouth to see the Tricorn Centre, a perfect example of 1960s neo-brutalism. The demolition crews beat you to it. Arguably the ugliest building in Britain, the Tricorn was a symbol of urban dislocation. Designed by Owen Luder, one of the post-war architects determined to inflict a concrete heritage on Britain, its fractured modernism epitomises the failures of a state-sponsored brand of corporate architecture.

Ted Bryant was that rarest of individuals, an architect with the integrity to live in one of the houses he had designed for the swarming masses of the new town. It was something of a novelty knowing the man who had designed our house. He stood out as an educated and cultured man who had enjoyed a distinguished career designing public housing in Liverpool and Sheffield. Then he spent five years living amongst the Pioneers in a small terraced house in Basildon before continuing his work, designing high-quality public housing in Manchester.

The architects were damned either way. If they lived among us, they were considered to be patronising; if they scuttled away at high speed from creations that were good enough for others but not good enough for them, they were criticised.

This was the era of Le Corbusier, the Swiss-born intellectual and architect who prophesied the megalopolis: soaring concrete structures in the sky housing millions of people in inhuman geometric symmetry, all made possible by the development of new building materials.

Le Corbusier may have been an intellectual but he had only the most limited understanding of human nature. Along with many of his Corbusierite disciples, he should have been tried for crimes against humanity. The only excuse for their work could be that such thinking was typical of the mid-twentieth century view that the state could plan and provide for the needs of the masses without considering what they actually wanted. Instead, the orthodoxy was prescribing what the experts perceived to be a necessity; a mindset that we are still struggling to get away from.

The political and social orthodoxy of the day was that better homes, particularly those built in the fresh air away from London, would make better people. The impulse was not a new one and it had been given paternalistic form with the construction of New Lanark, Saltaire in Bradford and Bourneville in Birmingham, one hundred and fifty years previously.

The ideal was given a clearer middle class shape in 1876 with the construction of the Arts and Craft Movement-inspired Bedford Park by Norman Shaw in West London. This was followed by building Hampstead Garden Suburb in the decade before the First World War under the inspiration of Henrietta Barnett. Both suburbs are now the haunts of the rich and are the opposite of the socially-mixed communities that their creators intended.

These experiments were followed by laying out the Hertfordshire Garden Cities of the 1930s – Welwyn and Letchworth, under the inspiration of Ebenezer Howard. These were built on the spacious principle that 'a garden is irresistible to a man of a wholesome mind'. Here a new way of life could be pursued free from the constraints of the grimy city with the spirit uplifted by the congruence of spaciousness and pleasing design. By the 1930s, Letchworth, in particular, had acquired a reputation for what George Orwell rather contemptuously called 'sandal and nuts' socialism. It was the Letchworth ILP Summer Schools, with their espousal of progressive utopian ideas, that goaded Orwell into his famous denunciation (in *The Road to Wigan Pier*) of 'every fruit juice drinker, nudist, sandal wearer, sex maniac, Quaker, Nature Cure quack, pacifist and feminist in England'.

For Orwell, the Letchworth middle class socialist was summed up by the two men who got on his bus while riding through the town. 'They were dressed in pistachio-coloured shirts and khaki shorts into which their huge bottoms were crammed so tightly that you could study every dimple. Their appearance created a mild stir of horror on top of the bus. The man next to me murmured, "Socialists" as who should say "Red Indians"'.

Every generation has its discontented minority looking for a different way of life. In the 1930s, they flocked to Letchworth, particularly those who had tired of the tyranny of the 'meat and two veg' diet of the inter war years. By 1935 the town boasted seven vegetarian restaurants at a time when the whole of London could barely muster the same number. For the 'simple lifers' who flocked there, the principle was even more simple – 'more air, less alcohol'. For Orwell, a meat-eating, chain-smoking, beer-swilling despiser of middle-class socialists, the lure of Catalonia must have seemed irresistible.

The garden cities – socialist and otherwise – provided the impulse for the cluster of new towns ringing London that were constructed in the fifteen-year period after the Second World War. The major difference was that Ebenezer Howard and Henrietta Barnet had been substituted for a 'we know best' state.

In hindsight it is difficult to share the optimism of the early planners in relation to human nature. During the past three years, I have visited Basildon, Bracknell, Harlow, Stevenage, Cumbernauld, Crawley, Skelmersdale, Hemel Hempstead, Milton Keynes, Peterlee and Washington. All of them are products of the New Town movement.

Those architects in Peterlee, committed to building houses with flat roofs using 'non-traditional building materials', might reflect on the reasons why, for the past two thousand years, houses have been built from stone or brick with an apex roof. These towns have, in general, but with some exceptions, resulted in a degradation of the environment. This is despite the fact that, in a minority of cases at least, attractive housing has been built using good quality materials.

The inhabitants have not always responded in kind. I recently walked along Stockwell High Road in South London past a social housing project that was low-rise, brick-built, and pleasing to the eye. Less pleasing to the eye was the graffiti on the walls, the smashed windows, the fencing that had been broken down, and the drug users' needles that had been left on the ground. For all the quality of the brick-built environment there was an air of despair. It is the sort of place where a pit bull terrier comes free with the housing benefit.

A recent visit to the new social housing developments in Kings Lynn shows that the problem is not unique to either new towns or inner city estates. It is clear that it takes more than good design, good intentions and the use of good materials to turn some aspects of human nature around. Other factors come into play. These are principally to do with education, attitudes towards community and feelings of self-worth. It also takes a reappraisal of the relationship between the individual and the state, and some stone-cold reflection on where individual responsibilities lie.

Whatever governments think they can do, they cannot will communities into existence. Rather they need to evolve with a little nudge in the right direction by light touch planners who have some idea about human nature. I await, with some apprehension, the Thames Gateway scheme to the east of London.

It did not have to be like this. I have been a regular visitor to Holland over the past thirty years. I am attracted by its man-made, reclaimed-from-the-sea qualities, and the relaxed, humane and heroic character of the Dutch people who, for centuries, have lived on the brink of watery disaster.

Holland is not perfect but it has gone significantly further than Britain in creating a human scale, aesthetically pleasing, responsive to social need environment. In Britain over the past fifty years the design of housing, both public and private, veers between either the bombastic, as in London Docklands, or, as in most new towns, it becomes a timid, imitative homage to what has been successful in the past. A visit to the Amsterdam island suburbs of Sporenburg and Borneo is an antidote to all of this; a reminder that housing can be low-rise, human-scale, high-density, and a mixture of public and private ownership.

Not that Holland has got everything right. For those who view it as a problem-free, social democratic, progressive, rational utopia, I recommend that they visit the new town of Kampen. Built in the 1960s on the flat land of the Mastenbroek Polder, it is a place where they have tucked away their Moluccan and Surinamese communities.

With a Muslim minority of 850,000, proportionately the highest in Europe, Holland is a multicultural society that is experiencing some discomfort. By encouraging Muslim children to speak Berber, Turkish and Arabic, successive Dutch governments have helped to fire the separatism they now abhor. With Muslims topping the wrong lists of the unemployed, domestic violence, criminality and school failure, there is now a fear for what the future will hold.

The gunning down of Pim Fortuyn by an ecological activist, and a warning from the Dutch intelligence service AIVD that the al-Qa'eda network is 'steadily taking root in Dutch society', has led many in Holland to feel uncomfortable with the practice of holding up their country as a shining example of liberal integrationist good practice.

London Docklands is an example of what can be achieved when government and the private sector do not have to worry about irritants like the poor. It also acts as a warning about the dangers of unrestrained, money-led demand in the formulation of housing policy. It is quite simply the grimmest, most soulless place in Britain, completely devoid of community: the symbol of an atomised society. The residents in their million pound penthouse flats hide behind their security gates and entry phones not knowing who lives above or below. It is difficult to walk along the empty streets of Dockland without feeling a sense of lost opportunity. Twenty years ago, there was an opportunity to create a dynamic, vibrant, mixed community that would serve the needs of inner London. Instead, there are only lonely streets and the smell of money.

However, there is some hope in Britain. In Manchester and Liverpool, the housing association, Urban Splash, has avoided the temptation to build boring breeze block houses on green fields in the search for easy profits. Instead, it is building attractive and innovative housing in areas of urban regeneration.

In York, the Joseph Rowntree Housing Trust is leading the way in a project that it hopes will prove private and social housing can be mixed and can make a profit. This assumes, perhaps naively, that better housing will make better people. Unfortunately, any housing project that is peopled by dysfunctional and anti-social individuals is doomed to failure.

Interesting developments are underway at West Malling, in Kent. The massive King's Hill Housing Estate is attempting to create the intimacy of the village atmosphere by holding the motor car at arm's length. It is not an organic community but, with twenty nine different house styles, it is not bland suburbia or a pullet cage, Brookside-style development. In the Sunley Homes section, timber-framed buildings are springing up that are factory-manufactured in Canada and assembled on site. They look very attractive but I worry for the future.

In Hackney, the Raines Dairy project comprises twenty-nine flats built in a factory and then assembled on site in five days. Supporters of these innovative developments say we must not keep harking back to the mistakes of the past. "Why not?" I always reply. The past is not only the best guide that we have to the future, it is our only guide. God made houses out of bricks and mortar for good reason. With the current generation of homes manufactured off-site (prefabs sounds too down-market) we have no idea what the future holds. They look wonderfully seductive, with state-of-the-art air circulation systems, anti-allergy timber treatments, solar heating and floor to ceiling glazing. What will the maintenance demands be in fifty years time? And will they still be standing one hundred years from now?

The simple answer is that no one knows. Experts tell us that we need to build 250,000 homes a year to satisfy demand, but that we only have the capacity to build 150,000 because we have huge shortages of key building workers. Therefore we have to import the products of a skilled Canadian labour force to make what we are no longer capable of producing ourselves. Where is our skilled labour force that can satisfy demand by using traditional methods?

They are, of course, all reading for degrees in Media Studies.

In Basildon, however, in the 1950s, we still lived in an age of optimism where anything was possible including building enough houses to satisfy demand. We did not know, however, that our freedom was being bought at the expense of others. We were sold the myth that the new town was built on empty, disused agricultural land waiting to be filled by those tired of London noise, dirt and overcrowding. This was a lie.

The area that today comprises the new town was a series of small towns and villages – Laindon, Vange, Pitsea, Nevendon and Basildon itself. These were viable brick-built communities containing something like twenty thousand residents, many of whom had their property taken from them with minimal compensation by a central government determined to build its New Jerusalem.

A photograph taken in 1949 shows a group of protesters gathered outside the offices that were the headquarters for those surveying the area in preparation for the announcement of new town status. Amongst their placards were 'Stop this Legalised Robbery', 'Freehold Property is our Birthright' and '1914-1918. 1939-1945 We Defended England. Now Does England Defend Us?' By a bureaucratic slight of hand land was purchased at low agricultural valuations and then sold for commercial and industrial purposes at a much higher rate

Once again the property rights of the minority were steamrollered by central government claiming to be acting in the interests of the majority. In the manner of a Chinese Communist government flooding the homes of a million people for the Three Gorges dam project in the name of the common good, the owners of legally-held freehold property found their rights stripped away. This was a soviet-style central planning with no acknowledgement of individual rights or liberties. More than five thousand people lost their property with no right of appeal. Whilst they were not sent kulak-style to some eastern gulag it could be argued that the gulag came to them.

Independent English men and women, a mid-twentieth century version of the yeomen of England, now found themselves, courtesy of the burgeoning new town, the clients of the state. The collusion between the politicians, the judiciary and the civil service ensured that one community was destroyed. It is a matter of judgment whether its replacement was in any way superior.

In the spirit of social improvement, The Becontree Estate in Dagenham had been built by the LCC in the 1930s to provide cheap labour for the Ford factory. For those who were a little more aspirational and keen to take the first hesitant steps into private ownership, the vast Harold Wood estate, an early experiment in mass owner occupancy a few miles to the north-east of Dagenham, was an ambition.

Ask the older residents of Becontree, as I have done, what they thought of being forced away from their East End roots in the name of improvement and they will tell you a sense of impotence and hopelessness was visited upon them. After the warmth and familiarity of the East End, living on the Becontree Estate became the wilderness years of their lives.

Even where the East End residents were allowed to stay put, the results were dismal. In Poplar, the activities of the Luftwaffe became the excuse for the wholesale destruction of long-established working class communities. Where once stood row upon row of mid- and late-Victorian terraces, the bulldozers moved in and flattened the whole area without a word of consultation with the residents. Occasionally the residents' voices could be heard in the background asking for the refurbishment of existing properties. Their voices were drowned out by those of ministers, planners and Fabian experts who believed in their own infallibility.

Out of the rubble emerged the Lansbury estate, a rather dismal showcase to mid-twentieth century paternalism, where ordinary people were told what was good for them.

My paternal great aunt lived a few doors away from the Snoddy family who, in 1951, amidst a blaze of publicity, became the first tenants in a development that, although well-meaning, became a denial of all that humanity and community stood for. To her dying day, my great aunt nursed the deepest regret that the destruction of her neighbourhood meant she no longer saw people she had previously seen every day of her life. It was not as though they had been bosom pals but rather that the everyday interactions that defined a community were denied to them. The people who comprised the fixtures and fittings of her life had been shorn away and she was the poorer for it.

The illusion of progress did not last long. My older cousin, Vincent, (my great aunt's son, so strictly speaking, a second cousin) was a fireman working in West Ham. In 1968 he was called to a gas explosion at the Ronan Point tower block in Canning Town. Three people had died and he helped to remove the bodies. Ronan Point, and other similar tower blocks, had been built as monuments to the vanity of a generation of post-war urban planners.

For the moment at least, the cruel deception that it was possible to humanely house working class communities vertically, rather than horizontally, was abandoned. Despite the light death toll, the disaster at Ronan Point turned into a victory for simple humanity over the bureaucrats of a dirigiste government.

On the matter of tower blocks, a simple question needs to be asked. Why, when I visit my friend, who lives in a very expensive flat overlooking Regents Park, do the lifts smell of lavender and stainless steel while the lifts in the tower blocks at Edmonton Green always smell of stale urine? Were they built that way?

Mrs Thatcher may have been wrong about many things – her hostility to trade unions, disdain for civil liberties and the encouragement of a suburban golf club mentality – but she was probably right about one thing: allowing people to own their own property encourages a sense of social responsibility resulting in a better physical environment that governments cannot replicate.

I discussed this issue with the father of a friend who spent his entire working life planning and developing Harlow New Town. My question was simple and offensive. When, and why, did it go wrong?

His answer was that the rot started in the early 1970s. The second generation of tenants did not have the same sense of commitment to the town as the original inhabitants. They did not see it as an opportunity for a better life. In 1950, the new tenants were grateful to the state. By 1970 the next generation was saying, "Is this all?" Those born in the new town had not experienced the deprivation of the East End.

"We tried to do too much. We denied them responsibility and they did not thank us for it. The paternalism of the state was taken too far." The fault, he said, lay with the planners and the civil servants for not even beginning to understand human nature. He said this, not in sorrow, or anger, but out of regret that a unique opportunity for social improvement had been lost.

Fifty years ago, in the stasis of the post-war years, it was assumed that the working class was not meant to be aspirational. Give them a watertight house, an elementary education, free health care and a modestly-paid job and the world could carry on indefinitely as if 1955 represented the end of history. Today, in the new, thrusting post-Thatcher Britain where we are all bewildered by the pace of change, it is a way of life.

*

It is difficult to overstate the optimism that was felt at the time for those who had escaped the grim cramped life of inner London. Within the authoritarianism imposed by a lack of choice, a whole new vista opened up to us. It was a grand view of gardens, parks, countryside, neat brick-built houses, open airy schools, bright modern shops and willing citizens revelling in the munificence of government – 'Bliss was it in that dawn to be alive.'

In 2003 it all looks rather different. Talking to the elderly of the town – those who arrived as young adults in the 1950s – there is now a pervasive sense of disillusionment that the dream failed to live up to their expectations. The promises of the good life have not been kept.

As Nigel Birch put it to Harold Macmillan at the time of the Profumo crisis: "Never glad confident morning again." It is now impossible to imagine that the state would ever again have the confidence and self-belief to create such a community in the hope that it could transform the quality of peoples' lives. We truly believed, fifty years ago, that it would be possible to build that shining city on the hill if we all pulled in the same direction. Lewis Silkin, the Minister for Town and Country planning, told a packed meeting in Basildon in 1948, the year before the construction of the new town began, "Basildon will become a City which people all over the world will want to visit. A place where all classes of community can meet freely together on equal terms to share common cultural recreational facilities."

Such was the optimism of what could be done. My research indicates that Mr Silkin had made an identical speech in Stevenage in 1946. The subsequent newspaper report contains the following quote – After the statement that "Stevenage will, in a short time, become world famous." – there was laughter from the audience.

*

And so we moved to Basildon, thirty miles to the east of London on the flatlands of the Thames Estuary. The area had already been the subject of two experiments in alternative living.

In the decade before the First World War, there had been a tentative attempt at a communal enterprise when Joseph Fels, the wealthy soap manufacturer, offered the use of Sumpner Farm to the Poplar Board of Guardians, in East London. The Laindon Farm Colony, as it became known, was founded with the intention that young men should be gainfully employed in the wholesome countryside away from the corrupting influence of the city.

The limits of the activities seem to have been digging a reservoir and constructing chicken sheds for the ubiquitous local poultry trade. With the coming of war in 1914, the enterprise collapsed and most of the young men volunteered to fight. For some of them, the experience of living in the Essex countryside was to be repeated with their involvement in the Plotlands community in the decades after the Great War. In turn, their children and grandchildren would become the first inhabitants of the new town that now covers Sumpner Farm.

In the years after the First World War, a generation of working class Londoners made the journey to the east. Many thousands bought a five pound plot of land from distressed farmers, and their agents, who emphasised the health-giving properties of the Essex air and the advantages of embracing the country way of life.

Several hundred bought plots from the Dunton Hills Estate that formed the core of what became known as the Plotland community. Plotlands-style residences were erected all over southern Essex from Rainham in the west to Fambridge in the east.

Whatever the defects of the Dunton/Laindon Plotlands community in terms of physical facilities, they were more than compensated for by the empowering sense of ownership that creating their own community had brought about.

It may be argued that the modern character of the southern half of Essex was moulded by this aspirational migration in the first half of the last century from some of the most deprived parts of London. Like the Diggers on St George's Hill three hundred years previously, they now owned their own little share of the riches of the earth: a small piece of England.

Responding to advertisements in newspapers like the Hackney and Kingsland Gazette, the reluctant Londoners would catch the LMS steam train out of Fenchurch Street and would alight at Laindon before walking the few miles to their plot. Those with a little extra cash would use Old Tom's charabanc for the journey from Laindon Station. Over the coming months and years, they would travel out at weekends and, using mainly scrap materials, construct their own paradise in the Essex countryside. Without proper drains and mains supplies, some of the Plotland houses, built on unmade roads, degenerated into less than perfect rural idylls attached to a septic tank.

The criticism that they were rural slums is a gross misrepresentation. Most of them were part of a neat and tidily-maintained rural paradise. With names like Iona, Hilltop, Glencrest, Maple Leaf, High Tide, Wendover and Coombe Cottage, they oozed a pride of ownership that was impossible to replicate in the vast mass of social housing built a mile to the east.

I was particularly impressed by Lansbury, in Fourth Avenue – a touching tribute to the great socialist hero of the East End. This rural idyll was built by the Young family who were East End Dockers five and a half days a week and rural pioneers in the flatlands of Essex on Saturday afternoons.

I once met one of the old Plotlands people during my wanderings of thirty-five years ago. I used to cycle out through the back roads of Laindon to the western end of the town where the Plotland community began. Old Joe had bought the plot in 1919 after returning from the Great War. He had stayed ever since.

For the first six months, Joe and his wife cycled out from Hackney at weekends on a tandem laden with tools, with materials strapped to the back. This was not so unusual. Mrs Simmonds, one of the older Plotlanders, travelled out from Plaistow on a tandem until the age of 84. For a year, Joe and his wife lived on the plot in all weathers. An old army bell tent was their home until they had acquired enough sheets of plywood, corrugated iron and timber to build the house that eventually became part of a small community of Londoners escaping the Great Wen to the west.

Some of the older residents at least recalled the assistance that the Plotlanders gave to each other while constructing their timber-framed houses. I suspect the unrestrained use of asbestos in the construction of these houses contributed to the early deaths of at least some of the inhabitants.

The house lacked mains plumbing. A bucket and a hole at the back of the plot garden was all they had. Joe explained that the house stood on ten feet of solid human dung as the contents had leached into the soil. It smelt like it.

We chatted a number of times and Joe told me that one of the best nights of his life was when they listened on a crystal set, while drinking distilled wheat moonshine, to the Welshman Tommy Farr challenging the great Joe Louis for the world heavyweight championship in America. It seemed incredible to a man born in Victorian times that he could hear a boxing match broadcast live over three thousand miles of Atlantic Ocean. He was certain Farr should have won but was robbed on points by the American judges. I looked up the fight later and learned that fight historians agreed Farr was a gallant but decisive loser.

Joe's father named him after Joseph Arch, the visionary agricultural leader from the 1860s. The name meant nothing to me at the time, but I marvelled at it later: Arch was a man who gave hope to those without hope.

Joe told me how his father had worked on the great farms near Witham in mid-Essex for a few shillings a day. The great moment in his life had been hearing Arch speak to a gathering of the poor and the oppressed. His poverty had been so intense that, as a child in the 1860s, he remembered living for months at a time on a diet of bread and raw onions.

In the years after the Crimean War, his father earned eight shillings week. A loaf of bread was one shilling! They could not afford tea so his mother would soak a crust of bread in boiling water to make an imitation of the beverage. It was against this sort of blinding, life-denying poverty that Arch spoke. Although Joe's father had been given hope, it was not enough to prevent him from dying in the workhouse and ending up in a pauper's grave. How Joe had ended up in Hackney, I did not know. Then, the distance in every sense between town and country was not the great gulf that it has now become.

I was struck by the way our lives overlap and link in. My great grandfather had been a boy servant in the household of Lord John Russell, a prominent Liberal prime minister of the mid-nineteenth century. Radical Jack, as he was known, could remember seeing Napoleon Bonaparte being taken prisoner en route to his exile in St Helena.

I, in turn, was taught at university by Conrad Russell, the great grandson of Lord John. In a vague sort of way I am therefore connected to Napoleon. Such is the continuity of history that draws and binds us all together.

When the winter came to Plotlands, Grove Avenue became impassable and I didn't visit. The following spring I went back but the house was empty and the plywood outer wall had been kicked in. Joe had died sometime between Christmas and New Year.

I pushed through the broken wall. Inside was the characteristic smell of the elderly – mothballs, furniture polish and Collis B liniment; the smell of age and poverty. I was struck by the porcelain washbowl on a mahogany stand, a reminder that these homes did not have mains plumbing. Against the far wall I found a George V half-crown piece that I still have today. When, many years later, I read George Orwell's essay, *How the Poor Die*, memories of that broken down house in Grove Avenue came flooding back.

My one regret is a minor but curious incident. Joe's older brother had died in the First World War and, more than anything else, Joe always wanted to visit his grave. When I was about twelve he told me that if I was ever in France I should visit his brother's grave and lay some flowers on it. He thought France was about the size of Canvey Island. Of course I was too young to have any sense of what he was saying and turned down the two shilling piece he offered me in the certain knowledge that I would only spend it on sweets. He told me all the details about where his brother was buried but I forgot them straight away. Now that I am familiar with the military cemeteries of Northern France, I occasionally think I should carry out Joe's wish. When time and leisure allow, I will undertake the necessary searches with the Commonwealth War Graves Commission. I owe that much to Joe's memory.

When Basildon New Town was built in the 1950s and 60s, Plotlands houses were demolished by the thousand. It is in the nature of government to resent people who show initiative, who create something for themselves that is not under the direct control of the state. The authorities propagated the myth that the whole area was a rural slum in need of demolition, that all the residents were elderly, and that the community was dying out. None of this was true.

In 1984, bullying local government pushed through a series of compulsory purchase orders that forced out the last residents and summoned in the bulldozers. It was not that the land was needed to build new social housing; it was simply that the Plotlands community did not fit in with the municipal vision of what the area should be like. Better a nature reserve than people living outside local authority planning controls.

By the August of 1984, the whole area was empty and waiting for the 'improvement' to begin. In that summer, I wandered along Hillcrest Avenue, Hilltop Rise and Glenwood Gardens. The names might have come from one of those tennis club encrusted, wealthy outer London suburbs yet all the houses were deserted, just waiting for the final destruction. They had the feel of an American Wild West ghost town from which, with great suddenness, the population had fled.

As I wandered past the neat little houses, I realised for the first time that, although the men and women that comprise government may be perfectly decent people individually, they are, collectively, given some sort of rationale, capable of acting in a grossly unjust manner. And here was the result of this misguided 'we know best' attitude.

For anyone who wishes to see a Plotland home, The Haven on Third Avenue in the Langdon Nature reserve is today preserved as a museum.

The name is a clue to the respite that such a home gave from the ceaseless energy of London. Its preservation is the local council expiating its guilt. Most of the visitors to the Museum and to what remains of Plotlands are elderly people accompanied by their families. It is clear from their gestures that they knew Plotlands when it was a flourishing community.

The most familiar sight is an elderly person stopping by a piece of scrubby land near one of the unmade tracks to indicate with hand gestures that this was where their little home once stood. Now it is just a barren plot filled with blackberry and hawthorn bushes. The accompanying families usually stand for a moment in silent reverence.

The remains now lie underneath the Langdon Country Park. The only things left are a few gateposts, piles of brick rubble and the remains of an old Anderson Shelter – relics of the hopes and dreams of thousands; this little Arcadia out in the Essex flatlands. The Archers of Canning Town, the Warren family of Bow and the Westons of Plaistow, all now gone, lie only within the confines of memory.

In my thoughts, there were only two sorts of Plotlands days; those of midsummer when it was hot and still and middle-aged men stood with their torsos burnt brick red from the sun, and those when the weather was wet and foul and the uneven, rutted roads were covered with deep puddles and the little houses seemed to sway in the November winds.

The nineteenth century historian, Thomas Macaulay, was almost right when he claimed that "An acre in Middlesex is better than a principality in Utopia." What he meant to say, of course, is that "An acre in Essex ..." It is easy to be nostalgic about a social phenomenon like the Plotlands community. It was not without fault but there was something intensely moving seeing this physical manifestation of the aspirations of ordinary people who, independent of the state, were determined to improve their lives. But is what replaced them any better?

The nature reserve, once part of Plotlands, is a reasonable social amenity. Great Berry is now an island of middle-class private housing that embodies most of the failings of modern urban planning. Lying to the west of Basildon, it is a private sector alter ego to the new town. This is Ford Mondeo land, a low rent 'Stepford Wives' suburban development serviced by a vast out of town Tesco store that stands out like a carbuncle on the Essex countryside. It is the embodiment of Blairite aspirational middle England.

In the middle of the wheat fields that lie alongside the rushing traffic of the A127 as it heads towards Newbury Park and Gants Hill, sits the archetype of how we will, increasingly, live in the 21st Century. Living in houses that resulted from the speculative activities of private building companies, the community of more than three thousand people is almost entirely lacking in social facilities. The churches, community centres, shops, pubs and parks that are necessary for any community to work are all missing. It is a community of sacrifice.

In return for owning their own house, for advancing a little further up the social ladder than their parents, for having a tidy back garden and a driveway for the Ford Mondeo (the huge Ford research plant is less than a mile away at Dunton), the sense of living in a naturally-occurring organic community has been sacrificed. It may be that the aspirational inhabitants of Great Berry have created a vibrant community but their task has not been eased by the banal thinking of those who have created their urban environment.

Three miles to the east of Plotlands, parts of the New Town are in trouble. The air of decay and depression is palpable. The reasons are complex but the core reason is because the town lacks the personal imprint of the experiences of the inhabitants. People are more likely to take a pride in where they live if they have constructed it with their own hands and had sweat pouring from their brow. In our age, this may be impractical but the lesson is that, unless people are engaged in crucial decisions as their communities are formed, any sense of ownership and engagement is likely to be minimal. This is a principle at the core of Mr Blair's communitarian vision.

Travel the road in South Essex that runs from Billericay to the north through Crays Hill, Ramsden Bellhouse and then to Wickford as it skirts around the northern environs of Basildon. This is a land of aspiration sprinkled with stardust where Essex dreams come true. The ranch-style mini-Southforks on the Thames sit in the flat and muddy clay pueblo of south Essex. This is where, last year, I bought an English bull terrier puppy from a couple so heavily tattooed that I called them (to myself of course) the illustrated bull terrier breeders. It doesn't have much of ring to it but it was accurate.

Was it my imagination or did I see Princess Anne cruising the lanes of north Basildon, hidden behind the tinted glass of her Range Rover looking for a new bull terrier? I can imagine her standing on the ranch doorstep clutching an old-fashioned handbag: "You with the tattoos, we have come about the dawg."

If Basildon is the half land, the staging post on the way out of the poverty of the East End, then the hacienda – little pieces of coastal Spain that lie to the north of the town – are the fully realised Essex nirvana.

*

After the Second World War, there was a desperate housing shortage. The construction of the new towns around London was one response. The East End of my childhood – Stepney, Bow and Bethnal Green – was filled with neat little prefabs built next to craters and bombsites. Made with an aluminium frame and complete with neat front gardens, they were only meant to last ten years but, in some cases, they have lasted up until the present time, and remain in great demand. I suspect this is because most of them were built by skilled German prisoners of war rather than the usual sloppy British workers. Of the 160,000 or so built in the immediate post-war period, just a few hundred survive.

Like the Plotland houses, they are a symbol of stunted working class aspiration. Detached from their neighbours but close enough to be part of a community, with their own front doors and gardens, the prefabs were a very English recipe for domestic contentment. The irony is that what was meant to be short-term was long lasting and popular, while what was meant to be long-term, the grim tower blocks, for example, was transient and disliked.

For connoisseurs of the prefab, the best remaining examples are in Ector Road in Catford, South London. For those in the area a reminder of the barrenness of post-war planners' imagination can be seen in the nearby Idonia Street flats in Deptford. These represent the British version of a Soviet-style attempt to provide decent housing for the workers.

A more satisfying solution to the post-war housing shortage was the Communist Party-organised occupation of palatial mansion blocks like the late-Victorian flats just to the north of Kensington High Street. Harry Olney, who briefly lived near us in Basildon, had been one of those Hammersmith King Street Communists who occupied the Duchess of Bedford Flats. The Attlee government, with its extreme tenderness towards the rights of private property, ordered the prosecution of the communist squatters. This resulted in much public sympathy for the squatters and the episode frightened the government enough to force the acceleration of the building programme for new houses.

Harry Olney and the King Street Communists were part of a generation given renewed self-confidence by the experience of war. Beaten down by poverty and unemployment in the 1930s, the final years of the Second World War and the publication of the Beveridge Report in 1942, gave the working class a new self-confidence. The Labour victory in 1945 temporarily created the illusion that the working classes were now the masters. It was, of course, a cruel piece of self-deception. Out of this ferment emerged the idea that the new post-war settlement would create a better material world and also allow the full liberating effects of education and culture to come into play. From now on, those with the ability and the inclination who were from the humbler strata of society could take their rightful place in the nation.

It was this new-found confidence that allowed the champion of the working man and woman, Nye Bevan, the Housing Minister and a man of absolute integrity, to insist that all new houses should allow the dignity of a toilet both upstairs and down. It was something of a mystery therefore that, in all the hundreds of Basildon Council houses that I lived in and visited, I never came across a second toilet.

The explanation was that the shabby and disingenuous Hugh Dalton, who succeeded Bevan in 1951, did away with the requirement on the grounds of cost. He took the view that the working classes should be grateful for having any sort of toilet, let alone two. I can imagine Dalton thundering: "Two toilets indeed, just who do they think they are?" What else can you expect of an Old Etonian socialist and the son of the private tutor to King George the Fifth?

Personally, I take the view that old Etonians should not be allowed to join the Labour Party. They are not to be trusted. I would, however, make a single exception for that fully paid-up member of the awkward squad, Tam Dalyell who is one of the last survivors of that grand, but dying, tradition, the independently-minded MP.

*

The lessons were no clearer fifty years ago than they are today. We did not realise then that it was upon the dreams of others that we built our New Jerusalem and tilled our rich earth (clinging Essex clay, as it was in our back garden.) We built ourselves a shining new country away from the teeming city and we felt like pioneers. The town was only one tenth built. Apart from a small parade of shops in Whitmore Way there were no shopping facilities. Instead, we rode in my father's Matchless motorcycle combination to Wickford. My father wore a long trench coat, goggles, gauntlets and a soft leather flying helmet. He looked like Toad from Wind in the Willows. To own and ride a motorcycle combination seemed to be an essential part of the 1950s experience. Dotted along the street were Ariel Square Fours, Panther Slopers and BSA Gold Flashes, all with enormous two-person family sidecars attached.

In the early 1960s, a motorcycle combination was an acceptable eccentricity. By the late 1960s the elderly combinations had been taken over by the sort of young men who today would be racing around in noisy modified cars glowing with eerie lights. The flight to the motor car was very rapid in the 1960s and resulted in a flood of cheap secondhand combinations on the market.

My older brother bought an Ariel Red Hunter combination for ten pounds. We removed the sidecar, attached a sturdy open wooden box in its place and, without the benefit of crash helmets, raced around the town – my brother riding the bike, while I sat in the box. I was proud to be described in a Basildon Standard editorial as a 'social nuisance of the first order'. This was before the nanny state had become excessively worried about safety although the battles over compulsory seat belts, drink driving and the wearing of crash helmets were to be fought over the next few years.

By this time many families could afford to run a secondhand Ford Anglia, perhaps a Morris Minor or a pre-war Baby Austin. Dotted in between the motorcycle combinations and the modest family cars were the equally eccentric bubble cars, those other means of budget transport that flourished up until the affluence of the mid-1960s. Heinkels, Messerschmitt and BMW, all companies central to the fallen Nazi state, made these flimsy microcars that offered an entertaining alternative to four wheeled motoring.

All were two-seaters with two alternative layouts. The BMW Isetta had two seats side by side while the passenger in a Messerschmitt sat behind the driver. I rode regularly in both and I was, and still am, convinced that the Messerschmitt, with its roaring engine and speed, was the closest sensation to flying an ME 109 without actually leaving the ground. Even now, I am struck by the irony that the success of BMW, the car of choice for the aspirant middle class, was based on the popularity of the Isetta, a bubble car aimed very firmly at the poverty end of the market.

The roads forty years ago were crowded with a much wider range of vehicles than today, even if many of the cars had one wheel less than a full set. The planners of the post-war years failed to anticipate the rise of mass car ownership during the affluent 1950s as the town was being built. The result was narrow roads with few garages, few parking spaces and large scale parking on the verges. Curiously, even after the rise of something approaching universal car ownership, the planners continued to build as if the motor car did not exist; as if the failure to provide parking would somehow will the wretched machines away.

We felt like the Waltons in *Little House on the Prairie* who had been cut off from civilisation for many months.

"Look! There's a Woolworths."

"A Woolworths!" we would chorus back.

Once while out walking with my father (it must have been around 1959) we came across a large sign in a field. It said, in bold letters. 'This is a vision of the future. On this site will be built the most modern shopping centre in Britain'.

Each day I would walk past the field and watch with fascination as the shopping centre emerged from the Thames flatlands. It was, indeed, a vision of the future but it failed to turn into that shining city upon the hill.

Today the town centre, with a variety of incongruous additions from the 1980s, is a monument to 1960s planning. It has now recovered from the corrosive Thatcher years when it was a mixture of bargain-buy shops and household chains. It is engaged in an uneven struggle with the Lakeside development, a few miles down the road. Lakeside in turn finds the life force being sucked out of it by Bluewater, built in a low-lying cement quarry, just the other side of the Dartford Crossing.

These places, displaced and dysfunctional, are the future of shopping in the southeast of England. They are nightmarish out-of-town developments, 'parking led' homages to the motor car and our consumer culture. Arriving at Lakeside on a Saturday afternoon, I experienced one of those pure 'South Essex' moments; an event that told me I was in a rather special part of the country.

A retired senior police officer had been signing copies of his memoirs in Ottakar's bookshop. The shop was crowded and the ambulance service and police were there. I made enquiries. The ex-policeman had been attacked and knocked unconscious; his blood had dripped on the carpet. It was reckless of him to brave such an environment boasting of his villain-nicking exploits. I still wonder if the attack was motivated by revenge or was it just literary criticism, South Essex style?

Lakeside and Bluewater now exist as illusions upon the landscape that slip in and out of view driving through the sodium glare that passes for light in this part of the world. The advertising hoarding tells me that Lakeside at night is 'magical' but I know that is a lie.

If Lakeside is the present, then Bluewater, out of territory for a purely Essex boy, is a distorted view of a weird retail therapy future. Approaching it at night across the Queen Elizabeth II Bridge is luminescent Bladerunner territory, a glow that can be seen from space. The centre is a pod lying on a Martian landscape. H.G. Wells, who lived a few miles away in suburban Bromley, would have recognised it as part of his view of the future.

Circling round trying to park, I keep passing the vast lighting display for Regus Global Outsourced Offices. I want to know what these are and what they say for our future. If I lived close enough I would want to cycle into the centre, a small gesture of defiance against the way the world is.

Bluewater does not recognise the concept of the bicycle. It is a car-driven American style shopping mall. This is hostile territory for cyclists. There are no bike racks. A sign tells me there is a car park for ten thousand cars but nowhere to leave a humble bicycle. I enter the space city of the future. This is where the body snatchers live; those who have taken over. In the cavernous Marks and Spencer I look for tell-tale signs amongst the staff. A display tells me that an 'exclusive Jimmy Choo shop will open soon'. The problem for such retailers is that, the instant they open in a mall like Bluewater, they cease to be exclusive.

The big question on my mind is what happened to the Dartford Warbler? Entombed and preserved in concrete I imagine.

*

There was a time for optimism but it slipped through our fingers in the early 1980s. By the late Thatcher years, Basildon was the town of Raquel's – the club where the tragic Leah Betts met her ecstasy-fuelled death. Many years before it was called the Mecca where, as a twelve year old, I saw Tottenham's finest – the Dave Clark Five. I had to leave after half an hour, blood coursing onto my borrowed Beatle jacket, having been punched on the nose.

Out of town sits the Festival Leisure Park, a dream-induced landscape of McDonald's, Pizza Hut, UCI Cinemas, TGI Fridays, Nandos, Jumping Jaks Nightclub and Hollywood Bowl. At night it has a dreaming quality to it, a temple to unrestrained hedonism not even leavened by a prosaic Homebase or Currys. I partially close my eyes in the darkness so that the image becomes a fuzzy-coloured blur.

A partial retreat into sanity is possible at the Chicago Rock Café at 'Bas Vegas'. The website guide tells us it has 'panoramic windows that offer a spectacular view of the vast car park where you can witness fights from the comfort of a slightly moist vinyl armchair'. It is true. Sitting there on a late summer evening in the gathering Essex twilight, I witnessed two fights, serious scuffles really, one of which resulted in the flashing blue light of an ambulance hurtling across the car park.

Queuing at the entrance to Jumping Jaks on a winter evening, I feel that I stand out. It is mainly young women, late teens perhaps early twenties, wearing small black dresses exposing acres of white goosepimply flesh. A small group of them, the worse for drink I assume, are chanting at me 'where did you get that hat, that dirty rotten hat?' I smile inanely and put the offending object in my pocket. Ice is just starting to form on the car windows. There is the obligatory puddle of vomit by the bushes. It is not the management's fault but it inadvertently sets the tone. I am frisked twice by door security. This reassures me. Inside a gob of chewing gum has been stuck beneath the table where I am sitting. I press my leg against it. The atmosphere in the half darkness is predatory, an endless boisterous, edgy happy hour with standard chart pop music, industrial strength lager and Bacardi Breezers. A vaguely sinister young man asks me if I 'want some puff'. I don't know what this is so I decline.

If I arrive before ten I can buy a drink and get one free. I sit there with the two drinks in front of me. Guard your drinks ferociously although I don't imagine that I am a high priority target for drinks spikers. The shaven-headed, earring-toting dealers are out in force. Or is it just my imagination? When you reach my age everybody under thirty looks like a drug dealer.

The bouncers also have clean-shaven heads and try to look menacing, but they cannot quite make it. The clientele are shaven-headed. In fact, I am the only one who has a full head of hair, excepting for the little patch that I artfully disguise.

Twenty years ago, a perfectly smooth pate indicated chemotherapy. Today it says dysfunctional and emotionally stunted.

Afterwards I go to the Nightingale pub. On the door is a sign 'Smoking allowed everywhere in this pub. If you don't like it go elsewhere'. It is my sort of place. There is no antiseptic altruism, no assumptions about the perfectibility of human nature to mar a good evening out.

For good or for bad it was not always like this. There was an indigenous south Essex culture. The young Vaughan Williams recorded that in 1903 he was invited to tea at the local vicarage in Brentwood, a market town ten miles from Basildon. It came as a moment of revelation to him when a fellow guest, an elderly farm labourer, sang *Bushes and Briars*, one of those ancient songs that taps into a folk memory that has existed for a thousand years. This glimpse into an atavistic past was to be the inspiration of Vaughan Williams' work for the next fifty years.

*

London is a monster that swallows its children. For more than a thousand years it has sucked in people and then occasionally, when it has gorged itself and sated its appetite, it spews them out again. A million people in Abercrombie's new towns are evidence of this. London not only consumes those sucked into the vortex but it consumes those around it.

Just as the freeholders of Essex were dispossessed by the building of Basildon, consider for a moment what happened to the villagers of Heathrow and Perry Oaks to the west of London. The sites of these pretty hamlets are now covered by what, in terms of air quality, is the most polluted part of Europe. Sitting on the western edge of Hounslow Heath, the arable land in the area was amongst the most fertile in the country. It was here that the Cox's Orange Pippin Apple was first propagated and then grown in vast numbers. As late as 1940, the RAC Gazette described the area as 'scented with gracious fragrance of green untainted country'. In the 1930s, a resident wrote that 'to be in Heathrow is to be in the historic bosom of the British Isles, with its pure sweet air of antiquity'. To be in Heathrow now is to be poisoned and blinded.

It was upon this part of Hounslow Heath that the Catholic James II assembled his menacing army that caused major alarm to the residents of London and helped to precipitate the Glorious Revolution of 1688. Yet all of this counted for nothing when, by subterfuge, the decision was made to build the airport in the 1940s.

As the Second World War was drawing to a close, it was clear that greater capacity for civil aviation was necessary. Fearful of a lengthy planning enquiry and wary of objections from the Department of Agriculture, Middlesex County Council, and from freeholders and tenants raising irritating issues like property rights, the Air Ministry cited emergency military needs and invoked the 1939 Defence of the Realm Act in order to make a compulsory purchase, with no right of appeal. Harold Balfour, Parliamentary Secretary of State at the time, admitted in his autobiography that the military justification was spurious. There were a number of military airfields in the south-east that were within comfortable range of Germany. It was simply an expedient, an abuse of power. So strong would the resistance have been that Balfour knew the only chance of getting the land was to cite a grave national emergency, even though one did not exist. From the very start the intention was to create a civil airport.

Today the shadow of destruction casts a blight over those villages and hamlets that escaped in the 1940s. Harmondsworth, with its Norman Church, its Georgian housing and, in particular, its unique fifteenth century tithe barn, the 'Cathedral in Wood', will be destroyed and disappear under the tarmac of a third runway. Thomas Gray could have written his famous elegy while sitting in the churchyard.

> Beneath those rugged elms, that yew-tree's shade,
> Where heaves the turf in many a mould'ring heap
> Each in his narrow cell for ever laid,
> The rude Forefathers of the hamlet sleep.

This is an historic area where John Dryden, John Gay, Jonathan Swift, Alexander Pope and Voltaire gathered at Lord Bolingbroke's home at Harlington, letting their genius flourish away from the fetid air of London. Now it will all go because we want the convenience of cheap flights on Easyjet and Ryanair.

There is no great commercial imperative here. It is simply that governments feel obliged to meet demand whether there is merit or not, irrespective of the destruction that will be visited upon ancient communities. The government anticipates demand for air travel will triple in the next thirty years. Does it have an absolute obligation to meet that demand?

Oliver Goldsmith summed it up more than two hundred and fifty years ago.

> Sweet smiling village, loveliest of thy lawn,
> Thy sports are fled, and all thy charms withdrawn;
> Amidst thy bowers the tyrants hand is seen,
> And desolation saddens all thy green
> One only master grasps the whole domain.

If the experience of the public inquiry into the building of Terminal 5 is a pointer to the future, then objectors to a third runway have little chance. Despite the overwhelming objections of witnesses, the inquiry found in favour of the new terminal thus putting the seal on the 'first great monument to unsustainability of the 21st century' and the biggest structure ever built on greenbelt land.

It is ironic that archaeological excavation of the site has revealed an area of rich and intense settlement stretching back 8,000 years, deep into Neolithic times. Once the current poisonous levels of atmospheric pollution are reduced, then it will be full steam ahead for a new runway, hang the environment and hang the loss of houses and villages.

Those not affected tend to say that national and commercial needs must come first but this is not a line of argument they would pursue if the runway was to be built over their house and their community. Sustaining what many people consider to be the greatest capital city in the world exacts a very heavy price.

> Ill fares the land, to hastening ills a prey,
> Where wealth accumulates and men decay.
> But times are altered; trade's unfeeling train
> Usurp the land and dispossess the swain;
> Along the lawn, where scattered hamlets rose,
> Unwieldy wealth, and cumbrous pomp repose.

I rode to Heathrow in the dark on an elderly Yamaha Diversion 900. I travelled along the diesel-scorched M25 cruising at seventy miles an hour occasionally letting the engine playfully surge a little faster, wary of speed cameras and the police. At night, the airport assumes the character of a sodium principality, sprawled out in a state of suzerainty for the rootless and the restless of the world. It is what Iain Sinclair describes as 'a Vatican of the western suburbs'.

I park the bike inside the concrete bollards on a flyover to protect me from the rushing traffic overlooking Terminal 2. In the daytime, Heathrow should be considered as Dante's fourth circle of hell; reserved for the avaricious. At night, standing on the flyover looking out over the endless streams of light, I am reminded of James Joyce; 'this battered cabman's face we call the world'. The face may be plastered with the make-up of garish sodium light but ravaged and battered it is.

A police car draws up beside me, its blue light flashing. They want to know why I have stopped. I explain that I want to admire the view. They hesitate for a moment, not quite sure if I am serious. They ask to see in the box on the back of the bike. It contains nothing but a waterproof suit and a lock and chain. They tell me to move on. I understand perfectly why they want me to do this but I resent not being able to stop and stand in the land of my birth.

*

Many years ago I had a motorcycle accident in Basildon. It happened before Basildon had a hospital of its own so I was rushed to Southend General Hospital with a variety of broken bones.

As I was lying in the road with the small finger of my right hand hanging off, contemplating the nature of life and death, a kindly man came out of a newsagent and gave me a bottle of R Whites Cream Soda. Then he lit an unfiltered Park Drive cigarette for me. He even shaded me from the sun with his newspaper. Such small acts of consideration lodge in the memory.

Some of my friends thought I had been killed and rushed to my house to hear the worst. At least, I hope they rushed; I suspect they probably sauntered casually in order to be disabused that I was merely rather bashed about. I was touched however by their concern as you never can tell what people really think.

As I later observed it was not the first time I had died in Basildon.

Chapter 3: The Unnoticed Diaspora

And not by western windows only,
When daylight comes, comes in the light,
In front the sun climbs slow, how slowly,
But eastward look, the land is bright.
After Arthur Hugh Clough

Arise and follow the star of the east.
Vladimir Mayakovsky, poet of the Russian Revolution.

I still retain a curious affection for my great aunt's outdoor toilet. There is something satisfying, and altogether purer, about defecating away from the house where you live, as if the environment has not been quite so violated. I recommend it and have an outdoor toilet high on my list when I view a house.

It was in my great aunt's small brick built outhouse that I was introduced to the pleasures of the *News of the World* hanging up in small squares on a hook on the wall. Then, as now, the News of the World was a salacious rag but it was a far racier read than either the *Daily Herald* or *Reynolds News*, the digests of most Pioneer households.

The Herald was a ponderous Labour broadsheet that, with its gardening columns and reports of bowls matches, was specifically written for the over 70s. Eventually it died from atrophy and lack of custom. It then metamorphosed into *The Sun*, which is one definition of irony.

Through the *News of the World*, I first learnt the details of the Profumo scandal; details that the television and radio news broadcasts were treating so delicately as to emasculate it of all its sordid human interest content. Christine Keeler might well have been a scout mistress as far as the BBC was concerned.

My problem was that the paper, when it reached the outdoor toilet, was cut into small squares. I would inevitably reach a sentence from the trial report like "... and did you have sexual intercourse with Lord Astor?"

only to find the answer lay beyond the ragged torn edge. I would then spend the next ten minutes fumbling in the semi-darkness trying to find the reply.

Those were the days of proper sex scandals. In comparison, the modern examples of unrestrained libido – David Mellor, Ron Davies, John Major, Tim Yeo and Cecil Parkinson – seem to be rather weak by comparison.

The Profumo scandal had all the ingredients of a Greek tragedy combined with the certainty that it would all end in tears. The basic ingredients – a cabinet minister with access to the most sensitive military secrets having a sexual relationship with a woman who was simultaneously romping with a Russian spy – seem almost too good to be true, even in our much more publicly sordid age.

Forty years on the scandal continues to cast a long shadow, with the principals, Christine Keeler and Mandy Rice-Davies, making occasional cameo public appearances. Profumo himself occasionally shuffles into the limelight from doing good works at Toynbee Hall in the East End of London like some minor but tragic Shakespearean character.

*

Those of us who moved to the early new towns did benefit from Nye Bevan's insistence on the use of high quality building materials. Fifty years on, houses that were built in the immediate post-war years remain in good condition and are highly sought after. In contrast much of the stock built in the late 1960s and 70s has either been demolished or degenerated into something not far removed from a slum.

The high post-war building standards were all part of the determination that new social housing should be superior to the dreary council estates that had been built in the 1930s. Visit any inter-war London County Council housing estate and it is difficult to imagine a more dispiriting environment outside the urban sprawls that surround the major cities of the ex-communist Eastern European states. It is as if the state and its agencies had said, "Yes you can have a tidy, warm, waterproof home but the price will be to crush your spirit."

There is no law that says that if something is ordinary, commonplace and functional, it has to be ugly and poor quality. That however, appears to have been the guiding principle of most social housing built between the early 1960s and the mid 1980s.

We lived in what the Americans would call a 'housing project' but without its connotations of poverty, drugs, gun crime and despair. The intention was the same: to provide reasonable housing for the deserving poor.

The house was a revelation for us. My mother was given a choice of three and finally she plumped for the solid brick-built four-bedroomed semi overlooking the countryside toward the Ford plant. We hunted the adders that sunbathed over on the newly-constructed sewage beds. After ramming a sharpened stick through the neck, I sawed the head off with a sheath knife while watching the headless bloody body flailing around on the concrete slabs. My mother objected faintly to the line of snake skins drying on the washing line and I always pacified her with the promise of a snakeskin bag. It never did materialise.

Coming from a two-roomed flat in South London, snake hunting and having our own garden, indoor toilet and bathroom, were riches untold. I seemed to be the only one unimpressed by the bathroom.

Forty years on, I still hanker for the public bathhouse in Bermondsey with its huge brass, faucet-style taps, mahogany doors, hot water that I used to run up to the overflow, miniature tablets of soap and the boiled white towels. Every bathroom since has been an anti-climax.

We were part of that post-war working class diaspora that has gone almost unnoticed by the sociologists and cultural historians. Like so many extended families from inner London, we were broken up by the vast impersonal forces of a political economy that, acting in the name of social progress, was prepared to consign ancient and established communities to the dustbin of history.

From the late 1940s, through the 1950s and into the 1960s, we were flung worldwide. The epicentre of our pre-war world had been a jagged line drawn between Bethnal Green, Clerkenwell and Poplar with outposts in Balham, Paddington, Mitcham and Islington. Twenty years later, the epicentre had ceased to exist.

I had uncles, aunts, first, second and third cousins in Canada, New Zealand, Australia, and South Africa. In this country the diaspora extended to Gants Hill, Basildon, Crawley and Hemel Hempstead. At the time it seemed as if this migration was both voluntary and a good thing, the search for a better life.

In hindsight, it seems that the move was involuntary; the desire for decent housing and a job negating any sense of voluntary accession. The price was the utter disintegration and dislocation of a family that was already in the process of being displaced from its inner London roots. Gone was the London of my great, great grandfather – a Swedish exile and friend to Karl Marx. His London was of costermongers, penny gaffs, music halls, the swell mobs and dodgers, the rookeries of St Giles and Old Nichol, the cheap lodging houses, glittering gin palaces, beer shops, ratting contests and a vast endless sea of displaced humanity. We had bred within our genes that sense of the early Victorian metropolis. Instead we exchanged it for foreign lands, a subtropical climate, the promise of a better life and, in my case, Basildon New Town.

This diaspora lacks a record of its history in the way that other groups have created theirs. I admire Black History month and the Holocaust Memorial Day. I am in favour of groups within our multicultural society acknowledging and reminding both themselves and the rest of society of their unique contribution. I only wish that the English working class, those who were flung far and wide by their post-war diaspora, had their own muse and chronicler.

They need their own defining moment, their equivalent of the Empire Windrush or the St Louis to give them a sense of the journey that they have made. The route out of the East End along the A127 and the A13 to the flatlands of south Essex, or north along the Great Cambridge Road out to Cheshunt and Waltham Cross, may not have been as long, or the hardships as great, but it has been just as significant in shaping modern Britain. This is the winnowing and selecting process that history imposes upon us. Through a sequence of cultural sifting, we choose to record and to emphasise some historical shifts and movements, but not others.

The most important demographic and social change of the last fifty years has been the process of embourgeoisiement visited upon the working class, particularly in the south of England. Yet this is a largely unacknowledged change. In a dominant cultural position, the indigenous white population lack the will, the impulse and the desire to define themselves as a distinct group in the way that Britain's black population does.

It is the burden of any majority group to be ignored and unacknowledged. If we look at the string of white working class settlements running east out of London, the impact of the movement can be seen. Travelling from the East End, we come to West and East Ham, for thirty years the home of Alf Garnett and a particular brand of stereotyped white bigotry. Alf would not like the way the area has changed. Outside the West Ham football ground, a few defiant Union Jacks fly from local shops signalling that they are a white owned business in a shopping parade that embodies what much of the East End has become.

Further east we come to Barking, Ilford and Dagenham before shading into the slightly more aspirational Gants Hill and Newbury Park and the vast ribbon developments of the inter-war years that follow the A127. Finally we reach Romford, Upminster and Rainham, the furthermost eastward refuges of the old East End before leaving the boundaries of modern London.

Heading towards the northern banks of the Thames there lie the bland and nondescript towns of North and South Ockendon, Grays, Thurrock and Tilbury. For the vast majority of the population of these settlements it is only necessary to go back two generations to find a strong East End heritage.

It was on these grey Thameside shores that Count Dracula purchased his Carfax estate just outside Purfleet:

> At Purfleet, on a by road, I came across such a place as seemed to be required, and where was displayed a dilapidated notice that the place was for sale. It is surrounded by a high wall of ancient structure, built of heavy stones, and has not been repaired for a large number of years.

I am attracted to the idea of the undead shopping at Bluewater, a few miles away from Carfax. I believe that I have seen the small tell tale puncture marks on the necks of the assistants at the make up counter at John Lewis

A few miles to the south of Basildon, on the edges of the Thames sits Stanford le Hope, a town that Joseph Conrad found sufficiently attractive to make his home in the 1890s. It was here that he wrote *The Nigger of the Narcissus*, arguably the greatest of his novels. There is something eerie about the idea of this Polish adventurer and dreamer writing, in his third language, after Polish and Russian, some of the greatest novels in the English language. He would sit staring out into the Essex gloom over the marshes and estuarine gravel to the north of the Thames.

From this vantage point Conrad could have seen the yawl from the opening scene of the Heart of Darkness as it sat anchored with 'the sea reaches of the Thames stretched before us'. It is difficult not to assume that, as Conrad narrated the tale of the pursuit of the unspeakable Kurtz along the Congo River, he did not see the barges plying their way up the Thames passing Stanford Le Hope as they made their way towards the heart of darkness that lay twenty miles up river.

A little further to the east, Laindon, Pitsea, Canvey and Benfleet emerge from the north Thames flatlands. Here the native east Saxon population intrude a little further into the gene pool. There will be very few families who claim to be pure 'Old Essex' stock who do not have two grandparents that were born in Bow, Poplar, Spitalfields, Bethnal Green, Shoreditch, Stepney or any of those other familiar East End districts.

As a series of communities with a linked heritage, the towns that sprawl out to the east of London have lost their way. There is no government-funded quango to champion their rights; no National Lottery grants to fund the exploration of their heritage; no list of blue chip corporate sponsors keen to be associated with the Essex working class. There is no project funded by the Welcome Institute to trace the dispersal of their gene pool, no Wembley Conference Centre beano to give them a sense of purpose or legitimacy.

They do not have a Primo Levi to record their misfortune and no Isaac Bashevis Singer to lovingly relate a lost way of life, as both did for the fate of the Jewish nation. There is not a Samuel Selvon to record the loneliness or sense of loss in their new way of life as he did for those West Indians who came to London in the 1950s and 60s. They need a George Lamming, who meditated on the sense of being different – that sense that the early West Indian immigrants experienced. Perhaps it is too much to hope for a Derek Walcott to muse on the feelings of rootlessness and movement, or an Alex Haley to tell the Essex working class where their 'Roots' lie. Sterling performers that they are, Chas and Dave do not seem to be enough.

The south eastern working class need a chronicler who will interpolate where they have come from and where they are going to. These are a people who need a name, a heritage, a history, an identity and a champion other than the BNP. The alternative is a culture that focuses around TGI Friday and the Multiplex cinema that obliterates the past until all the traces are gone. The process is constant and ongoing.

A young friend of mine, born in Edmonton in 1978, lived the early part of his life on the twentieth floor of a now demolished tower block in Edmonton Green. Within a mile radius lived his four grandparents and three aunts. Over a five year period, most had decamped up the Lea Valley to Cheshunt, Waltham Cross, Broxbourne and Goffs Oak. This is the north east passage for those who have fled out of this part of London. The remainder moved out into the further reaches of Essex. In a matter of a few years a tightly knit working class family had become part of the late twentieth century diaspora. They are a symptom of the increasingly rootless of our society.

The clear, but unspoken, message was that Edmonton, with its social problems, crime, poverty, multi-ethnic population and more than its share of asylum seekers, was no longer worth living in. My friend is now a councillor in Westminster, owns his own successful business and lives in considerable affluence in Battersea. He is a metaphor for an American-style social mobility.

Occasionally we went back to visit my aunt and uncle and three cousins in their cramped dockland house. Round about 1960, the term 'dockland home' had a completely different meaning to today's interpretation. My aunt lived in a small Victorian terrace in Bermondsey, near the Surrey Docks, with funnels of liners and cargo ships towering above the back garden. The exact spot is now the site of a riverside apartment block, complete with spectacular views of the Thames. One million pounds might now buy the most basic of flats.

So what happened to all the people who comprised that tightly-bound community, made up of a lattice of terraced streets next to the Surrey Docks? I was aware, even at the time, of a sense of loss; a dull insistence somewhere within my being that I had been torn away from my roots by those wretched central government planners who always knew best. The real failure of the planners was a failure of common sense: failure to acknowledge that the past needs to be recalled when deciding how people are to live.

When my aunt, uncle and three cousins sailed on the Canberra from Tilbury using the Assisted Passage Scheme to start a new life in Australia, I realised the pressures ordinary people were under – pressures that made them go from one end of the earth to the other for the chance of a better life.

Our twin experiences were the microcosm of the post-war disintegration of traditional inner city working class communities. It was simply a matter of degree. We emigrated thirty miles to the east while Auntie Olive travelled thirteen thousand miles to Perth, Western Australia.

Basildon was a classless society. It was the embodiment of 1940s Labour social engineering endorsed by 1950s paternalistic conservatism. This though was before the New Right neo-liberals took over the Conservative Party.

In those days of municipal socialism, new town style, everything was done for us. Every fifth year, council decorators redecorated the inside of the house, and every seventh year, the outside. Once every ten years, the kitchen fitments would be renewed with a choice of three styles. This, of course, produced the sort of dependency culture Mrs Thatcher railed against.

"Er ... could you send someone round with a screwdriver? A screw has worked loose on the door bracket." Incredibly, someone with a screwdriver always arrived the next day. This state of affairs provoked conversations like: "... and do you know I had to wait thirty-five minutes for a man from the council to come round and install a new Ascot boiler and water tank!"

No wonder local authority expenditure had brought Britain to the brink of bankruptcy in the 1970s. Mrs Thatcher and Keith Joseph, and their friends on the New Right, were frothing at the mouth about the corrosive effect of the dependency culture. There was a good side to this relationship. We were clothed, housed, schooled and fed in a way that was inconceivable to our grandparents but it came at a price.

Firstly, it was never enough. Although our material circumstances were beyond those of our parents and grandparents, the monster of materialism and conspicuous consumption had been awakened and the welfare state was never going to be able to satisfy it. An afternoon of self-aggrandisement in the local Marks and Spencer was never likely to satisfy this newly-acquired and very deep-seated lust.

However there was a deeper and more profound problem. We lived within a subdued authoritarianism that denied us control of our own lives and made us part of the mute crowd who looked on as others decided our needs. We could have a council house provided it was the one we were told we could have. And it would be decorated for us in the way prescribed in the council manual. We were not allowed to ask for a different pastel shade on the living room walls. We could have a job but it would be low skill, low wage in a factory on a local industrial estate. I could go to school and be educated but it would be the sort of education demanded by the state and at an institution deemed suitable by the state.

Although my brother and I failed the eleven plus exam we were sent to secondary modern schools at opposite ends of the town. This was in the name of efficient planning as a new estate was being built that would alter the catchment area of the first school we attended. To meet our personal needs, we should have been kept together but that was irrelevant to the grander scheme. Thus we became ancillaries to our own lives because the state had emasculated us of purpose and made the crucial decisions on our behalf.

The extraordinary fact is that, twenty five years later, the state (it is irrelevant what sort of government was in power) discovered, to its horror, that the policies pursued in the earlier period had created a culture of dependents. Thus we have a significant minority of the population who are content to be the passive recipients of whatever welfare crumbs may be thrown off the grand table of society.

In 1975, Sir Keith Joseph, coming from the right of the Conservative Party, made his notorious speech in Birmingham in which he advocated giving free contraception to the working classes to stop them from reproducing. For his foresight, Private Eye dubbed him Sir Sheath.

At the time, I thought of all those large happy families in their Basildon Council houses and I felt rather disturbed at the implications of what he was suggesting. Why didn't he just say what the eugenicist wing of his party really thought?

It seemed a curious, even repellent, analysis but a quarter of a century later the issues are not so clear. Joseph's view was predicated upon the Victorian notion that the poor are the way they are because of their own failings and that there is little the state can do for them. It follows, therefore, that the state has an obligation to reduce their numbers in order to alleviate the problem.

He was quite consciously rejecting the previous thirty years of welfarism, saying: "Look, this is where it has got us. These feckless and irresponsible young mothers are married to the state. We are making previously unviable lifestyles viable through our policies." Sir Keith was to have his eventual revenge on the working class for their prolific breeding. As housing minister under Harold Macmillan in the early 1960s, he was responsible more than any other individual for the tower block policy that destroyed so many traditional communities.

We cannot say we were not warned of the strongly moralistic tone the Thatcher revolution would adopt in the 1980s. In that sense, Joseph was the first to articulate clearly, on this side of the Atlantic at least, that not only was the newly formed welfare state creating a degree of security unprecedented in human history, but that, in a subtle and subversive manner, it was also changing age old patterns of behaviour and attitudes towards the state. The balance of the traditional relationship between the individual and the state was changing in a way that Sir Keith felt was damaging. He would argue that, by making viable long-term unemployment, single parenthood and dependency, the state was in the process of fostering its own destruction.

From a vantage point of a quarter of a century later, it is difficult to argue that he was entirely wrong. Today, right-wing social commentators such as the American, Charles Murray, do not shy away from making judgments about the deserving and the undeserving poor, and telling us that the rise of single motherhood is corroding the nation from the inside.

I remember a girl called Belinda who lived down the road from me and went to the grammar school. Sometimes we passed in the street and I would glance shyly at her. There was never a flicker of recognition that I existed. She was beautiful, remote, intimidating, a year older than me, and she fell pregnant in the sixth form. This was a quite staggering transgression. She became a non-person on the day that she disappeared, exiled to some remote gulag for fallen women, never to be mentioned again.

Not even her best friends knew of her fate. She had simply gone from their lives, never to return; swept away by the shame of her mother, the signature of her GP, the suspicion of moral imbecility, the concerns of the social workers, and the outrage of the church. In that pre-human rights era, she had no means of fighting back. Her fate was dangled in front of us to show what happened to girls who could not say 'no'.

This all happened twenty years before the advent of the Child Support Agency. The idea of male culpability was not part of the equation. "Belinda got herself in the family way," went the spiteful refrain as if we were witnessing the rerun of the virgin birth. "And she's from the grammar!" This compounded the offence as if girls from the secondary modern school had ever-welcoming, wide-open legs but not girls from the grammar school.

The impulse for a eugenicist solution to working class reproduction has not gone away, though it remains a peculiarly northern European instinct. Right up to the late 1960s, Sweden – that haven of liberal progressive social democratic values – was compulsorily sterilising its own citizens if they happened to be single mothers, mentally infirm, or criminally disposed. The quiet complicity of my family's country during the Second World War with Nazi Germany is often forgotten in the rush to load the Saab up with flat pack furniture from IKEA.

Across the Oresund, in Denmark, Professor Nyborg of Aarhus University is worried that the average intelligence of Danes is declining. The problem is that highly intelligent and educated Danish women are spending their time studying and earning money, not having children. Meanwhile, their stupid counterparts, who occupy the bottom twenty per cent of society, are at the behest of an over-generous welfare state busy having babies.

Given Nyborg's conviction that intelligence is hereditary, the result is that Denmark is producing more stupid people than intelligent people resulting in an overall decline in average intelligence. His solution is to use the powers of the state to persuade intelligent women to have more children while introducing financial disincentives for less intelligent women not to reproduce. This, of course, is perfectly logical, rational and acceptable if we can persuade ourselves that less intelligent people have no feelings; that they are of no value to society, and that we are happy in denying them their human right to have children. Professor Nyborg's problem would appear to be that he lives too close to Germany.

Unfortunately, the evidence stacks up steadily in favour of Keith Joseph and, quite possibly, Nyborg also. Sometimes we are presented with empirical evidence that draws us towards conclusions we find personally distasteful but nevertheless pander to our darker suspicions.

In America the economist, Steven Levitt, has examined why violent crime in America's cities has been falling over the past decade. The right tends to explain the trend as the result of tough 'law and order' policies. The liberal left favour economic growth and broader prosperity consistent with their view of the social causes of crime.

Levitt's uncomfortable conclusion is that Americans in the 1990s were seeing the beneficial impact of the historic 1973 'Roe versus Wade Supreme Court' ruling that effectively allowed abortion on demand. The result of this has been a culling in the womb of the underclass from which the majority of conventional criminals are drawn. As most very young single mothers come from the poorest groups in society, it is these women who are most likely to seek an abortion.

Once the termination had occurred, American society was deprived of the fodder that was fuelling its crime wave epidemic. In short, crime levels fell most sharply in those states where abortion levels were highest. This fact should come as no surprise but it inevitably draws us towards a eugenicist line of thinking. Levitt's findings are seen as statistically robust, if socially dubious, and have caused a great deal of hand wringing on both the left and right.

For most on the political right, abortion is an anathema but, at the same time, it proves their theories about a criminal underclass and offers a panacea to the crime epidemic that is gripping most western liberal democracies.

For the left, it is labelling people as criminal in the womb, an assertion that, even before a child is born, its fate is sealed. This does not fuel the demand that abortion should be restricted. Generally on the left, abortion has been seen as a symbolic issue defining a woman's independence: her sovereignty over her own body. Levitt's findings have served to stimulate demand for an extension of welfare in the belief that, through the largesse and intervention of the state, these children could be saved from their criminal futures.

The idea that the criminal underclass can be culled in the womb inevitably attracts the accusation that this is no more than covert eugenicism. The problem with Levitt is that we don't want him to be right but we know that he is. When he finds, through empirical research, that longer prison sentences and higher arrest rates serve to reduce crime, we experience the mordant satisfaction of proving the liberal left wrong. We also experience the grim pessimism for what this says about human nature.

Unlike most economists, Levitt seems to have no political axe to grind – in fact he appears to be completely apolitical. He just tells it as it is. Even for politicians on the right, the satisfaction is double edged. Every dollar spent on building bigger and better prisons is a dollar that has been taken from the hardworking, law abiding citizen.

Americans worry a lot about welfare and what worries them eventually comes to worry us. They are concerned that its collectivist ethos will undermine the creed of rugged individualism on which their country was founded. The general conclusion is that welfare starts out as a noble intention but ends up with a squalid result.

It is instructive to trawl through the raft of articles that have appeared in a range of American academic journals over the past two decades representing all political perspectives on the issue of welfare and the impact that it is having on the social fabric. The degree of emphasis varies but they all drive towards the same broad conclusion: that welfare is destructive of the individual and of the family and that, ultimately, it contributes to soaring crime levels.

The broad argument, taken from the NAACP report on crime in Maryland tells an increasingly familiar story: 'The ready access to a lifetime of welfare and free social service programs is a major contributory factor to the crime problems we face today.' The National Association for the Advancement of Coloured People is a left-leaning civil rights pressure group. Their literature then examines those social groups who are most likely to be involved in crime. This includes, amongst other groups, black children from single parent households who are twice as likely to commit crimes as black children from a family where the father is present (Bureau of Justice statistics).

The relationship is so strong between fatherless families and crime that it erases all factors such as low income and race. Thus single motherhood rather than race is identified as the key issue. Race is consistently acknowledged as a key factor but it is seen as subsidiary to the problems created by welfare.

The literature then asks why this growth of matriarchal single parent families has occurred. The consistent answer, according to a US Department of Health and Human Services study, is that 'a 50 per cent increase in the value of AFDC and food stamp payments leads to a 43 per cent increase in the number of births out of wedlock'. This finding was constant after factoring in a wide range of variables including income, race, education and urban versus suburban setting. Why should there be such a strong relationship between the two factors?

Again the literature is clear. The children of young single mothers are more likely to be involved in crime and 'providing additional benefits to single parents encourages births of children to unwed women' (Douglas Allen. Welfare and the Family: the Canadian Experience. Journal of Labour Economics 1993.)

A further highlighted, but aggravating, factor is the way that welfare has led to the marginalisation of young men, particularly young black men. Effectively they have been cuckolded by the state.

The hidden message of the welfare culture is that, when the welfare cheque pops through the letterbox, men become unnecessary to the family. This has had disastrous consequences: 'single men are five times more likely to commit violent crimes than married men.' (from Home Life to Prisons Life: the Roots of American Crime. Rockford Institute Centre on the Family in America.)

It is possible that these singles remain single because they are so violent. It is the consistency of the findings that depresses. These are not rabid, right-wing, free market journals.

The studies acknowledge the salient importance of race, education and income influencing social behaviour but all the time we are drawn back, with a nagging persistency, to the impact that welfare programmes have on individuals.

I want to live in a world where welfare works and solves the terrible problems that people face. We now live with a legacy of unintended consequences born out of the best of intentions. Sadly, it seems the experience of the last sixty years is that, for all the good welfare does for individuals, it inflicts profound damage on the rest of society.

Keith Joseph's welfare message has been largely accepted. The unthinkable of 1975 has become the orthodoxy of the twenty-first century. If the late Sir Keith had been able to gaze into a crystal ball in 1974 and see that, twenty three years later, a Labour government would force its own MPs to vote for a cut in benefit as part of a war on single mothers, then he would smile at his own prescience. He would also note that it was the party of irresponsible welfarism, as he saw it, that was pushing the measure through.

I dwell upon this point because, although the Pioneers were socialists, they had a strong sense of traditional morality. They believed in personal responsibility and knew the welfare state had the capacity to draw out the worst in human nature. The Pioneers, however, were not natural election fodder who, in the fullness of time, would vote for Mrs Thatcher in 1979. There was something that was too moralising, authoritarian, sanctimonious and smug about the Thatcher creed. The appeal of the overbearing middle-class housewife from Finchley who was so careless of civil liberties and trade union privileges was always going to be limited. However, that most typically-Thatcherite policy, the Right to Buy, did strike a chord amongst the Pioneers.

In a curious sense, the blunter message delivered by Sir Keith Joseph, free of Mrs Thatcher's abrasively nationalistic middle England sentiments, would have been more appealing. The problem was that Joseph was a Conservative and, in an era of deeply-ingrained class-based voting habits, that was always likely to be an insurmountable obstacle. Significantly Basildon did become a Conservative seat in the 1979 election but it was not as a result of garnering the very small number of Pioneer votes that were still there to fight for.

For nine consecutive elections, Basildon has been the barometer of the nation's voting behaviour, the embodiment of that thrusting C2 social class that enthusiastically took on board the Thatcher message. Of the fifteen general elections that have been held since the creation of the New Town only once, in 1964 when they elected the Tory Edward Gardener, has Basildon bucked the national trend. Even in 1964 Labour was only able to muster an overall majority of three.

As the election night results rolled in, the psephologists focussed on the town as the Sun reader's natural habitat. The embodiment of the Basildon spirit was David Amess, MP from 1983 to 1997. An instinctive, if unintellectual, Thatcherite, Amess was born in Plaistow, East London to a working class family and followed the London grammar school route to success. The high point came when, in 1992, he held Basildon contrary to national expectations. At that moment, we knew that it was all over for Neil Kinnock, John Smith, and company. The premature triumphalism of the Sheffield Rally was just a sour taste in the mouth.

The separation of Basildon from Billericay as a result of a recommendation from the Boundary Commission in 1980 created two constituencies where previously there had been one. Normal psephological analysis would have suggested that semi-detached suburban Billericay would have remained Conservative, which happened, while working class Basildon should have been rock solid Labour territory. This ignored the aspirational nature of Thatcherism that had a broad South Essex appeal. White van man, even before the term had been invented, was not interested in trade union dominated Labour-style social democracy. They wanted the Right to Buy, the promise of hard work rewarded, and a bracing dose of right-wing populism.

Mr Amess was just the man to provide this but being a man of astute judgment he could see the drift of events more clearly than the rest of us. Although he famously declared 'I love Basildon' it was not a sincere commitment. Before the 1997 election, he decamped to Southend West, a dozen miles to the east – a seat he inherited from the patrician old Etonian, Paul Channon. Clearly he was no fool. Having survived the 1997 Labour onslaught when all around him were falling to the ground mortally wounded, Mr Amess increased his majority in 2001 from two and half thousand to more than seven thousand. It is a shame for Basildon that their natural, instinctive MP scuttled down the A127 in the direction of the middle-class reaches of Southend West. For all his smugness, Mr Amess, up until the election of Angela Smith, was the only MP in more than 50 years who shared his constituents' south Essex background and their relentless aspirations. He was cut from a very different cloth to the Tory knights of the shires – Sir Bernard Braine, Sir Richard Body and Sir Edward Gardner – who represented the town in the 1950s when it was part of a much larger South East Essex constituency. Then Mr Amess ran away. For the moment at least Basildon's flirtation with Thatcherite conservatism is over.

His successor, washed in on the 97 floodtide, is Angela Smith. Bright, personable and a 'Blair Babe' to her fingertips, Ms Smith embodies the New Labour project. Her reward for loyalty and competence was to be appointed as a minister in the Northern Ireland Office. Feminine and consensual, she exudes an open classlessness that supports the fact she attended a local comprehensive school. She is a modern politician who owes her position of local distinction to her own abilities rather than Old Labour trade union patronage. Ms Smith can resist the charge, levelled at so many politicians, of being a carpet bagger. She is even more South Essex than David Amess who by comparison seems like a dinosaur from another political age. Perhaps Ms Smith, in her first year at Chalvedon Comprehensive School, conceived the desire to represent the people of Basildon at Westminster.

Ten miles to the east of Basildon, down the A127, lies Romford from which used to flow John Bull Bitter courtesy of the three hundred year old Romford brewery. Although it is just inside the boundary of Havering, Romford has the feel of an Essex town: young men with pony tails and girls wearing puffa jackets. The local MP, Andrew Rosindell, is indisputably Essex man. A formidable campaigner, he came to national attention while campaigning during the 2001 General Election accompanied by his Staffordshire bull terrier, Spike, complete with Union Jack waistcoat. I am assuming that the dog wore the waistcoat but it may well have been the owner as well. Sadly, but appropriately, Spike passed away on St George's Day 2002.

Mr Rosindell is a man of firm views. He advocates flogging for violent thugs, castration for rapists, and the return of capital punishment with the thoughtful concession that those convicted can choose their own method of execution. As for progressive clergy, he thinks they should 'pay more attention to the gospel than to the Guardian'. In fact, so right-wing are his views that even Iain Duncan Smith was sufficiently embarrassed that he asked him to resign from the overtly racist Monday Club. If the good folk of Basildon tire of Angela Smith then Mr Rosindell is the natural successor. Broadly speaking I am of the view that constituencies get the MP that they deserve.

The Basildon phenomenon has been sufficient to attract national attention. During the 1990s, Basildon Man became the focus of psephological attention to the extent that academics, Dennis Hayes and Alan Hudson produced a densely written academic study – *Basildon: the Mood of the Nation*. It looks as if my suspicions about Angela Smith are confirmed. She may be very worthy, and a minister, she may be local and personable, but there is not that spark of connection that existed between the town and Mrs Thatcher via the conduit of David Amess.

Tony Blair, from his Islington fastness, simply does not speak their language. There is no real point of connection. Now apathy and disengagement from all parties prevails. It is not Ms Smith's fault. The problem lies in the fact that the people of Basildon engaged in a semi-Faustian pact with a unique one-off politician and, quite simply, no other political leader compares.

I am not convinced by the idea of Basildon, as a bellwether constituency, leading the nation. It is just an instinctive desire to be on the winning side in the way that Rupert Murdoch's Sun newspaper backed Mr Blair and New Labour in 1997. There is no deep commitment involved but it is fun and novel being in with the winners.

A mile down the road from where we lived, the housing minister, Harold Macmillan, visited the town to celebrate the building of the one millionth council house since the war. One can only imagine what a patrician spirit such as Macmillan actually thought of such people living in such a house. He turned on the lights and said, "That's marvellous!" as if he had never seen electricity before. He shook hands and smiled at the new tenants as if he really cared for them and was delighted by their new house. He was a cunning old showman, even on this small stage. Perhaps he really felt a well-concealed contempt for them living in their little new town? Or did he glow because the working classes were being provided for by a far-seeing benevolent government?

The latter I suspect, given his words of sympathy for the miners during the strike of 1984-5. These were the grandsons and great grandsons of the men he had led in the trenches during the fight against the Kaiser, and he had not forgotten. It seemed the ultimate expression of an older style of paternalistic Toryism that is now stone dead.

The house that Harold Macmillan opened and departed as quickly as possible to get back to his stately pile in Stockton, now has its own mini-Doric columns and two fibreglass unicorns adorning the gateposts.

It was always part of the Macmillan brand of stately Conservative paternalism that the working classes deserved to be treated well but that did not mean having to meet them too often unless they were in the gamekeeper/domestic servant class.

Ten years later the Labour Prime Minister, Harold Wilson, came to see how we were getting on. He still retained some popularity even though a damaging national dock strike had just ended. The economy had not yet gone completely pear-shaped. Labour had just won the 1966 election decisively, England had triumphed in the World Cup, The Beatles bestrode the world of popular music, London was the swinging city of the world and it was the Summer of Love. This was probably the last time that we unequivocally felt good about ourselves as a nation. After 1967, it was the long slide into economic stagnation, poisonous industrial relations, problems in Northern Ireland, the class warfare of the 1980s, and the self-loathing that we have engaged in for the past thirty-five years.

As Labour Prime Minister, Wilson would have had a particular interest in Basildon as a new town. It was the embodiment of the 1940s Labour vision of how to build the New Jerusalem. He visited the Ford research plant at Dunton, next to the Plotlands community that was then still flourishing. Like Macmillan, he was a showman. The vaguely fashionable Gannex raincoat and the unlit pipe were all part of the image of Harold Wilson as trustworthy and reassuring as the avuncular family doctor. He was not, of course. He was having it off with his secretary and smoking a cigar when the cameras were not there, although not at the same time I hope. I don't know what he thought of Basildon. Not a lot I suspect but then he lived at 10 Downing Street and, when that was not available, at a plush house in Hampstead Garden Suburb.

There were no privately-owned houses in our new Utopia. This was in accord with the government orthodoxy of the day. Private ownership was to be discouraged in the name of housing for all. Local authorities not only refused to allow licences to build private housing but also fixed the sale prices of new houses. Most authorities only allowed private house building on a ratio of one private to eight council houses.

As late as 1959, Basildon Council rejected an attempt to build two private estates to meet private demand on the simple grounds that the demand should not be there. This was the embodiment of an overweening dirigiste state that viewed private demand as a denial of the ideal of state planning. We should have been content with what the state had to offer.

The professionals we all looked up to simply lived in bigger council houses. Along the side of some rough farmland, on what is now the golf course, they built a road full of five bedroomed detached houses, the sort that would now cost a million pounds in a smart north London suburb. These were for the doctors and the lawyers. The Development Corporation, by charging four times the rent it levied for the average three-bedroomed semi, was sending a clear message to the Ford factory workers: 'Keep Out.'

Even in our own New Jerusalem there existed a nomenclature who were not really part of the ethos of the town. But where there is demand, there is also supply and, by the mid 1960s, the town authorities had given up their campaign against private ownership. They allowed the construction of two estates containing nearly three thousand houses for those who now found that being a tenant in social housing was no longer agreeable.

This was a crucial moment in the decline of the Socialist Pioneers. They had come to the town with a burning belief in social ownership and holding things in common. Now, not only had the town reneged on this principle, but also the merest sliver of an idea had been planted in the minds of some of the Pioneers. The affluence of the 'You've never had it so good' years of the Macmillan premiership was rubbing off. The seed had been planted and was now germinating the idea that they could aspire to something their parents and grandparents never even dreamed about – owning their own house.

It was with a sense of shame and triumph that Ken Parker, a printer and our domestic expert on Proudhon's writings and theory, announced that he was buying a house on the Kingwood Estate. He was a serious-minded sort of person, one of the inheritors of that auto-didactic tradition that meant his bookshelves groaned under the weight of learned tomes of political theory, most of which, I am sure, he had read and understood.

The names were familiar – Sorel, Kropotkin, Bakunin, Kautsky and Bernstein – but they may as well have been an Austrian football team as far as I was concerned. In those days, when television was still in its infancy, we would play charades with him. Where I specialised in the popular films of the day like *Ben Hur* and *The Guns of Navarone*, Ken through much waving of arms and gesticulating would try to indicate dialectical materialism or the dictatorship of the proletariat. He would give me a withering glance as I shouted out "Dr No" and "Cleopatra."

Ken's argument for buying his own house was that this would vacate a house for another poor family to move in. The scramble to join the property-owning democracy was on and all the principles of solidarity, fraternity, the ideals of the friendly society, the building clubs and the co-operative society were jettisoned along the way. The issue split the Pioneers into those who bought a house and those who did not. Inevitably, they divided along lines of disposable income.

Those who stayed put in their council and corporation homes argued that they were remaining true to the Pioneer spirit but the reality was that they were too poor to buy and did not have the necessary £500 deposit. It was all part of the process that sociologists call embourgeoisiement; that people with a steady, if dull, job and regular wages aspire to leave the social class in which they were nurtured.

The 1960s desire to join the property-owning democracy was a symptom of this. It also meant that it was no longer possible to call round a man from the council to tighten up a screw.

On a recent visit to some of the old Pioneer homes of my childhood, I remembered the position of every house in street after street as if it were yesterday, yet I came across none of the original tenants. I marvelled at how compact a community we were, maybe fifty families in an estate of three hundred houses. Despite knocking on many doors and asking intrusive questions, with one exception, it was as if they never were; even their names had been obliterated by the intervening years. I looked at the neat brick-built houses and felt them to be empty and haunted. They had once contained the dreams and hopes of a better life. Perhaps they still do but it is no longer so apparent.

The single exception was in a street called Beeleigh West, one of many streets that had a pedestrian walkway rather than a road running past it. This was not foresight on the part of the town planners; they simply did not imagine our 21st century preoccupation with taming the motorcar. Back in the late 1940s, they did not anticipate mass car ownership.

The house had once been occupied by George Roberts the Pacifist, a Quaker who been a member of the ILP, a friend of George Lansbury, and a conscientious objector in the Second World War. As a child, I thought him a dull crank but I now realise that he was a noble man with powerfully-held ideals.

After a painful and protracted conversation with the tattooed and studded current tenant, I established that he was George's grandson, though it was clear he did not know what a Quaker was. Old George had died twenty years ago and his son now lived in Clacton. The young man helpfully offered the address but I declined and retreated in a state of confusion about how we change, the nobility of ideals, the corrupting nature of society, and how a spirit as pure as that of George Roberts could bequeath to the world such a gormless lump of tattooed, nose-studded, Sky television-watching blubber as his grandson. In intellectual terms, it was riches to rags in two generations. Still, I should not be too judgmental.

Tens of thousand of council tenants became property owners and I imagine all the old Socialist Pioneer properties are now privately owned because they were sound, well-built houses.

Next to my school, the prefabricated Siporex estate was built, or rather assembled, from parts made in Sweden. Within ten years it had become a slum that would have shamed the East End or even the outskirts of Warsaw, and it was demolished. This was the dark side of local authority benevolence

*

Basildon possesses an alter ego called Billericay. For nearly twenty years the towns were twinned in the same parliamentary constituency. It was not a happy marriage. Billericay was the epitome of prim, suburban, semi-detached middle-England. Where Basildon was local authority council housing, Billericay was Barrett homes in private ownership. For the folk of Billericay to admit to living within the same local authority as Basildon was like owning up to having a younger brother in prison.

"You live in Billericay? Is that close to Basildon?"

"Good God no. It is closer to Chelmsford."

The dubious nature of Billericay can be seen from their strange MPs. In the 1980s it was the spanking Harvey Proctor, customer of rent boys, believer in firm correction and general all round pervert. In 1987 he found himself at Bow Street Magistrates Court on three charges of gross indecency including spanking sessions with rent boys in his London flat. He was found guilty. To add to the pall of suspicion that hangs over the man he was also a member of the executive of the right-wing Monday Club, a supporter of a "vigorous programme of repatriation" (his words) and a friend to a number of strange and unnerving figures on the far right of British politics. I met Mr Proctor once in a non-spanking capacity. He had eyes like a dead cod.

There must be something wrong with a town that can vote for a character so flawed. After Proctor's rather hurried departure to open a gentleman's shirt shop, with financial assistance from Jeffrey Archer, he was succeeded by Theresa Gorman. She was significantly to the right of Mrs Thatcher, wore bright canary yellow suits, waxed lyrical about hormone replacement therapy and was one of the group of right-wing anti-European little Englanders known as the Whipless Eight; the group who made John Major's life such a misery in the 1990s. She found herself criticised by a Commons select committee for failing to record her activities as a landlord in the Register of Members Interests. The committee recommended that she be excluded from the House for a month. It takes some doing to be kicked out of the Commons, even on a temporary basis.

Today the physical distance between the two towns has diminished. Twenty years ago there were several miles of open countryside and farmland between the two, emphasising the very different nature of the two towns. Today the 'march of bricks and mortar' is epitomised by the Brookside-style private estates that creep up Noak Hill away from Basildon snaking towards the older town. This is a sign that one day we shall all be swallowed up by the insidious growth of southern England.

*

The Pioneers, on the whole, disapproved of television, seeing within it the capacity both to corrupt and to deflect us from our purpose. My father was particularly scathing about early game shows like *Double Your Money* and *Take Your Pick* on the grounds that we were being seduced into a world of trivia that had no obvious purpose. This did not stop him enjoying the early police drama, *Z Cars* nor did it prevent him following the advice of Barry Bucknell in *Do It Yourself* as he ripped apart a Victorian house and replaced all its 'ugly' original features. A cast iron fireplace with William de Morgan tiles was replaced with a nice 1960s British Gas coal effect fire. He also demonstrated a propensity for covering all those awful solid wood Victorian doors with a nice sheet of hardboard which was then painted white. At the time it seemed sensible but the Habitat-frequenting classes had not yet rediscovered the joys of Victoriana.

*

Having now spoken rather disparagingly of the area, I feel that I should now defend its integrity and illustrate its sense of what is right.

South Essex is a quality area despite being the butt of the Essex girl jokes and having a monopoly on the nation's stocks of white high heels. A minor incident illustrates this.

The play of *The Graduate* went on national tour recently and was booked to perform at Cliffs Pavilion in Southend. Those familiar with the production will know that the mature Mrs Robinson is required to appear nude in the seduction scene. Unfortunately for Southend, which is in effect Basildon-on-Sea, the coy actress concerned refused to (using that well-known South Essex phrase) 'get her kit off'.

A lesser sort of people would have shrugged their shoulders in weary resignation but not the people of South Essex. They threatened a boycott, planned legal action and organised a media blitz in an attempt to shame the blushing thespian into revealing all.

On the opening night, only two hundred of the sixteen hundred seats were occupied for a play that had been a sell out elsewhere. In south Essex it would appear that the motto is 'no bosoms, no audience'. I am sympathetic to those who demand value for their hard earned money. If one buys a ticket on the assumption that the leading lady is going to strip off, then I am afraid the artistic sensibilities of the actress concerned, Glynis Barber, must take second place to pleasing the punters.

'Sod the aesthetics, get yer tits out' seems to be the general sentiment. After all, she is what some of my unreconstructed Basildon friends would describe as a 'quality bird'.

Chapter 4: The Poor Man Pays for All

The history of all hitherto existing society is the history of class struggle.
Karl Marx and Friedrich Engels.
The Communist Manifesto.

Within the Pioneers there existed a powerful auto-didactic tradition. I am not claiming that all of them were widely read but a significant minority were, and most of them would have put to shame a modern political activist or undergraduate liberal arts student.

I have visited working class houses where the bookshelves buckled under the weight of bound hardback classic novels and worthy political tomes. Certain authors seemed to crop up with great regularity; Charles Dickens, Thomas Hardy and H.G. Wells were the favourites while a few of them might stretch as far as George Gissing and George Eliot.

The books were usually not just for show. George Roberts had intimate knowledge of the novels of Charles Dickens – not only David Copperfield and Oliver Twist. The less read Barnaby Rudge and Edwin Drood came well within the orbit of his erudition.

Some households had a few ageing orange-covered editions from the Left Book Club, usually G.D.H. Cole's *Intelligent Man's Guide through World Chaos* and John Strachey's *The Nature of Capitalist Crisis*. Ownership, if not actually reading, Walter Tresell's *Ragged Trouser Philanthropists* seemed to be obligatory. Having read Tresell's sole novel on Pioneer recommendation at the age of fifteen with its sentimentality and didactic tone it perfectly fits what Orwell described as 'a good bad book'.

Walter Greenwood's *Love on the Dole* was a favourite of the older Pioneers while a number of the younger ones were developing a taste for those gritty social realist novels characteristic of the 1960s by writers like Alan Sillitoe and Stan Barstow. I was given a copy of *A Kind of Loving* when I was sixteen. It still sits unread on my bookshelves.

In the wake of the famous 1961 Lady Chatterley trial for obscenity, it was *de rigueur* to have an unread copy of the D.H. Lawrence novel sandwiched between the collected works of William Shakespeare and a Readers Digest Omnibus. In some houses, the Penguin edition of *Lady Chatterley's Lover* would sit alone as the only book in the house conveniently falling open at the 'dirty bits' as we trawled it for the passages that had so offended the British establishment.

"Is this the sort of book that you would allow your servants to read?" the prosecuting counsel famously asked. We, of course, were the servants, or at least people like us. I cannot remember feeling obviously corrupted having read it at the age of ten although it was certainly a notch up in the sexual ecstasy stakes from my usual fare of Enid Blyton and Henry Treece.

I read just about every classic children's novel available, not out of enjoyment, but out of a sense of duty towards my father, who regularly presented me with these so-called classics of children's literature. Virtually all of them bored me. Captain Marryat, Kenneth Graham, A.A. Milne, Captain W.E. Johns, Richmal Crompton, and Lewis Carroll. But plod through them I did.

Captain Marryat elicits a particular shudder each time I park in Enfield Town and walk past a blue plaque on a white 1930s terrace telling passers-by that on this site stood the grand residence of Captain Marryat. I had a particular detestation for Arthur Ransome and his *Swallows and Amazons* and rather wished the boat had sunk with the loss of all life in order to prevent the possibility of a sequel.

In a perverse sort of way I enjoyed the Jennings and Derbyshire novels about high jinks in the boarding house at a public school. Quite why I should be engrossed by people whose lives were so privileged in a way that mine was not, remains a puzzle to me. It was only when I discovered the violent and racy novels of Mickey Spillane, Dashel Hammet and Raymond Chandler that I began to read for pleasure in earnest.

The following is the sort of dialogue that used to impress me. Mike Hammer was my favourite.

> I killed more people tonight than I have fingers on my hands. I shot them in cold blood and enjoyed every minute of it … they were Commies. They were red sons of bitches who should have died long ago. They never thought that there were people like me in this country. They figured us all to be soft as horse manure and just as stupid.

From One Lonely Night by Mickey Spillane

I suppose it is hardly surprising that, after six weeks reading English at university, my professor suggested gently to me that I should perhaps consider a subject closer to my heart. This was shortly after I had recommended the Ed McBain novels to him on the grounds that the subject of his academic interest, Edmund Spenser, lacked pace. He very kindly observed of me that, although I had a second rate mind, I told first class jokes. I suppose that is better than having a first class mind and telling second rate jokes.

A small number of the Pioneers owned the works of Karl Marx; that slightly sinister subsidised Moscow edition that simultaneously intrigued and repelled. However, the book that interested me more than all others was my father's copy of *The Rights of Man* by Thomas Paine; small, compact and densely printed in an Everyman edition.

For many years the book was simply part of the furniture, as decorative as the Toby jugs and blue Wedgwood on the mantelpiece

Although my own bookshelves are something worse than organised chaos, every book my parents owned had its own place. In hindsight, I think that the *Psychology of Sex* on the bookshelf between Robert Louis Stephenson and Thomas Hardy, was a vague attempt at sex education without having to go into the embarrassing details. If so, then it was a miserable failure as I never made it past page three, preferring to share the airbrushed outdoor photographs of young ladies playing volleyball in *Health and Efficiency* with my friends.

This publication, I should add, led me to believe for a number of years that women did not have pubic hair. It was only when I was sitting on what passed for a beach on Canvey Island that a woman who was changing dropped her towel to reveal an impressive mass of pubic hair. I was in a state of sober shock for several days afterwards but at least I was saved the sort of trauma the Victorian critic, John Ruskin, suffered on the night of his wedding to Effie Grey. He was rendered impotent and so disgusted at this deviation from classical purity that the marriage was never consummated.

The Everyman imprint holds a particular place of importance in the development of Pioneer literary tastes. While Penguin, through their Modern Classics and Pelican offshoot, may have pioneered the modern taste for cheap high quality paperbacks, only a relatively small number of them were to Pioneer tastes. Most of them were simply too modern.

The Everyman Imprint owned by J.C. Dent propelled the classics of world and European Literature into the houses and minds of ordinary working class people. Ever since the House of Lords had ruled the notion of permanent copyright invalid in 1774, there had been a market for cheap imprints of great books. J.C. Dent, of working class origins himself and firmly within the auto-didactic tradition, supplied that need better than any of his contemporary rivals.

Conceived with the idea of producing 1,000 volumes that were classics in the literary canon, there was a strong emphasis on the standards of English literature with occasional forays into non-European literature including Rabindranath Tagore and the Koran. It was by looking at the spines of the Everyman volumes on the bookshelves of the Pioneers, that I first became familiar with such names as Herman Melville and George Eliot although on only one occasion was I sufficiently inspired to read a volume. This was after having seen Gregory Peck as Ahab in Herman Melville's *Moby Dick*. I struggled through the first forty pages and then reasoned that, having seen the film, why should I bother with the book. I returned to it thirty years later after purchasing a copy in a Nantucket bookshop.

While the Everyman selections may not have been to everyone's tastes then or now, the experience of the Pioneers suggests that, assuming basic literacy and a modicum of curiosity, a new world of intellectual endeavour had been opened up. Ordinary working men and women could read and own the same books as a king, a millionaire or a Cambridge academic.

As part of the millennium celebrations, every secondary school in the country was given hardback editions of the 250 most important volumes out of the 5,500 that remain in print with the intention that they take pride of place in the school library. A worthy attempt, you may think, of re-establishing the idea of an English canon; the assertion of the almost heretical notion that some books are better than others and are worthy of preservation within the national consciousness. Toward the end of 2000, I visited the deputy headteacher of a local secondary school. In the corner of his office sat a dusty pile of boxes. During a gap in the proceedings, I sneaked a look. Inside, in pristine condition, were the 250 Everyman volumes.

This little incident sums up the problems of central government. It is relatively easy to fund from the centre and decree from the centre that every school will have this millennium gift courtesy of an overweening government. It is quite a different problem to force the school to display the books. It is a problem of a different order of magnitude to create an intellectual, cultural and educational climate in which books will actually be taken out and read.

This summer I took the Everyman edition of *The Count of Monte Cristo* with me on holiday. At the end, I thought I had read nothing better. My tastes have never been that demanding.

I have reflected many times on reasons why I was immune to the greatness of Herman Melville's novel. In many ways, I should have been natural auto-didactic fodder. I was literate, to the extent of being addicted to Ian Fleming's violent and charmless James Bond novels. (The films are weak beer in comparison. *Licence to Kill* is probably the film closest to the original Fleming spirit.) I came from a family that valued education and I had a natural curiosity about the world.

My conclusion was that I had been corrupted. Formal schooling had corrupted me with all the dreariness those thirteen years of servitude entailed. Being forced to labour through a variety of English classics alienated me from literature to the extent that, when confronted with a novel written by a representative of the English canon, I lost interest.

Tom Lexman, autodidact and Spanish Civil War veteran who lived to the rear of our house, told me he was glad he had left school at thirteen because he could now please himself what he did or didn't read rather than having knowledge forced down his throat 'by some nitwit school master'. On the whole, I retain the view that formal schooling, on odd occasions, may provide some useful elements of instruction and the rudiments of an independent social life but it also has a perniciously corrupting influence on the process of education. As the psychologist Burrhus Skinner wisely put it: "Education is what survives when what has been learned has been forgotten."

I was also corrupted by television. The first set arrived in our house in 1961 when I was eight. My father returned home one night with a twelve inch Bakelite Bush television perched precariously on the crossbar of his bicycle. From the outset, I acquired the television watching habit to the despair of my father who only wanted me to watch very specific and severely cultural programmes in contrast to my promiscuous instinct to watch everything until the national anthem was played.

In short, I preferred to watch Norman Vaughan hosting *Sunday Night at the London Palladium* rather than struggling through a classic of English literature. In contrast, my father, who was born in 1922 and did not see a television programme until he was nearly forty, would often prefer to spend his evening in the company of some serious reading matter.

The key difference between us was that I was born at the very beginning of the television age. In contrast he was born in the middle of that golden period, from the auto-didactic point of view, between the achievement of something approaching mass literacy in the early years of the twentieth century and the emergence of television in the late 1950s. Where I relied on the television for entertainment, my father in his south London working class home experienced the novelty of reading aloud – Wordsworth, Coleridge and Keats, all lying within the cultural orbit of the household.

As a youngster, he was taken to hear Harold Laski speak at Conway Hall, C.E.M Joad at the BBC at Portland Place, and Stafford Cripps at Toynbee Hall in the East End. I was taken to watch Spurs play. If I wanted to see any of those left-wing (or otherwise) intellectuals then I just had to watch Brains Trust rather than traipse up to some obscure venue in central London.

*

If Thomas Paine had been American or French he would be a national hero. In France there would be a Place de la Thomas Paine in every medium-sized provincial town and in America a Thomas Paine Shopping Mall. In England we are almost ignorant of him despite the claim that he was 'the first citizen of the world'. In the BBC 100 Greatest Britons poll he ranked below David Beckham, Boy George and Robbie Williams. Tom Paine should be grateful. William Wordsworth and Laurence Olivier did not even make it onto the list.

Collectively our memory has become threadbare to the extent that, as a society, we live in the 'here and now' with no means of connecting current events with those of the past. The plethora of history programmes on television exist in a disembodied state. They are separate from our awareness of where we came from or how we arrived here and, therefore, where we are going. There is an unconscious conspiracy to obliterate our national past. It may not be the aim but the likely consequence will be to emasculate the citizens of the future.

Inevitably, we will pay a heavy price for our carelessness. At every level we have become very forgetful of our national past and, as a result, we suffer in all sorts of unexpected ways.

We have a Prime Minister and a government who act as if the past did not exist. They fail to recognise that understanding the past helps us to shape the future. A government with an awareness of the Suez fiasco would never have embroiled us with such gung-ho enthusiasm in Iraq. Change Colonel Nasser for Saddam Hussein and the rhetoric is the same. The American government, with an even shallower sense of history, seems to have almost forgotten its Vietnam torment that may well be repeated. In this case there is a deliberate obliteration of the past. The 'V' word cannot be mentioned.

Within this scenario, education has been reduced to an adjunct of providing the low grade fuel to stoke the so-called knowledge economy. Any notion of education for individual enrichment and for creating a sense of national cohesion has all but disappeared.

The Pioneers used to tell each other that the purpose of education was to make us free. It would now appear that, in an age of universal education and unprecedented access to university life for the majority, the result, if not the purpose, of education is to enslave the citizen and to deny them choice in how they order and shape their lives.

I recently drove to Thomas Paine's birthplace at Thetford in Norfolk where they are curiously reluctant to own up to giving him his start in life. In the early 1960s, a suggestion was made to erect a statue in his memory. This provoked some vigorous and, on the whole, unenlightened opposition. The story made national headlines and was treated with incredulity in France and the USA where he is still regarded as a hero of both revolutions.

There is a statue now but it sits rather awkwardly in the prim little town with no sense that Thetford is proud of its most famous son. I expected to find a Thomas Paine Community Centre, a Tom Paine Park or Paine Avenue but the only reference I saw was the Thomas Paine Hotel. In a moment of feigned ignorance I asked the young woman behind the bar who Tom Paine was. She shrugged and passed him off as 'some local fella'. I was standing in the bar of the house where arguably the greatest of all Englishmen was born to find him dismissed as 'some local fella'.

If I went to Stratford-upon-Avon and asked the same question of Shakespeare would I get the same answer? He was only a playwright. I will not rest until the next time I cross into Norfolk and am greeted by the county sign 'You are now entering Tom Paine Country'.

I tried a similar ruse when I drove past the William Cobbett public house in Farnham, Surrey. Inside the bar was a magnificent confection of brass and mahogany.

"Who was William Cobbett?" I asked the barmaid. She was quite sweet and tried to answer before finally settling for the fact that he used to 'live up the road'. I thanked her courteously. I suppose it would have been unreasonable to expect her to know he was the greatest of all English journalists, a radical campaigner for the rights of ordinary people who, through his newspaper, the Political Register, was a profound irritant to a series of Whig and Tory governments that tried and imprisoned him for sedition.

Oh well I can live in hope.

Tom Paine came from the auto-didactic tradition that inspired the Pioneers. He designed the famous iron bridge that still sits astride the River Wear in tribute to just one of his remarkable self-taught abilities. *The Rights of Man*, written in 1791, is not easy to read, as those who have read him may discover, yet he is one of the most original thinkers ever to have lived. Despite hard commercial times, both Penguin and Everyman keep him in print today. This is ample testimony that he is for all ages.

Paine asked himself the same questions as the Pioneers did nearly two hundred years later. Why, in a country as rich as Britain with bountiful natural resources, fertile land and a hardworking and ingenious population, was there so much poverty? Why is wealth the preserve of the privileged few, most of whom do not work for it? Why did the majority of the population have no say in how the country of their birthright was governed?

Today we need to ask ourselves the same questions with even greater urgency before it is too late. The gap between the rich and the poor is becoming dangerously wide. Paine came to the conclusion, not unreasonably, that a defective economic and social system denied ordinary people their rights while allowing a small number of the privileged and unproductive elite to accrue the wealth produced by others.

Paine's book is one of the most sustained and devastating attacks on the political, social, and economic status quo ever written. In it he argued not only for democracy and equal rights, but also for a welfare stare that included child allowances and retirement pensions to be funded by progressive taxation.

Today the political establishment would greet such a book with a phrase like 'a timely and useful contribution to the national debate'. Then they would forget all about it. Paine lived in tougher times and found himself charged with sedition. He was in danger of his life and fled to France where he became a member of the French National Assembly. The British government declared him an outlaw and he never returned.

Having narrowly escaped the guillotine in France, in 1802 he fled to America where he had once been a national hero. Later charges of atheism reduced his popularity in that God-fearing country. Ten years after Paine's death in 1809, the Tory radical William Cobbett, who was a fervent Paine admirer, went to the USA and dug up his bones with the intention of returning them to Britain. Unfortunately he lost them on the return Atlantic voyage. It is somehow appropriate that the bones of 'the first citizen of the world' should have disappeared while on a transatlantic journey.

Paine inspired a whole generation of English radicals, early socialists, idealists and utopians who, in turn, inspired the Pioneers. The most influential of them was probably Thomas Hardy, a Scottish shoemaker who, in 1792, inspired by Paine's writing, founded the London Corresponding Society. It was aimed at artisans and working men with a subscription of one penny a week.

The chief object of the LCS was self-improvement and the vote. The resolution, passed on its founding earnestly entreated all members 'not to delay in improving himself in constitutional knowledge'. They literally believed knowledge was power.

The shape of Thomas Hardy's life was formed by tragedy. His father, a fisherman, drowned on the day Thomas was born, 3rd March 1752. All of his six children died in infancy and his wife died during childbirth in 1794 while their house was under siege from a Church and King mob encouraged by the Tory government.

The membership of the LCS was drawn from those intelligent, self-educated, politically-aware artisans who found themselves excluded from the existing political system. Despite its reformist, rather than revolutionary, demands, the LCS was banned and persecuted by a fearful Tory government that could not distinguish between moderate reform in Britain and the Jacobin excesses across the channel in France.

Hardy's demands were simple and moderate; that the working man should be allowed the vote and that the corrupt parliament should be reformed.

In 1793 Hardy and two of his supporters were arrested and charged with high treason. The reasoning of Lord Eldon, the Lord Chancellor and moving force behind the prosecution, a man who was against everything, was that a reformed parliament would want to challenge the power of the monarchy and would ultimately want to remove and execute the king.

The punishment for high treason was to be hung, drawn and quartered – a practice that was a hangover from medieval bestiality. Hardy and his co-defendants were in terrible danger, and they knew it. Only ten days before, Joseph Gerrald was beheaded in Edinburgh on a charge of high treason.

The prospect of this fate was offset by the fact that the prosecution presented no evidence. It was inevitable that a sympathetic jury would find them not guilty and Hardy was drawn in his coach by an ecstatic crowd through the streets of London. Three months later a celebratory dinner was held at the radicals' favourite tavern, the Crown and Anchor in The Minories next to the Tower of London.

Meanwhile, Hardy's cobblers business in Piccadilly had collapsed. Through the generosity of his friends and supporters he opened a new shop in Covent Garden, which at first bustled with business from those customers eager to catch a glimpse of the famous owner.

Hardy's moment of fame had passed, however, and he sank into impoverished retirement later to be rescued by the wealthy and eccentric radical, Sir Francis Burdett, who granted him an annuity for the remainder of his life.

Hardy died in Pimlico nine years later in 1832. The final irony was that, just a few months before his death, Parliament had passed the Great Reform Act which represented a concession to the demands that had put Hardy on trial for his life thirty eight years earlier.

Hardy remains an important footnote from the heroic period of English radicalism and the development of a working class consciousness. It is possible to stand outside Hardy's shop at 36 Tavistock Street, Covent Garden, and peer into the Turkish Restaurant that now occupies the building, even to imagine the radical old cobbler working over his last while reading *The Rights of Man* with an expression of outraged indignation.

There is something appropriate in this contrast between the old artisan London and its modern multicultural counterpart. It was no coincidence that Richard Tidd, one of the conspirators executed for his involvement in the Cato Street Conspiracy of 1822, when a group of misguided radicals attempted to blow up the Cabinet, was also a shoemaker. Cobblers are an admirable lot. They are representative of a sturdy breed of self-educated men of an independent disposition.

William Townshend, radical anarchist and member of the First International who lived in Tottenham Street, just to the north of Oxford Street in the 1890s, was in the same profession. In the early years of the twenty-first century, Tony Martin, the Angry Cobbler of Durham, is leading a dysfunctional city council a merry dance.

My father was friendly with a Labour Party man called Ted Bryant who had worked for fifty years as a cobbler. After retirement he continued to repair our shoes in his garden shed where he had a metal last clamped within the jaws of a metal vice. I always took great pleasure when he nailed on new cleats so that I could make sparks on the kerbstones while walking to school.

Not having thought of Ted for many years, my memory was jolted recently when I was browsing through a book of British folk songs. Ted had a soft, thin voice and would sometimes sing as he played his plaintive accordion. The only song I remember him singing was *The Poore Man Payes for All.*

Ted, who must have been born in the mid-1890s, learned the song from his grandfather who, in turn, would have been born about 1830. Perhaps he had learned it from his father or grandfather. It makes a biting pre-Marxist statement about how the rich have always sponged off the labours of the poor. For those historians of the left who argue that class consciousness did not emerge until the early decades of the nineteenth century and that we cannot properly talk of socialism in England until the 1860s, I offer them *The Poore Man Payes for All.* I am sure that Ted only sung the first two verses but it seems useful to recount the others and reflect on how little the world has changed since 1770, the year in which the song was anonymously composed.

> This but a dreame which here shall insue,
> But the Author wishes his words were not true.
>
> As I lay musing all alone

upon my resting bed,
Full many a cogitation
did come into my head:
And waking from my sleep, I
My dream to mind may call:
me thought I saws before mine eyes,
how poore men payes for all.

I many objects did behold
in this my frightfull Dreame
a part of them I will unfold:
and though my present Theame,
is but a fancy, you may say
yet many things doe fall
Too true alas! for at this day
the poore man payes for all.

Me thought I saw (which caus'd my care)
what I wish were fable
That poore men still inforced are
to pay more than they are able:
Me thought I heard them weeping say,
their substance was but small
For rich men will beare all the sway,
but poore men paye for all.

Me thought I saw how wealthy men
did grind the poore men's faces,
And greedily did prey on them,
not pitying their cases:
They make them toyle and labour sore
for wages too too small;
The rich men in the taverns rore,
but poore men paye for all.

Me thought I saw a userer old
walke in his fox fur'd gowne,
whose wealth and eminence control'd
the most men in the towne:
His wealth he by extortion got,

and rose by other's fall,
He had what his hands earned not,
but poore men paye for all.

Me thought I saw a Courtier proud
goe swaggering along,
That unto any scarce allow'd
the office of his tongue;
Me thought were not for bribery,
his peacock plumes would fall;
He ruffles out in bravery,
but poore men paye for all.

The Common Muse
Me thought I met, sore discontent,
some poore men on the way
I asked one whither he went
so fast and could not stay.
Quoth he, I must goe take my Lease
or else another shall;
My landlord's riches doe increase
but poore men paye for all.

It would be easy to dismiss this as a just a piece of eighteenth century doggerel but it contains a profound message. The shame is that we cannot pay personal tribute to the perception, wit and insight of the author because he remained anonymous.

In the first seven years of a Labour government, the number of millionaires, excluding their property, has increased nearly four-fold; the gap between rich and poor is wider than at any time since the 1930s and we are told that nearly one third of all children live in poverty. We have been bludgeoned into a state of political torpor that we blithely accept as the way of the world.

*

My paternal grandfather's mother was a Thompson, part of the extended Thompson family who, it would appear, flourished in the environs to the north and east of the City in the late 18th and early 19th century. Some of them had infiltrated the old Huguenot silk weaving trade and lived in Fournier Street and Weaver Street, the latter now being covered by an urban farm. The site of the main Thompson residence in Folgate Street is today occupied by a particularly dispiriting 1950s LCC block of flats. Elizabeth Thompson's grandmother, also called Elizabeth Thompson, was born in 1807. In the parish records for St Luke's church, her father is listed as a Henry Perkins, a market gardener from the St James Estate at Walthamstow. His date of birth is given as 1770. The lists of the London Corresponding Society members show a Henry Perkins of St James, Walthamstow who is described as being of the 'artisan class'. Is he my great, great, great, great grandfather? Probably, but I cannot say for certain although he is almost certainly related to me.

It would appear that the Thompsons and the Perkins, as well as being in the business of supplying fresh produce to the City, were also respectable political radicals. Although I like to think that my ancestors were part of the London Corresponding Society, there niggles within me the lurking suspicion that the Thompsons and the Perkins, the Greens and the Dawsons – my distant London ancestors of more than two hundred years back – were at the head of that furious Church and King mob of whom I cluck so disapprovingly.

On the evening of 5th October, 1985, when living in the northern part of Wood Green, North London, I looked out of my bathroom window at the yellow flames illuminating the sky over the Broadwater Farm Estate in Tottenham. I had already listened to the radio news broadcasts covering the events of that terrible evening and, being of a curious disposition, I cycled in the direction of the flames. As I approached the estate I was stopped by a police officer at a roadblock and told to 'piss off' – an expression they learn at the police training college in Hendon. He was understandably upset. The news had just emerged that P.C. Keith Blakelock had been hacked to death by an angry, savage mob on the estate.

I was struck by the fact that the mob never changes. It is always an angry seething mass devoid of moral sense and stripped of pity for those who are its victims. It is as if individuals can abdicate responsibility for their actions through their collective endeavour. The mob, in a near Hegelian sense, assumes a life and discretion of its own which is greater and more terrible than the sum of its parts.

I was reminded of tragic events on a larger scale that had taken place more than two hundred years previously. Family legend has it that one of my ancestors, a man bearing the surname Green, performed the Newgate

Polka as a result of participating in the Newgate Riots. This particular polka was the London slang for the actions of those who had the misfortune to be hanged outside Newgate Prison, the site of which is now occupied by the Old Bailey. The polka description is presumably a reference to the victim's writhing and jerking movements at the end of the rope as he is slowly strangled to death.

The riots took place early in June 1780. A march organised by Lord George Gordon against the repeal of anti-Catholic legislation got out of hand. Having started as a peaceful march from St George's Field's, Southwark, to the Houses of Parliament, it turned into a week long rampage in which poor and ragged London vented its anger on first the Catholics, then the Irish, then any foreigners who happened to be convenient. Curiously, only in a modest way did they vent their anger against the real cause of their misery and suffering – the existence of the rich and the privileged.

While observing the racially-based disturbances in the late 1990s in urban centres as varied as Wrexham, Oldham, Bradford and Burnley, it was again obvious that the rioters did not strike at the real cause of their disadvantage but at those racial minority groups who happened to be close at hand. Astonishingly, rioting can flicker and spread like some vengeful fire into previously tranquil areas.

In the course of seven days, the Gordon Riots affected most of London. Two hundred and one years later, what should have been a localised disturbance in Brixton, south London, turned into widespread urban rioting that affected the most innocuous parts of London. Even bland, respectable, semi-detached Southgate, hardly on the front line, experienced the riotous mob smashing windows in the High Street and turning over cars until their mothers called them in for tea. This suggests that civilisation and order, as we like to see it, are only a very thin veneer. Severe disorder, even in the most benign of circumstances, is only just around the corner. In my imagination, at least, there exists a feral mob on a permanent state of alert waiting for the opportune moment when the defences of respectable society are lowered then the signal is given out 'let the rampaging begin'. An evening spent observing the centre of any medium-sized British town on a Saturday evening is proof that the problem does not all lie in my fevered imagination

Significantly, the actions of the mob in 1780 were transformed into an attack upon the political, economic and social elite of London. The hated

Newgate Prison, always a symbol of cruelty and oppression, was burned to the ground quickly followed by the prisons at the Fleet, Borough, Clerkenwell and Kings Bench. The mob then attacked the house of the magistrate, Sir John Fielding, in Bow Street and the grand residence of the Lord Chief Justice, Lord Mansfield, in Bloomsbury Square on the grounds that he was insufficiently anti-catholic.

Given the oppressive and brutal nature of the eighteenth century judicial system, I find it hard not to have some sympathy with the frantic desire of those who wished to destroy the symbols that so tormented them. This was to be the undoing of my ancestor.

The mob then attacked Downing Street before launching a bloody assault on the Bank of England which was repelled by a volley of musket fire from the clerks inside. It would appear that the riot burnt itself out through a combination of exhaustion and the destruction of Langdale's Gin distillery in Holborn. This led to scenes of mass drunkenness on the part of the rioters, many of whom, literally gin-soaked, were turned into human torches as the distillery was fired.

I knew very little of these events until my maternal grandmother, who was born at Lambeth in 1886, retold a story she had been told as a child. Her father's grandfather had apparently been hanged for being part of a huge riot that destroyed London. The dates however were not quite right.

Allowing thirty years for a generation, my grandmother's great grandfather would have been born in 1796, sixteen years after the riot. Allowing for another generation, and given any sort of oral family history (the generations are always ill-defined) and the possibility of late fatherhood, then it is entirely possible. Sometimes, when untangling working class history, small intuitive leaps are necessary. I was sufficiently intrigued to undertake the long trek to the Public Record Office at Kew where old Home Office papers, and those of the Lord Chancellor's department, are stored.

It was immediately apparent that the reference to the Newgate Polka was part of a working class residual memory. Newgate was destroyed in the riots and the executions afterwards took place at Smithfield and Tyburn on the site of Marble Arch. However, some of the executions were summary and took place on the site of the offence. Three apprentice boys were hanged outside the home of Lord Mansfield whose house had been attacked.

The hanging of apprentice boys is a powerful feature of eighteenth century justice. The Tyburn records indicate that half of those executed in this period were apprentices. The authorities feared and demonised the apprentices and their capacity for random and destructive violence, perhaps taking the view that, if the apprentice boy mob could be controlled, then the whole of society could be controlled. Those who advocate a strong stance on youth crime will probably approve. The three hanged outside Lord Mansfield's house certainly committed no further offences.

There was a feeling of hopelessness about my task. The list of the condemned contained familiar London names – Pearson, Tanner, Borrowby, Parwell, Hammond and Turner. However another name caught my attention. Edward Dennis had been condemned to hang but had then been reprieved in order to execute his fellow rioters.

My indefatigable cousin, during her researches into our family history, has uncovered a family by the name of Dennis who lived in Islington and then Wood Green in the mid- and late-nineteenth century. Their line was that of Thomas Dennis who married the youngest daughter of my great, great grandfather and whose progeny now extend to New Zealand, Australia, Canada and Cheshire. They are my cousins four times removed. It was Thomas Dennis's grandfather who happily strung up his fellow rioters and earned a commendation from the Lord Mayor of London, who also gave him five golden guineas.

I suspect I will never know for certain, but I take some comfort that this distant kinsman of mine stood so firmly for order and authority in such a tumultuous century. He was a survivor in a difficult age. It does not disguise the fact that he was one of those who burnt the private chapel of the Sardinian Ambassador in Lincolns Inn Fields and made a significant contribution to the destruction of Georgian London.

There is a pleasing symmetry. I was one of those who stood as a curious observer, from a vantage point behind the neo-classical columns of St Martins in the Fields, and watched the Poll Tax Riots in Trafalgar Square in 1990. A famous English historian of left-wing disposition has tried to explain such outbursts of rioting and anger in terms of (what he calls) 'moral economy'. He argues that a mob on the rampage has some innate sense of what is right and wrong and that, being powerless within society, the only way to express this, to right the wrongs, is through direct crowd action. He may well be right but I would challenge him to defend the actions of some alleged anarchists in Trafalgar Square who were attempting to decapitate a police officer by ramming a long metal pole through the side window of a police car, and then tell me this was the action of a crowd seeking moral justice.

The problem with Marxist historians is that, while they nearly always possess high-level analytical abilities, they are usually devoid of common sense. An eminent sociologist claimed that the Trafalgar Square riots were a cry for help by the dispossessed. What I witnessed was nothing more than a cry for a riotous good time in that grand old London tradition.

Substitute the firing of the Bavarian Embassy in 1780 for the burning of the South African Embassy in 1990 and there emerges a satisfying, if wholly reprehensible, sense of continuity. The press blamed the anarchist contingent for the trouble. Such statements overestimated both their numbers and their simple capacity for violence. The reality was that the crowd in Trafalgar Square were responding in kind to police aggression and violence. Unfortunately the television coverage gave very little emphasis to the police action that precipitated the deplorable events.

Chapter 5: Education in the East

If a nation expects to be ignorant and free – it expects what never was and never will be.
Thomas Jefferson.

My headmaster lived in a small terraced council house just half a mile from the school. It was a sign of the times that we thought it normal for the headmaster of a large secondary school to live in a two-bedroomed local authority house, cheek by jowl with those he was gallantly attempting to educate.

On days when I did not cycle to school, I walked through the maze of alleyways that took me past his back gate. David Brookman took the same route while doing his paper round and each morning he hocked up (what he called) 'an oyster' and left it hanging tenuously from the gate latch.

I must have been reaching a sensible and mature stage because I asked him, "Why do you do it? He's done you no harm."

"Because I want to," Brookman replied. "Do you want to make something of it?"

Observing the rings that adorned his fingers like knuckledusters, I did not pursue the conversation.

So many conversations of my childhood were similarly punctuated by the violently aggressive question, 'Do you want to make something of it?' Our town was a fighting town in which the strong flourished. An old friend and I tried to recall our abiding memory of growing up in Basildon in the 1960s. Independently, we both reached the same conclusion: the violence. It was though of the 'fist and boot' variety rather than the 'knife and gun' approach to settling personal disputes

The inevitable consequence was the casual, yet cynically extreme, violence witnessed at the Rettendon killings of 1995 when three South Essex drug dealers were 'executed' in a Range Rover parked in a lonely lane near Basildon. The title of the film that resulted, *Essex Boys*, says it all. It seems that old habits die hard. In 2002, while in Foyle's bookshop looking for a book on applied linguistics, a half-witted customer objected to me using a mobile phone in the shop. My instinctive reaction was, "Do you want to make something of it?" God knows what I would have done if he had said 'yes' but he didn't and he slunk off muttering under his breath. The fact is, you can take the boy out of Basildon but you can't take Basildon out of the boy. To be honest, I later felt some shame that I was unashamed by this little incident.

*

Despite the justification of occasional usefulness, I have never warmed to the culture of the mobile phone. I can only think of one moment when they have given me any pleasure and this involved the destruction of one.

About five years ago, I was travelling in a fairly crowded carriage on a train to Twickenham to watch England play France. A weasel-faced young man insisted on sharing the rather unpleasant details of his sexual conquest from the night before with a friend via his mobile phone. I rather suspect it was mainly immature fantasy but, distressingly, he was also sharing the sordid details with the rest of the carriage, including several matronly, middle-aged women who were grimacing with disgust.

When he recounted, to his hapless friend, how he had asked her if she 'took it up the arse' it became more than we could collectively bear. A very large man, who resembled an England second row forward from the early 1980s, marched over to the young man in question. Without comment he removed the mobile phone from his grasp. If I could remember his name I would be delighted to include it, as I feel that he should be rewarded from the public purse. The rest of the carriage looked on in breathless silence.

The offender attempted to rise from his seat. "What the **** are you doing?"

The aggressor – about six foot five inches tall and probably weighing twenty stone – forced him back into his seat with a massive hand. The carriage was of the more recent type without opening windows. As a result the man forced the phone through one of the ventilation slits. It disappeared into the void.

The youth then said he was going to call the '*******' police' using the phone of his spotty friend sitting next to him.

"If you do that," replied the man calmly, "then the same thing will happen to that phone."

At this stage I began to clap and the rest of the carriage joined in the applause. A woman sitting opposite observed that: "There is a God after all."

As we pulled into Twickenham station, our very large saviour alighted while his victim, spotting several policemen standing on the platform, made a move to get off.

"Block him!" shouted one of the large man's companions.

Instinctively and collectively, we moved to block the exit route of the two young men for a full minute, thus allowing our hero to escape into the massing crowd heading for the stadium. I observed to the young man that if he had extended a little consideration to his fellow members of the travelling public then he would still be in full possession of his mobile phone.

"Why don't you **** off, you ****!" he spat out at me, his face twisted with rage.

I have reflected on this lawless incident many times over the last few years and each time I think of it I smile with unconscious pleasure.

This was truly the 'moral economy of the English crowd' in action. Like their eighteenth century predecessors they were acting to defend what they believed was morally right in the face of an assault upon their values. Substitute the price of bread or the payment of tithes to the Church of England for the pursuit of civility and consideration, and we have the same impulse. It was a collective and spontaneous action by a group of law-abiding, decent people, representing what is sometimes, slightly mockingly, called Middle-England. They acted to protect those values that they held most dear with a modicum of consideration for others. Thus, they felt perfectly justified in blocking the path of the gormless young man despite the fact that he had been the victim of a mobile phone mugging.

As those middle-aged anarchists, the Chappists, tell us, we should all engage in random acts of common courtesy. No doubt the police, in their hapless way, would have prosecuted our heroic stranger and suggested his victim could join a support group where he could get counselling, courtesy of the taxpayer, in order that he could overcome the trauma of his ordeal.

Half an hour later I was walking through the Twickenham stadium car park filled with Rolls Royces and Range Rovers belonging to the wealthy who were indulging in those grotesque pre-rugger picnics that have come to characterise England home games – a show of 'rub it in the face of the plebs' privilege and vulgar conspicuous wealth.

One can take only so many red-faced shouting men, waving champagne bottles and stuffing themselves with canapés and lobster before one feels tempted to take out a direct debit and become a full time member of Class War. Despite the best efforts of many people, rugby union in England remains a 'posh boys' sport'.

*

My education has never quite recovered from having lived in Basildon New Town. Primary school was idyllic. Through the haze of memory it reminds me of those pictures of a Soviet Newtown during the five-year plans, with happy and healthy children, mother and baby clinics, sanatoria and people riding ancient heavy bicycles through pedestrian underpasses.

We sat in rows and chanted our tables but it never seemed like a hardship, as we knew of nothing else. Forty years later I can still do long division but it has never been any use to me.

The exception to this happy picture occurred on my first day in infant school. It was solemnly explained to us that, if we wished to go to the toilet, we must always ask the teacher for toilet paper which she tore off an Izal roll that hung behind her desk. On my second day, to cries of "runny bum" from the boys, I asked for the toilet paper.

"How many sheets do you need?" the teacher asked.

The question perplexed me for the number of sheets would depend upon the nature and consistency of the motion. I came from a household, indeed a culture, where we had unlimited access to toilet paper based upon need. I cannot remember my form of words but I made this point in some way or other and was rewarded by being hit across the hand with a ruler.

The town was a microcosm for the old eleven plus system. The Butler Education Act of 1944 had swept away the old elementary schools and fee-paying grammar schools. Instead, they introduced the tripartite system whereby, at the age of eleven, children sat a test called the eleven-plus and were assigned to one of the three sorts of secondary schools.

Working class children went to a secondary modern school where they endlessly sawed up pieces of wood and in the more rural areas tended the school farm. Middle class children attended the grammar school where they learnt Latin and told themselves that they wanted to be accountants. Clever practical children went to a technical school but few were actually built and they rapidly sank from sight.

Labour had the chance, in 1945, to deal with the problem of the independent sector but they shied away from the issue. With the ink barely dry on the 1944 Butler Act, the situation was propitious in the name of the New Jerusalem to rid the country of the educational apartheid that had disfigured it for the last century.

With a leader from Haileybury, and his successor, a self-conscious Wykhamist, they declined. Even that grudging hero of the Socialist Pioneers, Stafford Cripps, was a Wykhamist. I have learnt in life that they get everywhere and they are always so very smug. The commitment to socialism by these sort of people was of the variety that everyone had an entitlement to a good set of false teeth but they had no interest in storming the ramparts of class privilege.

Ellen Wilkinson, the combative and radical Minister for Education, suggested that the state take over the public schools. Her lover, Deputy Prime Minister Herbert Morrison, dismissed her suggestion as a 'female tantrum'. His grandson, Peter Mandelson, carries on the tradition of familial condescension. The result of Labour's moral cowardice in the 1940s is that we now have the largest independent sector in the world and a cruel and damaging division between the state and private sectors.

The omens will never be as good again. The pernicious influence of the independent sector is constantly with us. An example is a small group of independent schools, led by Eton College, representing no more than 3 per cent of school pupils in England and Wales. They have publicly challenged the usefulness of the GCSE exam and this triggered, within twenty-four hours, a national debate about the value of the exams, fuelled by the privately-educated editors and journalists of the Daily Telegraph, The Times and the Daily Mail. The case they presented ignores the fact that the GCSE is a qualification that suits the vast majority of children.

When the headmaster of Eton describes GCSEs as being of no more value than scout badges, he denigrates the efforts of hundreds of thousands of children. Sadly he is taken seriously.

If a large coalition of schools representing a majority of state school pupils questioned the value of the qualification then an official from the Department of Education would make a pompous statement along the lines that they were 'a vital part of the government's long term strategy for maintaining standards and engaging young people in a culture of learning'. To use a cliché, it is the tail wagging the dog.

At a very early stage in my primary school education, there was a serious attempt to inculcate in all of us an awareness of our lowly position in society. The school I had been assigned to had not yet been built as the town was expanding so rapidly. I was therefore sent to a traditional primary school over which presided a dried-up stick of a headmistress to whom I took a strong dislike.

Children in the school were divided into 'serfs' and 'lords and ladies' on a ratio of about twenty to one. The task assigned to those pupils appointed as 'lords and ladies' was to lead the 'serfs' by moral example and shop their fellow pupils to the headmistress.

Needless to say I found this situation unacceptable, as did my friend, Animal. We were not conscious socialists but we were instinctive egalitarians and fighters against injustice. It was like Tsarist Russia where the secret police (the Okhrana) informed on the peasants to the officials of the Tsar. In an outburst of revolutionary insurrection, Animal and I, together with a large number of very undeferential serfs, waylaid our Lord and Lady. We threw our Lord into a ditch of stinging nettles and, I am embarrassed to admit, we removed the knickers from our Lady and threw them on top of a tall bush. It was our version of the Peasants Revolt but with no heads hacked off.

The next day, as the dried-up old stick was liberally dispensing corporal punishment, Animal and I avoided any chastisement by virtue of the fact that we were members of another school and the headmaster of our school-to-be appeared not to be unduly bothered by the incident. I suspect he was secretly quite amused.

In all my years at school, at a time when there was still a significant addiction to corporal punishment, I was never once beaten. This was due to a combination of luck, superior intelligence, and knowing how to divert attention from myself. It was not due to any deficit of beatable behaviour.

When a boy in my class lit up a cigar and began puffing ostentatiously, my only thought was that he would get everything he deserved for his stupidity. He was duly dragged down to the headmaster's study for a caning. Yet one of the more depressing experiences of being in a secondary modern school at this time was that every break period saw a queue of boys standing outside the office of the deputy headmaster waiting to be beaten. Occasionally, Animal and I would stand outside and listen to the whistle and thwack of the cane, and the resulting squeals of pain. We decided this was simply part of life.

Fortunately I was never faced with the ominous question: "Which hand do you write with, boy?" For those who were, it was a signal that the inquisitor was about to disable the other hand.

Strangely, it never seemed to occur to our school beater that it was the same miscreants who returned to his office each day for the routine treatment. Consequently, he failed to realise that the punishment was obviously not working. For anyone who hankers after the good old days, with education as it should be, I recommend they join the queue outside the child beater's office.

To his credit, our beater did not indulge in the old hypocritical rubbish of 'this is going to hurt me more than it will hurt you'. His was the more pragmatic view that it was going to hurt the victim a lot and would not hurt him at all. Possibly he might even enjoy it. I remember being repelled by the sight of fresh wheals that had just been inflicted on the buttocks of a boy in the school toilets. They were dark red, as thick as my thumbs and filled with blood.

Girls were, on the whole, immune from such abuse. Their rather different nemesis came in the slight, hunched form of the shrunken, humourless senior mistress. Her spiteful nature was illustrated by the fact that she would make recalcitrant girls roll up the sleeves of their blouse, grasp their wrist in her left hand and slap the forearm with such vigour that she appeared to levitate off the ground. It was as if the cathartic effort of reddening the forearms of girls twice her size put the harridan in a temporary reasonable mood before her brooding, shrewish nature once again forced her to demand: "Roll up your sleeve, girl." Irma Griese had nothing on her.

Punishment was usually administered for a specific serious offence like 'talking in assembly' or 'being in the toilets at the wrong time'. Bizarrely, it was also administered for the much more generalised offence: the need to 'buck your ideas up'. This underlined an educational philosophy that certain individuals needed a beating in order to motivate them. Sadly, it was the case that some individuals did work harder as a result.

"Gosh as a result of Mr Thrashem giving me four strokes of the cane I got an 'A' in my French and Latin exams. Thanks, Mr Thrashem. I couldn't have done it without you."

As George Orwell mentioned in *Such, Such Were the Joys*, his rather intellectually-challenged classmate, Hardcastle, who was desperate for a scholarship to Uppingham, received a severe beating for doing poorly in the entrance exam.

"I wish I had received that caning before I went up for the exam," he exclaimed afterwards.

A not dissimilar philosophy was applied rigorously at Friern Barnet Grammar School, a grim day-school for boys close to where I now live in north London. It was one of those dubious institutions that hide under the prep school umbrella and attract the patronage of parents who are fearful of the local comprehensive schools. In 1989, the headmaster drew the attention of the national press by forcing a boy into a contract whereby he agreed to achieve a certain average percentage mark in his school exams. The penalty for failing to achieve the mark was a bracing dose of corporal punishment that drew blood, the wrath of the mother, and the attention of the press in an unseemly court case. This flogging in the quiet suburbs of north London led to the premature retirement of the headmaster who, under current law, would now be in prison. It also led to the eventual merger of this latter-day Dothebys Hall with a more liberal institution.

The beating of small children was just accepted as an unavoidable fact of the British way of life. Geoffrey Fisher, freemason and Grand Chaplain to the United Grand Lodge of England was appointed Archbishop of Canterbury in 1945 despite the fact that it was widely known that he had a sadistic addiction to caning small boys that was fed when he was headmaster of Repton. The failings of Fisher were testified by the publisher Victor Gollancz, Roald Dahl and many other staff and pupils who dubbed him 'Flog 'em Fisher'. It was not an impediment that prevented him from rising to the holiest of positions that he held until 1961.

Such painful experiences are surprisingly commonplace for anyone over the age of thirty-five. As a result of articles I have written on the subject, I have received wide-ranging correspondence from people who are still outraged by their treatment.

One correspondent attended William Collins, a secondary modern school near to Kings Cross in the early 1970s. The school had been singled out for its excessive use of corporal punishment and had been the focus of unwelcome media attention and a damning report from Her Majesty's Inspectors. My correspondent told of an insidious and depraved culture in which the decision about a child's beating was largely determined by parental attitudes.

"And what would your parents say if they knew that you had got the cane today?"

If the reply was "My mother will be up here with a rolling pin and will knock seven bells out of you" the child would be unmolested.

If, on the other hand, the reply was "They will be mad and I will get some more at home" that was green light for an endless series of beatings that only ceased when the boy left school – usually at the first opportunity when he reached the age of fifteen. In general, boys from middle class supportive families avoided being beaten while those children who were vulnerable and were from working class or single parent families were remorselessly abused. It was the same philosophy that George Orwell described at St Cyprians, his ghastly Edwardian prep school where the boys of parents who earned more then £2,000 a year were never caned.

A correspondent who, in the 1960s, attended St Ignatius, a boys Catholic School then situated in Stamford Hill, North London, told me of a priest, the tolly man, whose job was to beat children using a long strip of black leather known as the tolly. The system was operated by chits issued by offended teachers that designated the number of strokes. Failure to report in good time to the tolly man, complete with chit, merely increased the severity of the punishment. He recalled one boy who was beaten every day, and every day he cried. Another person recalled he was beaten every Thursday afternoon because he was 'evil'. His parents knew of his misery but were adamant that he should remain because the school had an excellent record of getting pupils into Downside, the Catholic public school.

As Philip Larkin observed;

> They fuck you up, your mum and dad,
> They may not mean to, but they do,
> They fill you with the faults they had
> And add extra just for you.

These famous lines show a prescient wisdom. Every teacher in the land should have this verse emblazoned across their classroom and every school report that is sent home should have it printed at the top.

An older correspondent recalled his time at Queen Elizabeth Boys' Grammar School in Barnet in the late 1940s. On one occasion, the headmaster was outraged when the guilty boy would not own up to breaking a window. The rather excessive solution was to take the entire school year out onto the field. The headmaster caned every boy on the principle that at least the guilty individual suffered.

I can corroborate this story as it was recounted when I joined the teaching staff at the school. The sad part is that it was told in a triumphant spirit as proof of the quality of the 'old school'. I am all for tradition but not at the expense of obliterating the possibilities of the future.

My wife's brother-in-law told me he was horrified when he bumped into his old housemaster from Uppingham Public School when he was a guest at a wedding. Although he was in his late twenties, he shook involuntarily when in his presence, such was his memory of the brutality of the man.

My own brother-in-law attended King's School in Grantham, a grammar school with its own boarding house. There he was routinely beaten. He left school at the age of fifteen with not one shred of his great potential fulfilled. His experience was made even more unpleasant because the senior pupils, the house captains, were allowed to beat the younger pupils in the name of learning leadership skills. Inevitably it turned into an episode of unpleasant and painful bullying. When he recounted his experiences to me, such was the rage he still felt that he said, very calmly, if he ever bumped into a teacher or fellow pupil who had abused him, he would, without compunction, break his nose, or worse. One of the more bizarre, but sinister, aspects of his experience was being invited with a group of boys to a teacher's house where they donned blue PE shorts and then wrestled with the teacher on the living room floor.

Even girls were not immune from this sort of abuse. My mother, who later in life was a school secretary, recalls the headmistress of her all-girls secondary modern school kept a cane permanently soaking in a hand basin in the ladies cloakroom to keep it springy and supple and always ready for immediate use, which was frequent.

I have always been strongly against corporal punishment as an affront to human dignity. In 1986, on the eve of Prince Andrew and Lady Sarah Ferguson's marriage, I walked through Westminster on my way to Parliament to witness the debate that would lead to the abolition of corporal punishment in state schools in Britain. The pavements were crowded with devoted royalists, all with their garden chairs and airbeds, bedding down for the night in order to get a good position for the next day's festivities.

It was not to our credit that this socially-progressive piece of legislation was being debated. It was the result of those interfering softies at the European Court of Human Rights who had ruled that the fun must stop. Predictably, a stream of snivelling, conceited, perverted and overfed Conservative MPs spoke in the chamber testifying that being beaten at school was a character-forming experience, an experience that had made them the men they were. The men they were was a powerful argument for instant abolition. The sight of Conservative MPs wanting to have their fleshy bottoms beaten while dreaming of matron (Hattie Jacques style, I imagine) is the most revolting sight I have ever seen in politics, including my dealings with the racist far right.

When the division came, the abolitionists won by a single vote. Within minutes, two puffing and rather flushed Conservative MPs arrived, too late for the division having been held up by the traffic around the Palace of Westminster. Had they arrived on time, the abolitionists would have lost.

For those pupils still wishing to be beaten, it was then necessary to attend an independent school until the complete ban came in 1997. Incredibly, a group of Evangelical Christians in Liverpool launched a case at Strasbourg in the belief that the human rights of parents were being breached by being denied the opportunity to send their children to a school where they could be beaten. I sometimes nurture the deepest suspicions about Christians.

To their credit, the European Court threw the case out at the first reading. It could only have emanated from Britain. It was suggested that if a pupil at one of these evangelical schools deserved a beating then the approving parent could be requested to attend the school to personally administer the punishment. Legal apparently but quite perverted.

*

Basildon had two grammar schools, a technical school and eight secondary modern schools (one was a bilateral school, which counts as two schools). It was a rather curious social policy decision that it was felt necessary to impose a selective system in a town that was almost entirely working class. In 1949, the year the town was founded, there was already a significant level of unease at the failure of the newly-introduced tripartite system. At the time, there was talk of children being 'golden' – able to think in abstract terms, 'silver' – capable of high-level technical skills, and 'iron' – those who comprised the lumpen mass and could do nothing but labour. We did not even qualify as bronze. Somehow that stage was missed out in the pursuit of base metal.

The core of the problem was that no one ever defined, in honest terms, the purpose of secondary modern schools in an educational sense. If a child was not academically-gifted or technically-able, then what was the purpose of education? They skirted round the question and, in desperation, Ellen Wilkinson claimed, in 1947, that the new schools would be characterised by 'laughter in the classroom, self-confidence, and growing everyday, eager interest instead of bored conformity'. In other words, the secondary moderns could do what they liked provided they did not disrupt the grammar schools. The reality was that most of them were old elementary schools with a fresh coat of paint and a new sign at the front gate.

I was 'iron' – deeply tarnished and very rusty. I was assigned to a secondary modern school. The first, and most immediate impact was that my best friend went to the grammar school and, although we lived only two hundred yards apart, we never spoke again. A system of apartheid operated via selection every bit as efficient as it was in South Africa in the bad old days. I may as well have lived in Soweto and my friend in Johannesburg for the gulf that opened up between us. I often reflect on why I lost my best friend, feeling that, in some way, it was my fault. I noticed that he always walked the longer way to school to avoid coming past my house. I later learned that his mother told him not to talk to secondary modern boys because he would never get to be a solicitor. It was as if we had an infection.

I recently looked up his entry on Friends Reunited and he is now a systems analyst, whatever that means. Another is a public relations consultant while a third lists himself as a drinks sector analyst. What do these people do? What in God's name is a drinks sector analyst? Imagine what my old friend might be if he had never met me at all – Lord

Chancellor, Admiral of the Fleet, Archbishop of Canterbury?

I went through a fiction before I went to my new school when I was interviewed by a besuited flunky at the education offices.

"I don't want you to feel, Magnus, that you have failed your eleven plus."

I sat there in silence.

"No, the purpose of the exam is to show what sort of school you are most suited to and the results show that you are most suited to Nicholas Secondary Modern."

This was extremely comforting, of course.

"Anyway there will be another chance to get into the grammar school if you choose to sit the thirteen plus."

At this point, I should have said, "And will they be sitting an exam in the grammar school at 13 to see if they can transfer to the secondary modern?" But I didn't. I merely sat there in a mute deferential way, quietly pleased at the prospect of going to a school that did not set homework.

All the children of Pioneers failed the eleven-plus and went to secondary modern school, with one exception. Brian (we used to call him Brains) passed and was held in some awe by the rest of us. When he was expelled for refusing to get his hair cut, it somewhat tarnished his success. The headmaster held a termly inspection of all the boys in the hall. The silence was occasionally punctuated with the word 'cut' when a few wisps of hair hung slightly over the collar. Brian, exhibiting the sturdy Pioneer spirit of awkward principled independence, refused and was expelled.

In those days, headmasters were little sawdust Caesars against whose arbitrary rulings there was no appeal. Perhaps the head saw some flaw in a feckless character for it was Brian's fate to become a heroin addict for more than twenty years and spend some time in a secure unit before he awoke from the nightmare and decided that he wanted to be a bespoke furniture maker. Again, the Pioneer destiny can be seen in the desire to be a skilled and independent artisan in the tradition of Thomas Hardy, William Lovett and Francis Place. I don't know how much progress he has made in his new chosen profession but I wish him every success.

I was different from the rest of my friends who lived in the same road and in the surrounding streets. I was the only one who was physically whole.

Douglas Boyle was missing an ear. I stared, endlessly fascinated, at the small bud where the ear should have been. Inevitably, he was called Lugless Douglas. On the other side of the road, Alan Prufrock had no front teeth after being kicked in the face by a horse. Many years later, while reading T.S. Eliot's *The Lovesong of Alfred J Prufrock*, I would think of his pink, toothless leering grin. "Mornings, Evenings, Afternoons, I have measured out my life with coffee spoons." In the opposite direction lived the Smedley family. Keith, who was too stupid to be my close friend, was minus two fingers on his left hand. We never did find the reason for the missing digits but it was rumoured his father had taken an axe to him when he was roaring drunk from the filthy liquor he produced on a still in an old outhouse somewhere over the back of Laindon.

The Smedleys were 'Old Basildon', that is, they eked out a living running a small poultry farm before the new town was built. They would have made a family of Appalachian hillbillies look intelligent. I know it sounds unkind, but it is true. The reality is that, despite being less than thirty miles from London, there were small pockets of rural deprivation in the area, reinforced by non-existent educational opportunities and, before the new town was built, little prospect of reasonable work. As a result the gene pool became very limited.

My most interesting friend was Fred Murrow who lived above the local parade of shops. Fred lost an eye in an airgun accident. With a few more able-bodied, if not entirely mentally alert, friends, we formed our own happy little gang and succeeded in turning ourselves into a minor social nuisance. We specialised in such anti-social activities as knocking on doors, letting down bicycle tyres, setting off random fireworks (what has changed?) and forcing potatoes into car exhaust pipes. Tame stuff, I know, but it kept us amused.

Ours was a childhood that came right at the end of the period of unrestrained outdoor play that was ended by television, the motorcar, Playstations, the meat grinder of school tests, neurotic parents and the fear of strangers.

> Boys and girls come out to play,
> The moon doth shine as bright as day.
> Leave your supper and leave your sleep,
> And join your play fellows in the street.
> Come with a whoop and come with a call,

Come with a good will or not at all.

We were completely territorial and kept to our own little patch mainly because there were many bigger and tougher gangs of boys who were not only physically whole but also mentally agile. In the violent world of street gangs, we were easy prey. Over a period of years, I got to know an area no larger than a quarter mile square with an intimacy that will never be repeated. I knew who lived in every house, who owned every car and motorcycle, and who owned all the stray dogs and cats. I was familiar with every hiding place, back alley, side turning, garage, shed and allotment.

This was the map of my childhood. Such local knowledge was useful because, occasionally, other gangs would come looking for us knowing that a bunch of maimed halfwits would make easy prey. The most feared of these was the Roydon Bridge Gang, led by Glenn Keeley, who later went on to have a distinguished soccer career with Ipswich, Newcastle and other clubs. He punched me in the stomach once. Not everyone can claim to have been beaten up by a top professional footballer and I hold no grudge. Whenever he and his equally large and forbidding brothers hoved into view, we disappeared. We knew our place.

However there was strength in our weaknesses. Confrontations were sometimes defused by the issue of Fred's missing eye. For his party piece he would remove his glass orb and allow us, or any rival gangs, to look into the socket. It was better than being punched in the stomach. With true Thatcherite entrepreneurial instinct I took him under my wing and explained that he should be charging for such an entertainingly grotesque piece of amusement. I immediately became his manager. For one shilling apiece, or half a crown for a group viewing, he would pop his eye out as we gawped into his red pulpy socket. Helpfully I would have a torch and magnifying glass to hand for those who were interested in the finer detail.

I know I should have agonised about this matter and struggled with my socialist conscience yet, with torch in hand, I exploited this poor benighted soul as heartlessly as any bloated, greedy capitalist. And I was taking half the money. Any Pioneer would have explained I was taking the Marxist theory of surplus value to an extreme. I was stealing from my friend. And did I care? Of course not, my conscience was clear.

Fred went to a special school called Moat House because he still could not read or write by the time he was approaching school leaving age.

Unfortunately, his mother did not take kindly to my efforts on behalf of her son and complained to the headmaster. Although this issue had nothing to do with him, I was summoned to his office on a Monday morning.

"I have had a most disturbing complaint." He then went on to outline the details.

I nervously eyed the cane propped in the corner and was alert to any movement in that direction. I thought of the wisdom of my friend, Barry, who always wore two pairs of underpants to school to guard against the possibility of being beaten on his tender buttocks. The red punishment book was ominously close but I was comforted by the fact that it was closed.

"We were raising money for the Oxfam One Million Pound Campaign, to help those poor people in Africa," I excused myself lamely.

His eyes closed to narrow slits as he stared suspiciously. "I was not informed of that fact. Very well, if you give me the money, I will send a school cheque to Oxfam."

I made to leave his office. "Next time boy, next time," he said ominously, glancing at the cane in the corner. I was informed by gloating friends that one's fate was sealed if the punishment book was open and the number of strokes to be administered was indicated by a series of neat little ticks. Offences were various and never straightforward. Insolence was always 'gross', disobedience was always 'flagrant'. Harmless and amusing additions to a biology text book were 'indicative of a corrupt and depraved cast of mind'. My record of 'disgusting behaviour in the boys toilets' was not what you might think. I was sitting in a hand basin, as one does, smoking a cigarette and chatting when it came away from the wall and crashed to the floor.

After the Fred Murrow incident, I resolved to have as little to do with the headmaster as possible. Richard Branson must have started somewhere. Not that I was alone in possessing a basic entrepreneurial instinct. My little friend Wingnut, a nickname derived from his sticky out ears, organised a small but elaborate betting circle of which I was an eager participant. It was based either on the length of morning assembly or on the number of times the headmaster would remove and replace his glasses. For a shilling, I would sit in an agony of suspense discreetly timing the length of the assembly which was, unfailingly, a prayer, a hymn and a bollocking about some minor transgression or other.

Imagine my joy on the day the glasses came off and back on eight times, as I had predicted.

The headmaster, poor man, was under the illusion that we sat in the assembly hall in rapt silence because we were transfixed by the pearls of wisdom he was laying before us. On the day of my triumph I had odds of twelve to one which yielded a decent return. We knew that, although there were odd occasions when the glasses would stay firmly in place, or would be removed just once or twice, this would only happen a few times a term. For removing them once we were offered odds of fifty to one. Tempting but, in my view, having spent many years squandering small sums of money in provincial betting shops, attractive odds are not by themselves enough.

Wingnut, a few years younger than me but from my street, was a sophisticated bookmaker and I have no doubt that is his chosen profession. Sadly, I can no longer remember, and perhaps never knew, his real name.

*

Smoking was prevalent in the mid 1960s. All my teachers, it seemed to me, smoked. Mr Marks stood at the cricket nets giving us batting advice while puffing at a thin wispy Sun Valley roll-up. In primary school the secretary once sent me to the newsagent down the road to buy a packet of ten Bachelors. Mr Menzies seemed indescribably sophisticated because he smoked Passing Clouds with their oval shape and aromatic smell. Occasionally, just to be different, he would smoke Sweet Afton instead.

A young and rather attractive female English teacher marked herself out as not being cut from the common cloth by smoking Balkan Black Sobrainie. In PE lessons, I was once sent by the Head of Physical Education to cadge a Park Drive from the groundsman. I think I was chosen in the belief that I was one of the few pupils who would not smoke it on the walk back.

In a history lesson, our teacher smoked contentedly at the front of the classroom with his feet on the desk, staring at the ceiling, and blowing smoke rings while we copied details about how Arkwright's Spinning Jenny worked from the textbook. The yellowed forefingers of chain smoking adults was a constant feature of my childhood to the extent that the ability to roll a cigarette and the acquisition of a stained digit was a rite of passage on the journey to early manhood.

*

Football matches were something of a trial. Playing a neighbouring school we walked to a pitch about a mile away. Memory tells me it was always cold and wet with a ripping wind coming up the Thames Estuary. Naturally the PE teacher drove up there. If the weather was particularly inclement, he parked his Triumph Herald immediately alongside the halfway line so that he could referee the match from inside the car.

During one particularly vicious downpour, he explained that he would flash his lights to indicate any offence and we should go over to the car to hear his decision. This match was played under a deep black, thunderous sky. The headlamps flashed in the stygian gloom and I wandered in a sodden state towards the car. I could see the tip of a cigarette glowing orange in the darkened cabin. The window wound down an inch or so. "Sorry, lads, just trying to tune in my new radio … hand slipped."

Cricket was equally problematic. For the first few years, my place in the side was not secure. I rotated the twelfth man position with a boy greatly inferior in ability to myself. Imagine my delight when he was run over by a car in Wash Road. Both his legs were broken and he spent 13 weeks in Broomfield Hospital, in Chelmsford. At times like that, I believe there is a God after all.

A similar, but much darker, incident had occurred a few years earlier in late primary school when a boy called David, who was from another school, bullied me unmercifully. Despite my best efforts, our paths often crossed and he either twisted my arm until I cried, kneed me in the testicles, or punched me in the stomach. My torment ended when he was killed on a railway line. My joy was overwhelming and I felt not the slightest scintilla of guilt in rejoicing at his death. Even now, nearly forty years later, I feel a quiet sense of satisfaction at his demise and I feel it without guilt. He was a very unpleasant boy and the chances of him becoming an adornment to humanity were negligible.

Our cricket fixtures were always a problem. The grammar schools would not play us and I did not realise there was an independent school eight miles up the road.

"I've got a match for you against Runwell, lads," said the coach.

"Runwell?" I replied. "I didn't know there was a school there."

The coach was ominously silent and I thought no more of it until the directions we were following, having alighted from the bus, took us into

'Runwell Secure Unit for the Mentally Ill'.

"We're playing in a loony bin," said the captain.

"It's probably against the staff," I reassured him. My notion was cruelly quashed when their opening batsmen came out sharing a pair of pads between them. The right-handed opener had his only pad on his right leg and, at the end of the first over, urinated in spectacular fashion at the non-striker's end before running back up the pitch with his knob hanging out.

Still I must look on the bright side. I bowled like the wind that day with seam, swing and movement and I have never bettered the 7 for 9 figures I achieved despite playing thirty years of cricket.

On the rugby field, we were a tough and effective unit. The key to our success was the scrum, which was rock solid and never went down. This was credited to the methods used by our coach. For reasons that are beyond me, there always seemed to be a used sanitary towel on the school playing field. Normally, we would just throw it at each other and run away shouting, "Jam rag! Jam rag!" On at least one occasion the coach broke off a twig from the hedge and placed it under the scrum. We were desperate not to collapse it although, from my normal position of lock or flanker, I viewed the discomfort of the props and the second row with a degree of amusement.

"What's up boys?" Coach would say in his thick Welsh accent. "Scared of getting a jammy in the face?"

I have since examined the RFU coaching manual in great detail and have yet to come across this strategy as a recommended technique for keeping the scrum up.

*

My sex education at school was non-existent. My main information came from watching local dogs copulate on the school field. During one particularly bleak English lesson, a pair of stray mongrels began the process of mechanical reproduction. It was a dark overcast day with a thunderous sky and we were reading the Song of the Lotus Eaters. The rain was sheeting down as the dogs shagged without respite for more than half an hour, the male dog stopping every few minutes, resting on the back of the bitch, the plumes of its breath hanging in the air while she stood bored and uninterested until the dog pulled itself off and slunk away. We said nothing but I could see the shifty, panicky glances of the teacher as her eyes flashed in the direction of the field.

I felt a little sorry for her. She did not know what to do and was clearly desperate for the wretched creatures to go away. To stop would be to draw attention to them. She knew we could see and realised we were paying scant attention as the poem was read. In a modern classroom, I imagine there would be a round of cheering and applause when the dogs finished their performance. In a more restrained age, we sat there in mute, slightly embarrassed silence, gloomily surveying the prospect in front of us. There was a post-modern bleakness about the scene that somehow summed up life in a secondary modern school grooming pupils for the unskilled labour market in Basildon new town.

Despite the lack of ambiguity concerning our eventual position in the labour market, there was something curiously uplifting about the literature that we studied in English. My recall is very precise.

Amongst the representatives of the English canon that we read and studied in the first three years were *Oliver Twist*, *David Copperfield*, *The Black Tulip*, *Lorna Doone*, *Silas Marner*, and *Wuthering Heights*. For drama, we studied Sheridan's *School for Scandal*, Goldsmith's *She Stoops to Conquer*, *Julius Caesar*, *Macbeth* and *Dr Faustus*. Amongst the great poets that we were exposed to at an early age were significant portions of the work of Blake, Wordsworth, Tennyson, Keats, Shelley, Thomas Gray and, almost inevitably, Coleridge's *Rhyme of the Ancient Mariner*. I cannot claim to have understood any of these to a significant level but at least we were given a chance. We learnt nothing of literary criticism or textual analysis but we did learn to enjoy an enormous amount of poetry, much of which would now be regarded as archaic. I thrilled to Robert Browning's *How They Brought the Good News from Ghent to Aix*.

> I sprang to the stirrup, and Joris, and he;
> I galloped, Dirck galloped, we galloped all three.
> "Good speed," cried the watch, as the gate bolts undrew;
> "Speed," echoed the wall to us galloping through
> Behind shut the postern, the lights sank to rest
> And into the midnight we galloped abreast.

Then I closed my eyes and, for a moment, I was thundering across the Flemish lowlands in the company of Dirck and Joris. When I began teaching a decade or more later in a reasonable suburban comprehensive school, the two books that caught my attention amongst the new canon being studied were *Suedehead* and *Skinheads Put the Boot In*. Upon querying this, I was fed the usual claptrap about studying texts that were relevant to the lives of children.

The headmaster of our establishment nurtured the illusion that he would turn us into young gentleman. "Just because you are at a secondary modern doesn't mean that you cannot have a few airs and graces." To this end, on a Wednesday afternoon during our third year, he took us for a ballroom dancing lesson, bringing a great pile of 78 records from his home. For a reference point, the afternoon I learnt to do the foxtrot was the same afternoon Gary Sobers and his cousin David Holford made the famous stand that saved the West Indies from defeat against England in 1966.

The headmaster soon realised it was a lost cause but he was determined to teach us matters of protocol and etiquette. The girls would sit on the far side of the hall and the boys would be required to gravely approach a girl and formally request, "May I have this dance, please?"

This procedure turned into an unwitting lesson in humiliation. Even now, at a distance of thirty-five years, the basic kindness in my soul prevents me from mentioning any names. The girls must have slightly outnumbered the boys for, at the end, there would always be a female surplus consisting of the fat, lumpy, spotty ones, the one who smelt (stank, really) of urine, and the only black child in the whole school. Continually being referred to as 'Chocolate Drop' had induced in her a state of melancholy autism. I never saw her stony face smile nor did I hear her speak once. Perhaps the thing that kept her going was being immensely strong and that she was the Essex girls' discus champion.

I related this sad state of affairs to my father who immediately said, "You know what you must do, don't you?"

I did but I dreaded his words. "No, I can't."

"But you must. Think of the hurt you will save her."

It was all right preaching a generosity of spirit but this was taking things too far. The following Wednesday afternoon, I strode over and asked her gravely, "May I have the honour of this dance?"

For a moment, she stared at me with a mute, inscrutable expression then, in a movement of graceful athleticism, she grasped me around the waist. Yes, she was strong alright. I felt as if I was being carried violently around the dance floor with my legs trailing underneath me.

For the next week, I endured the taunts of 'nigger lover' and 'what did you dance with Sambo for?' I explained that she had feelings, and that it was humiliating for her to be left sitting in a chair every week. In short, I attempted to appeal to my tormentors' better nature. Sadly they did not have one.

My torment reached crisis point when, one night as dusk was approaching, I was crossing Gloucester Park near the Town Centre. About a hundred yards behind me were three of my tormentors, led by a menacing, but blubbery, boy called Hulk but whose real name was Paddy. He was one of a number of bullies at the school.

It was a foggy night and, although the path across the park was well lit, I felt scared and vulnerable. The three boys caught up with me, shouting, "Have you shagged Chocolate Drop yet?"

At this stage, my story divides into two versions: one is the more mundane reality of what actually occurred; the other is the fantasy of what I wanted to happen.

For the moment, I thought I could get away but two of the boys – Smedley and Watts – had cut across a small hillock so I was now trapped on the path. I bent down and picked up a pebble about the size of a golf ball. Hulk approached, oozing a cheery sort of menace, small folds of fat bulging over his collar.

"Hi, Hulk," I said. "What do you want?"

"You, you lanky streak of piss," he replied. I knew then I was in for a beating. Smedley and Watts were about twenty yards behind me. In one of the rare moments of clear thinking in my life, I decided I had only one chance. I strode quickly towards Hulk. "What's the problem?" I asked. "Have I ever done anything to you?"

Before he could reply, I smashed him on the nose with the stone concealed in my right fist. I knew it had to be hard and that it must be on the nose. He had to go down or I would be in serious trouble. The effect was spectacular. His nose flattened and immediately began spraying blood as he went down in a heap squealing, "The ****'s broken my nose." I now panicked beyond any sort of reason and, driven by fear and dread, I kicked him in the face as hard as I could while shouting. "Now ******* leave me alone" before running down the path and into the darkness. Behind, I could hear Hulk shouting while Smedley asked, "Shall we get him?"

I arrived home in a lather of sweat and fear worrying about how I would avoid Hulk's unwelcome future attentions the next day at school. I needn't have worried, at least, not immediately.

As I entered the playground the following morning, I could see Hulk standing next to Smedley and Watts talking to a group of small boys. He had a bandage across his nose, both eyes were blackened, and he had the lace mark from my Dr Martens boot imprinted vividly on his cheek.

"How many of them were there?" asked one boy.

"Six," replied Hulk. "I flattened two of them but the others got me down. But one of them is in hospital now. Cowards they were; kicked me in the face. If there had just been four of them I would have sorted them out."

I admired him for turning a disaster into a triumph. He wasn't going to admit that weedy little me had broken his nose in Gloucester Park and I was not going to point out any inaccuracies in the tale. That helped matters but the menace remained. I volunteered to become a library monitor and spent most lunchtimes issuing books. Hulk would occasionally join me and make remarks like, "You're ******* dead meat, you ****!"

I could never resist a jibe about Hulk's inability to read. "How's the extra English coming along Paddy. Read a book yet?"

For a while I feared some sort of family vengeance. The fact that Hulk's father was in Chelmsford Prison was some comfort. His mother was what television producers now call a 'neighbour from hell'.

It was soon obvious that Hulk wanted to keep his humiliation to himself. As he lived on the Powell Estate at the other end of town, the chances of bumping into him were not great. Nevertheless, I worried about it for years and, even when I came back from university and walked to the town centre, I would glance around nervously searching for his bulky presence. Once I spotted him standing outside Marks and Spencer and I beat a hasty retreat through the market area. I expect he is a perfectly upright citizen now.

Sadly the above is a fantasy version. Every word is true up to the moment that Smedley and Watts attempted to cut me off on the pathway in the dimly lit park. I nurtured this version as a fantasy of what I would like to happen because they persecuted me. The reality was that I turned and ran over the hillock into the darkness and made good my escape. Having just finished tenth in the town's cross country championship, I knew I could show them a clean pair of heels.

*

It did not do to have a sensitive nature. Coming out of an English lesson I cautiously confessed to a friend that I had enjoyed reading the poem we were studying. On that particular day something in me thrilled to the imagery and power of William Blake's *The Tiger.*

> Tiger, Tiger, burning bright
> In the forests of the night:
> What immortal hand or eye
> Could frame thy fearful symmetry?

Today the lines seem almost over familiar but at the time they were both unique and revelatory.

"Are you a poof?" my friend asked.

After that I kept quiet about my growing appreciation of poetry. This was the first indication of what I have come to see as the unmanliness of education. Being educated beyond a certain basic level was not a desirable masculine quality in same the way as being able to hit a good free kick in soccer, or downing a pint of beer in one, or squeezing the red ball past the black into the pocket.

When I was reading English literature at university, this point was brought home to me as I sat in a seminar group studying Coleridge's *Frost at Midnight* surrounded exclusively by rather serious young blue stockinged women.

> The Frost performs its Secret Ministry
> Unhelped by any wind. The owlet's cry
> Comes loud—and hark, again! Loud as before.
> The inmates of my cottage, all at rest,
> Have left me to that solitude, which suits
> Abtruser musings: save that at my side
> My cradled infant slumbers peacefully.

"You got all those birds to yourself, I see," the porter said to me with a nudge, smoking thin spindly Old Holborn roll-ups as I exercised my desire for proletarian company. This was true but Samuel Taylor was the sole object of their attention.

The moment my masculinity was questioned because I liked William Blake was the moment my estrangement from my contemporaries began. It was not a conscious process. It was incremental in that I slowly saw I was not one of them. This was not because I was feverishly studying *Songs of Innocence and Experience* in my bedroom while they were downing pints of lager in the Double Six but because a certain barrier was growing between us. At first I convinced myself that this lay solely inside my imagination until the day that the aggressively unpleasant Tony Day, who had borrowed money off me that he had no intention of ever repaying, announced as I joined a group hanging around in the town centre, "Here's that ******* poetry poof."

I suddenly felt very lonely and did not know who my friends were.

A few weeks later I was uplifted by Tom Lexman, who had fought in the International Brigades in the Spanish Civil War and introduced me to W.H. Auden, C. Day Lewis and the almost indescribably exotic Federico Garcia Lorca.

I do not wish to give the impression of being wholly ungrateful for the education that was conferred upon me. I had the benefit of having a wonderful English teacher, the sort who might appear in one of those celebrity interviews 'My Best Teacher'.

At the start of my upper sixth, he handed me a brown envelope with the words, "I think that you might enjoy this." It was an Olympia Press edition of Henry Miller's *Tropic of Cancer*. This was 1969 and, despite the failure of the authorities to secure a conviction in the Lady Chatterley's Lover trial, many famous works of English literature were still emerging from under the censor's cosh. It is a sign of the times that, in 1960, possession of Lady Chatterley's Lover was an offence punishable by imprisonment while, thirty-five years later, it was the gentle Sunday evening serial featuring Sean Bean's bottom bobbing up and down.

By 1969 *Cancer* was legally available but there was something clandestine and exciting about being given it in a brown envelope in the Paris Olympia edition. I still wonder what made my English teacher, now sadly dead, feel I would enjoy this particular book filled, as it is, with the most explicit sexual scenes imaginable, even if they are of a straight perve nature.

The Olympia Press books were very distinctive with their nearly square format, green covers and black lettering. While Miller and many other authors were banned from publication in Britain and the USA, it was possible to publish them in France in English. The result was that, in the 1950s, tourists and British and American soldiers smuggled copies into England fuelling an increasingly brisk black market trade.

By the time I left school, at least six of these suppressed works of English literature had been passed to me by my teacher and scrupulously if not over-eagerly read. Indirectly, I have to thank Maurice Girodias, the maverick and faintly disreputable owner of Olympia Press. By the late 1950s, he had a reputation for having the best DB (dirty book) list available. But for his unerring eye for literary talent, he would be remembered for no more than being a minor publisher of smutty books. The loan of *Tropic of Cancer* was followed by *Tropic of Capricorn* in the older and more valuable 1930s Obelisk Press edition owned by Jack Kahane, father of Maurice Girodias. A taste for literary pornography must have run in the family. I was then exposed to Vladimir Nabokov's *Lolita*, which I did not enjoy, William Burroughs *Naked Lunch*, which I tried to enjoy, and J.P. Donleavy's *Ginger Man*.

It is a sign of just how repressive 1950s English censorship was that Donleavy's hymn to gentle onanism should have been suppressed with the full weight of the law. The upshot was that I left school with an excellent knowledge of twentieth century literary pornography but was completely unemployable.

In hindsight, it would seem that my old teacher took a considerable risk. It was highly unlikely that my very Tory headmaster would have approved of these attempts at intellectual liberation. Today, I would not dare to pass any sixth former a Henry Miller book despite our infinitely more liberal moral climate and the fact that they are available in every high street bookshop. The most I dare do is point them furtively in the direction of the volume of Lord Rochester's verse that sits unread on the top shelf of the poetry section in the library.

This is the mystery of teaching and the intimate personal dynamics that exist between teachers and taught. If just once during the thirteen or so years of compulsory schooling to which we subject our children, the vital spark of personal connection can be ignited, then there is some chance of it being a life-changing process. The problem is that this process does not reduce to a ready formula that the Teacher Training Agency can produce in a glossy and expensive pamphlet and force upon every school.

I am very confident that providing a liberal supply of high class pornography is not on the TTA list of desirable teacher characteristics. In hindsight, I was done a disservice when my inspiring teacher convinced me I would enjoy studying English literature. Alas, this was not strictly true since I found it rather dull once the filthy bits had been taken out. As for the matter of Henry Miller's Tropic books. I have returned to them recently and still cannot decide if they are great novels because of the pornographic content or despite it.

My memory is now fairly threadbare but my brother's, at his different secondary modern school, is better. He remembered Basher Beaumont for both his violence and his longevity.

His violence was random and unplanned. Boys who displeased him were usually out of lessons, walking on the wrong side of the corridor, running, making a noise, cutting corners over the grass or simply being in the wrong place at the wrong time. All were potential targets for his random acts of brutality which took the form of cuffing, slapping, pushing, pulling sideburns, striking with a piece of wood that he had concealed up his sleeve or, if the spirit so moved him, beating with an outsize plimsoll. Obviously Basher would now be in prison or on List 99 but he commanded a curious sort of respect in that he cared enough to be so violent towards his charges. It is a sad fact that some of my contemporaries judged the effectiveness of a teacher by either the threat or the reality of beatings.

Basher's longevity was phenomenal – forty-four teaching years from 1924 until his retirement in 1968. He began his campaign of relentless violence in the year that Ramsey MacDonald formed the first Labour Government; he retired the year before a man landed on the moon and the year that Russian tanks rolled into Czechoslovakia.

During that period he had witnessed a sexual revolution that began with the virtual outlawing of contraception and ended with free love and the birth control pill. All of which, I suspect Basher disapproved of. In the intervening years, he had held back the forces of barbarism by his cuffs, slaps, punches and slippering in order to preserve what was great about Britain. New Left, New Right, Situationists, Baader-Meinhof, Red Army Faction, Weathermen, Symbionese Liberation Army, Dutch Provos, Kabouters, deschoolers, hippies, yippies, Angry Brigade, Post-Modernists Trotskyists or Soledad Brothers: all of these manifestations of late 1960s counter culture, Basher would have sorted out with his slipper. At his final assembly, he went through the usual prayer, hymn and a bollocking routine. We had the same hymn book with 703 hymns, arranged alphabetically, starting with *All People That On*

Earth Do Dwell and finishing with *Ye Holy Angels Bright*. It felt like all the world was ordered and everything was in its place.

On reflection, my brother realised that Basher had some kind of pastoral responsibility although, at the time, he thought he was just some kind of hired thug whose job was to impose discipline on the unruly kids from the council estate. His idea of sensitive pastoral care in the face of a personal problem was to shout, "Stop playing with yourself, boy!" before slapping his charge round the back of the head.

After the Grosvenor Square Riots, Basher explained patiently to the assembled pupils that, if the police had the powers to birch the ringleaders, the nonsense would have been nipped in the bud. For the unaware, the riot in Grosvenor Square was an anti-Vietnam War demonstration outside the American Embassy in 1968. Events got rather out of hand and shocked the political establishment and most of the press. Although we were only thirty miles away and should have been against that unjust war, it somehow did not impinge upon our conscience or awareness. Both the war and the demonstration may as well have been happening on the moon.

Thus I finished five years of secondary education still sealed in the tight cocoon of childhood and oblivious to the fact that there was a world of infinite complexity and richness all around me. My final report stated that I was 'capable of performing simple tasks if kept under close supervision'. My reflection on the past thirty or so years is that this observation was a broadly accurate assessment.

Chapter 6: Failing the Eleven Plus

Education in England remains an exercise in class prejudice.
George Orwell from The Lion and the Unicorn.

My wife, who is very much a product of a girls' grammar school (nice handwriting and good table manners) recalls that the cleverest girl in her primary school lived on a council estate and talked common. She flew through her eleven plus exam and then failed the interview. It was explained to her parents that their daughter really would be better suited to attending the girls' secondary modern school where they could cater more appropriately to her needs. For her, at least, this was her first meaningful introduction to that rat's nest of privilege and disadvantage known as the English education system.

Forty years ago, the purpose of the education system was clear and unambiguous. Education was a winnowing process whereby the wheat was sorted from the chaff. This contrasts with what we hope it might be one day, a process whereby each child achieves their maximum potential.

The very superior grade of 'wheat' went to the independent sector while the ordinary 'wheat' went to the grammar schools. However, for the small amount of 'wheat' that was produced from the threshing process, a large amount of 'chaff' was left on the barn floor destined to be swept into the secondary modern schools where they would be held for four years until they were deemed old enough and mature enough to enter the unskilled labour market.

Forty years later, our educational process is still about sorting 'wheat' from 'chaff' via the great rafts of examinations and tests that children have to take over the course of their school lives. In no sense can this system be deemed good for children except the very small number who are at the apex of the system. Even then, it tends to produce an unwholesome and uninformed sense of superiority.

I never had that system inflicted upon me. I only took one test from the age of five until the age of sixteen – this was the eleven plus that I failed, a failure that obviated the need for me to take any further exams.

I can only recall one occasion when I was let out upon the outside world after this ignominious fall from educational grace. A group of us were taken to meet our contemporaries at Brentwood Public School in the interests of 'social harmony' and 'bridging the class divide'. I imagine the Brentwood pupils were probably told before our arrival, "These people are representatives of the English working class. They are the sort of people that you will boss about in future life. Establish your authority over them."

I had no awareness of the existence of such a school, or such a group of people as the middle class and only the dimmest glimmerings that there were people seriously wealthier than ourselves. I had once met Edward Gardner, the Tory (and I mean that word in the proper sense) MP for South East Essex. I could remember thinking to myself, 'this guy is posh.' He visited our school and I was sent to greet him on the principle that I was capable of walking in a straight line and would not try to steal his wallet. Having never met anyone of his social status before I gave a small jerky bow to which he responded with a quizzical look before accepting it as a natural response to someone of his standing.

On the day before our visit to Brentwood School, Terry, aka Animal, announced that we were going to see, 'Some rich ****s in ******* Brentwood.' (The working classes have always sworn horribly and we were no exception. I remember two occasions in my childhood when the police arrested people for swearing in public. It is a sign of the general coarsening of our national life over the past thirty years that we now accept public use of language that previously resulted in criminal charges. I hold the BBC primarily responsible for this regrettable state of affairs.) Upon arrival at Brentwood School I had some dim inkling of journeying into unknown territory on an anthropological expedition amongst natives who might well be hostile and did not speak my language. We were greeted by the head boy, a fairly typical prep school meathead who looked like he ate on behalf of the rest of the school. With his fleshy features and his superior air he would, if he had been born thirty years earlier, have been out in India shooting natives.

"And where do you chaps hail from?" he asked.

"You what?" I replied.

Animal did not like him. "I'm gonna nut that ****."

I suggested that might not be a good idea. The Master – we could not refer to them as teachers in such an august institution – was an altogether different creature to the nicotine-stained, yellow-teethed, grizzled specimens that passed for pedagogues in Nicholas Secondary Modern. This one was about two metres tall, completely bald and carried with him a small lap dog. I suspect he was a sex offence waiting to happen.

Having taught in a well-known independent school and met many people who have been educated in the private sector, my general conclusion is that, with few exceptions, they are for children who cannot cope in the state sector and need the artificial advantages that such an education affords. In England to attend a non-state school has become a badge of social superiority. It is a shameful comment about our society that the type of school a child attends confers considerable advantages in later life and that we only allow access to these institutions to those who, on the whole, have considerable personal wealth.

On the day I first came across the species, my only memory was of discussing rugby with one of the boys. I wanted to ask if they practised scrummaging over used sanitary towels but I suspected this was not an acceptable entrée into polite conversation. In an attempt to stimulate conversation, the master asked if we'd "had any of those coloured chaps turn up at your school. You know those Pakis?" He was referring, in his own strange way, to the Kenyan Asians crisis of 1968 when about 20,000 Kenyans of Asian descent were expelled from the country and were accepted by Britain. Predictably, the tabloid press worked itself into a frenzy at the time. I nodded mutely, having not the slightest idea what he was talking about.

"We've got an Indian chap," he continued. "Lovely batsman, beautiful timing. His uncle's a Maharajah, you know."

That was all right then. They had done their bit.

My best friend's sister, who went to an all girls' secondary modern school, had a similar experience. Once every month, she was sent for an afternoon at the private Ursuline Convent School in Southend. There she learned such skills as washing up, how to lay a table, greeting visitors and arranging flowers. Whether she was being prepared to be a good housewife, or for life in service, was never made clear. Her mother had invested a considerable amount of her meagre income in elocution lessons (so that she did not talk common) and, it would appear, attending the private convent school may have been part of a master plan for social advancement.

Her first day at the Convent School was St Ursula's Day and that happy occasion was celebrated by an arcane ceremony in which the girls, in their neat pinafore dresses, paraded on the front lawns (they did not have fields or anything as common as a playground) clutching posies of flowers while weaving ever more intricate patterns. It was like a cross between the first form at Mallory Towers and a Nuremberg Rally. I later learned that the family dentist was a member of the same golf club as the chairman of governors at St Ursula's. Whilst in the process of filling every tooth in her head, he realised she was a young woman of some intelligence and refinement who, in his opinion, would benefit from exposure to the nice girls of St Ursula's. I am not sure if it had the desired effect or merely induced a lifetime inferiority complex.

Our school system has changed very little over the past thirty-five years. I took a group of sixth form students to a citizenship conference at the Institute of Education in London. As we stood waiting for the lift, the door opened to reveal a group of meaty, prematurely-corpulent young men. Their blazers told me they were from the City of London School. The lift was full and, as the doors closed, the words 'comprehensive school scum' drifted out followed by an outburst of coarse laughter. We stood there for a moment in depressed stunned silence. Next to us, a workman in a smart blue overall who had been repairing the fire alarms, observed, "What a bunch of ****s." It was difficult not to agree with him. The irony of them attending a citizenship conference was not lost upon me.

No matter what public face the independent sector schools adopt, in private they teach and encourage these sort of destructive social attitudes. It is part of their hidden curriculum to believe themselves to be superior. I have sat in enough common rooms in a variety of independent schools to know just how socially regressive, snobbish and, in many cases, simply puerile are the attitudes of a significant minority of staff. As George Orwell put it in *The Road to Wigan Pier* more than sixty years ago, "I suppose there is no place in the world where snobbery is quite so ever present or where it is cultivated in quite such refined and subtle forms as in an English public school. Here, at least, one cannot say that English 'education' fails to do its job."

As long as governments accept the existence of the independent sector in education, then they are explicitly denying the principle of equality of opportunity. It is impossible to view it in any other light. As most governments are pragmatic and moderate, in the end they reason that the price of such radical political action is not worth paying.

The Friends Reunited website provides an illuminating insight into the long term impact of differences in educational opportunity. I am amazed how many of my contemporaries emigrated, not only to the dominions but also to the USA. Out of curiosity I have emailed a number of them, most of whom I never knew, to ask why they left and never returned.

Firstly I was struck by the fact that everybody replied. In most cases they were complete strangers, bound only by the fact that we had attended the same secondary modern school. The answers were uniformly the same. Working class children from a secondary modern school in the 1960s had little chance of getting a fair start in life. All my correspondents praised their new home for giving them the chance that England, with its class society and its system of education, denied them. They wanted to tell me that life had given them a new start; that despite the most unpromising of beginnings they had taken life by the scruff of the neck and made something for themselves.

One boy who played football with me in primary school now trains horses on a ranch in Montana; another go-getter has a comfortable life selling powerboats in the Bahamas, and I am envious of the former classmate who now runs a vintage car restoration business twenty miles from Esjberg in Denmark. What a long road it has been for them. I was also struck by the wistfulness of their replies. On the surface they say that life is marvellous and they have no regrets but there is something within the cadence and rhythm of what they say that suggests what might have been. Another life may have been there for the taking but for the decisions that were made. I thought I discerned a sense of resentment that they had to travel half way round the world, abandon friends and family in order to make a decent life for themselves. There is one poignant entry from a boy who I can just remember if I dredge some deep recess of my memory. 'Why did I have to go so far to find myself? Why did it take so long?'

I have trawled the websites of all the schools in Basildon looking for familiar Pioneer names and there is a sadness about it. Some people are desperate to impress and go through a list of mind-boggling tedium concerning all they have done in the intervening years. When they claim to be the chief executive of a company you know it has only two employees because they would otherwise say: 'chief executive of a company employing forty thousand people.'

A very simple exercise allows us to peer into the past and observe the advantages, and indeed disadvantages, that are bestowed upon us from an early age. For my year at Nicholas Secondary Modern School, only 22 from 180 ex-pupils have registered on the site. For the two local grammar schools the figures are 92 and 108 respectively for the same intake. Why the difference? I suspect it is nothing to do with IT literacy or access to computers. It is do with life chances. If you went to a secondary modern school any time between 1944 and today, then you have been rejected and told that you are second rate. In the 1960s the system was very unforgiving. Being sent to a secondary modern school mapped out your life route and it was not likely to be a journey through the breathtaking uplands. For large numbers of people, secondary modern school was a miserable experience they escaped from as soon as possible with no intention of renewing old acquaintances.

For the small proportion of people who have done well, there is an impulse to register on the site and effectively say, "Look how well I have done even though I only went to a secondary modern school." The great majority remain hidden with no desire to tell the world their humble educational origins.

The large uptake from the grammar schools suggests a level of satisfaction with life that makes them feel confident enough after thirty plus years to say, "Look, I have done well. I am happy for you to know it and I am happy for you to get in touch with me." Personally, I preferred the entry on one of the grammar school sites that said, "I hated you all when I was at school and nothing has changed." The entry has now been removed presumably in the interests of the general bonhomie and goodwill that Friends Reunited exudes. I am not bitter for myself but I am bitter for all those hundreds of thousands of talented and intelligent people whose lives were blighted by the selection process and I do not exaggerate. I have contacted and spoken to hundreds of people who went to secondary modern schools. Many of them say the experience ruined their lives. It blighted family relations and gave them an inferiority complex which lives with them to the present day. One man told me that he and his brother did not speak for twenty years because he failed and his brother passed; another told me that so intense was his father's disappointment that, as he lay on his deathbed, he imagined his father was still reproaching him for that abysmal failure nearly forty years earlier.

My friend, Peter, was promised, like John Prescott, that he would get a new bicycle from his father if he passed. Like the Deputy Prime Minister he failed and the bike was never mentioned again. Each day, we caught the school bus together from a lay-by opposite Halfords. Each day, he would walk past the bicycle that he could never have. In my imagination, I still see Peter staring wistfully through the plate glass window at the gleaming bike he was never destined to own. Through responses to articles I have written I am witness to the unknowing destruction that ill-conceived and prejudiced government policies have wreaked on the lives of vulnerable individuals. In many cases these people spend the rest of their lives coming to terms with their rejection and their feelings of failure.

It seems barely credible that a nominally Labour government should be allowing – sorry, encouraging – the return of selection at the same time that it mouths the platitudes of equal opportunity. In many inner London areas, the moneyed middle classes have abandoned the state comprehensive system entirely. The consequence is that many schools, although retaining the title comprehensive, have become 21st century secondary modern schools by default with all the hopelessness that implies. In 1996, David Blunkett told a Labour Party conference: "Read my lips. No selection under a Labour government." When pressed, he claimed he meant it as a joke. He's such a funny guy.

In 1997, Labour offered parents the illusion of choice by inventing a ballot system so biased in favour of keeping selection that, one by one, highly organised and motivated local campaigns have been forced to give up the unequal struggle. It is difficult to argue that this is anything other than a cynical betrayal of what parents in Trafford, Kent, Buckinghamshire, Lincolnshire and other areas where selection is widespread, were promised. Seven years later, selection is spreading under a Labour government.

Swathes of the country, like Kent, that time warp of a county, have always been selective with no sign of central government intervention. To visit the schools of Kent, as I have done, is to witness an exercise in pure class discrimination. The grammar schools of Folkestone, Dover, Rochester and Chatham are, with a few exceptions, full of the children of the affluent, graduate, professional, middle classes. The High Schools, as they now call the secondary moderns, are full of the children of the poor – those of modest educational achievement, those living on benefit, those who are long-term sick, the children of asylum seekers and, above all, those who have special needs.

For the unfortunate affluent, whose children are consigned to a High School, the option remains to buy into the private sector. As a result Kent has evolved its own strange independent sector. I am not talking about the Tonbridges and the Benendens, but a string of small, relatively low achieving schools (about 50 per cent grades A-C at GCSE) that cater specifically for the parents of children who have failed the eleven plus. For parents who cannot face the social stigma or the educational deprivation of their children attending a High School and can just about muster the £4,500 a year fees, then escape from the consequences of selection is possible. For families who live near the county borders and know how to manipulate the system, escape is an option. They flee into the comprehensive systems of Surrey and Sussex and even, for some, across the Thames into Essex.

The better off Kentish people bequeath their prosperity to their children via the prism of the grammar schools. The poor bequeath to their children their poverty. It is no coincidence that OFSTED inspections reveal Kent has more failing secondary schools than any other local education authority in the country, and that England's lowest performing secondary school (in Ramsgate with 4 per cent grades A-C) is part of the Kent authority. In 2003 there were 17 Kent schools where less than 30 per cent of pupils scored five A-C grades at GCSE; the highest number in the country. Kent calls these Community Schools, attempting to pretend they are comprehensive schools. In reality, they are the worst type of secondary modern schools.

The Audit Commission's report for 2003 is equally damning of Kent. Of thirty-five county councils responsible for education in England, thirty-two have shown improvement. Kent is not among them, scoring below those of deprived London boroughs like Tower Hamlets, Newham and Brent. Despite much talk of 'parity of esteem' the reality is a chasm between Kent's different types of schools. Kent's councillors and officials like to maintain a fiction that the grammar schools and the secondary moderns are very much the same except that the grammars are for children who are a little more academically gifted. The free school meals figures indicate the extent of the deception. For the grammar schools the figure is 2.5 per cent and for the secondary moderns it is 17.1 per cent.

Those who support selection in Kent argue that there is strong competition to get into the secondary moderns. It is hard to imagine a child being offered a Playstation 2 as an incentive to fail the eleven plus and be sent to a secondary modern school. For the Dr Jekyll of the grammar schools, there must always be the Mr Hyde of the secondary moderns – a fact that those in favour of selection never admit.

Apart from the grammar schools that exist in selective areas, there are also a small number of stand-alone grammar schools. Through a variety of historical quirks and slights of hand, they have survived the move to comprehensive schools that took place around them. If we can ignore the issue of equal opportunity for one moment, then it is possible to argue that these schools do not damage the education of those children who fail to gain admission in the way that the grammar schools of Kent or Buckinghamshire do. The stand-alone grammar schools usually draw over such a wide area that it may be argued they do not damage the local comprehensive schools to any significant degree by 'stealing' their most able students. They do, however, create a sufficiently unhealthy obsession with gaining admission that there are often ten serious applicants for every place.

The statistical argument over which sort of school produces the better results is an irrelevance. More than any other area of social policy, the education statistics are abused and manipulated to fit an argument. The key question is not educational. It is a moral issue concerning what sort of society we want to live in. Do we want a society that offers equal opportunity for all, or do we want one that offers substantial advantages for the few, wildly celebrating its success while castigating the have-nots for their failures?

There are many ragged issues at the edge of the debate. A friend of mine had his nose broken at his Leeds comprehensive school (16 per cent grades A-C at GCSE) for bringing a copy of The Times into class. In an educational milieu, in which reading the Daily Mirror was seen as dangerously highbrow, to brandish a copy of The Times was like showing a red rag to a bull. As a result, my friend passionately defends grammar schools on the grounds that they allow individuals with special needs (i.e. they are academically gifted) to flourish without being beaten senseless by the less gifted. I am inclined to agree with him but for two objections.

Firstly, how can we ensure that those who are selected are selected on the grounds of true ability rather than because their parents are graduates, have come from bookish homes, can afford private tuition, or have demonstrated a degree of proficiency on a musical instrument? Secondly, how can we guarantee that those children who are not selected will be placed in an environment in which they are allowed to flourish as well? I regret, as we have discovered over the past sixty years, there are no easy answers to these questions.

In the bright new dawn that marked the end of the Second World War, anything seemed possible. The introduction of selection and the eleven plus were clothed in the language of equal opportunity and were presented to the nation as giving bright, working class children a chance in life. Part of the tripartite system's attraction was that it was clearly superior to the system of elementary schools and fee-paying grammar schools that preceded it. Today, sixty years later, selection is little more than an exercise in class discrimination.

From the London metropolitan perspective, it is easy to forget that Northern Ireland retains selection on province-wide basis. In a society where maiming and killing was once an everyday occurrence, the issue of what sort of secondary school children should attend always took second place. It is a sign of a return to something approaching normalcy that Northern Ireland is now having the debate that took place in the rest of the United Kingdom nearly forty years ago.

Both sides abuse the statistical argument for their own ends though it is not really relevant. What is relevant is the commitment to giving each child an equal chance in life. Uplifting, but at the same time pathetic, is the case of William McQuillan who was assigned, aged eleven, to a secondary modern school – Priory College, Holywood – having been turned down by Bangor Grammar. They rejected him again at the age of thirteen. Applying for the third time, after having gained good GCSE grades, the principal asked William why he was trying yet again.

"To prove you wrong," was the reply.

Three years later William was at Oriel College, Oxford, reading for an English degree. The question remains: why did the education authorities in Northern Ireland have to make life so difficult for William before he was allowed to realise his potential? He reminds me of my old friend, Graham, who failed his eleven plus, failed his thirteen plus, yet achieved four grade As at A-level, gained a first in Chemistry from Manchester, completed a PhD, became a university lecturer, and is now a very senior research scientist at Shell. I felt a twinge of envy when he told me that, being in charge of the team that supports Ferrari, one of his less onerous duties was to travel round the world and watch every Grand Prix.

Back in Northern Ireland, the huge irony is that the fate of selection and the grammar schools will be decided by the eleven plus failure – former Derry butcher's boy and self confessed IRA terrorist, Martin McGuiness.

In 2003, schools were told they could select on the basis of aptitude not ability. I have yet to hear anyone credibly explain the difference. The arguments I hear now are identical to those I heard in the company of the Pioneers almost thirty-five years ago. We have tremendous difficulty in this country accepting the very basic principle that all children are of equal worth. Nearly forty years ago, Anthony Crosland, Secretary of State for Education in the first Wilson Labour government, announced, "If it's the last thing I do, I'm going to destroy every fucking grammar school in England and Wales and Northern Ireland." A product of the public school system himself, it may be significant that he did not announce 'he was going to destroy every fucking public school in the country'. He was quite content to leave the independent sector alone. The cynical might suggest that, while he was prepared to remove what had, by and large, become a middle-class perk, he was not prepared to apply the same reasoning to the fee-paying schools of the upper middle class.

Is it just coincidence that both Crosland and the current Secretary of State for Education, Charles Clarke, are the products of Highgate, that most unenlightened educational institution? It is the sort of school that requires male job applicants to bring their wives with them to interview. I assume this is to guard against appointing a member of staff who is married to some runny-nosed slattern who would be an embarrassment to the school. We are, of course, still waiting for Crosland's 1965 promise to be kept with no sign of early fulfilment. I recently wrote a letter to Charles Clarke expressing my disappointment at the failure of the Labour government to act decisively on the issue of selection. I was not discouraged by the reply. "When grammars school are looked at, we must indeed look at the impact those schools have on non-selective schools in the area." Clarke added that the government was aware of the 'damaging effect the existence of the eleven plus has on those pupils who fail to gain places at a grammar school'. I am aware that the reply was probably composed by someone on a DfES youth training scheme but, given the strength and transparency of these views, the surprise is that government refuses to act to resolve the issue.

Intelligence is not a virtue; it is a characteristic we are born with. What we do with our endowed intelligence may be a matter to occasion judgment as to individual worth. The unintelligent person has the same intrinsic value as the clever individual and, in many practical ways, may make a more valuable contribution to society. Karl Marx wrote in *The 18th Brumaire of Louis Napoleon* that 'History repeats itself, the first time as tragedy and the second time as farce'. I experienced that tragedy and now I believe I shall witness the farce.

I have taken my experiment a little further by contrasting the lives of five of my contemporaries selected at random from my year's entry in the Friends Reunited records. I then selected five random entries, again from my school year, at an expensive fee-paying boys' independent school in north London where I taught briefly. Curiously, the common room (never called the staff room at such a revered, if not quite premier league, institution) was full of people from off-centre educational backgrounds. I suppose parents do not pay tens of thousands of pounds in school fees for their children to end up as teachers.

The first five from my secondary modern school were:

> a restaurant worker (the word is horribly misspelt);
> a groundsman no more than a few miles from the school;
> a mini cab driver;
> a window cleaner;
> a manager of a plumbing supplies shop.

All worthy occupations, you may think. If nothing else, they are all in work.

My first five from the public school were:

> the managing director of Heathrow Express;
> the head of research and development at a major but unspecified pharmaceutical company;
> a consultant at University College Hospital;
> a partner in a London firm of solicitors;
> the author of a series of foreign travel books.

I thought perhaps my sample had been unrepresentative; perhaps I had just been unlucky. I tried another three from each site.

My old school came up with:

> a boy I remembered who had taken early retirement on the grounds of ill health at the age of 48;
> a refrigeration engineer;
> a mechanic at the Arriva bus depot.

At the independent school the additional three were:

> a senior civil servant in the Crown Estates Office;
> a strategy manager for Barclays bank;
> a Professor of Applied Linguistics at the University of Leicester.

Given that the school specialises in educating the brutish sons of prosperous north London accountants, you might think these three had not turned out too bad.

What conclusion did I come to? Was my inquiry just stating the obvious? Was it possible that they were just cleverer? Could it be my contemporaries were just so lumpen and sunken that they could not climb out of the mire?

It is likely that money had given the privately educated students a huge early advantage or perhaps their education was simply of a superior nature. Had family connections, or networks established at school and university, given the Old Londonians a decisive advantage? It is difficult not to feel the poignancy of the contrast between their lives, particularly if you accept, as I do, the old philosophical notion of tabula rasa – that we are all born in a neutral state with life waiting to imprint its experiences upon us. Ignatius Loyola famously said, "Give me the child and I will give you the man." I suspect he was right.

Girls, in particular, were very badly served by secondary modern schools. Their only hope of salvation was to have come from a supportive family that valued education and had not yet been clubbed into defeat by the system. I have analysed two hundred entries for all eight secondary modern schools in Basildon for my year and the results are uniformly depressing – a denial of human talent and ability. With very few exceptions, they have failed to make any sort of career for themselves. A few are now teachers and nurses but nothing beyond that.

The list of occupations is routine and uninspiring. In terms of aspiration, it was not so much a denial but rather one of discouragement. In my email correspondence, I have come across many examples of young women from the 1960s who were told by their teachers and parents to be realistic in their choice of occupation.

It was a bit different for boys in that they had the traditional expectations placed upon them that they would work for the next forty years and would be bread winners for their families. For them, there was a route through craft apprenticeships and engineering that in some cases led to management of their own businesses. For others, joining the police acted as a conduit for working class ability and ambition. Going into the armed forces with their separate, public school educated officer class, was a less wise choice. Several of my friends joined the army but, in their late twenties, found themselves cast adrift on civvy street with no obviously marketable skills, apart from the ability to idle away vast amounts of time for no constructive purpose.

For working class young women, there was simply no expectation that they would do anything other than marry, have children, and then perform part-time lowly-paid factory or shop work. The symbols and the practices of their subjugation were the typing classes where they sat in serried ranks clattering away at old Imperial machines, like mindless automatons learning a skill that would soon become redundant.

Not that it was much better for the boys who were shunted into metalwork classes to learn how to torture a piece of metal into the shape of an ashtray or a G-clamp. Presumably someone thought we were all going to become blacksmiths.

A familiar pattern repeats itself when looking at the grammar school websites for the same years. This time, the girls are teachers, doctors, civil servants and local government officers. In a significant number of cases they have married men who are affluent enough to support them.

Looking at entries for girls from a well-known London day school with which I am unconnected the contrast is even starker. The girls have become doctors, surgeons and barristers, government policy advisors, fund managers in the city, literary agents and publishing executives. There is also one judge and, of course, there are ladies who lunch.

It is a sobering experience to see, in such terms, the denial of equal opportunity that passed, almost without comment more than thirty years ago as if it was simply an inevitable fact of life. I have met so many talented, intelligent and humane people in my life who have made a success of their professional lives despite failing their eleven plus. From MPs to nuclear physicists to solicitors, they somehow managed to survive. This leads me to the same conclusion. What was the point in making that judgment on them at that early stage in their lives? Why did society have to make it deliberately hard for them and why, in those benighted areas of the country that still practise selection, do they continue to make it so hard?

Educational opportunity, particularly at secondary school level, remains absolutely pivotal in perpetuating the sort of society that Britain is. I am sitting with the printed details for the governing bodies of three London secondary schools in front to me.

The first one is for University College School, in Hampstead. It is an expensive, pleasant, liberal London day school that can boast Joseph Chamberlain and Will Self amongst its alumni. The list of governors includes four knights, a Lord, three professors and a barrister. The second list is for a sought-after London grammar school. There are no titled members but there is a healthy smattering of BAs and MAs and people with solid professional qualifications; the sort that might sit on the membership committee of a suburban golf club. The third list is for a London comprehensive school in the Borough of Waltham Forest that, at present, has five unfilled staff vacancies. Regrettably there is not a Duke, a Marquis or a Baronet listed amongst the governors and two of the positions remain to be filled. Neither do any of the members appear to possess any educational qualifications but I suspect this is simply the sort of misplaced egalitarianism that London local government tends to favour. For anyone naive or deluded enough to believe that class no longer matters in Britain, this simple exercise is a reminder that the class barrier is alive and well, and as pernicious as ever.

It was perhaps inevitable that the eleven plus and selection processes would be challenged in a town like Basildon – a town founded on roughly egalitarian principles. Most people were pragmatic and sensible enough not to accept the 'working class ladder' nonsense that was touted in defence of grammar schools. The reality was that the grammar schools were ninety per cent middle-class with the odd clever working class misfit thrown in. Conversely, the secondary modern schools were comprised almost completely of children from working class families. When the end came it was bloody and entertaining.

In 1968, a group of parents went to a tumultuous meeting held in the hall of the local grammar school. I felt uneasy even entering the building as if someone was going to run up from behind and say, "Oi you! This is not for the likes of you. Out you go!" It didn't happen then but it has happened a number of times since. But then, I do go out of my way to provoke. The atmosphere was tense and hostile because the Council was about to announce its scheme to introduce a comprehensive schooling system within the town. The grammar school lobby was outraged. A plump, overfed woman denounced the scheme as a socialist plot to destroy educational standards. Another spoke of the end of a fine tradition. The reality was that neither grammar school was more than ten years old. The father of my lost friend spoke of grammar school children having to mix with unsuitable types, i.e. the likes of me. Within a week, there was a 'Save our Grammar School' organisation. Strangely, I do not recall a 'Save our Secondary Modern Schools' organisation.

The issue soon became so heated that the Director of Education, who actually lived in Billericay, comfortably outside of the town, had his windows pelted with stones. Dog mess was pushed through his letter box by outraged grammar school parents. On the first day that comprehensive children were admitted to the old grammar school, a group of parents stood at the front gate and made a half-hearted attempt to block their admission, Little Rock style.

The Pioneers were confused about the issue. Almost to a man and woman, they had attended elementary school and had left at fourteen. Some of them – a minority – saw the grammar school as a bastion of middle-class privilege which they would not want for their own children. Others took the educational establishment viewpoint that a grammar school was a ladder for able working class children to better themselves. Some swallowed the disingenuous Harold Wilson argument that the new comprehensive schools represented grammar schools for all and therefore offered the best of all possible worlds. Perhaps the original opponents of comprehensive schools were right.

Thirty-four years later the old grammar school, Fryerns, having endured a quarter century as a declining comprehensive school is now a rather shrunken and low achieving community school. The low point came in 1998 with a torrent of bad publicity that the pupils had persistently racially abused a teacher and that the headteacher and local education authority had stood idly by.

There was always something very petty and parochial about the local grammar school. I associated it with rotary clubs, old students' associations, freemasons, bumptious Home Counties solicitors, overfed accountants, and that petty snobbery that disfigures small-town England – the first step to joining the crypto-fascists at the local golf club.

It was exclusive but with no real awareness of its own humble position within the great chain of being. One of my correspondents told me how she and her friend transferred to the sixth form of the local grammar school in order to take A-levels. For the two years they attended, they were not allowed to use the sixth form common room but, instead, had to use a demountable hut in the playground reserved for the ex-secondary modern pupils.

These were the days when getting five O-levels came close to guaranteeing a job for life. Such an achievement was regularly quoted to me as a touchstone of success. I can claim little personal hostility toward the school, but I detested the uniform – the royal blue blazer and particularly the school cap with its yellow badge. In the first year the boys still wore shorts and looked like a bunch of gormless 'Just William' look-alikes.

It was not jealousy. I was quite content at my school, mainly because it made very few demands upon me. I disliked their air of superiority, the awareness that I knew they were looking down upon me. When they refused to play us at sports fixtures, my loathing was complete. Even the independent school in Brentwood granted us the occasional fixture.

To my surprise, I found myself almost a member of the reviled institution. I had little choice. I had conceived the idea of going to university even though I did not know what a university was. A friend of my father's, an Indian gentleman straight out of an R.K. Narayan story, proclaimed himself to be a BA (failed) of the University of Bombay. I was intrigued and decided that I wanted 'some of that'. My only route was to study A-levels at what had once been the local grammar school. The rot had already set in, at least, that is what I thought, but I had not realised that greater events were swirling around me.

Basildon was at the forefront of the comprehensive revolution and at the moment I was due to transfer to the grammar school, my old secondary modern became a comprehensive and acquired a sixth form of sorts. I was both promiscuous and unprincipled in that I accepted places for sixth form at both the local grammar schools. This cheap duplicity of attitudes was paralleled in my social life when I had two girlfriends on the go simultaneously. I never had the heart to hurt the feelings of either and thus convinced myself that my moral duty lay in attempting to keep them both happy. It was physically arduous and sapped my vital spirit. On the issue of which sixth form to attend, I was not so morally discerning. On the first day of term, I turned up at neither institution and, instead, sloped off to my old school.

The former grammar school went into precipitous decline. The new first year was the first of the comprehensive intake and there were clear signs of breakdown in the order of what passed for civil society within the institution. After two years, half the student body in the lower years were from the tough estates that surrounded the school. It was clear they were not interested in being part of a grammar school for all. A friend of mine, who transferred to the grammar school from Craylands Secondary Modern on the other side of town, told me of his history teacher, who could not cope with the new clientele. On the cusp of retirement, he perhaps saw something in his new charge that influenced his decision.

One day, my friend was summoned into the stock room and was earnestly presented, as a rite of passage, with a dog-eared Historical Association pamphlet on Charles I. After that, the elderly teacher walked out of the school and was never seen again. Although my friend had little interest in the matter, he realised he had been 'chosen' above the potato heads that made up the rest of the class.

As the comprehensive revolution cut a swathe through English secondary education in the late 1960s and 70s, a whole generation of teachers, nurtured and raised within the grammar school tradition, found themselves rudely awakened to some of the more basic facts of educational life. As the council children poured through the doors of the previously exclusive institution, the grammar school masters, with their gowns and mortar boards, found some of the old certainties slipping away. There was to be no return to the comfortable old ways.

In 2002, I visited the condemned lower school building which the local youth periodically set on fire. The Council, in that clumsy inefficient way unique to local authorities, had partially fenced off the building leaving a gap through which I squeezed. The school had been built in that familiar 1930s elementary school style. It now felt like a run down relic; plates of boiled mince, tapioca pudding, periodic beatings, separate entrances for boys and girls and outdoor toilets. Most of the windows had been boarded up; those that hadn't had been smashed. It was merely waiting for the bulldozers to complete the final execution.

As a concept, selection looks terrific in the abstract; the notion that, at the age of eleven, you administer to all children a series of reliable, discriminating tests in order to be able to decide what sort of education to offer them. It makes perfect sense that society should try to offer its citizens in the making an education that is appropriate to society's need. Even if we assume, for one moment, that the intention of the principle was good, even noble, as opposed to old-fashioned class discrimination, the end result was still full of hidden cruelty. The naked judgment of the system that says 'you are a failure and have nothing to offer' is traumatic because it also says that you have no potential. Scratch beneath the surface and there is something fascistic about selection. It is the division of people into 'inferior' and 'superior' but, instead of using race as the criteria, a spurious measure of intelligence is used.

For those of a conservative and unimaginative disposition, selection is a comfort blanket; a reassuring reminder of how the world should be. In this world, the working class knew their place while irritating notions about fairness and equal opportunity could be ignored. As Orwell put it, 'It is a reminder of a world where the king is on the throne, the pound is worth a pound... and, at the outposts of the Empire, monocled Englishmen are holding the savages at bay'.

It is something of a mystery as to why, in a town that was meant to embody a new and classless Britain, a system of selection was visited upon it that was almost entirely about separating, for educational purposes, middle class and working class children. This was only a few years after the 1944 Butler Act. There still remained a vestigial belief that the eleven plus offered a form of equality of opportunity. In places where selection remains standard practice today – most of Kent, much of Buckinghamshire and Lincolnshire, Tameside, the city of Gloucester and a few free-standing grammar schools in North London – this working versus middle class divide still exists. The answer probably lies in the prevailing political and educational orthodoxy. In the 1950s only in a few select places such as Anglesey and Leicestershire was the comprehensive revolution starting to take root.

Twenty years later, the story was very different. When the new town, Milton Keynes, was being built in northern Buckinghamshire it was in a county that still practised selection. For the middle classes of Aylesbury,

High Wycombe, Amersham and Beaconsfield this was probably an attractive system. The working class, socially-aspirant inhabitants of Milton Keynes realised, however, that selection was unlikely to work in their interests and therefore agitated against it when the new town was being built. The result is one of the best and the most progressive comprehensive school systems in the country.

After 1944, generations of children were scarred by bad judgments about their ability at the age of eleven. Some were so incensed they were driven to achieve something extraordinary in order to prove the system wrong but the vast majority gave up and settled for second best in their lives. Now, children and, in some cases, grandchildren of this generation of educational rejects are being visited upon the system. This negative experience of education is in many cases transmitted to their children who carry their anti-educational attitudes into schools. In this sense the sins of the politicians of sixty years ago are being visited upon the children of today.

R.A. Butler, architect of the 1944 Education Act, could never have conceived of this. He thought he was creating a bright new future for the children of Britain but, as the saying goes: 'The road to hell is paved with good intentions.'

I attended a lecture recently by a member of Enfield Education Authority who, I suspect, had never taught a class in her life. I was informed that all teachers must apologise to the children in their charge for the harm that had been inflicted upon the English working class by the educational establishment. Additionally, I was informed that, when children from these so-called deprived backgrounds behave in an anti-social and disruptive fashion, they are engaging in a legitimate form of class protest at the dominance of middle class mores within the educational orthodoxy. And there was silly old me thinking they were just being foul-mouthed, inconsiderate and selfish.

The problem in Basildon was that, when they let the drawbridge down and admitted local children into what had been a grammar school, irrespective of ability and need, those schools went into terminal decline and then self-destructed. Whose fault was that? It should have been a place of hope and opportunity but it became a synonym for hopelessness. Was it the fault of the school? Did they carry on dishing out a grammar school education unaware of the changing clientele? Was it the fault of the pupils and parents? Did they arrive with an attitude that was hostile towards educational achievement and authority? Was it the fault of society? Had the swirling economic and social changes of the 1970s and 80s undermined the purpose of education so that it was no longer a ladder of opportunity? Looking through the broken windows, I could see all those eager children wearing their royal blue caps, keen to do well, keen to make their parents proud of them, knowing that they were on the well-trodden route to becoming middle class. For them there was once hope that has now gone.

So what now is the route to becoming middle class? Is this a desirable social objective? Probably, given that the chances of becoming unemployed, seriously ill, committing a serious criminal offence and not being a burden on the state are all dramatically reduced upon entering the hallowed ground of the English bourgeoisie.

In 2003, 89 per cent of the population in England and Wales attended comprehensive schools, 3 per cent attended grammar school and 8 per cent were educated in the independent sector. These figures hide some disturbing bald facts. In the Borough of Kensington and Chelsea, 54 per cent of children were educated privately while a dozen miles to the east in Barking and Dagenham, according to government figures, not a single child was privately educated. It is more likely there were not enough to register as 1 per cent. Despite these discrepancies, the vast majority of the population received broadly the same sort of educational experience. Has this contributed to the process of embourgeoisiement? The route is now very unclear in comparison to the straight shining road offered to some more than forty years ago. To others, the pathway went through brambles and the briar patch. The most obvious answer is that affluence brings with it property ownership, a sense of having a stake in society, and a belief that such a society is worth preserving. How governments create affluence and, more importantly, ensure it is spread fairly evenly without trampling too outrageously on the rights of the individual, is the most difficult question of all. It is clear, from our experiences of the last fifty or so years, that there needs to be a degree of inequality in society in order to provide incentive for aspiration and self-improvement. The extent of inducing an acceptable degree of inequality, whilst preserving a healthy society, is one that must overwhelmingly concern us.

Each year, I scrutinise, with some care, the league tables of school performance published by the government. My first port of call is always those tables relating to Essex. For the last eight years, my old school has been one of the worst performing secondary schools in Essex. Perhaps there should be an educational equivalent of relegation into the Ryman league for such a dismal performance. According to the Daily Express in 1999, with just 5 per cent of pupils gaining 5 grades A-C at GCSE, it was in the bottom ten of all schools nationally, and had been for a number of years. Six years ago, in response to this continuing failure, the school was closed down temporarily. Merged with an equally failing institution, it was refurbished and renamed the Sir James Hornsby High School. Did this change things? Not a great deal. It is still one of the worst schools in Essex because it still has the same sort of pupils attending, those from families who place a low value on education and are caught in the perpetual cycle of low achievement. They do not even have the usual excuse of ethnic diversity or English as a second language.

In the interests of fairness, I should record that, in 2003, it achieved 23 per cent A-C grades at GCSE which sent it shooting up the school improvement tables but not enough to have the parents of south Essex beating a path to its door. Knowing teachers as I do I am sure that this reflects an almost superhuman effort on their part. Perhaps the Conservatives are right. Throwing money at a problem is not enough. It is necessary to somehow change attitudes.

Also worthy of note was the fact that the lowest achieving mainstream school in Essex was the old grammar school, Barstable. Thirty years ago, parents would have forfeited their right arm to get their child into that school. Today, it is shunned as a failing school, languishing as the very worst in Essex, bottom of the class, with just 10 per cent of pupils gaining 5 A-C grades at GCSE in 2003.

*

I have slightly misrepresented my position in attending a secondary modern school. I was being prepared for factory life but not necessarily unskilled work. At the age of 15, I began to ponder the future and the prospect of finishing school. Unusually, I was being allowed to stay on for a fifth year for an undefined purpose as we were not allowed to take O levels. I suspect that it may have been my obvious and complete lack of suitability for the world of work.

I spoke to several of the older Pioneers. Their advice was uniform. "Get yourself a trade. Get an apprenticeship and you'll never look back." My problem was I did not want an apprenticeship but I was reluctant to ignore the accumulated wisdom of my elders. By this time, I had developed an interest in William Blake and I knew all about the Dark Satanic Mills. The pressure was considerable so I went along to the main Ford factory at Dagenham for an interview to become an apprentice. I can date it very precisely in 1968 for it was the day the Ford Escort was launched and, despite my near total lack of interest, I was given an Escort bonnet badge.

Coming from a socialist egalitarian background, I found myself both puzzled and perplexed at the elaborate hierarchy prevalent in British factories at the time with different canteens and facilities available for different grades of worker. A man in a brown store coat spent half an hour outlining the dining facilities would not be available to us.

"It wouldn't be right" he said when I questioned why all employees did not use the same facilities. "It wouldn't be right!"

What did he mean? An offence in the eye of God? A breach of the law? Against the company rulebook? A grave transgression of fundamental morality? No wonder our Ford Cortina kept breaking down. When he said it was now time for lunch (I still called it dinner), I promptly made for the canteen. He pulled me up short. "That's not for the likes of you, sonny." The likes of me! What did he mean? Did I have a large brand mark on my forehead that said working class? No wonder the Japanese ran all over us in the 1970s. While Datsun focussed on producing reliable cars, Ford were more worried about who used what canteen.

Many years later, a similar incident occurred at Lords cricket ground where I was watching the first England versus Sri Lanka test match. Having entered the ground, I went to get a decent seat in one of the stands. One of the many blazered-buffoons from St Johns Wood shouted, "Oi! That's not for the likes of you." There must be something about me and there certainly appears to be something about Lords. There is no other place in England that has the ability to make me feel like a second-class citizen in my own country and that includes Henley and Ascot.

The upshot of my apprenticeship interview was that Ford, with great perception, wrote my father a letter explaining that I was not really suited to the idea of a craft apprenticeship. To be honest, I would have feared for the future of Ford if they had accepted me. The truth is, Dagenham is now dying, most of the engineers have been laid off, and I would have been redundant at fifty, probably ready to start a second career collecting trolleys in a B&Q car park. Having been rejected, I returned to school with no clearer idea of where the future would take me.

The stigma of rejection still hovers.

I recently had lunch with the Master and some Fellows of Peterhouse College, Cambridge. Some of these Cambridge Colleges are now becoming seriously concerned about the number of public school meat-heads they admit. On the whole, they do their best to keep them out but public schools have always been very adept at disguising mutton as lamb.

The lunch was something out of *Porterhouse Blue*. We ate in a poorly-lit, oak-panelled dining room with small deferential men scurrying around serving us from ancient silver tureens. When I was asked what school I had attended, I am afraid that I lied and claimed 'a small rural grammar school in Essex' as my alma mater.

The words small, rural and Essex were true enough but I could not bring myself to tell these learned men from this august institution that I had attended Nicholas Secondary Modern School. I was in the company of Lord Wilson of Tillyorn, a former diplomat and a distinguished linguist, a fellow who specialised in intellectual history, and a professor whose specialism was nineteenth century German philosophy so you may wonder what we discussed over lunch. The answer is that, at their instigation, we discussed the merits of candidates on Celebrity Big Brother.

Of course, had I not been there, they would have been discussing Wittgenstein or Forbach but I suppose the moment I hoved into view the cry went up, "Here comes one of the plebs, let's make him feel at home." Distressingly, I was not familiar with any of the candidates involved in Celebrity Big Brother while the Master (always referred to as Master which makes him sound like something out of Star Wars) was disconcertingly well informed. I felt rather left out of the conversation and would probably have made a better fist if we had discussed Wittgenstein.

All in all, the lunch yielded none of the stimulating conversation I would have expected from such intellectual men. I suppose they must have Big Brother running continuously in the Senior Common Room. The Master may even have one of those amusing stand-up cards on his office desk with the message: 'If you don't smoke then I won't fart'.

*

As I was driving out of Cambridge through the southern environs in the late afternoon darkness, I was aware of stationary police cars with flashing lights on both sides of the road. Police officers on foot were vigorously waving the traffic on. To my left was the Cambridge Crematoria into which swept at speed a darkened hearse accompanied by silent police cars to the front and rear. Two men with cameras leapt forward and there were several intense flashes in the dark before they were hustled away by the police.

As I drove into the darkness of southern Cambridgeshire, the six o'clock news on the car radio announced that Myra Hindley had been cremated that evening in Cambridge. I reflected, as I drove down the M11, on the cruelty of life, the capriciousness of fate, the squalor of the press, and what course Myra Hindley's life might have taken if she had not met Ian Brady.

Chapter 7: Tom Lexman's Shed

When you come back to England from any foreign country, you have immediately the sensation of breathing a different air.
George Orwell. The Lion and the Unicorn.

We carry a new world here in our hearts. That world is growing by the minute.
Bueneventura Durutti.
Anarchist leader during the Spanish Civil War.

Sheds were an important part of my childhood. Every self-respecting man had a construction of some originality and, at times, luxury either at the bottom of the garden, attached to the side of the house or, less often, remote and alone on an allotment. Rarely were they used for something as mundane as the storage of bicycles, lawn mowers or garden tools; sheds were a little kingdom for the man who had no other realm.

The houses in Basildon were small and the families were often large. After a day at work in one of the factories – Standard Telephone perhaps, or Marconi, or Yardley – the shed was a retreat from the worries and cares of the world where hobbies could be indulged; hobbies of the sort that have now, by and large, disappeared.

Whatever happened to fretwork, budgerigar breeding, carpentry, tending allotments, choral singing, stamp and coin collecting, woodcarving, crocheting, knitting, basket weaving, model making, pottery and, perhaps most curiously, grown men making metal Meccano models driven by Mamod steam engines?

This was the last gasp of George Orwell's gentle unassuming England of little men pursuing their lives away from the gaze and out of the grasp of intrusive government. It was an England of playing darts on wet Sunday afternoons, cups of strong tea, Carnation tinned milk, luncheon meat sandwiches, Camp coffee with chicory essence, growing grotesquely large vegetables, games of dominoes and cribbage, and listening to the Light Programme on a crackly radio. This was the fading England of totes, dog races, football pools, Woolworth's, the flicks, Gracie Fields, Walls ice cream, potato crisps, Celanese stockings, pin tables, cigarettes, and Saturday evenings spent in the four ale bar.

Some individuals still pursue these hobbies but they have become minority activities about which one only makes a very guarded admission. People still eat Walls ice cream, play darts and do the football pools but such conduct is no longer emblematic of a way of life. To admit, in the third millennia, that one is a philatelist or, even worse, a numismatist is to invite sheer puzzlement at best or, more likely, derision.

Such quaintness has been swept away by television – that great numbing, soothing blanket that we have allowed to be draped over us. For those who doubt the corrosive nature of television, may I direct them towards Robert Putnam's seminal study of the decline of American civic culture – *Bowling Alone*. What happens in the USA tends to happen here about ten years later and Putnam allows us slivers of information that only point in one direction.

One example will suffice. In his survey, those who listed watching television as their primary form of entertainment were twice as likely to gesticulate at other drivers and half as likely to be involved in a community welfare project. Television erodes our humanity and the connections we have with the rest of society. However, we did not give in to the monster in the corner without a fight.

My father, when he eventually conceded the principle, bought a single channel device that was manufactured before the advent of commercial television. Thus we were protected from (in the order that my father listed them) Coronation Street, Popeye, Double Your Money, Sunday Night at the London Palladium and Saturday afternoon wrestling with Mick McManus and Jackie Pallo. Although he was a firm advocate of Reithian values, I can think of no obvious harm that Coronation Street ever inflicted to justify its high position in his demonology.

For myself, I saw no sinister purpose that extended beyond watching *Picture Book* on Mondays, *Andy Pandy* on Tuesdays, *The Flowerpot Men* on Wednesdays, *Rag, Tag and Bobtail* on Thursdays and *The Woodentops* on Fridays but perhaps I was missing something.

And so it came to pass that the shed was an escape from the newly-popular television, a place to listen to Radio Luxembourg on a transistor set. There, in the calm of a warm summer's evening, fathers – but never mothers – would sit smoking Black Cat, Craven-A, Bachelors, Park Drive or Buckingham cigarettes while listening to one of those 1960s comedy programmes like *Round the Horn, Much Binding in the Marsh* or *The Navy Lark.*

Nearly all the cigarettes came cheap, or in some cases free, from the old Carreras factory on the A127, now replaced by a Homebase and McDonald's restaurant. For some of the older generation, smoking cigarettes was a little suspect, a rushed pleasure indulged only by ruffians, spivs, and a certain sort of upper class cad; the type Terry Thomas played in those 1950s black and white films. The older folks' slower burning pleasure was to suck on a pipe with a comfortable bowl full of St Bruno Ready Rubbed and reflect about life and the world. But pipe smokers were obviously a dying breed because where are they now? Taken by mouth cancer, I suppose.

The construction of sheds was rarely standard. Pioneers were not the sort to buy an off-the-peg shed and erect it at the bottom of the garden. No, each structure was unique and idiosyncratic, incorporating a wide range of designs and building materials. Some Pioneers had a Plotland heritage and a large helping of the working class ingenuity that enabled them to turn their hand to most practical activities. They would never understand how specialised and impractical we have now become.

Three months ago, I replaced a rear brake light bulb in a neighbour's car and he still hails me as an all-conquering mechanical genius. The rest of the street now know that I am a man who has mastered the mysteries of changing car bulbs without serving a Ford apprenticeship.

Mervyn Pelman's father had an astronomical observatory at the bottom of his garden. To most, it looked just like a shed but with a home-made dome on top of it through which jutted a large ancient brass refracting telescope of impressive but uncertain vintage. We could gaze triumphantly at the rings of Saturn and marvel at the moons of Jupiter bobbing around ceaselessly in the sky thanks, in no short measure, to the lack of an adequate stand. In the corner of the shed were copies of the Amateur Astronomer series by Patrick Moore (yes, he really has been around that long) resting on top of the other essential requisite that no good astronomer could be without – a crate of Jubilee Stout and Mann's Nutbrown.

Fred Warrior laboured for ten whole years building his shed from what appeared to be disused railway sleepers. At the end of his exertions he had created a structure that took up half the garden and looked as if it was capable of resisting the nuclear attack we were all expecting in the early 1960s. For us, it was as unique and original as the Hanging Gardens of Babylon.

At the time of the Cuban Missile Crisis, we joked with Fred about reserving a place in his shed. Inside the shed, he kept crates of tins of baked beans and Spam, jars of stewed apple and old military-style jerry cans that he kept full of water. Once a month he emptied the cans over the flowerbeds and refilled them. They needed to be fresh for the coming nuclear Armageddon.

Mr. Warrior was the driving force behind the 1962 civil defence exercise when we were reluctantly persuaded to simulate emergency procedures in the event of nuclear attack. In October that year, with the Cuban Missile Crisis unresolved, this did not seem to be an unreasonable precaution. As the sirens wailed insistently, we made our way to some large open storm drains about half a mile away. Some people were swathed in bandages, daubed with red paint, and were carried on stretchers by members of the St Johns Ambulance complaining constantly, "You're ******* heavy. You can walk until we get in sight of the drains."

Even at the age of nine, I was not convinced of the value of this particular exercise, which involved standing in nine inches of cold dirty water for thirty minutes and then emerging to the prospect of a nuclear winter. I was all for taking my chances in the coalbunker although the delivery of a ton and a half of Coalite forced me to consider the alternative of using the brick-built tool shed at the back of the house.

With its three inch thick wooden walls, permanent electricity supply and a Baby Belling stove, Mr Warrior had effectively declared independence from the rest of his extended family. Always a fan of *Rawhide* and *Gunsmoke*, he wandered round his garden wearing chaps and a pair of imitation silver pistols in the style of Rowdy Yates. Sometimes he would sit on the shed porch sorrowfully plucking out a rendition of *Oh, Susannah* on an ancient banjo as if he was at home in the Appalachian Mountains with his bottle of moonshine and a bowl of hominy grits. Then, when reality once more intruded, he went off to the Ford radiator factory to prepare the cooling systems for Consuls, Anglias, Zephyrs and Zodiacs.

Ray Clark's father had a row of optics on the back wall of his shed from which he dispensed measures of whisky. As I recall, he was the only customer in this rather unique bar.

Russell Jones' mother (yes, there was a woman with a shed) had her own little brewery; a small brick-built structure where she produced her own beer as well as vast amounts of wine made from tea, nettles and potato peelings. My first hesitant introduction to alcohol was the result of liberal quantities of Mrs Jones' tea wine. Of all the sheddist occupations, it may be argued that hers was the only one of any value and it may be significant that she was the only woman I have mentioned.

Eddie Vincent, only two years older than me, had his very own shed that he filled with what he called motorcycles. In reality, they were merely a large number of boxes filled with motorbike parts. Given a large amount of time and considerable mechanical expertise, they could probably have been assembled into several running motorcycles but they never were. On the odd occasion I visited with my older brother, he would hold in the air such arcane objects as an Ariel Red Hunter big end, a Triumph Trophy swinging arm, a Norton Dominator Rocker Box Cover or an AJS alternator and I would nod in mute enthusiasm and acknowledgement of something for which I had no understanding. To this day, I still cannot explain those four objects.

Our own house backed onto houses in another street so we shared a rear garden fence. Several Pioneer families lived in the street behind us together with an old man called Tom Lexman. I say he was old, because that's the way he seemed at the time but mature reflection suggests that he was probably in his early sixties when I knew him. Unless he has been blessed with extraordinary longevity, he must now be dead.

Tom was not quite a Pioneer but he was a fervent socialist, a former member of the Communist Party who regularly regaled us with tales of the General Strike and the treachery of Ramsey MacDonald, the first Labour Prime Minister.

He reserved a particular venom for Philip Snowden, the Labour Chancellor of the Exchequer in the National Government of the early 1930s, who turned out to be the hammer of the poor rather than their saviour. "After the revolution," he would say, "the first thing I would do is put that Snowden up against a wall and have him shot." As Snowden died in 1937, it would have been difficult but Tom never struck me as the sort to scrutinise The Times obituary column on a daily basis.

Despite his left leanings and instinctive sympathies, Tom, like many of his working class generation, had discovered the liberation that self-taught intellectual freedom brought but he could never bring himself to wholeheartedly support the over-doctrinal approach of the British Communist Party.

A general sympathy for the underdog, and an instinctive revulsion at the juxtaposition of poverty and privilege in British society in the early 1930s, initially propelled him in the direction of Marxism. His spirited intellectual independence meant he was never likely to be impressed by the doctrinal bombast of Harry Pollit, General Secretary of the Communist Party of Great Britain. Even more repellent to him was Rajani Palme Dutt, the emotionless, desiccated editor of Labour Monthly for more than fifty years. The sort of theological absolutism exhibited by Palme Dutt, the ascetic Stalinist 'Pope' of British Communism, cast a baleful influence over British Marxist politics. Most working class people were rightly suspicious of any political ideology that threatened to increase the power of the state. British Marxists, well drilled in the catechism of Das Kapital, may have been very good at silencing critics but they were poor at persuading fellow travellers to join the cause.

Tom was a fellow traveller but he was blessed with a healthy degree of scepticism and common sense. Very few of the Socialist Pioneers were Marxists although many had a healthy respect for the old man while rejecting the baggage that came with him. Some had experienced the dogmatism of the British Communist Party in the 1930s and were repelled by its cavalier treatment of the individual and its blind adherence to the Moscow line.

For someone as spirited and critical as Tom, the aridity of Marxist doctrine was never likely to appeal seriously. Any attempt to explain society in terms of a materialist conception of history was never likely to convince someone who had fought in the Spanish Civil War and had been in the thick of the carnage at the Battle of Jarama. What Tom, and his generation of left-wing egalitarian idealists needed was a humane proletarian Marxism that addressed their needs and perceptions as individuals. What they got was the ghastliness of the Moscow-inspired lexicon of democratic centralism, revisionism, deviationism, politburo and the Comintern. Men like Tom Lexman, who fought all their lives to be free from the limitations of their circumstances, were hardly likely to enter willingly into another form of intellectual slavery.

Tom represented what was almost the last throw of that grand auto-didactic tradition that is now dead. The rear of his shed was lined with builders' planks that passed as makeshift bookshelves containing, I imagine, in excess of a thousand volumes. Here I was introduced, for the first time, to *Palgrave's Golden Treasury*, the Arthur Quiller Couch *Oxford Book of English Verse*, *Samuel Pepys' Diary*, Samuel Johnson's *Lives of the Poets* and Goldsmith's *History of England*. On a lighter note there was Walter Scott's *Ivanhoe*, many volumes of Robert Louis Stevenson, *Gulliver's Travels* and *Robinson Crusoe*. In short, this was the library of the interwar autodidact ranging from the novels of A.J. Cronin and Richard Llewellyn to Plato's *Dialogues* and Gibbon's *Fall of the Roman Empire*.

In my naive childish sort of way, I asked him which was his best book. Without hesitation, he replied that he did not have a best book but, for him, the writer who towered above all others was Thomas Carlyle, at which point he handed me a copy of *The French Revolution*. I stared at it incomprehensibly for a few moments before placing it on the floor. The idea of reading a book of more than fifty pages, especially one with no pictures, had never occurred to me. I was a big fan of the Commando Library, a series of small compact comic books based upon the Second World War in which the square-jawed British hero would deal out justice to the Hun with lines like: "Take that, Fritz!" and "Fight like a man, you squarehead swine!" That was my sort of literature.

I cannot claim to have read any of Tom's books, or experienced some sort of cultural epiphany as a result of the many hours I spent in his shed. The reality was that I gained far more pleasure from listening to Radio Luxembourg and firing a catapult at a target in his garden. However, I did take home, at his suggestion, Bertrand Russell's *History of Western Philosophy*. Its appeal was enhanced by the fact that Tony Hancock, in his self-improving phase a few weeks earlier, had struggled for half an hour to get through the opening page.

The thick blue volume sat on a shelf in the kitchen for three months, constantly reproaching me for my ignorance, before I returned it with an admission of my failure. There was little point in pretending otherwise as I knew he would ask me a searching question if I claimed to have read it.

Many years later, although I had not the slightest inkling at the time, I realised that Tom's craving for knowledge was also a crusade for a way of defining himself within a hostile world. He had been born into the poverty of the East End and, although of obvious ability, he had no means of distinguishing himself; no way to establish an identity through his knowledge and his learning. For a man who spent the first twenty years of his working life following orders, reading and the generation of ideas gave him an intellectual independence within an industrial and depersonalised world in which he was just one cog in a very large machine. The life of the mind somehow liberated him from the menial circumstances of his life. Like John Keats, the moment he read Chapman's *Homer* for the first time, he knew what Cortez must have felt like the first time he stared out across the wide blue Pacific Ocean from that peak in Darien. (In fact, Keats confused Cortez with Balboa.)

Tom was part of a way of life now completely lost but movingly recorded in historian Alan Bullock's biography of his father growing up in 1920s Bradford. Dissenting, purposeful, and high-minded, it is based upon a liberal individualist principle of self-improvement that fifty years of the welfare state and universal access to education have swept away.

It did not strike me as strange that Tom and his friend (whose name I no longer remember) would sit together in the shed discussing whether or not Dickens' reliance on coincidence in the plot of *Nicholas Nickelby* was fanciful or whether Harriet Beecher Stowe had exaggerated the wicked treatment of Tom in *Uncle Tom's Cabin*. They were merely two men who had left elementary school as thirteen year old boys, ostensibly poorly-educated, and were discussing literature in the manner of undergraduates. A comparison with the undergraduates of my acquaintance, whose literary penchant is for *FHM* and *Loaded*, is not really possible.

At the time, I thought little of such matters but, many years later, I reflected on the literary tastes that were exhibited in my version of *Uncle Tom's Cabin*. Now I realise just how conservative were the reading tastes of Tom Lexman's generation. Much of the content of his bookshelves would not have been out of place in the London home of William Lovett or in William Cobbet's cottage.

Even in the first half of the twentieth century, *Pilgrim's Progress* was still read and revered as a 'guide to life' almost as if the modernists did not exist. *Ivanhoe* was preferred to *Ulysses*; Dickens, Thackeray, Hardy and Kipling were there aplenty, but everything seemed to stop suddenly with John Galsworthy. There was no Joyce, Hemingway, Eliot,

D.H. Lawrence or Virginia Woolf. Perhaps the impediment was their perceived inability simply to tell a good story. It may have been the fact that the Workers Educational Association classes Tom had attended forty years earlier had not yet discovered the modern movement.

I am puzzled by the juxtaposition of Tom Lexman as a fellow traveller of the Communist Party, volunteer for the International Brigade, and the conservative Daily Mail-reading literary tastes of his alter ego. He came from the Jewish East End where there had long existed a tradition that admired the liberating power of literature and culture.

Rudolph Rocker, the great East End anarchist leader, taught his followers that the purpose of education was to make people free; to liberate them from the constraints that shaped and stunted their lives. Society could only progress, and people could only be truly free, if each generation was allowed to shape its own ideas through its cultural emancipation. Thus, he argued, culture was not the creation of a particular class but was achieved through the common efforts of successive generations from all social classes. Capitalism could therefore be destroyed, not through a Soviet-style purging of the western cultural canon, but by redistribution to all social classes through a universal cultural education.

The key for Rocker, and his disciples like Tom Lexman, was that each individual must be in control of his own development rather than being the passive recipient of a high culture whose characteristics were determined elsewhere. It was through this creed of auto-didactism that Rocker claimed the true emancipation – freedom that would be achieved within society. They believed quite simply that great literature makes you truly free.

Tom Lexman was also a connoisseur of classical music. On a small camping table in a corner of the shed stood an old wind-up record player beside which stood a massive pile of 78 classical recordings. The pile contained what we might call standard classics – favourites like Beethoven, Mozart, Brahms and Chopin. Moderns were unrepresented which may have been due to disapproval or possibly lack of access. It is easy to forget just how restricted the airwaves were a mere thirty-five years ago.

The BBC had a complete monopoly on legal broadcasting which meant the severely cultural Third Programme was the only source of broadcast classical music. Not that there was a plethora of popular music available – the sole arbiter of this type of music was the BBC Light Programme which, after much agonising, eventually became Radio 2.

The Third Programme did not even embrace the Reithian ideal of bringing high culture to the masses. Instead it sought to exclude them by appealing only to a university-educated cultural elite. It catered solely for those who already knew the code that allowed them entry to the world of classical music and the appreciation of high art. Then, as now, it has a regular listening base of about one hundred thousand, 0.2 per cent of the population. As was the case forty years ago the pleasures of the few are paid for by the long-suffering licence fee payer.

For cultural aspirants who found Milton's Comus inaccessible, the answer was 'tough'. Just as it was tough on Tom Lexman and his friend as they sat listening to the Third Programme in pursuit of cultural enlightenment. They would make remarks like: "Well, I don't think much of that." after sitting through a broadcast of *Waiting for Godot*.

When he told me they were broadcasting Shaw's *Man and Superman*, I ignored the Shaw bit and confidently expected Clark Kent and Lois Lane to appear. I was to be disappointed.

"You mark my words, lad," he would say to me. "One day, when we are all educated, this sort of stuff will be listened to in every living room in the land." This, of course, was the triumph of optimism over experience. Even in the mid-1960s the signs were clear. We preferred the Beatles to Beethoven and *Take Your Pick* to the *Brains Trust*.

Tom Lexman's prediction has been almost exactly reversed today. We are hugely more formally-educated as a society than we were in the 1950s and 60s yet we prefer *Big Brother* to *Arena* and *Blind Date* to *Late Night Line-up*. I have reached the conclusion that the more the state insists upon educating us, the less we know. I am reluctantly driven to support Kingsley Amis's assertion that, in the case of television broadcasting, more does mean worse.

I was never quite sure if Tom and his friend genuinely enjoyed their classical music sessions or whether they merely felt they should, in thrall to the belief that, if they listened long enough and hard enough, enlightenment would come to them. A little like jazz and me I suppose. I still listen to Charlie Parker, Bill Evans and John Coltrane in the belief that one day a little light will switch on in my head and, out of discordance, all will be revealed.

*

Somewhere, waiting to be written, is a PhD thesis on the importance of canary breeding in working class culture between 1850 and about the mid-1960s. It is all over now, of course; another of the many leisure activities swept away by television and the revolution of information technology.

Albert Steadman, who lived not far from Tom devoted his leisure hours to breeding Border canaries; his father was one of the breeders who developed the Norwich Fancy in the nineteenth century.

Albert: the name has the ring of the early twentieth century about it. When did you last meet someone under the age of eighty bearing the name Albert? It is the old man in *Steptoe and Son*, an extinct London dock, the other half of Queen Victoria, a piece of triumphal Victorian architecture, and the 'square' setting for a television soap opera.

Like a small number of his generation, Albert Steadman was obsessed with unpasteurised milk as the panacea for our modern ills.

"You pass that Green Top to me, boy," he would say with a solemnity born of reverence.

Pasteurised milk was a symbol of our disconnectedness from nature; the bastardising, through industrial intervention, of a wholesome natural product. To insist upon Green Top unpasteurised milk was just one small way of fighting back.

The pursuit of the canary is the symbol of a lost working class. And Albert was a canary man. At the back of his house was a large porch inset into the house on to which he had built a timber-framed and mesh extension full of cages, with a small flight out into the garden. Using the rear porch door, he could walk straight into his little kingdom. In addition, he had a wooden shed full of canaries, linnets, greenfinches and siskins, all housed in small hand-made wooden cages.

He was though no ordinary canary man. For the last twenty years of his life he devoted himself to reviving the lost, and now forgotten, London Fancy.

I must have been an odd, and very dull, child for I would sometimes prefer to sit and talk to Albert about his birds than go out and play football. He told me the London Fancy had been the great canary of the London working class, and that his grandfather had exhibited at the Crystal Palace when it was moved to south London. The breed had gone into decline as fashions changed in the early twentieth century and a marauding stoat wiped out the last birds in the 1930s. How close he got I do not know.

Albert showed me an old mezzotint of the London Fancy. They were striking birds, long and elegant in the body, yellow and buff (or as he put it, jonquil and mealy) with black tail and flight feathers. The birds that hopped round in his many cages may, or may not, have been replicas of the London Fancy. I was not too interested in the exact science, more that the process of such a simple act of creation could come to define someone's life.

Albert talked of lizards, lutinos, siskins, rollers, mules, inos and opals. Such was the language of a working class passion that enthralled both my grandfather and great grandfather and old Albert himself.

It has now gone the way of jellied eels, music hall, flat caps, pearly queens and 'Doing the Lambeth Walk' though you may argue that a bizarre version continues to live on in the television set of Albert Square.

Back then, it was part of a working class culture that flourished between the rise of the concept of leisure time in the second half of the nineteenth century and the emergence of a mass television audience in the early 1960s. Albert, as well as being a Pioneer, was one of the last of that type. He was a representative of that generation; class-conscious, self-taught, politically-aware, proud of all that he stood for and determined never to doff his cap to any man.

*

For the sake of convenience I shall refer to Tom's other friend as John. Although they were bosom pals in a curmudgeonly sort of fashion, Tom was suspicious of John because he had been to Ruskin College and had, therefore, formally acquired some book learning. The suspicion ran deeper than it appeared on the surface and was characteristic of working class attitudes to the adult education offered by the Workers Educational Association and Ruskin College.

Founded in 1899 by three philanthropic Americans, Ruskin College originally specialised in correspondence courses mainly covering economics and politics. It soon became a residential college, loosely affiliated to the Workers Educational Association, using the services of a large number of sympathetic Oxford Dons while remaining fiercely independent of the University.

The questions raised in many proletarian minds about these projects, either partially or fully funded by the state, were: Were these attempts to offer a belated education to the working class simply a means of social control? Were they a low plot to distract the workers away from the purity of Marxist thought unsullied by the bourgeois assumptions of tutors and lecturers.

The official view was that they were a valuable opportunity for ordinary working men and women to acquire at least the basics of an education that, if they had been born fifty years later, would have been theirs by right.

Tom could never make up his mind. He valued the independence of being able to pick any book off the shelf and discuss it with his friend, John. There may have been a patina of envy at the rich experience of spending a few weeks in Oxford, even if the tutors believed in the principle of a liberal humane education as opposed to crude Marxist indoctrination. For many like John, the gruelling reality of wading through Das Kapital was a sure cure for any oversimplified application of Marxist principles. Though they retained the suspicion that the state was seducing them with kindness, they were equally drawn by the prospect of intellectual emancipation at the University that represented both a citadel in defence of the existing status quo, and a finishing school for the British ruling class.

I now know that Tom was Jewish although this was not apparent to me at the time. There was a slight Semitic resonance to his name and a wiry swarthiness that suggested his origins in the huddled East End.

Tom had been witness to if not an active participant in the Battle of Cable Street in 1936 against the inflammatory attempt by Oswald Mosley's Blackshirt fascists to march through the heart of the East End. The date, coincidentally 5th October, is the same as the Broadwater Farm Riot. There is often a symmetry to London violence. In the harshness of the 1930s Tom's political views had been formed and he found himself, a year later, in hot, dusty Spain again fighting against fascists with (what he called) 'the Cable Street Lads'.

I knew nothing of the war but was aware that a few people at school had gone on some of the early package holidays to the Mediterranean coast. I somehow assumed that fighting in Spain was akin to brawling with the Spanish police on the beaches of the Costa del Sol.

A few years later, I read in the newspapers that General Franco, the ghastly fascist dictator of Spain, was partial to the habit of executing opponents by garrotting. I later saw a demonstration of the principles of garrotting on television and it seemed suitably unpleasant. I picked up some references to the Spanish Civil War and realised this was the conflict Tom Lexman had been involved in. I resolved to find out more and cultivated a grudging relationship with him.

Tom had been born in Bethnal Green at the turn of the century, had attended the Jewish Free School in Spitalfields and, at the age of thirteen, had been apprenticed to a tailor. In the wake of the 1929 crash and the spread of a world wide depression, he asked himself that most fundamental of questions: Why are some rich and some poor? More pertinently he asked why he was poor when others had so much. No satisfactory answer presented itself and so, in 1932, he had trooped along to King Street, Hammersmith and joined the Communist Party.

After the battle of Cable Street, he was fired with the spirit of anti-fascism and applied to join the swelling band of British volunteers fighting in Spain. Arriving in Boulogne with no passport, he was spirited to Paris before he caught the train to Barcelona where, curiously, he became involved with the Trotskyist POUM. I didn't understand the significance of this then but, given the anti-Stalinist position of the POUM and the official line of the British Communist Party, this was a contradiction that, with greater awareness, I should have explored.

I did not have the words to ask Tom why he went but I did later ask my father.

"For the money," he replied, "and the adventure," he added after a moment of hesitation.

For Tom, it wasn't a poet's war or an intellectual's war. I probably do him no disservice to say that he had never heard of Stephen Spender or W.H. Auden at the time. For him, it was an alternative to depression, unemployment and the dole, with the prospect of soldiering in what seemed to be an exotic, even remote, country for a cause to which he was sympathetic.

I am uncertain how strong his ideological commitment was but I suspect it had shallow roots. By early 1937 he had joined, under an assumed name, the British battalion of the XV International Brigade near Albacete. It is likely that, instinctively, he was closer to the heterodox Popular Front than to the hard line communists. My father knew he had been friends with a number of ILP volunteers. As the basis of his association with the Pioneers was his empathy with ILP ideals, rather than any staunch communist views, this seems to be consistent.

For all of them, their innocence was lost in February 1937 at Jarama. When these eager but tender young volunteers were caught on an open hillside, they were cut to pieces by Franco's best troops. Despite terrible leadership and chaotic organisation, Tom survived but from that moment the scales fell away from his eyes. Several times I heard him sing the song but I had no understanding of its significance.

> There's a valley in Spain called Jarama,
> That's a place that we all know so well.
> For 'tis there that we wasted our manhood
> And most of our old age as well.

This song is now familiar, very familiar, but at the time it seemed fresh and new.

Having survived the Moorish rifle fire, Tom deserted the International Brigade, along with many other deserters, and ended up in a Republican prison near Ablactate. Disillusioned with the Communist Party he felt he had done his bit. He had gone out as a volunteer and wanted to be able to leave as a volunteer. Unfortunately, the Republican government took the opposite view and issued a decree incorporating the Brigades into the Republican Army, thus placing them under military discipline.

Tom never came to terms with the new emphasis on hierarchy and saluting officers. He had gone to fight fascism in Spain not to salute men who were no better than him. Not that he had much respect for his communist leaders either. In particular, he disliked both his local commander, Will Painter, and Harry Pollit, the head of the British Communist Party, whom he accused of having no concern for the lives of the men but an excessive concern with following the Moscow line.

Tom was unexpectedly released, along with a group of other volunteers, following the intervention of the poet, Stephen Spender. I assume the group of British prisoners, including Spender's lover, Tom Hyndman, took no further part in the military action. Tom knew though of the military disasters at Teruel and Brunete, and the desperate battles along the River Ebro. It was here that his Cable Street comrades died.

I pieced this together talking to Tom, my father, and his close Pioneer friend, Harry Winton. It wasn't easy and I have made a few assumptions that a proper historian would frown upon. No one could tell me how Tom came back to England although, by mid-1938, he was back in Bethnal Green working as a tailor. I was never able to find out why he abandoned the East End as he never married and did not have the excuse of children as a reason for moving to Basildon.

At the time I discussed these matters with him, I understood little of the issues involved. I did not even understand which two sides were involved in the battle. Of late I have returned to the matter and reflected on the irony of a group of Stalinists fighting for democracy and liberty in Spain.

Did he not question the rights and wrongs of the literally murderous campaign that was waged by communists against the POUM Trotskyites and the Anarchists who were all nominally on the same side? These were fundamental questions and I assume he must have accepted them as part of the compromise necessary when combat is waged against a greater evil. If our integrity is to be absolute then we will do nothing.

When the Spanish Communist leader, La Pasionaria, told the departing Brigades, "You are legend." Tom was already back in England but he would probably have agreed with her. Otherwise there would have no point in the Cable Street lads dying on the banks of the River Ebro. He told me once they would 'live on in the glorious memory'.

He was wrong. After the victory of Franco and the Nationalists in 1939, Spain was subjected to a terrible and oppressive right-wing nationalist dictatorship that lasted up until the Generalissimo's death in 1975. Apart from the half million Spaniards who died during the war, in the years afterwards Franco arranged for the execution of a further 100,000 Republicans. Another 40,000 died in concentration camps.

The British government was, on the whole, content to ignore what was happening in Spain, being more concerned with the communist dictatorships to the east. For some Pioneers, this was a matter of concern that went beyond other issues. The events in Spain had the same significance for the Pioneers' generation as those born thirty years later who were radicalised by events in Vietnam in the 1960s.

While many 1960s Britons were experiencing the pleasures of a Spanish Mediterranean holiday for the first time, there was a darker aspect to the sunny side of Spain and the endless drunken bellowing of Viva Espana. Conventional histories of the war tend to portray it as the struggle of a Spanish form of nationalistic fascism versus the Republicans and Communists who stood shoulder to shoulder in a common cause. They often ignore, or skim over, the success of the Anarchists organised by the CNT FAI syndicalists in governing (if that is not a contradiction) Catalonia in the period before the war. Forget the bearded bomb-throwing anarchist stereotype: this was a serious attempt to organise a viable and fair society along different lines from those that produced the extremes of wealth and poverty characteristic of pre-revolutionary Spain.

The opinions of historians vary regarding the success of the anarchist experiment in Spain and the extent to which a humane way of running society was prematurely destroyed by the forces of reaction. It is certain that Franco and his supporters were sufficiently alarmed by the CNT FAI experiment that, right up to the 1970s, they were terrified of anything and anybody that smacked of anarchist ideals. The result was an increasingly frenzied period of repression for anyone who opposed the Franco regime.

This reached a low point in 1974 with the public garrotting of Puig Antich, a Spanish anarchist convicted on the flimsiest of evidence. This final barbaric deed by a dying regime revolted even a British government that had shown considerable enthusiasm for prosecuting Spanish exiles and their British sympathisers.

*

Between 30th May and 6th December 1972, a period now almost forgotten, the longest criminal trial in British history took place: the Stoke Newington Eight were accused of being part of an international anarchist terrorist conspiracy to bring down the British government. This was a reaction against a modest wave of non-fatal bombings that occurred in the early 1970s. The most widely publicised of these was the destruction of the residence of the Home Secretary, Robert Carr, in the plush north London suburb of Hadley Wood, half a mile from where I now live.

The bombings allegedly committed by the Stoke Newington Eight were linked to groups as diverse as the Angry Brigade in England, the Tupamaros in Uruguay and the Spanish Anti-Franco MIL GAC, all supposedly co-ordinated by the International Revolutionary Solidarity Movement.

This is not to claim that any of the eight were innocent although four of them were found 'not guilty'. Rather it is to highlight the way in which the British government tolerated a barbaric regime and the enthusiasm with which they prosecuted those who opposed it.

In 1997 there was a small ceremony on the Embankment in London marking the sixty years since the formation of the British section of the International Brigade. Just seven veterans and their families were present, all of them close to ninety, wearing black onion sellers' berets, and withered with age. Two were from Glasgow.

I tentatively asked some of them if they remembered Tom Lexman and was met with blank stares while they dredged the deepest recesses of their memory. One man closed his eyes and I imagined he was going back to the horrors of the wars. Perhaps it was just the boredom and the heat that lay so heavily upon his memory.

When Ken Livingstone was elected London Mayor, I wrote to him suggesting that he might consider erecting a memorial in memory of those hundreds of Londoners who fought in Spain. I thought it would be just his sort of thing. I eventually received a reply from a minion saying that, in the interests of political balance, they would also have to commemorate those Britons who went to Spain and fought on the fascist side which would be offensive to many Londoners. If nothing else, I am delighted that Ken Livingstone's office is interested in political balance.

I then wrote to the Department of Culture (am I alone in trembling at the totalitarian implications of that name?) to suggest that the empty plinth in Trafalgar Square be occupied by The Duchess of Atholl as a symbol of the suffering of all women in war. Although not a major figure, the Duchess had sacrificed a modest political career in the Conservative Party in the interests of promoting the Republican cause. More importantly, she was 'of the right gender' as press reports suggested only women need apply for the vacant plinth. I thought it was politically right and enough to, at least, warrant a reply but none was forthcoming. The spot has now been taken.

A year ago I visited Cable Street. There can be no street in London that is more laden with memory. I found a small copper plaque covered with a green bloom attached to one of the buildings commemorating the volunteers from the street who fought in Spain.

They are nearly all gone and no one remembers and no one really cares.

Chapter 8: Why Governments Always Fail

Liberty is not a means to a higher political end. It is itself the highest political end.
Lord Acton.

Until August 1914, a sensible law-abiding Englishman could pass through life and hardly notice the existence of the state, beyond the post office and the policeman. He could live where he liked, and as he liked. He had no official number or identity card. He could travel abroad or leave his country forever without a passport or any sort of official permission. He could exchange his money for any other currency without restriction or limit. He could buy goods from any country in the world on the same terms as he bought goods at home. For that matter a foreigner could spend his life in this country without permit and without informing the police.
A.J.P. Taylor English History 1914-1945.

Government, even in its best state, is but a necessary evil.
Thomas Paine.

The history of British social policy over the past sixty years provides us with perfect examples of the folly of all governments that has led to British people, in Western Europe at least, being almost uniquely misruled.

One government tells the British people not to worry for the future. It assures them 'We will look after you from the cradle to the grave'. It discourages individuals from owning their own property by telling them that the state will provide them with housing. A welfare state is created and the people are told 'All of this is yours. We will take the responsibility out of your lives'.

The following government from a different party endorses these principles and, as living standards rise, it soothingly reassures British people that the state will continue to provide for them. Twenty years later both parties turn round to the British people and say: 'Sorry, we got it wrong. You should want to own your own house, don't expect to live on the old age pension, don't clog up the waiting lists, don't be a burden on the state, don't become part of the dependency culture, get on your bike and find a job, you parasite.'

For one generation, wanting to provide for themselves brings the accusation of selfishness. For the next generation, failing to provide brings the accusation of fecklessness. No wonder there is a deeply-ingrained cynicism about politics; no wonder election turnout is gently falling to dangerously low levels. This is not because people have lost interest in politics – it is because what is on offer has so little appeal.

However, try building an airport runway near a pretty Essex village or opening a hostel for paedophiles on a suburban housing estate and people will re-engage quickly enough.

Enoch Powell once said: "All political careers end in failure." He was probably right but he could have added that they start in failure as well.

Democracy has almost ceased to exist in this country. It is not so much the infrequency of voting, but the fact that voting makes little difference. The problem with politics is … politicians. A commonplace observation perhaps but it goes straight to the heart of the problem with our form of democracy. We've all heard the remark that the trouble with political jokes is they end up getting elected.

The two main parties do not offer a genuine choice and local government has become an agency of the centre. Where we desperately need a democratic process in the delivery of those services that determine the shape of peoples' lives, we find that, instead, an unaccountable quango exists, usually chaired by a friend or the close relative of a leading politician, and in receipt of a handsome wage out of taxpayers' money.

Politicians all too easily forget that all government money is money that belongs to the people, money that is held on trust. Governments do not generate wealth, people do. Governments take the rewards for other peoples' efforts, and use it for purposes that the electorate do not support. The catch-all phrase 'better public services' is simply not precise enough. Fairly typical is the new Welsh Assembly. Its sixty English-speaking members have the services of thirty seven full time translators, paid for out of general taxation, creating demand where very little exists. This is not to deny the right to tax. It is simply a plea that it should not be done so recklessly. Income represents in monetary terms the hours of an individual's labour. Tax is the confiscation of a slice of our lives

Sometimes politicians try to pretend they are something else. In 1978, Jimmy Carter was elected as American President on the pretence that he was a peanut farmer from Georgia rather than a venal Washington insider.

Twice in the 1990s, Ross Perot tried to persuade the American people to elect him on the basis that he was just an ordinary 'down to earth' billionaire rather than a politician. In Italy it is less damaging for Silvio Berlusconi to be seen as a dubious businessman with Mafia links, rather than a conventional politician.

In Britain, in particular, the party system so tightly regulates entry into political life that it is all but impossible to enter politics without the backing of the party machine. The charismatic, and hugely wealthy, James Goldsmith discovered this when he floated the Referendum Party in 1997. The existing parties had already pulled up the drawbridge to prevent entry to outsiders.

There are some signs of cracks in the party machines. In Middlesbrough, Ray Mallon has partially broken Labour's grip on the North East. In London, Ken Livingstone keeps adding to his reputation as a radical, pushy, risk-taking outsider while spending vast amounts of taxpayers' money unencumbered by the embrace of party.

A significant proportion of politicians are hypocrites. They just cannot help it, just like the dog returning to its vomit. Whether it is MPs awarding themselves large pay rises while urging restraint upon the rest of us, Labour cabinet ministers living in the grand style at the taxpayer's expense, or John Prescott telling us to ride bicycles and use public transport while himself owning two Jaguars, it is a two-faced philosophy.

Nowhere is this more clearly illustrated than in the field of education where the general strategy seems to be to get your child into a top-performing state comprehensive school and then discreetly buy as much private tuition as possible. Where does not matter: it can be, for example, that you live in Islington and send your daughter over to Hammersmith, or send your son to a top-performing state school on the Brompton Road. The key point is that you display the socialist badge of honour, educating your children in the state system, preferably at a comprehensive school.

The exception to this, on the front bench, was Harriet Harman who sent her son to a Kent grammar school even though the official government line was that comprehensive schools were perfectly good enough for the rest of us. We also have the curious and perplexing case of Diane Abbott, left-wing backbencher, member of the Campaign Group, general all-round activist and campaigner for social justice who has consistently berated her fellow MPs for sending their children to independent schools. The revelation that Ms Abbott sends her son to an independent fee-paying school, complete with cap and satchel, met with a certain amount of disappointment in the Labour Party. The disturbing aspect of the issue is that, when I pointed this out to some intelligent but broadly apolitical friends, they evinced not even a flicker of surprise. "What do you expect? An honest politician?" was their response.

Since 1997, I have been contacted by three Labour ministers asking if I will privately tutor their children. It would appear that I have a reputation. It is always women, in one case a Parliamentary Private Secretary, who do the contacting. Clearly, the Labour Party still casts high-profile working women in the nurturing role. In addition, I have been approached by a well-known Labour peer and two left-wing journalists who, in theory at least, support comprehensive education. The unfairness of the situation is illustrated by my own lack of moral principle.

I took a phone call from a gentleman merchant banker who explained that his daughter's place at Oxford was in some jeopardy because her A-grade in history was not secure, despite attending the most expensive fee-paying school in London. I declined to be of assistance but wished him well in his search

"I will pay you one hundred pounds an hour for your services for as many hours as you deem necessary," he insisted.

"What's your address?" I replied.

It is the hubris of all governments that I find most irritating. I would like to see politicians who are more humble. It would please me to see Tony Blair and the rest of the cabinet cycling from No 10 Downing Street to the House of Commons for Prime Minister's Question Time. Their bodyguards could cycle with them. There is no immutable law of politics that says that politicians have to travel around in chauffeur-driven

Jaguars.

There is no need for senior civil servants to award themselves silly titles and honours merely for doing the job they are very well paid to do. It is merely a lazy, self-serving convention that reminds us we are constitutionally only one step removed from being a bizarre Ruritanian tin pot state. I would like to see politicians and civil servants remind themselves again and again that they are the servants of the people. They need to be reminded of the old Jeffersonian notion that governments are formed with the consent of the people and have no separate existence. I would like to see the citizens of this country collectively assert the principle that Abraham Lincoln first announced seven score years ago in the Gettysburg Address 'that government of the people, by the people, for the people, shall not perish from this earth'.

It may be convenient for ministers to hide behind the fig leaf notion that they are the servant of the crown; that they are Her Majesty's government. Every drop of petrol that goes into the fuel tank of the Jaguar is paid for by the taxes that individuals and businesses in this country pay to the exchequer.

It is sign of the immaturity of our democracy that we have not reached the American view of government that it is not just the representative of the people but it is the servant of the people. Having been present on many occasions when cabinet ministers and senior politicians have condescended to visit those who elected them and who they represent I am always staggered at the sheer sycophancy and flummery that is exhibited on such occasions.

Some time in the early 1970s, I viewed with some disdain the events surrounding the visit of Ray Gunter to open a factory on the Pipps Hill industrial estate in Basildon. Mr Gunter had been a south Essex MP and briefly had been a very undistinguished Labour cabinet minister. I was shocked to see that a roll of rather plush red carpet had been rolled out for the visitor. This man was a jobbing politician whose career fizzled out into mediocrity, if it ever reached that level. Yet he was being treated as a cross between the Pope, the Emperor of Japan and the Queen of Sheba. I should have shouted, "Get off the carpet and get on with your job." But I did not.

The town centre of Basildon is dominated by Brooke House, a block of flats named after Henry Brooke, a rather undistinguished and unpopular Conservative Home Secretary and former Housing Minister of the early

1960s. The obvious question is to ask why the authorities of the new town felt obliged to engage in such an act of obsequious deference in what was, in theory at least, an increasingly meritocratic age.

The problem is compounded in that when they become elected our major political figures become locked in deadly rivalries that become more important than the policies they espouse. Hugh Gaitskell versus Nye Bevan entertained us in the 1950s while George Brown versus Harold Wilson defined the political life of the 1960s. This was followed by the Heath versus Thatcher feud that embittered the Conservative Party in the 1970s. This then spilt over into Heseltine versus Thatcher a decade later. In the 1990s, we were treated to John Major versus what, at the time, seemed like the whole of his party to be followed by that clash of giant egos, Blair versus Brown, in the first decade of this century.

And what were these rivalries about? Can any more than one person in a thousand say what it was that Brown and Wilson and Heath and Thatcher were fighting about beyond the hissing sound of punctured egos?

As the sociologist Joseph Schumpeter pithily expressed seventy years ago, 'Democracy is the rule of the politician.' In the 1930s, this view was expressed as disinterested fact. Today it is suggestive as a critique of all that has gone wrong with our political system.

We have, to use an American term, become a polyarchy. The rights of citizenship are conferred upon a significant proportion of the population, sufficient in numbers to create something that looks and smells like democracy. The reality is rule by a relatively small elite to the exclusion of the majority. However, the sort of polyarchy that pluralist theorists such as Robert Dahl and Charles Lindblom described fifty years ago were those whereby citizens were excluded from the political process.

Today, a large proportion of the population, probably a majority, have withdrawn voluntarily from their compact with society out of disillusionment. They nurture the pessimistic belief that 'they are all the same. It makes no difference; therefore I will disengage from the process because it is of no concern to me'.

As a result of being pummelled into indifference, we have even given up the soft murmur of protest. In December 2003, the government officially named Labour-run Plymouth as the worst run local authority in England on the grounds that it was the only council to drop from the Weak to the Poor category in the government scheme of classification.

Two days later, the councillors of the Devon city voted to double their attendance allowances from £4,500 to £9,500 on the grounds that it would attract a wider range of people to stand as councillors. The Plymouth Evening Herald chose not to run the story as it was not sufficiently newsworthy. In a civic culture worthy of the name, the people of Plymouth would have taken over the running of the city themselves.

*

I rode my motorcycle past the decaying and battered fabric of the Millennium Dome on the Greenwich Peninsula. It stands as a monument to the vanity and purblind vain glorious incompetence of our politicians. It is also a permanent reproach to the failure of our system of democracy that the citizenry of this country have been so reduced that they cannot exact some form of accountability for such obvious policy failures. John Prescott told us that we should judge the Labour Government on whether or not they made a success of the Dome. Our judgement has yet to be exacted.

We see this on a larger scale in the three main judicial enquiries that have taken place into the behaviour of politicians in the past decade.

The Scott inquiry, in the early 1990s, over the illegal export of weapons to Iraq revealed a self-serving and deceitful political culture in which everything was acceptable provided that you did not get caught. Perhaps the single most damning revelation to come out of the inquiry was the admission by officials of Sir Geoffrey Howe at the Foreign office that the British government had covertly supplied Saddam Hussein's regime with weapons-related equipment even after the Kurdish town of Halabja had been subjected to a gas attack that left at least five thousand dead. It should be remembered that one of the key justifications offered by the Blair government for Britain supporting America in the war against Iraq in 2003 was that he had gassed his own people.

Howe's justification for keeping the illegal trade away from public view in the late 1980s was to prevent an 'emotional misunderstanding' that might threaten Britain's corporate interests in the Middle East, the promotion of which had been central to British government foreign policy. The 'emotional misunderstanding' was, of course, being horrified at the gassing of thousands of innocent Kurds and then supplying the same regime with the equipment to make even more terrible weapons.

The three years of the Scott Inquiry showed the Foreign Office at its most contemptuous in terms of public opinion. Whilst the march of democracy has impacted upon most government departments in the past hundred years, the Foreign Office remains impervious. It is loftily disdainful of the notion that it is the servant of the people and in any way accountable to them. It is as if foreign policy is far too important that it should take into consideration such issues as human rights or public opinion.

Last September I visited the Foreign Office as part of the Open House scheme where various government departments open their doors to those who pay for them. Metaphorically at least, I am sure the staff were counting the spoons afterwards. In employment terms, the Foreign Office has been, and largely remains, a feather bed for the privileged middle class. Despite Richard Scott's scathing judgments, no politician at the end of the process held up their hand and said, "I am sorry I made a mistake." Instead we were treated to the treacly self-pity of Sir Geoffrey Howe and the disdainful, almost Gallic shrug of Alan Clark's shoulders.

For many people, the abiding image of the BSE crisis was the hapless John Gummer cajoling his reluctant daughter into publicly consuming a beefburger for the benefit of the media, to prove that beef was safe.

The Phillips inquiry into the disaster revealed a culture of complacency and secrecy over public health that should have finished the careers of those involved. Instead, we were treated to the Panglossian view that somehow everybody had acted for the best. Mistakes had been made, it was unfortunate, but now we must get on with things and not make too much of a fuss.

From the start, Lord Phillips stated that his intention was not to blame any individuals. Instead, a two year inquiry that cost £27 million and resulted in a 4,000 page report, found no one was at fault, despite the deaths of at least one hundred people and bills for the taxpayer amounting to £5 billion and rising.

Within the Phillips report, we entered the bizarre world that 'the government did not lie to the public about BSE' because, when Ministers pronounced that 'beef was safe to eat' they believed their own claims, even though they had wilfully ignored advice to the contrary. In this world BSE, and its human equivalent CJD, was an accident that was beyond the ability of government to prevent.

There are two key points to be made here. Ministers did receive advice of a looming disaster but they were selective in their listening choice. Both Professor Richard Lacey, leading microbiologist, and Dr Harash Narang, who attempted to develop a urine test for BSE, found themselves victims of a campaign of defamation and intimidation orchestrated by politicians, sections of the media, and agribusiness in an attempt to undermine their credibility.

The second point is the failure to apply that underrated quality, common sense. The practice of feeding meat and bone meal to the national herd was profoundly unnatural. It may not have been scientifically provable that BSE would emerge but it was always likely given the practice of feeding cattle the remains of other cattle.

This was an economy that was solely concerned with producing cheap dairy products and resulted in rejection of safer, more expensive vegetable proteins. Even after it became clear that MBM was the agent that was spreading BSE; even when its use was banned, the government still gave the animal feed industry five weeks to use up existing stocks in order to limit economic damage.

It is difficult to avoid the conclusion that the main purpose of the Phillips inquiry was primarily to protect the commercial viability of the meat and rendering industries. Protecting public health was a secondary consideration.

As with the Scott Inquiry, no civil servant, politician, or private or public company has been reprimanded, or made to face any form of legal action, as a result of the BSE disaster.

While politicians of all hues may wring their hands in despair at the mass of dependents they have created with the policies of the last sixty years, there is a sense in which such a condition is in their interests. Politicians may sing the praises of civic involvement but it is to be defined on their terms.

A critical, questioning, politically-literate population is not in the interests of any political elite. Such a population may start to ask awkward questions such as why is the gap between rich and poor now widening at a faster rate than during the Thatcher Years? Why do we tax the rich so lightly? Why are MPs allowed to award themselves such generous pension and pay rises? Why do we give in to Republican terrorists in Northern Ireland while standing firm against Muslim terrorists internationally? Why do we allow the security services to infringe our liberties at will? Why do police powers increase while accountability lessens? Why do we allow the children of the economic and political elite to be educated separately from the children of the rest of society?

Better for politicians is a population obsessed with winning the National Lottery and guessing who is going to win *Big Brother* rather than one that challenges fundamental political assumptions. The main purpose of voting appears to be to preserve a fig leaf of democratic legitimacy.

The figures are alarming. The Labour government may have won the 2001 election on a respectable forty-three per cent of the vote but once the fifty nine per cent turnout and the eighty per cent voter registration level is taken into account, then the result looks rather different. The reality is that only twenty-two per cent of the adult population voted for the present government at the last election and seventy-eight per cent either voted against it or, more likely, did not vote at all. In some of the poorest constituencies in the country turnout hovers at the one third mark. The irony is that those who are most dependent upon the state are the most disengaged from it. In what is starting to look like a post-democratic age we are not presented with ideological choice. Rather we are simply asked who we think will be most competent at managing the country.

It is possible to argue that, of all western European democracies, Britain has been uniquely misgoverned over the past fifty years. The failure to join the European Economic Community, as it was in the 1950s, stands out as a particularly dismal moment. Our problems with Europe have stemmed from this initial reluctance when we could have joined on advantageous terms rather than going in as the resentful laggard in 1973.

Our political leaders of both main parties were too obsessed with the British Empire as a trading partner. In hindsight it seems absurd that we worried about Australian apples and New Zealand butter on such a fundamental issue. For most of the British political elite, the prospect of joining the EEC was akin to an act of treason. In the overwhelmingly insular words of Hugh Gaitskell, the Labour leader: "It means the end of a thousand years of history." The political elite still clung to the 'Island Race' mentality

At this crucial juncture, the British people deserved better leadership than the one provided by an anally-retentive Wykehamist leader of the opposition and an 81-year-old Prime Minister who was convinced of the racial superiority of the British people. To have had observer status at the momentous 1955 Messina Conference, and then to have failed to join, seems to be an act almost criminal in its negligence.

With its emphasis on free trade, many in the Labour Party saw Europe and the trade unions as an employers' club that would do down the workers. By the time the British political ruling class had realised their error, General De Gaulle, that most Gallic of French presidents, was in the driving seat and we had become the permanent outsider.

The decision by the Attlee government in 1946 to develop a British atomic bomb stands as a bleak moment and a further symptom of the collective neurosis of our governing class at the loss of great power status. We still find ourselves saddled with the illusion of being a world power that needs, to use that overworked phrase, to 'punch above its weight'.

The British attack on Egypt in 1956 was launched because the Nasser government wanted the Suez Canal back on what Britain saw as the spurious grounds that it 'ran through Egyptian territory'. It was a unique miscalculation. The Prime Minister, Sir Anthony Eden, and most of the Conservative Party, was unable to distinguish in Colonel Nasser the difference between an Egyptian nationalist and a Middle Eastern Hitler.

For a generation that had been nurtured on the myth of Empire, beliefs died hard. Some even remembered the 1898 Battle of Omdurman, the one where, as Corporal Jones told us on many occasions, the 'fuzzy wuzzies didn't like it up 'em'. There was still the rather desperate belief in ruling class circles that Britain could remain a great power: 'Greece to America's Rome,' as Harold Macmillan romantically put it. Being slapped down by the United States in 1956 over Suez and told to behave ourselves was a lesson that was only partially learned. Even in the twenty-first century, we have only been able to partially divest ourselves of the idea that we are a great imperial power.

In the late nineteenth century, the British marched into various African kingdoms using the excuse of local misrule. Today the justification is the same. Substitute Iraq for the Ashanti, Saddam Hussein for Cetawayo, King of the Zulus, Osama bin Laden for the Mahdi of Sudan, and the Mau Mau or the Dervishes for al-Qa'eda, and the formula is no different. The weapons may be more lethal, the media may be more all-embracing, but the motivation is the same – to produce compliant nations that are well disposed towards the West.

In the 19th century we talked about spreading Christianity: in the 21st century we talk about spreading democracy and the free market instead. Beneath each motive lurk other much less generous reasons. By riding on America's coat tails, Britain basks in the illusion of being a major player. Adventures in Afghanistan and Iraq are not a new version of socialist internationalism. They represent a throwback to imperial ideals and notions of British supremacy.

I had convinced myself that Mrs Thatcher represented the last of that generation of leaders who would have remembered the British Empire as a significant political issue. She would have been twenty-two when India became independent, and a young MP for Finchley when Harold Macmillan made his 1961 'Winds of Change' speech. It would appear I am mistaken, however. Tony Blair can have nothing but the faintest of memories of Empire yet the imperial imperative has been bred into the calcium of his bones. Imperialism was wrong one hundred years ago and it is wrong now.

*

What were the decisions of economic policy made in the 1950s, 60s and 70s by successive governments that led to the destruction of the British car and motorcycle industry, symbols of our manufacturing base? As late as 1960 it would only be a slight exaggeration to say that Britain, with twenty seven different manufacturers kept the world supplied with motorcycles. A decade later, all but three of the firms had closed down and Japan had taken over the British markets.

Sometime in the mid 1970s, I joined a group of motorcyclists who assembled weekly at Beech Hill in Epping. We would admire each others' bikes, mainly Triumph Bonnevilles and Trophys and Norton Commandos, together with the occasional Moto Guzzi and BMW Boxer. When a rider arrived on a four-cylinder Honda 750, he may as well have landed in an alien spacecraft, so formidable and advanced was the technology.

We laughed, of course, over our cup of tea and liver sausage roll from the food caravan and convinced ourselves that getting covered in oil and having to make impromptu repairs at the roadside was part of the experience of riding a British motorcycle. It was part of our defensive posture that riding a motorcycle that was well made and technologically advanced compromised our masculinity. Primarily our problem was one of attitudes.

In the 1950s, the complacent plutocrat, Lord Docker, owner of BSA, Britain's largest motorcycle manufacturer, swanned around in a gold-plated Daimler while his wife, Lady Docker, cut a swathe through what passed for London society.

Meanwhile, the Japanese, in particular Honda and Yamaha, were focussing on innovative design, reliability and giving the public what they wanted. The first Japanese motorcycles had square headlamps and we laughed because we knew that proper (i.e. British) motorcycles had round headlamps. By 1962, Honda was producing more motorcycles than the whole of the combined British motorcycle industry but somehow, in our deluded state, we ignored this unpalatable fact.

By then it was too late for the British manufacturers, even for internationally-recognised names like Norton, Triumph and BSA who were trying to meet the Japanese head on.

Any motorcycle enthusiast over the age of fifty will be familiar with the symptoms. The gaudy Triumph Bonneville of the early 1970s compares unfavourably with the aesthetic beauty of the Bonneville that had adorned the previous decade. On a more prosaic level, the solidly-engineered BSA C15 of the late 1950s, a no frills 'ride to work' 250cc machine was transformed into the lurid and tacky BSA Barracuda of the 1960s that, frankly, nobody wanted. Secondhand values in the classic bike market reflect a posthumous judgment on the respective merits of British motorcycle industry offerings in the 1950s and 60s.

Much the same can be said of the car industry. Britain had a huge post-war lead compared to war-ravaged Europe, but it was squandered. Poor management and design, militant unions and indifferent workforces were all factors. No government can get away from the primary responsibility that a pall of complacency hung over British manufacturing industry until it was all but destroyed.

In 1960, the British motorist was driving around in such cars as the Hillman Minx, the Austin Cambridge, the Ford Consul, the Vauxhall Cresta and the Vanden Plas Princess with the odd Renault Dauphin and Saab 95 thrown in for good measure. A decade later Hillman, Singer, Sunbeam, Morris, Riley, Standard and Wolseley had all gone. Instead we were driving Datsuns, Citroens, Peugeots, Audis and Fiats.

What were the economic decisions made by governments in France and Germany that meant they retained huge indigenous car industries while Britain was forced to look to the Reliant Robin to fly the flag?

The sad story is summed up in the little vignette that when Jim Callaghan was Prime Minister from 1976 to 1979, he patriotically insisted that both his official cars should be Rovers. During his three years in office they had to be returned because of 34 major mechanical faults. When one finally came back from being repaired, he rolled down the window and the glass fell into his lap. This manufacturing disaster has just been accepted with a 'that's life, it's the free market in a global economy' shrug of the shoulders. "It was just one of those things. Nobody's fault, we just couldn't do anything about it."

There was an almost racist assumption that the disciplined and conscientious Japanese worker was always destined to produce a superior product to the slovenly British. Somehow, to be free and work shy was seen as an acceptable price for producing an inferior product that nobody wanted.

Anyone over the age of forty should be able to remember the Austin Allegro and the Morris Marina. These were produced in the dog days of British Leyland and represent two of the worst cars in automotive history. While the Germans and the Japanese hit upon the idea of producing cars that were reliable, well manufactured and, in varying degrees, of pleasing design (yes, I have driven a Datsun Cherry), British Leyland hit upon the novel idea of putting a square steering wheel in the Allegro. God made steering wheels round for a good reason.

In 1979, I went on one of my occasional trips to see the tennis at Wimbledon. Slipping away at the end on a rather elderly, but reliable, Honda CB 72, I came across a broken-down car beside which were standing two well-known male doubles players, both looking none too pleased. The car was a British Leyland Austin Ambassador produced courtesy of the British taxpayer in the 1970s and part of the official fleet that ferried the top players around. It is not impossible, but it somehow seems unlikely that two top tennis players at the German Open would be stranded at the side of the road in a broken down Mercedes.

*

The disaster of the partition of 1921 that divided Ireland into a Protestant-dominated North and republican South was a terrible error that has led to eighty years of bloodshed. When in the late 1960s the Catholic minority in the North started to make a fuss, successive governments prosecuted an unwinnable war that could, with foresight, have been avoided in the first place.

It remains a permanent stain upon a succession of Labour and Conservative governments that, up until 1969, they blithely ignored the injustices that were being visited upon a sizable minority of the population of the United Kingdom. It now appears that part of the tactic for winning that unwinnable war was to collude with one group of terrorists in order to murder members of another group of terrorists.

Thus the state demeaned and degraded itself in the pursuit of the illusion of victory in a war that was wholly avoidable. One of the more shameful facts about this particular tragedy is that it only rose to the top of the political agenda when, in 1971, the IRA moved their bombing campaign to the British mainland. As long as the outrages and the killings were taking place in Northern Ireland it was seen as a localised issue. Once the bombs began to go off in Birmingham, Aldershot, Guildford and in particular, London, with an appalling loss of life, then it became a matter of national political concern. Successive revelations in the post-Good Friday Agreement period, evidence of collusion, 'shoot to kill' policies, imprisonments on falsified evidence, and the failure to investigate past atrocities properly, have all served to undermine the legitimacy of the British government.

*

The welfare state, for all its virtues, has had a corrosive effect on that traditional British virtue of self-reliance and personal responsibility. We have now created successive generations who, when problems occur, look not to themselves as a matter of first recourse, but to the state.

Expanding welfare is like building new roads to ease congestion. The demand simply increases and the problem repeats itself. We are told that, despite spending nearly one third of our gross national product on welfare payments, poverty is still a feature of the life of a substantial minority of the population. It seems that the more we spend, the greater the poverty becomes.

In 1945 the government was optimistic enough, some would say foolish enough, to believe in the abolition of poverty. Today we accept the poor as the baleful, glaring, unwanted guests at the orgy of consumer spending that has fired the British economy for the last twenty years.

As I was born in 1953, I am part of the generation that was told on a drip-drip daily basis that we have an absolute legal and moral entitlement to all the benefits and services of the state for free. This view was hammered into me, and those of my generation, with such resolution that it became extraordinarily difficult to challenge the notion.

I shook with rage when I first heard in 1974 that I would have to pay twenty pence for a prescription. My absolute entitlement was being ripped away from me by a wicked government, so I thought. I had to pass across that psychological Rubicon where I first accepted the idea that I might have to contribute in some way for the services that were supposedly provided for me by the state.

There is, of course, no such thing as the state in this sense. I am not imagining some neo-Hegelian construction that hovers above us and gives focus and purpose to our lives; it is my fellow citizens, the little building blocks of the state, through their taxes who provide all of these services for free.

Having now paid for my own dental treatment for the past twenty or so years, it seems rather odd that I should expect someone else to pay for it. I accept that if I was genuinely unable to pay then the state should legitimately give me some assistance, rather than allow my teeth to rot and fall out.

At a distance of thirty years, it now seems quite bizarre that, not only did the state pay my university tuition fees, it also paid me a living income for four years and, as final proof of its bountiful nature, I was paid social security benefit during the holidays. And was I grateful? No of course not. It is not within human nature to be grateful for that which is easily given. I even asked the state to dig once again into its deep pockets and pay for me to train to be solicitor. It did, without hesitation or demur.

What has changed in the sixty or so years since the welfare state was created is the loss of a sense of shame. For those of my grandfather's generation, brought up in late Victorian and Edwardian England, there was a deep stigma attached to any form of state assistance. The Smilesian sensibilities of an older generation told them that state assistance bore the tag of the workhouse.

For my parent's generation, who came to maturity in the 1940s, the welfare state was what Beveridge told them it was – a safety net that would provide for them in times of need. For my generation, it was an entitlement that offered a reasonable, if low paid, alternative to work. For a significant number of people who are twenty years younger than me, it is a crutch to support a way of life; a supplement to existing income; a badge of dishonour to be flaunted at those who support them. Nearly one hundred years ago Lloyd George spoke of those who were 'too proud to wear the badge of pauperism'. Not only is the language alien today but so is the concept.

Somewhere in the last fifty years there has been a failure of public education whereby the sense of shame that Lloyd George hinted at has gone. By quite consciously and deliberately creating a culture of entitlement, successive governments have ensured that the proportion of our national wealth that is spent on welfare provision has assumed a magnitude that is both ruinous and irreducible. Simultaneously, they have served to undermine the self-respect of the individual and the notion that we are all bound together and must contribute for the universal good. We have succeeded in cultivating the opposite message, that we must take from the commonwealth in order to promote the individual good. Perhaps Sir William should not have repeated the phrase 'cradle to the grave' quite so often.

*

I lived, for a while, in the United States in the early 1970s and was staggered to learn from my hosts that their household rubbish was not collected weekly as a matter of routine by the municipal authority. Instead, they had to contract into a service for which they paid. This was a dizzying revelation. The surprising thing was that, not only did my hosts accept the fairness of this arrangement but it struck them as outlandish that, in England, my rubbish was collected for free. What sort of strange country was this Europe my hosts asked. It was not for free, of course, but the payment was not filtered through the agencies of the state.

I should add that, in Rochester, Upper New York State, the weekly rubbish collection was conducted in a way that was far more efficient than the English method. Rubbish was not strewn down the path and onto the pavement and I was not called a 'wanker' when I politely pointed out this fact. My hosts assured me that, in the week before Christmas, there was no knock on the door from the normally surly and uncommunicative refuse operatives fulsomely wishing them a Merry Christmas. It is simply a matter of what we are used to. The only boundaries in these matters are the conventions of our own thinking.

The ambiguity of our attitudes towards the state and what it should, or should not do for us are summed up in the cases of two of my neighbours.

A friend who lives a few streets away gets very agitated at the failure of the council to clear the leaves and the horse chestnuts that fall in front of his house. He writes letters and telephones the council and generally has very limited success. I gently suggested to him recently that perhaps it would be easier if he cleared away the leaves himself. I may as well have been speaking Martian to him. In his mind, there is a very clear line as to what is the council's job and what is his job. Clearing away leaves and horse chestnuts is the job of the council therefore he could not possibly do it.

My neighbour is a very fine man. He is full of integrity and general goodwill towards the world. He is about sixty years old and was therefore born in the early 1940s. He came to an awareness of the world during the first luxuriant flowering of the welfare state, during the early years of the post-war consensus. Like every other member of his generation he was drip fed about what the state could do for him in a very insistent way and therefore he is a victim.

Contrast this with a neighbour who lives about fifteen doors away. He has a particular dislike of the state or, at least, the way the state manifests itself in the form of speed cameras. He asked me to sign a petition against some speed cameras on Stagg Hill on the road to Potters Bar. I politely declined and asked him would it not be simpler just to observe the speed limit and thus be saved the frustration of trying to persuade awkward people like me to sign petitions.

His view of the authority of the state is that it is an unjust impediment to him driving as fast as he wishes wherever he wishes. This state is not the benign one that fails to clear fallen horse chestnuts but a harsh and oppressive one that restricts individual liberty. In the end, most of us cherry pick what we want from the state and hope that it will not be too much of a nuisance in our lives.

The all-encompassing nature of state activity becomes, in some contexts, very apparent. I recently spent three hours in Newcastle Crown Court observing three different cases.

The first was a case of a wife accused of assaulting her husband's girlfriend. The second case concerned a man who had attempted to burn down his own house. In the third, a man was accused of stealing a concrete mixer from the front of a neighbour's house.

All the defendants looked pathetic, dishevelled and damaged. It was difficult not to conclude that there should be some other way of dealing with these people rather than using the full majesty of the law. None of the cases was resolved; all were adjourned within forty minutes of proceedings opening. The most common reason seemed to be that either an important piece of paper was missing or a key witness could not be found. I was assured that this was not untypical.

I was overwhelmed by the sheer numbers of well-paid professional people involved. In fact, I just do not know what the middle classes would do for employment but for the criminality of the working class. There was the judge, obviously paid a handsome salary, and the clerk of the court. Both struck me as humane and dignified individuals. There were the barristers, up on their hind legs for both the Crown Prosecution Service and the defence, and being paid one hundred and fifty pounds an hour from taxpayers' money for what seemed to be quite modest skills. Rumpoles of the Bailey they were not.

It was of course essential that the solicitors of the clients were also present in court.

Then we come to those professionals whose specialist services and expertise keep the court system going. In one case, an expert witness on lighting conditions at the time of the offence was due to appear but the ubiquitous piece of paper was missing. For the arsonist, a psychiatrist was later called. As one case concerned children, there were Children and Family Reporters and separate solicitors appointed by the Children's and Family Courts Advisory and Support Service. As one of the children involved had spent a period in care, there were also two social workers representing the local authority.

There were the Witness Support Officers of the court ushering people in and out, and representatives of the Meditation and Reparations Services in the case of the stolen concrete mixer. Officers from the National Probation Service, including those responsible for community punishment, were involved in the assault case. Constantly present were guards from Group 4 Security and a handful of police officers hanging around waiting to give evidence.

Out of this vast amount of time, effort, expertise and expenditure that I witnessed, in the panoply of activity that constitutes an English Crown Court, not a single issue was resolved. So if you are ever worried about what happens to the huge amount of taxes that we, as citizens, pay to the government be assured that it is being put to a good use. It keeps the indigent middle classes of the English legal system afloat.

*

Within the new world that we now occupy, the terms left and right have become a misleading guide to secure our safe journey across the increasingly choppy ocean of British society. During the French Revolution those who sat on the right hand side of the National Assembly stood for the monarchy, the established church and tradition; those who sat on the left hand side of the assembly stood for the people and the principle of equality.

For two hundred years these basic theoretical concepts have provided our analytical guide across the rocky landscape of politics within an industrialised western economy. The compass is now unreliable and the needle veers and swings wildly.

Forty years ago, left meant flat caps, trade union solidarity and nationalised industries while right meant blimpish colonels, the Monday Club and choleric Conservative backbench MPs.

We have now broken away from the moorings and the old certainties have gone as the rickety old vessel drifts across an increasingly choppy ocean. To be left or right has no resonance or associations. They have become labels without apparent meaning. Thus my criticism of an overweening state could come either from the libertarian left or from a free market right.

We find the Liberal party of Gladstone and Asquith to the left of Labour while the neo-liberal free marketeers cluck approval of New Labour policies. As the storms begin to lash, we need new directions and new ways of looking if we are to avoid smashing the old timbers upon some very jagged rocks.

The significant divisions are no longer between right and left and, increasingly, they are not between the political parties. Instead the key divisions are now within the parties. They are between traditionalists and modernisers, libertarians and authoritarians, centralisers and decentralisers. In the long term, the future will belong to the libertarian modernising decentralisers but, in the short and possibly the medium term, we will have to suffer government by a variety of traditionalist authoritarian centralisers. Slotting somewhere into this scenario will be the ongoing, but increasingly important, non-party battle being fought between the informed citizens and governments that consistently betray their interests.

For two hundred years we have fought impassioned battles between right and left over complex and abstract principles of social justice, the distribution of wealth, and personal liberty. Now it is reduced to a conflict between those who like the Nike swoosh and those who do not.

Eventually it will become apparent that governing without consent in a way that usurps all power to the central government and denies freedom to the individual, will always fail. This is the consistent message that emerges from the twentieth century. The danger is that, by the time we realise this, it will be too late.

No government can now assume itself to be safe in office no matter how big its majority or how impressive its lead in the opinion polls. The electorate have become very fickle and no longer exhibit the same unquestioning party loyalties that victimised their grandparents. It is possible that, in little more than the twinkling of an eye, the political landscape will change. Processes and movements that used to take thirty or forty years to happen now occur in months.

Less than fifty per cent of British voters profess loyalty to a particular party. We, the voters, are now harlots available to the highest bidder. It is not inconceivable, given the right political circumstances that the Liberal Democrats could leap with one bound from being the also-rans of British politics directly into political power.

It is not fanciful to suggest that Britain has the feel of the mid-period Weimar Republic about it. The Golden Years are passing but we have barely noticed. We live in a state that has overreached itself in its ambition and, in the manner of Icarus, has flown too close to the sun. The process is aided by a civil society that is too engrossed with enjoying itself while authoritarian figures wait in the shadows.

Adrift on a sea of hedonism and consumer credit we are in danger of failing to notice the rocks. There is no coming post-New Labour Hitler. I am not quite that despondent, but there are powerful forces at home and abroad that have little time for democracy and will not hesitate to impose their will upon us if we do not show that we care enough. This process is aided by a Labour Party that, betraying the extreme left-wing backgrounds of some of its key members, has created a twenty-first century version of Lenin's democratic centralism. The party decides and it expects everyone else to follow unquestioningly.

The frightening thing is that we may not even notice. How cavalier and blasé we have become about that precious condition called liberty. When we read of the brave battles fought by the Suffragettes and the Chartists for a stake in the running of society, then the inevitable question of 'what went wrong?' is raised.

Why do we care so little now? Have we given up or is it the politics of contentment, the politics of despair, the politics of 'what difference does it make', or the politics of 'I don't really care because I can afford to buy that plasma screen television that my grandfather could not even have dreamt about'? We have almost, without noticing it, slipped into a Roman-style bread and circuses welfare society. Read 'ever rising living standards' for 'bread', and 'Sky Sport, Premiership football and the National Lottery' for 'circuses'.

The problem arises when, as is inevitable, the state can no longer deliver. We have in effect become a Danegeld state at the mercy of the barbarian hordes or, at least, the prospect of uncontrollable levels of civil unrest unless the gold can be paid. Just how far down the slope towards a discreet dictatorship do we have to slide before we take note? Most importantly, will it then be too late?

The ever-increasing powers of the police and the security services are not so much directed at conventional criminality but rather as to what the state should do when faced with the disintegration of civil liberties and fail to recognise the symptoms.

Visit any British high street as the pubs close on a Friday or Saturday evening. The scenes of drunken mayhem offer just a small taster of what is to come. Having had an operation on my foot recently, I visited a pub in Barnet High Street by way of recuperation. As I was limping heavily past a bus stop, a drunken youth came up to me and screamed into my face, "What are you? Some sort of ******* cripple?"

My friend, who is in his mid-eighties, was seriously injured at the Salerno Landings during the Second World War. Although he was able to work after the war he never learned to drive because of the extent of his injuries. His indicator of the decline of the country is that twenty years ago when he arrived at a bus stop he would be allowed onto the bus first. Now he is always first to the bus stop and last onto the bus.

If our current civil society is Rome, then the barbarian Goth hordes are banging at the gates and we are waiting passively. Perhaps there has always been a ragged sense that we are looking over the precipice, the feeling of ennui, an air of foreboding that we are looking at terminal decline. Today we embrace and elevate the barbarians. As the Greek poet C.P. Cavafy observed when writing of the decline of the Roman Empire, "the barbarians were a kind of solution."

One hundred and forty years ago, Matthew Arnold wrote in his great poem *Dover Beach* of the long dragging roar of the world becoming steadily more desolate.

> Nor certitude, nor peace, nor help for pain;
> And we are here as on a darkling plain
> Swept with confused alarms of struggle and flight,
> Where ignorant armies clash by night.

Governments urgently need to re-educate the electorate as to what they can realistically expect from the state. The number one lesson is that, in the long term, living standards cannot go on rising indefinitely and that the state has only the most limited ability to improve peoples' lives. The expectations, however, are so deeply ingrained that no conventional party dare make the point to the electorate because, in a childish sort of way, we judge governments by their ability to make us happy. For the majority of the electorate, the happiness quotient is judged by material prosperity.

When Harold Macmillan told us, "You've never had it so good." he was simply stating a belief in the capacity of government to make us happy. Forty-four years later, we are three and a half times more prosperous. In 1959, the average worker had to work fourteen months to be able to buy an average car. Today the average worker only has to work four months.

Yet are we three and a half times happier? I suspect not. This is a feature of overarching modern government. Two hundred years ago, the early classical economists, Thomas Malthus and Adam Smith, recognised that governments could promote prosperity but individuals gifted with the capacity to choose and make rational decisions had to make their own happiness.

The Pioneers existed at that curious ideological intersection where conservatism, socialism, anarchism and liberalism met. They were socialists in that they valued the traditional ideals of fraternity, mutualism, equality, community and co-operation. Their anarchist instincts showed in their deep and abiding suspicion of all government activity and their passion to be free from the control and constraints of society. They were conservatives in their reverence for a limited form of tradition and in their neo-liberal belief in self-help and sturdy independence. Their liberal instincts were apparent in their desire for freedom and an unshakeable belief in individual autonomy.

Not that they thought of themselves in these rather high-flown ideological terms. They simply thought of themselves as organising their lives in a dignified and practical manner whereby they were as free as possible to be the masters of their own destiny. They recognised, very wisely, that governments do not have the capacity to make us happy whatever the illusions that the government and its agencies may nurture. It is one of the tragedies of our age that we have been sold this particular lie.

The Pioneers also recognised, in an unconscious way, that the Jeffersonian ideal of the pursuit of happiness is misconceived. Happiness is not something that can be acquired through specific actions like buying a new car or going to a particular restaurant, although both of these experiences may provide transitory pleasure.

Happiness comes through right living, through good living in the Aristotelian sense of Eudaimonia. Put more simply, we cannot pursue happiness but happiness can pursue us through our actions and our conduct. To pursue such a viewpoint is an act of faith. It is certainly easier to believe that winning the lottery or buying a new pair of shoes will give us what we want because right living, in contrast, requires a lifetime of devotion.

Chapter 9: The French Revolution Lite

Freedom is always and exclusively freedom for the one
who thinks differently.
Rosa Luxembourg.

There exists within all of us the capacity to be truly free. The Pioneers
knew this instinctively and, in a slow and hesitant fashion, they struggled
towards it. In doing this, they were following their great intellectual
predecessor, Ralph Waldo Emerson, although it would be fanciful of me
to claim they had either read or, in many cases, heard of him. I cannot
even claim to have seen copies of *Self Reliance* and *The Conduct of Life*
on their extensive bookshelves.

But this is somehow irrelevant. It is a symptom of their heterodox
beliefs that they could embrace individuals as different as Emerson, Tom
Paine, Robert Blatchford and Pierre Proudhon. It illustrates not so much
an incoherence but rather a refusal to be ideological beyond the pursuit
of what they considered to be a right and just life.

Although no longer in fashion in the 1950s and 60s, Emerson summed
up the spirit of Pioneer enterprise based upon ideas of self-reliance,
self-worth and each man being his own personal god: "That is always
best which gives me to myself. The sublime is excited in me by the great
stoical doctrine, obey thyself."

No Pioneer could have stated more clearly, or with greater economy,
their central doctrine. Significantly, today and for the past one hundred
and fifty years, Emerson has been exalted, lionised and appropriated by
men and women of the left and the right. This brings into further question
the integrity of these old-fashioned political divisions.

Emerson tells us that when we give ourselves to ourselves we then
achieve the outlook and the personal autonomy that enables both
self-realisation and the enrichment of society. In order to avoid a state of
selfish chaos, he further tells us that: "All sensible people are selfish, and
nature is tugging at every contract to make the terms of it fair." Each of us
therefore arrives at a balance between what we need to make ourselves

whole and what society needs to make itself work.

The philosopher's stone is discovering where the point of equilibrium lies; defining the dynamic between personal autonomy and the realised self and the need that we all have for fraternity, community and love. There is the wariness of binding ourselves too close in a way that threatens our integrity.

"Who so would be a man must be a non-conformist." Here Emerson is demanding of us that we be different. Why is it that we are all born original and unique and then spend our lives struggling to prevent ourselves from becoming copies of each other?

At the same time, Emerson recognised the dangers of unbridled autonomy: "Make yourself necessary to someone" he sternly lectures but our engagement with society must be on terms that we define.

Perhaps Stephen Gough was guilty of not knowing where the limits lie. Mr Gough, better known as the Naked Rambler, became something of a minor celebrity by determining to walk naked (except for his boots, rucksack and bush hat) the 847 miles from Lands End to John O'Groats in protest against society's blinkered attitudes towards nudity and as an assertion of his right to freedom of expression. Unfortunately, the various police forces of Scotland were not schooled in the teachings of Emerson and Mill and arrested him on six occasions Nor are the magistrates great admirers of the principle of unrestricted liberty. They sent him to prison. However, his three month sentence was perhaps a kindness as winter was approaching and there was a distinct nip in the air.

I first read Emerson thirty years ago and have now come back to him in the last year. I am more aware of the wisdom, the prescience of his words and the impossibility of classifying what he is saying beyond the fact that it accords with our vision of what society should aspire to. When he tells us that 'a foolish consistency is the hobgoblin of little minds' he is distinguishing himself from the multitude and acknowledging the myriad range of his own unique genius.

I am now more aware of both the complexity and familiarity of his arguments. I had to read numerous passages three or four times until I understood the reason for their familiarity. As Emerson himself put it: "In every work of genius we recognise our own rejected thoughts: they come back to us with a certain alienated majesty." Emerson in his writing provides us with a pabulum that is generally missing in modern life.

*

We are witnessing the slow disintegration of society and the signs are all around us. Like the onset of serious disease, the first symptoms elude us, or we ignore them.

In the winter of 1983, I was standing outside the front door of 23 Cranley Gardens, Muswell Hill in North London watching the police investigate the contents of the drains at that ill-fated house. Dennis Nielsen, the lonely civil servant and mass murderer, had just been arrested and the news had spread quickly. I lived less than a mile away in Elms Avenue, Muswell Hill. Fired by a sense of morbid curiosity and an awareness of the infinite nature of human depravity, I cycled over.

I observed the contents of the thick black plastic sacks that sat in front of the house with a mixture of revulsion and a pathetic knowledge that they contained the remains of what had once been human souls. Here was the terrible signature of a man who had murdered many young men just because he did not want to be alone.

He was a man whose loneliness within the vast impersonal forces of society was so complete that he was compelled to go down the road of butchery and murder. After ten minutes or so, the police told me to 'go away' though they did not use those exact words.

For the first time I realised that not everyone was as lucky as me in having a close family and good friends. Some float and bob about in this sea of people that we call society until they feel that they are drowning. The dislocation is all around us. To listen to dozens of mainly young men and women trilling away on mobile telephones on the early-morning rush-hour trains into London is to be reminded of how we are losing the ability to talk to each other. We are becoming an atomistic society where fractionated citizens relate to each other through the ether of the airwaves while ignoring their neighbours, their communities, and those around them.

Take, for example, the 2003 phenomenon of flash mobbing. Significant numbers of young people in their twenties and thirties, usually between one hundred and three hundred strong, co-ordinated through mobile phones to 'spontaneously' gather in an open public place, usually a large department store. They then acted in a peaceful but bizarre fashion before dispersing. After a few minutes, they disappeared as quickly as they had appeared.

Typically, a flash mob might appear in a large furniture store, stand on one leg for thirty seconds, burst into spontaneous applause and then leave. In Dortmund, a flash mob assembled in front of a washing machine display, ate a banana each, and then dispersed.

The name is interesting. The original flash mob (sometimes known as the swell mob) were the disreputable gangs of low life, sporting gentlemen, and aristocracy who peopled the first half of nineteenth century England. They were united by a mutual interest in horseracing, gambling, dog fighting and the Fancy – the name given to those who followed the grisly sport of bare-knuckle fighting. In comparison, the modern flash mob, with their bananas and mobile phones, seem to be very weak beer. Their excuse? We do it because we can.

What does this post-technological development tell us? It is largely a phenomenon limited to those between twenty and forty because they are the most likely group to be in possession of a mobile phone that is actually switched on, fully charged and in credit.

Most mobsters, it would seem, work in IT or some sort of recruitment consultancy. They are the children of Tony Blair's knowledge economy. It reflects the age group in society who are the most deprived of the benefits of living within a traditional supportive community. Do these transient gatherings, marshalled through the ether, represent an inchoate desire for community? Are they an expression of the need to be part of something? Is it a substitute for something that is missing in their lives?

The main point is that young people in this age bracket are, with exceptions, deeply conformist in their attitudes towards fashion, work, money, authority and society as a whole. This is not their fault given that the pressures are immense. A capitalist society cannot function with everyone acting as autonomous individuals possessed of their own free will. It is in this early period of their adult lives, after the carefree years of childhood have been left behind and they are struggling to carve out a place for themselves in the world, that the pressures to conform are greatest.

I sometimes feel quite depressed after talking with people under the age of thirty. It is as if they have watched too many episodes of *Friends*. Something is lost between each generation. Some might argue it was ever thus but the process seems to be accelerating. I can have perfectly sympathetic and lucid conversations with people who are twenty or thirty years older than me but I find it difficult to locate common reference points with people who are twenty years younger.

I went for a drink recently with a friend who is about thirty. He kept glancing at his mobile phone. In the end I found myself shouting, "Leave the bloody thing alone, turn the ******* thing off. Concentrate on me not some bastard in the distant ether who has nothing better to do than send you half-witted text messages."

In this context, I can see the attraction of flash mobbing. It is not illegal but it has a subversive edge to it; it is the French Revolution Lite, as one American participant observed. There is a risk-free, clandestine, non-conformist appeal; the comforting feeling that a small select group of individuals are part of something that the rest of society does not understand.

I must assume this is at least part of the motivation for the Chaps. These are the tweedy, grumbling revolutionaries who, in 2003, from beside the Oscar Wilde Memorial in Trafalgar Square, launched a display of Chappist indignation at the state of Britain.

The anarchic journal, *The Chap*, tells us that Britain is on the edge of a precipice, looking out onto a dark void. The targets of their anguish are the 'symbols of corporate banality; fast food emporia, American-style coffee shops, sportswear purveyors and lager shebeens'. Like so many of us, they yearn for a gentler, less abrasive age. They are prone to committing random acts of common courtesy.

Their preferred method of destroying McDonalds is to enter the restaurant and ask for a table for two with a pleasant view.

Unfortunately, the Chaps have a rather off-putting preference for Oxford University, tweed suits and wearing cravats. There is something disquieting about it all; they are imbued with an unsettling cultural snobbery. It is commenting on the state of the nation but I am not sure what it is saying.

Grizzled cultural commentators would inform us that flash mobbing and associated activities are not new. They would point to 1960s 'happenings' of the alternative culture, 1920s surrealist gatherings, and the Paris art school Situationists of May 1968.

None of this matters if you have no awareness of the past and you believe that what you are doing is original. We crave safe ways of asserting our individuality that will not compromise the security of our position in the world. In this way we can be a revolutionary just for a few minutes before the comfortable warm waters of conformity lap around us again. The flash mob is neither nihilistic nor political. It is tempting to claim that it is meaningless except that would be to encourage the post-structuralists to lecture us that everything has meaning; the meaningless of the phenomena has meaning.

In 2002, the social commentator, Howard Rheingold, wrote in *Smart Mobs*: 'The Next Social Revolution predicted the increasing importance of what political scientists have dubbed new social movements. These operate outside the conventional structure of politics and are sustained by the technology of the mobile phone and the internet. They are of course a deep and persistent symptom of the disillusionment with mainstream politics and conventional social patterns.'

Rheingold had highly motivated radical political groups in mind like the fuel tax protesters who, in 1998, reduced the government to such a state of funk. What he did not anticipate was the deep yearning to be different, a difference that technology has revealed whether it is standing naked on the escalator at Selfridges as part of photographer Spencer Tunick's vision of the world, or the flash mobbery of waving a banana in the air.

The problem is that most of us are too scared, or have too much moral sense, to become part of a real mob like that of Brixton in 1981, Broadwater Farm in 1985 or Trafalgar Square in 1990. Instead those who suffer the nagging little question 'Is this all life has to offer?' engage in a zany simulacrum of the real mob that is ideology-free and poses no threat to the political status quo. Then, after a brief bout of flash mobbery, they all go back to the banality of the computer screen.

Earlier this year, I was riding a motorcycle past the BBC studios at Elstree when I noticed, in the distance, that a substantial crowd had gathered at the entrance. As I approached it became apparent they were carrying placards in which they were proclaiming the names of their chosen hero. Those gathered in the crowd were, as far as I could judge, exclusively under the age of 25. Having my finger very firmly on the pulse of popular culture, I realised immediately that I was witnessing one aspect of the Big Brother phenomena. As I rode slowly past, I found I just could not help myself. The words came welling up from within me. "You poor sad bastards!" I shouted. "Get a life."

A policeman standing by the crowd gesticulated at me and proceeded to write down what I assumed to be my registration number in his notebook. For several weeks afterwards, I expected to receive a court summons for some offence like 'inciting a crowd of simpletons under the age of twenty-five' or 'insulting the dignity of Big Brother'. However, serious questions remain. What was missing from the lives of those young people that they felt obliged to stand on a busy street in bleakest Hertfordshire and hold up placards displaying the names of people they had never met? Why did they expose themselves to the ridicule of people like me?

Such diversions are a symptom of the disintegration of the normal social nexus that has prevailed for hundreds of years. It is the emasculation of the ideal of citizenship that people find themselves in thrall to such a vacuous activity that is a denial of our commitment to each other. I later discovered that those young people who gathered in Elstree were expressing their support for the participants in a pop talent contest but the same principle applies.

We live in an increasingly crowded and depersonalised world in which the pressures to conform are sometimes almost overwhelming. I observed a young man who had the Nike swoosh marked on his scalp – a shaven area within a very short haircut. I assume he was sporting this mark as a statement of individual identity within an impersonal world. The irony was not lost on me, though, that he was making a powerful statement of conformity; an expression of his place in the world within the Nike family. Perhaps, therefore, it was a statement of belonging.

With the decline of familiar institutions and groupings, family, formal religion and class, here was a statement of the future based upon a notion of global corporate identity. Within a dislocated world of job insecurity, shifting transient communities, the mass movement of labour, the merging of class boundaries and family breakdown, Nike offers that comfortable, warm feeling of being part of their world. Here, in less than a square inch of revealed pink scalp, were this young man's views on youth culture, globalisation and celebrity, combined with a rather supine acquiescence in the face of 21st century trans-national capitalism. He was probably also saying something about his admiration for such Nike luminaries as David Beckham and Tiger Woods.

Emerging at the start of the twenty-first century, we have a version of 1930s Italian fascist corporatism with the ideology of racial superiority and 'all hail the leader' replaced by the cult of celebrity and an uncritical consumerism. This new corporatism offers a revealing transect through society.

McDonalds provide the food, Sky Sport the entertainment, Nike the clothing, Sony the music, Vodafone the means of communication, and Peugeot the soft-top car. This new corporatism allows some choice, and a certain reformation of the permutations to create the illusion of choice while simultaneously establishing conformity. Perhaps Adidas for the clothing, Ford for the soft-top car, Playstation because we can no longer cope with books, Pizza Hut for the food, MTV to be numbed into unconsciousness, and Orange to talk to someone in the distance because you don't want to talk to anybody nearby.

It is all part of the process of establishing identity without the normal reference points that punctuate peoples' lives at the beginning of the third millennia. This is a very complex business, especially for companies whose existence depends upon the ability to identify, define, redefine and profit from what is fashionable; or, to use the new replacement youth-friendly all-purpose word – 'cool'.

Cool is the holy grail of turn-of-the-millennia marketing. It is the instrument whereby global brand names burrow into our unconsciousness. It defines what is desirable and undesirable. Children worry about what is cool. For a moment, as they go through the front door, there is that stabbing little concern that what they are wearing is uncool.

"Don't worry," I say. "You can't go wrong with Matalan."

In a down-market sort of way, Nike is safe because it has succeeded in persuading a sufficient slab of the teenage and twenty-something population that wearing their brand is acceptable if not actually fashionable. I mean acceptable in the sense that for the insecure it is risk-free at the cost of obliterating identity and judgement.

And me? I positively enjoy it. In my world I define what is fashionable and I am not dependent on the brand name kulturkampf that has dominated marketing over the past fifteen or so years.

Other brands lead a more precarious existence. McDonalds teeters on the brink between being a greasy hamburger chain and a fun young person's brand. It just can't make it as a lifestyle illusion despite their glossy new hamburger palace in the Strand. If you are in danger of letting this happen, just close your eyes and allow a vision of the grotesque Ronald McDonald to float into view then everything will be alright.

I spend a portion of my time trying to persuade young people that British Home Store is a cool brand in an ironic detached sort of way. It's a hobby of mine. I enjoy preying upon their insecurities. I explain that to wear a BHS jacket (or as I used to put it before their departure from Britain, a C&A jacket) is to put themselves in touch with inner city values and energy while buying a shopping centre product.

In this complicated world of mine, I explain to my breathless audience that the Millets label is so uncool that to wear it denotes a self-mocking ironic awareness. This denotes that the wearer of the garment is truly cool in the way that the owner of something naff like Calvin Klein or Nautica never can be.

I explain to my young friends that they can be at the forefront of the trend that is known as kitsch marketing where the 'knowing' have an unassailable advantage over the 'unknowing'. When I explain this I sense their fear, their uncertainty, and the air of suppressed panic that perhaps what they are wearing is not cool after all and they have got it all wrong. They look at the logos, the stitching, the shiny fabric; they smell the cheap polyester and realise with a sense of flooding relief that it is all right. They are cool after all. They aggressively tell me that I am just some '******* nutter who knows **** all'. In trying to persuade them that British Home Stores is cool, I am speaking a heresy that suggests the underpinning to their world has collapsed.

If Tommy Hilfiger, Diesel, Polo and DKNY – all of whom comprise that emporium of tat known as branded culture – want a cool hunter to tell them what the next big thing will be then I am their man.

The key battle of the future, at the radical cutting edge of citizen politics, will be fought between the informed, aware citizen and the brand giants who increasingly seek to blur the boundaries between television and advertising, education and indoctrination, and fantasy and reality.

The nadir of the notion of 'cool' came in the early years of the Blair government when it decided to co-opt into the idea of youth culture and came up with the toe-curling idea of Cool Britannia. The instant Oasis stepped over the threshold of Downing Street they became as hip as a pipe and slippers. The only way to redeem themselves would be to vomit on the carpets and urinate in a pot plant.

Watching politicians try to be 'cool' reminds me of an overweight uncle doing the Twist at a family wedding during the Chubby Checker era with his bottom bursting out of his shiny trousers.

My train of thought now turns to one of the most important question concerning the nature of our existence. How do we establish our personal identity within the thronging masses?

More than a hundred and fifty years ago, the liberal philosopher, John Stuart Mill, famously wrote on this matter. He warned us of the rise of Nike and McDonalds: "He who lets the world or his own portion of it, choose his plan of life for him, has no need of any other faculty than the ape-like one of imitation. He, who chooses his plan for himself, employs all of his faculties."

Despite what some modern philosophers tell us, the answer to the establishment of individual identity is through personal memory; those experiences, thoughts, impressions, instincts and dreams that represent the signature we imprint upon the world.

Memory is the accumulation of experience or at least some of our experiences. It is also the editor of that which makes us unique. We filter and shape our life experiences into a seething whole that makes us what we are. The odds seem to be stacked against us. The new corporatism is endowing us with a false, or rather a shallow memory in which we perceive not through our own experiences but through the world of television, brand names and celebrity culture.

We are lost souls, we crave identity, and we crave meaning. We have allowed ourselves to be weakened by a consumer culture that sells us the message that we need to own a particular brand of clothing, or drive a certain make of car and then we will be happy and fulfilled. The problem is that, for a significant proportion of us, this does not bring us happiness or fulfilment. By then we have lost the personal resources to seek other routes to accomplishment. Faced with a lack of choice we then haul ourselves back on the consumer bandwagon in the belief that our next expensive purchase will produce the true happiness that we crave.

Because we are irrational beings, we ignore the fact that expectation has triumphed over experience. Mill again warns us of the dangers: "In some such insidious form there is at present a strong tendency to this narrow theory of life, and to the pinched and hidebound type of human character it patronises. Many persons no doubt sincerely think that human beings thus cramped and dwarfed are as their maker designed them to be...."

Through a perverse regenerative process, we create meaning and focus through the comforting familiarity of brand names that hold in front of us a secure and undemanding world that meets our ideas of status and self-image.

The Nike family is uncritical and supportive. The swoosh demands nothing of us but our money and our loyalty. It makes no demands in terms of commitment and behaviour while feeding us the illusion that we are sharing in the fabulous world of Ronaldo and Edgar Davids. It is, in effect, a palimpsest of the mind; a cruel illusion that sustains us through these dark times. Every time I see the Nike tick I am reminded of how far we have come down the road to a society that is less than human in its aims, values and aspirations. It is only through the reclamation of our individuality that society can hope to progress.

To revisit J.S. Mill for a final time: "... it is only the cultivation of individuality which produces, or can produce, well-developed human beings, ... it brings human beings themselves nearer to the best thing they can be."

So what can we do about it?

Very little I fear. The question assumes that we want to do something about it which is extremely difficult if we are not aware of the problem. Yet each of us is entitled to make our own little gesture.

My personal manifesto is as follows. I try very hard not to buy anything that I have seen advertised in the belief, probably mistaken, that I am making some little statement about these matters. I buy Grenson shoes made in Northampton, not because I particularly like them or because I feel like waving the Union Jack: I buy them because I refuse to collude with Nike and their ilk.

This is not because they pay twelve-year-old Indonesian children sixteen pence an hour for their labour or because Northampton shoe workers are reasonably well paid. In fact, Nike are one of the better employers in the developing world. In Vietnam they pay, on average, 54 dollars a month which is one third above the national average. Many ordinary people in Vietnam experience relative job security and affluence courtesy of Nike. If I boycott Nike's products then some of these people may lose their jobs.

In the end, the arguments are so complex and varied that a compelling case can be made either way on the issue of globalisation. The real exploitation of labour in the developing world is usually by local companies paying dirt wages to produce unbranded trainers destined for European supermarkets and cheap sports store outlets. In comparison, most of the brand name sports marques are model employers who have too much to lose through open and naked exploitation.

My hostility to Nike is based upon anti-Americanism and a hostility to the idea that prosperity can only be had by following the American model. In the world that is emerging, regional and national differences are being obliterated under the crushing tread of American economic imperialism.

I am old-fashioned enough to like the idea of companies that actually make things while being repelled by the increasing reality of companies who make nothing but attempt to sell us a 'brand' while franchising their manufacturing process into low wage dependent economies.

The Philippines is becoming to the western world at the beginning of the twenty-first century what that sweated-garment industry of the East End was to England in the late-nineteenth century. Independent sovereign governments find themselves under the control of vast trans-national companies with a global reach who are the negation of the idea that individual nations decide their own destiny.

For me, with my pockets full of money and more motorcycles than I know what to do with, it is a luxury to criticise a system that delivers higher living standards. It is at a price that, from my personal point of view, is too high.

I own two scooters – a PGO and a She Lung – makes that nobody has heard of. They are made in Taiwan by workers who earn three quarters of the European average wage in the car industry. I am trying to persuade my wife to replace her Renault with a Malaysian-made Perodua because they do not have an advertising budget. I am looking to buy a Ural motorcycle from the Dnepr works in the Ural Mountains because they do not advertise and their workers are, by Russian standards, very well paid.

It irritates me that nine per cent of the cost of a mainstream Ford or Vauxhall is fatuous advertising. If I see any products advertised on television particularly McDonalds, Coca Cola, Sony, any large supermarket, any insurance company, and any make of car, then I will go a considerable distance out of my way not to patronise them. I have to pinch myself again and again when I am told that advertising works. The products I favour are those of sufficiently high quality that are produced on a small scale. They sell themselves by virtue of meeting the needs of the buyer.

Marks and Spencer were selling what appeared to be a perfectly serviceable, brightly-coloured beach towel for £12-99. Poundstretcher had on their overstocked shelves a rather thin and coarse, but nevertheless adequate offering for £5·99. Louis Vuitton were selling a towel that was rather gaudily-coloured but was fit for its purpose for £185.

Clearly, the Louis Vuitton product was a superior beach towel to the other two. After all it came with its own carrying bag and was of a sufficiently high standard to meet the critical demands of a Premiership footballer. However, was it fourteen times better than the Marks and Spencer towel as it cost fourteen times more? The answer, of course, was 'no'. It was twenty per cent larger, the pile was certainly a little deeper, and, taking into account the little carrying bag, I would judge it to be twice as good as the Marks and Spencer towel. Therefore, it should have cost £26. This judgment of course takes no account of such matters as label and status and how we perceive ourselves in the world.

The more we undertake this sort of appraisal, the more we assert our individuality in a hostile world. It probably makes no difference but it keeps me amused. When I explained this to a friend who is a solicitor in a company that has, amongst its clients, a well-known advertising agency, he accused me of not playing the game. If everyone acted and thought like me then capitalism (shorthand for the exploitation of the poor) would no longer work, he explained.

"But that is the whole point," I replied. "Those clever, talented, creative people who work in the advertising industry should go and work in something that is socially useful; something that benefits humanity as a whole."

It is not that I am against capitalism; it is probably the only economic system that works tolerably well. I am opposed to its wastefulness and the way that it tries to obliterate human identity and choice. A world without capitalism would probably be a significantly worse place than it is today. What is necessary is for every citizen to place it in a position of critical suspicion, to make the assumption that we are being manipulated and that the value of our labour is being stolen from us by 'those who reap not, neither do they toil'. Every time I see a celebrity endorsing a product I add it to my private list of those things that I will not buy.

I can recommend, by the way, that everyone should ride a Ural motorcycle for a while at least. It is like rumbling down the roads on a Soviet Five-Year Plan. It is a reminder of why the Soviet Union collapsed in 1990; a reminder of a world without choice. Urals are direct copies, albeit modified and somewhat refined, of BMW wartime R71s, constructed to agricultural standards with what can best be described as leisurely performance. They may have a certain nostalgic charm to some but, on rational grounds, the comparison with a modern Honda or Kawasaki means that, in any proper free trade economy, production would cease tomorrow. They are a reminder of just how far the Russian economy has to go that the factory deep in the Ural Mountains continues to churn out these obsolete, but strangely charming leviathans, adding to the three million or so that have already been produced.

For those who are unsteady on two wheels and want to experience the automotive consequences of socialism, then try driving an East German Wartburg Knight, a Russian Moskovich Neva, or a Polish FSO Polonez. It gets worse. The Aro, the Tatra, the Syrena, the Chaika and the Zil were all makes of eastern European car that failed to make it to Britain with the exception of a modest number of Tatras that were a cut above the communist competition. All of them were terrible cars, albeit possessed of a certain quirky charm made viable by a simple lack of choice.

Nevertheless, I am intrigued by the Hungarian Aro. Its body was made from a composite of pig fat and chicken feathers. The Syrena featured a floor hatch for fishing on frozen lakes. I have not seen that featuring on BMWs list of ruinously-expensive extras.

However, do not be deceived by driving a Lada. They are positively sophisticated in comparison to the two mentioned above.

Soviet-style socialism may start out as a noble aspiration but the reality is the humiliation of driving along in an East German Trabant made out of Formica while the rest of Germany cruises past in their sleek Mercedes and BMWs.

Chapter 10: Rivers of Blood

Here even the newsagents are white.
A member of the BNP telling me of the advantages of living in Thurrock.

I confess to being a benign, but narrow, English nationalist and I blame it all on Walls Ice Cream.

As a child, the wall of my bedroom held a map of England produced by Walls. It showed all the counties, major towns and cities and I used to stare at it for hours on end. It was only a map of England though. As a result, I can tell you without hesitation that Uttoxeter is to the northeast of Stafford and Morpeth is on a more northerly latitude than Carlisle. However, I cannot tell you if Glasgow is west, north, east or south of Edinburgh, whether Renfrewshire shares a border with Lanarkshire, or if Flint is in North, South or Mid-Wales.

On my map, the places occupied by Wales and Scotland were blank. Walls may just as well have printed 'Here be Dragons' for all I knew of what occupied the empty spaces.

My sense of what it was to be English was first challenged by Enoch Powell's 1968 'Rivers of Blood' speech when he warned the white English, in quite sensational terms, of the dangers of unrestrained mass immigration. Most people who have condemned Powell have not read the full text of the Rivers of Blood Speech. I have and I can confirm that it is unpleasantly, indeed offensively racist although in the 1960s our antennae were less finely tuned on these matters.

There is also a precision, an intellectual rigour behind what Powell said that makes the speech, nearly forty years later, compelling reading. It was also compelling at the time. He received more than one hundred thousand letters of support. Powell's final vision was that of the classicist. 'As I look ahead, I am filled with foreboding. Like the Roman, I seem to see the River Tiber foaming with much blood.' It is the fascination that the snake has for the rat.

When, in the summer of 2002, there were riots with a strong racial element in Burnley and Oldham I heard once again the old Alf Garnett refrain from those of a certain age: "Enoch was right. He tried to warn us."

Until the time of this most notorious intervention, I had given little consideration to the issue of race and nation. It had simply not occurred to me that negritude or any other ethnicity should be a disqualifying factor in basking under the protection of the British crown.

When, in the mid-1970s, I saw the black Bermudan winger, Clyde Best, being taunted at Upton Park by West Ham fans throwing bananas, there was aroused within me a very basic, vestigial instinct about fair play and a breach of good manners. It did not help that the stewards joined in.

On the other hand, I had no hesitation in addressing my black friend, Peter, as 'Sambo' while we told each other Rastus and Liza jokes. Both of us seem to have survived that trauma without too many side effects.

Despite spending most of my time in a secondary modern school learning woodwork, I was interested in these matters. I discussed it with my parents, my teachers, my neighbours, my friends and many of the Pioneers. Their view was generally consistent that 'Powell had a point' even if they did not like the way he expressed it. For others, perhaps less liberal and less educated, the view was expressed with some regularity that 'It's all up for decent white people in this country. I'm off to Australia, New Zealand, Canada, South Africa etc before it is too late'.

An unfortunate feature of modern Britain is that many of the things that Mr Powell predicted thirty-five years ago are now a fact of everyday life. Such is the climate in our open liberal democracy that it is very difficult to discuss such matters, even in the most cautious of terms, without attracting the accusation of racism.

I often talk with elderly people, those who are 'rich in years' – to use a euphemism. It is rare not to find a fading sense of a nation in decline but perhaps this was always the fate of the elderly. A question that I always ask is, 'What politician from the past fifty years do you particularly admire?' I also ask them to exclude Churchill. Only four names are ever mentioned. Margaret Thatcher comes up with some frequency. Tony Benn is mentioned occasionally and Nye Bevan even more rarely. By far the most popular choice is Enoch Powell. These people are not maliciously or consciously racist but they do retain a nostalgic fading memory of Britain as it was. They view Powell as the only politician who attempted to defend that particular vision and was foolish or brave enough to articulate their concerns. Admiration for Mr Powell has become, for those over a certain age, the political loyalty that dare not speak its name. He is one of only five post-war politicians to appear on the BBC poll list of 100 Greatest Britons. All the Prime Ministers, bar Tony Blair and Margaret Thatcher, have been forgotten but Mr Powell remains an object of a curious atavistic loyalty.

At risk of courting some controversy, it was a mistake of social policy to allow virtually unrestricted immigration into Britain between 1948 and 1970 without reaching some sort of judgment about the likely impact this would have on inner city working class communities, and on relationships with the indigenous population.

Amongst all political parties, it was a policy of hoping for the best and making, perhaps unjustified, assumptions about the basic decency of human nature. The 1971 British Nationality Act, and all subsequent legislation in this area, has been a tacit admission by governments that the twenty-year open door was a mistake.

It is possible to argue that working class disillusionment with the political elite took hold as a result of this policy failure. For many inner city working class communities, immigration was not an abstract exercise of economics, labour markets and social justice. Rather it was a real issue in which they saw their communities transformed without consultation, explanation or apology as a result of decisions made by those whose lives were not affected.

The old paternalistic Tory compact had been broken. The unspoken agreement up until the 1960s was that the British working class would allow themselves to be ruled by their social and political superiors provided they ruled in the spirit of noblesse oblige. To allow the destruction of traditional working class inner city communities without consultation was a betrayal of a political contract that had existed since the 1870s.

The electoral success of the British National Party in the first few years of the twenty-first century is a symptom of breaking the compact. This is an ominous and undesirable development but one that was entirely predictable. Politicians now need to work hard to reassure this disaffected constituency to prevent the infection spreading.

This is not to say that there was always direct resentment of this change, though for my friend's grandmother it was a matter of puzzlement that, in the course of fifteen years, her street filled up with what she regrettably referred to as 'darkies'. I would go round to her house to watch ITV when we had a television that could only receive BBC. Her hero was Cecil Rhodes and she would sit in front of the television watching her favourite programme *The Black and White Minstrel Show* while making remarks like 'look at those darkies go'. I was never sure if she actually realised they were white men blacked up.

Somehow it is possible to forgive the attitudes of the elderly. Twenty years ago I was emerging from Gayton Road on to Hampstead High Street in an elderly Renault 16 that had no reverse gear. There was a sharp rapping on my side window. It was an old woman demanding that I take her to Birchington Road, Kilburn. I obliged as I was in no great hurry and she was in a state of some distress. I drove through the north London streets ever mindful that I must not get into a situation in which I would need to reverse. She was Polish; her father had been a well known Communist leader. They had fled the country in the late thirties sensing the horrors that were to come. Many of her extended family had died, either in German or Russian camps. They were caught hopelessly in between.

She invited me into the tall narrow house into which was packed a lifetime's collection of the cultural memorabilia of Mittel Europa. She was bitter, not because of the war or living in exile, but because the 'filthy niggers' were taking over her street. She could not find it in her heart to accept that both she and her new neighbours were in exile and that their hearts lay elsewhere.

What distressed many ordinary people as the immigration debate first surfaced in British politics was the airily dismissive lack of concern of the liberal elite. This was compounded by the state of political paralysis that ensued when the realisation dawned that there was a problem.

Irrespective of political parties, the inescapable platitude now is of the virtues of multiculturalism, not because it is intrinsically good or widely wanted, but because there is no other way. In the other direction lies a road that leads towards race war – American style separatism and, ultimately, the flag that flies over Auschwitz.

When the historian, Andrew Roberts, interviewed the Home Office Ministers of the 1950s responsible for immigration policy during those years, all, without exception, expressed regret at their failure to impose restrictions and felt that in some way they had let down the British people. The unforgivable feature was the lack of any decision-making process. Successive Home Office ministers in the 1950s failed to confront the issue because they represented constituencies that were not affected by this mass movement of peoples. Additionally they had a fear of offending the governments of Jamaica and India that would lead to the break up of the Commonwealth and a further diminution of Britain's role in the world.

For some more liberal conservatives, it was also about expiating guilt over Empire. For Britain's naive ruling class, the belief that the new immigrants would be plugging a hole at the lower end of the unskilled labour market was justification enough. It never occurred to them that the children of these immigrants would, quite rightly, not be prepared to accept a similarly low position in society. At successive cabinet meetings during the 1950s the issue was raised and then put aside as too difficult to deal with.

Britain is not an organically immigrant society. There has been no equivalent to the American melting pot where people crossed the Atlantic specifically to become American, discarding their past along the way and, within a generation, becoming part of the American Dream. It is not possible to become British in the way that it is possible to become American. There the process of assimilation is central to the national experience.

In contrast, groups have come to Britain with the intention of resisting assimilation. The cultural imperatives of their position, history and outlook have made them hostile to the idea of being absorbed into British society. The result has been the steady exhortation over the past thirty years to embrace the multicultural ideal; a notion that tends to appeal to intellectuals, ministers, civil servants and those on the left, but it has little resonance with the bulk of the population.

The resulting cultural friction left governments not knowing which way to turn. As a result the problem was not discussed for more than twenty years. For political leaders the issue became too difficult, too volatile and open to accusations of racism so it was ignored. By default, our political class allowed race and immigration to become a monopoly issue of the extreme right to the extent that it was not possible for the liberal mainstream to engage in the debate.

There are only two possible solutions to the problem of deep-seated cultural abrasion: an acceptance of valid differences between groups while subscribing to the same basic laws and values, or a long experience of destructive conflict. It is far from clear at present which path we shall go down.

It is a curious exercise to try to imagine a counterfactual history of a post-war Britain in which mass immigration had not occurred.

The orthodoxy has been that the mass immigration of the 1950s and 60s breathed new life into an ailing body giving birth to a vibrant multiculturalism. The dark underbelly is a sinister gun culture and the nagging suspicion that, for a small minority at least, loyalties lie elsewhere other than the country of their birth and citizenship.

Superficially, the exercise is easy. Without Asian shopkeepers we would not have had our 'open all hours' 24/7 culture. A visit to any northern European country that has not experienced mass immigration quickly serves to remind us what Britain used to be like. Beef stew would not have made the transition into beef Madras and we would still be eating an awful lot of steak and kidney puddings and fish and chips. What would the British High Street or any suburban parade of shops look like without the obligatory ration of Indian restaurants and takeaways? Where would we go to act in a boorish and anti-social fashion after drinking eight pints of lager on a Friday night?

We have to assume that the National Health Service would have collapsed about thirty years ago given its high degree of dependence on the skills of doctors and nurses from ethnic minority backgrounds. This may not have been an entirely bad thing in that it would have forced successive governments to grapple with the intractable issue of how to reform a system of health care designed in the first half of the twentieth century to meet the needs of the twenty-first century.

For too long, meaningful reform has been delayed by the availability of cheap labour. There is a long running and complex, but ultimately unprovable argument that the availability of a huge pool of low-wage immigrant labour in the 1950s and 60s prevented the modernisation of the British economy in a way that made it impossible to compete against the more efficient and automated labour markets of Germany and Japan.

If the 1948 British Nationality Act had not been passed, the politics of the British Right would have been very different. We have to assume that, without mass immigration, Enoch Powell would not have made the 1968 speech that brought his mainstream career to a premature end. This in turn means he would almost certainly have been in the Heath Cabinet in 1970-74, given his previous shadow cabinet status. Perhaps he might have been Chancellor of the Exchequer because of the premature death of Ian Macleod and the less than impressive record of his successor, the almost entirely forgotten Anthony Barber. In this case, we would probably have been introduced to the bracing stringencies of neo-liberal economic policies a decade earlier than actually occurred. There is a possibility that the economic disasters of the 1970s would not have happened under a Powell Chancellorship and this, in turn, suggests the probability that Edward Heath would not have lost the first 1974 election given that it was a knife edge result.

Once we assume a second Heath term, then the possibilities would be endless. Most obviously, there would not have been the drive to unseat him as leader in 1975 and Mrs Thatcher's appeal to those red meat Conservatives desperate for change would have been delayed by half a decade.

Even if the implosion of 1974 had not happened, it is unlikely that Powell would have joined the Ulster Unionists despite Heath's strong pro-European credentials. That was the last desperate strategy of a man in the wilderness. The appeal of staying in office would have been too strong.

Would he have backed Thatcher against Heath? Probably, despite his reservations about her and the permanent grievance that she had 'stolen' his right-wing monetarist ideas. Powell would not have been an equivalent to Keith Joseph – a selfless right-wing free-market guru looking for the chance to serve. He would have been too powerful and charismatic a figure to ignore. I suspect he would have finished his career as an interesting but marginal figure holding an important, but lesser, cabinet position like Trade and Industry, finding an excuse to resign before the 1983 election. There is a sense that he might have viewed himself as an English De Gaulle but the political circumstances were never sufficiently auspicious to have that role thrust upon him.

A reasonable assumption is that the politics of the extreme right would have been different without the 1948 Act. Oswald Mosley's career would not have been given a late fillip (as happened in the 1959 election) as it was exclusively based on opposing West Indian immigration. We have to assume that the unpleasant parties of the extreme right would have lacked impetus to the extent that the National Front would not have been formed in 1968. It is likely that they would have remained a splintering of primarily neo-Nazi anti-Semitic groups that commanded tiny levels of support rather than the significant organisations they later became.

What is even more difficult to decide is how would the development of our inner city areas have changed if the mass immigration of the 1950s and 60s had not occurred?

These judgments are made more difficult by the coincidence that, during the peak years of immigration, Britain's inner cities were being ripped apart in a Soviet-style exercise of mass destruction that was either driving the white working class away from the inner cities or allowing them to stay on in alien vertical tower block communities.

The prevailing view of the last thirty years has been that the black and Asian immigrants from the New Commonwealth occupied those areas of the inner cities that were no longer wanted by the white working class. The reality is much more complicated. The view that the white community of Southall moved out on a Tuesday and the Asian community moved in on a Wednesday is clearly nonsense. The process was incremental and, for both sides, involved a painful adjustment.

When my aunt and uncle left Brixton in the late 1960s and moved to Market Harborough in Leicestershire they were not abandoning a Mad Max landscape of urban desolation for the green fields of middle England. They were leaving behind a respectable, stable, lower middle class area because, for good or for bad, they felt that the place they had lived all their lives was being taken over and they had had enough. Compulsory multiculturalism was not to their taste.

The process of transforming inner London has been a complicated one in which race has been an important, but perhaps not central, issue. Like a pantomime villain, the phenomenon of gentrification stalks across central London and the inner suburbs. We hiss and boo at it while making clucking noises about the destruction of traditional communities. We thrill to the transformation of areas that until recently had exhibited a monotonous lower middle class uniformity. We are curious about streets where it is not possible to buy a bag of screws but where we can drink in chrome and stainless steel wine bars, linger in picture galleries, be spoilt in delicatessens and eat in alfresco diners.

This avaricious and aspirational gentrifying class descend like clouds of locusts. Forty years ago it was Islington and thirty years ago it was Fulham. In the early 1980s, Wandsworth came within the purview of this floating nomadic group of merchant bankers, advertising executives, and people who are something in the media. Nowhere is safe. As long as the existing housing stock is of a reasonable standard, and the journey into the City or the West End is significantly shorter than the train or tube journey from the outer suburbs, then all districts are vulnerable.

At the time my great aunt was decamping from Brixton her younger sister believed herself to be safe in the Bellevue Road area of Wandsworth, a Pooterish suburb of late-Victorian terracing at the south end of Clapham Common. For close on one hundred years, the area had been a stable lower middle class/superior working class community. Then it was discovered by those who were spilling over from Clapham and Battersea. With the assistance of some entrepreneurial local estate agents, who helped to rename the district Bellevue Village, the area underwent a transformation of bewildering and frightening speed.

Having previously been a land of H.G. Wells, clerks and shop assistants it is now the haunt of Gap-clad children with names like Ethan and Chloe. Gone are the Sierras and Montegos of the 1980s. The parents of the young fashion icons drive huge four-wheel-drive off-roaders and the occasional sporty Alfa Romeo.

The problem with this sort of locust like gentrification, is that it destroys traditional communities while being unclear about what to put in their place. The incomers may choose to live in London Fields for its traditional working class community, Brixton for its ethnic diversity, or Canning Town because, although it is a dump, it is a reasonable distance from the City.

Academic research suggests, however, that they do not form new communities. Instead, they stretch out and attenuate existing ones. The spatial difference between the old and the new communities may be minimal but the difference in terms of income, education, life-style and attitudes tends to be enormous.

This is reinforced by a fear of allowing Jack and Emily to use the local schools in some areas. While nationally only 8 per cent of children are educated at independent schools, in some inner-London boroughs the figure exceeds 50 per cent. The notion of living in a gentrified bubble is accentuated by the habit of socialising with old friends from outside their new area rather than forging new ties.

It may be suggested that Thameside Essex does not take naturally to the pluralistic diversity that is encouraged in twenty-first century

Britain. The 2001 census, the first to offer an optional indication of sexual orientation, reveals that Castlepoint, the local authority to the east of Basildon has the smallest proportion of gay men and women in the United Kingdom. Only 0.04 per cent of the population (amounting to eighteen people) ticked the requisite box. I recounted this fact to a mildly-homophobic Basildon friend.

"I know," he replied. "We have all their names and addresses."

I gently chided him for making such a remark even in jest.

It was not without significance that in September 2003 Thurrock returned the eighteenth councillor for the British National Party despite having no significant ethnic minority population even amongst the newsagents. It is now clear that the BNP is achieving success in two very different types of area.

Firstly it has succeeded in towns like Oldham and Burnley in the north of England where there are very significant Asian populations and a perception amongst the white working class that it has lost out. Secondly, the BNP has succeeded in areas like Cheshunt (in the Lea Valley) and Thurrock that have white working class populations where some of the voters are sending out the message that 'this is our territory and we intend to keep it that way'.

A significant proportion of the population in both Thurrock and Cheshunt nurture the grievance that they were driven out of the East End of London by the mass immigration of the 1960s and 70s. They have engaged in a tactical retreat, redrawn the battle lines, and are in no mood to concede more territory.

Thurrock is only a few miles from Tilbury. Many of the voters are the children and grandchildren of the dockers who in 1968 marched to the House of Lords in support of their hero, Enoch Powell. They demonstrated their support for him outside the House of Commons by chanting, "Get the Jew boys out." Some of them were old BUF East End activists from the 1930s, now very likely long dead. They were not quite the people he was aiming to reach with his message in a final attempt to define Britishness in a nationalistic quasi-racial fashion.

This unwholesome local government BNP victory also illustrates my second point that there is a price to be paid for our political indifference. The successful candidate (who has Italian grandparents – it would be too much to expect the BNP to be rational) was elected on a turnout of less than 22 per cent with slightly over 30 per cent of the popular vote. This means that less than seven people in a hundred voted for him. Such are the mysteries of democracy.

*

It is true that, in many parts of the country, a preponderance of newsagents are of Asian origin. More than twenty years ago I knew Vinesh Mistry, my newsagent in Mill Lane, West Hampstead better than most. Mr Mistry was a slight, diffident, dignified and cultured man. One day I entered his shop carrying a copy of John Stuart Mill's *On Liberty*.

His face lit up as he recognised the green Everyman edition. "Ah!" he said. "You are concerned that your fellow man can be free?"

Then I was not but now I am. I nodded in agreement with him. It transpired he had studied moral philosophy at the University of Nairobi and had been one of the twenty thousand or so Asians forcibly expelled from Kenya in the late 1960s who had settled in England. From then on, every time I went into the shop, I would receive his personal greetings and he would ask me how I was getting on with Mr Mill and recommend me to Mr Locke and Mr Bentham while the man behind would shout out for 'twenty Embassy Regal, mate, and the Sun'.

When, many years later, I read R.K. Narayan's *Malgudi* novels on life in small town India, a vision of Mr Mistry swam into view.

*

The derelict and declining inner city areas of the 1960s would not have remained that way without mass immigration. The experience of London Dockland demonstrates the transformation that demand and money can bring about. It also illustrates how soulless certain areas can be without their own communities. Given the pressure on public transport systems, and the demand for inner city living, it seems inconceivable that areas such as Brixton and Tower Hamlets would have fallen into dereliction. Given a supply of half decent housing stock, and reasonable proximity to the City and the West End, then any area would have become the focus of an Islington-style gentrification.

This is not criticism of what has happened in Southall, Tottenham and Walthamstow. They are all dynamic and viable communities in the way that Docklands is not. It is simply to state that it is a deliberate misreading of another version of history to say that they would have remained urban wastelands without the benefits of mass immigration.

It is probable that the white working class communities of Britain's inner cities would have remained and would not have been tempted out into the suburbs and the dormitory towns. A combination of local authority and central government investment would have improved the housing stock and the infrastructure rather an allowing an American-style depopulation of the inner areas. They would have developed into something different but equally viable.

*

There have been some high points in Britain's post-war history but it is doubtful whether Harold Wilson's decision to stay out of the Vietnam War was enough to erase the failures of his three premierships.

There is a view that Britain undertook a graceful retreat from Empire in the late 1950s and 60s. Admittedly it was not as clumsy, rushed and curmudgeonly as that undertaken by France, Belgium and Spain but it is a matter of degree and judgment.

Enforced decolonisation resulted in bitter civil wars and terrorist campaigns in colonies as diverse as Cyprus and Malaya. It would be useful to ask the families of those colonial subjects who were executed by the British in the 1950s if they felt the withdrawal was conducted with good grace. We have conveniently forgotten the mass hangings after group trials of Mau Mau suspects in Kenya in the late 1950s.

A number of social policies, including the abolition of capital punishment and the decriminalisation of homosexuality, reflect well upon an increasingly tolerant and inclusive society although the fact that such individual policies have to be highlighted is an admission that there are few greater successes that we can point towards.

The decision to end selection and introduce comprehensive schools in most parts of the country was a noble, but probably failed, attempt to produce greater social justice without necessarily raising educational standards.

For all its problems, the introduction of the National Health Service brought about a standard of health care that my grandparents in the inter-war years could only have dreamt about. Such praise however is double edged. The National Health Service was appropriate to the needs of fifty years ago but the lethargy of governments in dealing with its problems means that it is ill-suited to dealing with the health demands of today.

I knew relatively little of the Pioneers' thoughts about these events. Discussions about current politics were usually very parochial and centred on issues such as 'what sort of pipe Harold Wilson smoked' and 'was George Brown really a drunkard or did he just fall up and down stairs as a matter of course'. A few years later, in the late 1970s, I lived in the same block of flats as George Brown in Kensington Park Road, Notting Hill and, on numerous occasions, I shared a lift with him. A more sober and restrained individual you could not wish to meet. I desperately wanted to ask him in the silence of the stainless steel lift what difference it would have made to Britain if he, rather than Harold Wilson, had been elected leader of the Labour Party after the death of Hugh Gaitskell in 1963, assuming, of course, that he had then gone on to win the 1964 General Election.

Given the grave disappointment of the 1964-70 Labour government it remains an intriguing 'what-if?' of recent political history if we could have looked to Prime Minster Brown instead. However, his reputation as a tigerish, right-wing social democrat who could be drunk at any time of the day or night rather intimidated me. I contented myself by reading the 'Emergency Procedures in Case of Lift Breakdown' as we descended or ascended in gloomy silence.

What I should have asked George, but what I was not to know, was: "Is it true that Harold Wilson is having it off with his political secretary, Marcia Falkender?"

I feel let down in this matter. My father admired Harold Wilson more by virtue of the fact that he was a Labour Prime Minister rather than for any personal qualities he possessed. Yet he was performing the mattress quadrille with his political secretary Marcia Falkender (a female Alistair Campbell) when he should have been focussing on better ways of running the country for the benefit of people like me.

Perhaps I was naïve but I did not think that politicians had sex. I assumed they were so busy doing whatever politicians do that somehow the testosterone was just not there. How wrong I was. This avuncular, cheery, pipe-smoking man with his Labrador and Gannex raincoats, the man who resigned out of principle from the Attlee government in 1951 because of the introduction of charges for spectacles, was cavorting about in bed with a woman who should have been taking the shorthand notes. Marcia Falkender treated our Prime Minister like some 'over the hill' pimp who had lost control of his girls. According to Joe Haines,

Wilson's press secretary, her hold over him was so complete that when, unknown to her, he slipped away from a House of Lords reception and made his way back to Downing Street, she followed him back screaming, "You little ****! What do you think you are doing?"

The only surprise in the sorry saga is that Wilson did not take up the offer of his personal doctor to do away with Marcia Falkender and make it look like natural causes. Was our ignorance of these matters due to a more deferential press and a less rapacious media thirty years ago? Or has it always been this way but somehow the really juicy stuff does not get out?

We only saw the pictures in the Daily Mirror that they wanted us to see – those of a cheery Prime Minister, his loyal wife Mary, and a cabinet of decent pipe-smoking chaps who looked more like a group of slightly battered Oxford Dons than contestants in some seedy sexual Olympics.

No election had ever been fought on one of these issues. There was a referendum in 1975 about whether Britain should withdraw from the EEC but that was more about getting Labour out of a political hole than furthering the spirit of consultative democracy.

The phrase 'I am sorry, we made a mess of that' is not in the politician's lexicon. Norman Lamont's defence of his handling of the Black Wednesday events in 1992, when, in a few short hours, £20-billion was lost from the national coffers in a vain attempt to fight the forces of the free market, exposed an arrogance and a contempt that is both breathtaking and depressing. Despite this he is now Lord Lamont.

The working class in this country has little reason to be grateful to the state. For hundreds of years the only state manifestation for ordinary people was to punish and imprison them, take money from them in the form of taxation, and occasionally force them to fight in defence of the state. Finally, they were expected to accept, in a spirit of compliance, a lowly position in society that would not threaten the position of the privileged elite.

In the nineteenth century, the state introduced the workhouse to the working class, with all its attendant horrors, while offering little in return. There still lingers in the minds of the elderly a vestigial fear of 'ending up in the workhouse' or suffering 'a pauper's burial' This fear was part of the folk memory of working class people in the early twentieth century that they passed on to their children.

There is no equivalent fear today because our relationship with the state has fundamentally changed. There is little sense of state provision as the position of last resort when all other remedies for failure have been exhausted. The phrase 'we shall all end up in the workhouse' is now meaningless.

In the early years of the twentieth century, the British state sent the working class to be senselessly slaughtered in their hundreds of thousands on the Western Front. Those who survived found themselves stigmatised and cast aside by the application of an inhuman means test in response to the poverty and depression of the 1930s. When called upon to sacrifice themselves once again in the Second World War, the working classes were rewarded with the sop of the welfare state. This produced the conundrum that it encouraged the vast expansion of power of the instrument that had previously oppressed them.

Today the state overarches our lives in a way that would have been practically impossible in the 1930s. The symbol of this over powerful state is the ever spiralling levels of taxation that are thrust upon us. In 1914 the total amount of tax paid on national income was less than 8 per cent. In 2003 it is 44 per cent. Economists predict that by 2010 anyone on an average income will be paying a marginal rate of tax of more than 50 per cent.

There is a restlessness about the state as it pursues its relentless quest to fine tune the engine of society. It is like the lapping of waves as the tide rises, when water fills every crack and crevice in the rock face. The end result is always the same, either the partial solution to the problem or the creation of a new problem that will surely demand future intervention.

One minor example may help to illuminate the issue.

In 2004 the Department for Education and Skills employs 4,800 civil servants. Despite my extensive enquiries, it is impossible to establish exactly what they do beyond administering the very small number of City Academies that by various nefarious means it has conjured into existence. The Academies are the educational equivalent of secure gated communities, designed to reassure the worried middle classes that the state system is safe. 'Come on in,' they shout. 'We've kept the hoi polloi out.'

A key function is to rename themselves from time to time at a cost of many millions of taxpayers' pounds. In 1998, the Department of Education and Science became the Department for Education and Employment that in 2001 became the Department for Education and

Skills. Its pre-1944 predecessor, the Board of Education, employed 380 civil servants overseeing the education of approximately the same number of young people as now. And they did not have any computers. To all intents and purposes, the DfES has the appearance, and probably the usefulness, of an outdoor relief scheme constructed for the indigent middle classes.

This problem is replicated throughout the vast and overblown civil service. They are a non-productive sector of the economy. Their numbers have increased by nearly twenty per cent since 1997 yet there is very little evidence that they have become twenty per cent more effective in administering the country. Their extravagance and lack of financial accountability is at times difficult to comprehend.

Operating without the disciplines of the free market and buoyed up by the certainty that extravagant indulgences will be endlessly subsidised by the long-suffering taxpayer, the DfES blunders on, forever raiding a bottomless pit of money in an expensive search for a meaningful role in the world of education.

One of my many moles within the civil service told me of a series of crackpot training exercises organised for new entrants at the Treasury. Below I have itemised only the first three.

1. Building towers of wooden blocks blindfolded and spending the next hour analysing the behaviour of different people in the team.

2. A two-day team building beano where the entrants had to build a wine factory out of hoops and plastic guttering and then produce large amounts of coloured water (wine) which had to be delivered to a supermarket across a hypothetical swamp using planks and logs.

3. Taking a card from the Pumpkin Box (*it was Halloween*) placed in the middle of the room and filling in the name, background and job description of the person next to him so that the entrants could introduce each other to the rest of the group. The big question to be discussed was "HONESTY? We're all civil servants, we're all going to be honest ....what does that mean?"

And you thought all these management team-building and bonding exercises were just an invention for satirical comedians to lampoon human foolishness.

The consequence of such expansion, extravagance and ambition on the part of the state is always the further restriction on the liberty of the individual, even if we are not quite aware of it at the time.

When Gordon Brown announced in 1997 his grandiose vision of abolishing child poverty in this country within twenty years, he was demonstrating the almost touching faith that conventional politicians have in the power of the state to solve intractable social problems. Despite this vaulting Brown ambition, I would be prepared to wager a very significant sum that, come the year 2017, using the same measure as was used in 1997, the proportion of children living in poverty will barely have changed. This is not because I approve of child poverty. Rather I view it as such an intractable problem, bound up in the nature of individual behaviour, that its eradication lies beyond the reach of the state. This indicates that I am probably not a socialist although I would like to be one.

A similar level of ambition highlighting the ability of the state to manipulate the individual can be seen in the 2000 document produced by the Further Education Funding Council for 16 to 19-year-olds. It tells its audience that 'learning outcomes ... must primarily identify changes necessary in individual behaviour'. This ascribes a rather sinister view of the relationship between the state and the individual.

Lord Palmerston would have been amazed at this never-ending, searching restlessness. When asked after his victory in the 1859 General Election what the new government's legislative programme was, he replied, "None. We cannot go on legislating forever."

Almost every self-respecting modern politician would profoundly disagree. Not to legislate, not to be constantly looking for new excuses for interfering in peoples' lives, would deny a politician his or her reason for existence. We are all under the lash of the state. By its nature, it is an attempt to impose the collective will upon the individual; a transgression into the private realm that violates the sense of self and degrades our ability to achieve self-realisation.

We live in a state that spends record amounts on defence yet we are insecure. We spend vast amounts on social security yet all it does is perpetuate poverty. Police numbers are at an all time high but crime is out of control. Every year the National Health Service consumes record amounts of our national wealth yet we become less healthy. It is increasingly apparent that the state creates rather than solves problems.

In general, the Pioneers accepted Thomas Jefferson's maxim: 'That which governs best, governs least.' A few would have taken it further and accepted the Henry Thoreau view: 'That which governs best, governs not at all.'

Theirs was a pessimism about the role of the state borne out of bitter experience. Yet there was also a contradictory expectation that the state had a moral duty to provide for its citizens. Hence the overwhelming commitment of the Pioneers to the National Health Service as an emblem of working class emancipation that had been made possible by the man who, for many of them, was a hero; the embodiment of campaigning decency in a grubby world – Nye Bevan.

With its principles of equality of access and free at the point of use, the NHS was a central pillar of the vision for the creation of a more just society. It is an emblem of our way of life and a commitment to social justice that is as much a part of the British birthright as bitter beer and discussing the weather. Even Mrs Thatcher was forced to say through gritted teeth in the 1980s, that: "The National Health Service is safe in our hands." At the time, very few of us were convinced she really meant it.

The Pioneers were the living embodiment of the historian R.H. Tawney's dictum that 'the British Labour Party owes more to Methodism than to Marx'. If we, for the moment, remove the words 'British Labour Party' from the equation and substitute the words 'British left' then a more accurate summary of the contribution of non-conformity to British socialism becomes apparent.

The Pioneers were no exception to this principle. Some, I suppose, were militant atheists, and at least one was a Roman Catholic. A few like my father were low Church of England and in doctrinal terms indistinguishable from most forms of dissent. There was one Quaker, George Roberts, a man I came to know well, and a significant group – a solid phalanx of maybe a dozen families – who were Methodists. They worshipped at the Unity Methodist Chapel in Pitsea at the eastern end of the town.

Why was there a preponderance of Methodists when I can recall no other branches of non-conformity – Unitarians, Congregationalists, Baptists or Christadelphians – being present in any serious numbers? The answer, I suspect, as with most things, lies in history. The English working class retain a powerful residual memory and, on the whole, the Church of England is not remembered with fondness. Memories of the clerical magistrates, the foxhunting parsons, and vicars vying as the social equal of the squire and factory owner, clung on well into the second half of the twentieth century.

For every socialist vicar like Stewart Headlam in Bethnal Green, there were dozens of clergy insisting that the poor sit in the hard pews at the back of the church to make way for the quality folk at the front. All that business about the poor and the meek inheriting the earth was theoretical as far as many of them were concerned. Only in the last forty or so years has the Anglican Church decided it is the conscience of the nation and that this might involve it in upsetting the politicians.

The urban working class had little time for the hierarchy and formalism of the Church of England, and even less time for the arcane notion of predestination and mediation by a privileged clergy. Methodism, when it emerged in the eighteenth century, filled the void – particularly in the urban areas – that was left by the failure of the established church. The result was that in London, where most of the Pioneers came from, those who had religious faith tended to come from a Methodist dissenting tradition. They were attracted by the Arminian view, strong within Methodism, that we give precedence to free will without contradicting God's authority.

The Pioneers believed that on earth, given the right environment and good fellowship, each of us is capable of realising our full potential without the interference of external authorities.

Methodists rejected the idea of a hierarchical church in favour of the notion that each individual can make their own path to heaven irrespective of what the fox-hunting parson said or did.

One old man who I remember very clearly, Ron Duckton, had worked as a farm labourer for more than fifty years and had lived in the area long before the new town was built. Retirement did not come easy to him and he worked as a groundsman at Gloucester Park until he was nearly eighty. I was employed there during one of the long summer breaks.

Ron worshipped at the Primitive Methodist Chapel at Nevendon, a construction made from timber and corrugated iron with the legend 'The Word Is Life' emblazoned across the front. Many years later when I read in *Cold Comfort Farm* the descriptions of the Quivering Brethren, I was reminded of Ron and that irritating brand of biblical fundamentalism that preys upon the minds of the poorly educated.

Despite my affection for the Pioneers, I have always found something disquieting about the endless splintering that Protestantism is prone to. I am very relaxed about Quakers, Catholics, Unitarians and High

Anglicans. I can just about cope with Congregationalists, Presbyterians and those low Church of England types and on a good day I will even tolerate Baptists and Methodists. The Plymouth Brethren are off the scale with their holy self-righteous exclusivity. I am though wary of those who too obviously flaunt their religious credentials.

I think it started in 1978 when I was teaching on a supply basis at a comprehensive school, now demolished, in North West London. My suspicions were aroused when the headmaster, having told me my duties, pronounced 'God be with you' before I went off to meet my first class. It was a kind gesture but it was also an un-English thing to do, an act of suspicious piety. A few weeks later I arrived one Monday morning to be ushered into the staff room by a besuited flunky from the education office. The rest of the staff were sitting quietly while, at the front, waiting glumly, the Director of Education, looking like a down-at-heel funeral director announced that the headmaster of the school, who was also a Methodist lay preacher, had been arrested and charged with indecently assaulting a number of young boys. He was an 'Oxford' man to boot which all goes to show you never can tell.

The offences had not taken place in school but had occurred when he was exercising his Methodist authority from his home in Rickmansworth. The curious thing was how many staff claimed to know of his unpleasant predilections from the way he behaved with children at school. This raised the awkward question about why they did not make their concerns apparent before the police were involved.

The headmaster was sentenced to four years in prison.

Chapter 11: Politicians are not what they used to be

Democracy is the rule of the politician.
Joseph Schumpeter.

A good politician is quite as unthinkable as an honest
burglar.
H.L. Mencken.

Having observed Harold Macmillan working the crowd in his grand
paternalistic style during a visit to Basildon, I could not help but contrast
his masterly performance with that of Michael Portillo, with whom I had
lunch thirty-five years later. I knew within ten minutes that Portillo
would never be leader of the Conservative Party let alone Prime
Minister. Consumed by the flame of ambition, he had no interest in those
around him because he felt they could not advance his cause. Any
attempts at small talk were curtly deflected. A golden rule in politics is
that you have to at least pretend you have an interest in the lives of those
who you claim you wish to serve. At that, Macmillan was a master.

It is difficult to be perfect all the time and it is not a skill that can be
taught at Central Office. Portillo's nemesis came on that hallowed
evening in May 1997 when he lost the safe Tory seat of Enfield
Southgate to Stephen Twigg, the Labour minister for schools who does
possess this gift.

The parents of a friend, both life-long Conservative voters, were
touched that Mr Twigg had come round to see them because they had a
problem with their housing benefit. "He really cared about our problem,"
the mother told me before proclaiming her intention to break the habit of
a lifetime and vote Labour in 2001.

It is nice to know that occasionally in politics an individual can make a
difference to the lives of ordinary people. I recently met Stephen Twigg
in the briefest of circumstances. Although our paths had crossed briefly a
year before, he treated me as an old friend and I surprised myself by
finding that I believed him. I actually felt good about myself that this

important man remembered me, or at least gave a very good impression that he did.

"Hello," he said as he pumped my hand. "Good to see you, Magnus."

He has that ability to make you feel that you are an important person in his life until he moves out of sight and the searchlight moves on to the next person. His other strength is that he has the ability to talk to young people in a way that neither patronises nor condescends. In fact, the man is in danger of giving politicians a good name.

In contrast, Michael Portillo was almost contemptuous of the questions the sixth formers put to him during the last dog days of the old apartheid regime in South Africa. Inevitably, many of the questions were on British policy. As we walked away, Mr Portillo turned and asked me, "Why are all sixth formers so obsessed with South Africa?"

"Because they have an interest in social justice?" I tentatively suggested.

Before the conversation could develop further, he slipped into the black official car and was whisked away in the direction of Southgate.

Mr Twigg, despite his ministerial status, had no official car. Instead, I walked with him to the bus stop where he waited for a W6 to take him the three miles to his Southgate constituency. I also noticed he was carrying a small parcel of foil-wrapped homemade sandwiches. There was something appealingly humble about this and I do hope he does not become corrupted by the political machine.

*

It is an indisputable fact that I have been slighted, ignored and overlooked by some of the most famous politicians of the last forty years. An exception to this was R.A. Butler or, as I knew him, Lord Butler of Saffron Walden. He was the epitome of decent, broad-minded Conservatism, which was probably the main reason why he never became leader of the party despite his seniority and outstanding political abilities.

Having created the modern system of state education, courtesy of the 1944 Education Act, Butler became an outstanding Chancellor of the Exchequer in the 1950s but he failed to become Prime Minister after the resignation of Anthony Eden in 1957. Passed over in preference to Harold Macmillan, he was overlooked again in 1963 when Macmillan resigned. This time he lost out to the aristocratic Alec Douglas-Home who was the last proper toff to be prime minister.

Contemporaries and historians still argue about what exactly happened in those days before the Conservatives did anything as vulgar as electing their leader.

My friend Raymond's uncle was a gamekeeper on an estate in Finchingfield in North Essex, close to Saffron Walden. One of his duties was to organise the summer partridge shoots. I was sometimes invited up to act as a beater for the shoots over which Lord Butler genially presided. These were the days when the aristocracy were quite uninhibited about flaunting their privileges. This bevy of inbred rural Conservatives were so upper-class they seemed to be deformed. When they spoke, the whinnying sound was quite unintelligible.

Lord Butler was a benign presence who would speak to everybody, me included. He was what my university friend's grandmother would call 'a proper gent'; someone she could look up to and respect. She hated being represented by a Labour MP, someone who was no better than she was. It was contrary to the natural order of things.

Her MP in Bethnal Green was Peter Shore who, she conceded, was not the average trade union loudmouth and was, in fact, 'a bit of a gent' which made it all the more puzzling that he should be representing Labour. Given that the most famous residents of her Bethnal Green constituency were the Kray Twins, or at least their mother who they would visit for homely cups of tea, she was lucky neither Ronnie nor Reggie was her MP. Their popularity in the 1960s East End meant they would have strolled in to Parliament whatever party they chose to represent.

Perhaps it is a sign of the changing times that, in the 1880s, the most powerful moral influence in Bethnal Green was Stuart Headlam and his socialist church, the Guild of St Matthew, while by the 1960s the most powerful influence was the Kray Twins and their criminal friends.

In 1995 and then again in 2000, I stood in Bethnal Green Road and watched as the funeral cortège of first Ronnie and then Reggie was hauled towards St Matthew's church by six black-plumed horses. In death, as in life, they performed with some style. Followed by twenty-six stretch limos, cameras, television crews, and with a police helicopter hovering overhead, it would have been understandable if the innocent bystander had thought the Queen Mother was on her way out.

It was the East End equivalent of a state funeral. The crowds were solemn and reflective and, it struck me, elderly. This was the East End as it used to be – white, tight knit and hard faced. I spoke to several people and they had nothing but good words to say about Ronnie and Reggie as the embodiment of the East End as a community. Their past indiscretions were overlooked as being the actions of decently-minded professional criminals who only murdered their own kind when they asked for it.

Go to the York Hall in Bethnal Green on a boxing night and it is possible to find East Enders who claim that they knew Ronnie and Reggie personally. They will tell you that they were 'diamond geezers' who looked after their mum and made the streets safe. I suspect it is all just a fantasy. What about the mothers of George Cornell and Jack 'the hat' McVitie, both brutally murdered by the Krays?

Standing at the back of the crowd at the funeral, I asked some of the more elderly people who looked as though they might be capable of giving me a civil answer, if they lived locally. They smiled when I told them that my great grandfather had been married at St Matthews.

The answer in all cases was 'no'. It was far too dangerous, they said. And it was not what it was before – all now bought up by yuppies. In some cases there was open resentment of the Asian community who, in their view, were 'taking over'. These ex-East Enders now lived in Cheshunt, Waltham Cross and Goff's Oak.

One couple had come down from their retirement home in Clacton for the day, but they told me they would not be staying; it was dirty and their cat would need feeding.

It is appropriate that both Ronnie and Reggie ended up at Chingford Mount Cemetery as this north London suburb on the edge of Epping Forest has proved, during the past sixty years, to be a popular first staging post on the north east passage for those families wishing to escape the East End of London.

The graves are surprisingly low key amidst the dereliction of the cemetery. Ronnie and Reggie lie together under a black granite slab a few feet away from older brother, Charlie, and next to their beloved mother, Violet. It is a quiet and calm final resting place that contrasts with the criminality and reckless violence of their lives. Someone has left a small bouquet of fresh flowers on the grave of Reggie and Ronnie.

*

At the end of the shoot at Finchingfield, Lord Butler would come round and personally give a green pound note to the men beaters and a red ten shilling note to boys like me who had assisted. For each of the men he had a cheery word and for the boys a pat on the head.

Forty years ago, the Conservative Party knew how to behave. Since then it has lost its way and, to use a very British phrase, it has ceased to be a party of estate owners and has become a party of estate agents. The Conservatives are not what they used to be. They are now dominated by men who, in Michael Jopling's wonderfully snobbish phrase, have had to buy their own furniture.

During the 1983 General Election campaign, I was standing in Wood Green, North London, with a group from the Socialist Workers Party. Their mole in Conservative Central office had told them Michael Heseltine was visiting for a photo opportunity. As the gleaming Jaguar rolled to a halt at the kerbside, Heseltine leapt out with an excess of athleticism for a man in his fifties, and was greeted with a chant of "Tory Scum!"

Despite the fact I was not chanting, his gaze fixed on me. For a moment I froze. With his blond hair and blue eyes, I instantly thought of Reinhard Heydrich, the Nazi overlord, the 'Blond Butcher' whose death precipitated the destruction of the Czech town of Lidice and all its inhabitants. I am sure Michael Heseltine is a perfectly decent man in his own way but, for that moment, he was striding along in a Blackshirt uniform looking for all the world like the embodiment of the Teutonic Aryan ideal. An unpleasant element seems to have crept into the Conservative party since the days of Macmillan and Butler – or was it always there, hidden behind the scenery?

On another occasion, my friend from the SWP had been reassured that the chances of stumbling across opportunities for casual sex were better with the hard left than with any other part of the political spectrum. Sadly, for him, this was not to prove the case. I suppose the exception to this is the right wing of the Conservative Party but as far as I am aware he is not a homosexual.

This time we were waiting in Chingford for that 'semi-housetrained polecat' Norman Tebbit to arrive for a constituency meeting. As he emerged from the ministerial Rover 800, the cry of "Tory Scum" went up once again.

Tebbit turned to look at us. It was like being surveyed by someone from beyond the grave. Have you ever noticed how dark and dead his eyes are? He turned to move on while one of his minders snarled, "You're just a bunch of faggots, poofs and lesbians." Now, while, with one or two exceptions this was true, is it any way to talk to constituents?

Harold Macmillan would have made a joke of it and patted us on the head and we would probably have felt a bit better about the world.

But politics is not what it used to be. We do not admire politicians any more. In fact, quite the reverse is true.

When did we have a political leader who could uplift and inspire us in the belief that they were better than us and could make a difference to our lives? We have lost that sense of politicians as 'moral leaders' but then perhaps we should never have had it in the first place. The idea that a party leader, or a Prime Minister, can stir us today in the way that William Gladstone did in the nineteenth century when he launched his Midlothian Campaign, seems to be quite laughable. We elect politicians in the hope that they will govern us competently when, in an ideal world, we would elect them to provide inspiration in our lives.

My father became excited when Labour narrowly won the General Election of 1964. "You wait," he said, "you'll see some changes now."

Sadly the changes – devaluation of the pound, a prices and incomes policy that tried to cap the wages of ordinary workers, and attempts to limit the powers of trade unions – were not the ones he expected.

The only politicians who ever met with the Pioneers' express approval were Stafford Cripps and Aneurin Bevan. Cripps died in the year that I was born but I occasionally heard of him referred to in approving terms on the grounds that any socialist expelled from the Labour Party must have had something about him. His sheer moral superiority and eccentric, ascetic, vegetarian, teetotal principles so distanced him from conventional politicians that he was able to exercise a curious fascination over a section of the British public unused to the idea of living on carrot juice and nuts.

Nye Bevan, the driving force behind the National Health Service, was an inspirational figure because the Pioneers had been the first generation to benefit from its creation. One Pioneer told me how, when his mother was very ill in the 1940s, his father struggled to pay the cost of treatment. As the years passed, his mother became more and more ill, and his father became poorer and poorer until, finally, his mother died and his father's business went bankrupt.

"Now with Nye in charge," he said, tears welling in his eyes, "no one will ever suffer again like my poor old father."

Apart from the appeal of The Lady to those red-meat, extra-chromosome Conservatives, who is there now to inspire us among the dreary functionaries, apparatchiks and factotums of contemporary politics? I can think of only one figure who is prepared to show us, in a clear and unequivocal fashion, that the duty of politicians is to improve the lives of the people they represent. Unfortunately he is approaching his eightieth year and predictably is reviled and mocked, and occasionally patronised, by the pygmies of the Labour establishment.

Tony Benn is an extraordinary figure, a throwback to the ethical socialist tradition of the early labour movement. When he was Viscount Stansgate he campaigned, successfully, to be allowed to throw off his hereditary title. He then became a cabinet minister in the 1960s and embarked on an odyssey of self-discovery that is the complete reverse of the normal trend.

For most of us, the passage of the years leads us from Guardian-reading youth to Daily Telegraph-reading decrepitude. For Tony Benn this has not been the case.

As a rather posh sounding Anthony Wedgwood Benn, he was the acceptable face of Labour radicalism in the 1960s who gave us the Telecom Tower as his contribution to Harold Wilson's technological revolution. As the far more proletarian-sounding Tony Benn, he has been the standard bearer for decent humane left-wing socialism for the last twenty years.

My heart gladdened when I read that in 1992 he introduced a bill into the House of Commons to create a socialist commonwealth and replace the Queen with a president elected by MPs. Not surprisingly, this rather contentious measure failed to engage the house and it never came to a vote.

Contrast this with his extreme nervousness in 1964 when, as Postmaster General, he very tentatively suggested to the Queen the possibility that her head might not appear on some stamps. Such an outrageous suggestion was, of course, crushed by those who saw it as the first step on the road to the Royal family riding in a tumbril towards the guillotine.

I have seen him speak a number of times and I am always stunned at the affection, indeed the adulation that he inspires amongst young people. I saw him during the 1983 election campaign speaking in a packed school hall in Southgate, North London. That mere fact makes him sound very dated. The idea that a major politician would speak to an audience of less than a thousand people without the prospect for photo opportunities and sound bites is alien to modern politics. Gone are the days of Quentin Hogg rounding on hecklers unconcerned as to whether it would make a good sound bite for the evening news. I saw him at Lancaster in the February 1974 election. A section of the audience were chanting, 'Hoggy, Hoggy, Hoggy, Out, Out, Out.' His response to a question that the Heath government had deliberately provoked a confrontation with the miners was: 'Shut up, you moron.' Politics and in particular general elections have become stupendously dull. All that we now remember of the 2001 General Election is John Prescott in Rhyll practising his left hook on an egg throwing demonstrator and Tony Blair being berated by the partner of a cancer sufferer while visiting a hospital in Nottingham. The rest is a dreary tedium.

In contrast Tony Benn held the audience entranced as he sketched out his vision of milk and honey socialism in the journey to the Promised Land. At the end of the meeting, a group of young people climbed onto the stage. While some engaged him in conversation, most were content to touch or stroke the sleeve of his jacket in an almost religious state as if they imagined themselves to be touching the hem of his garment. They wanted to be able to tell their grandchildren, 'I touched the great man.' It was a wonderful sight for an old cynic like myself for it reaffirmed that one person can make such a difference to peoples' lives and the way they see themselves.

During the 1970 General Election campaign, I went with a few of the older Pioneers to hear him speak in Basildon. The day is very clear in my mind. I sat my last A-level exam, listened on the radio to England being beaten by Brazil in the Mexico World Cup, dozed in the sun and then went and saw Tony Benn.

Not all were impressed. Old Alf Finch regretted the lack of socialism by example. "That bloody Wedgie Benn. He's one of them aristocrats pretending that he's not. He's got a bloody country estate up near Maldon with servants and all."

In essence it was all true. Benn's father, a Labour Cabinet Minister in the 1920s, had been made a hereditary peer so he was not quite aristocracy but it was close enough for any full-blooded socialist. Anthony Benn had been a reluctant Viscount Stansgate before sloughing off the unwanted peerage. But for the death of his elder brother during the war, the title would have passed him by.

There is a rather grand family home near Maldon on the banks of the River Blackwater complete with a walled estate. I imagine there is at least a housekeeper or a gardener. What Alf didn't mention was the grand family home in fashionable and eye-wateringly expensive Holland Park, West London, worth, in today's inflated property market, many millions of pounds.

But does it all matter? Do our socialist leaders need to wear a hair shirt, take a vow of poverty, and live in a trailer park before we can take them seriously? Is it any of our business? The man is not a billionaire plutocrat with mansions dotted around the world. He is simply in the position of having inherited wealth and, through his abilities, has earned a considerable sum of money over the years. He is not a saintly, impoverished George Lansbury type but then he never set out to be.

What should he do with his wealth? Give it to charity? Donate it to the Labour Party? Turn Stansgate into a centre for asylum seekers? He would then be accused of engaging in cheap gesture politics. As Mr Benn has discovered, it is a hard business casting aside privilege, particularly if you number Josiah Wedgwood and Charles Darwin amongst your ancestors.

We have had four generations of Benns (with and without the 'Wedgwood') in the House of Commons. The last three served at cabinet level. I have tried to calculate the chances of this happening in a random way. My calculator could not cope with the figures but it is many billions to one.

Obviously the inheritance of privilege had something to do with it but Mr Benn did throw over his peerage and sent his children to Holland Park Comprehensive School. Then, I'll be damned, his eldest son, Hilary, became a cabinet minister. That's life I suppose.

It is a difficult issue but, having thought about these matters on and off for the past thirty-three years, I am not sure that Alf Finch had much of a point.

I do find it odd that I have thought about Tony Benn periodically ever since 1964 when he revolutionised my stamp collection by introducing the modern style of commemorative stamps, and yet he has never even heard of me.

In fact, for some odd reason, I find that he is never that far from my thoughts. He now lives as a Roman-style tribune, the champion of the poor and the disadvantaged, a politician who is prepared to make the sharp moral distinction between right and wrong. He has become the universal representative for all of those who feel disengaged from society and unrepresented.

A steady stream of a thousand letters a week is a standing reproach to both the failures of our political class and our system of representative democracy. Benn also engages in what the radical historian Raphael Samuelson calls 'ancestor worship'. In order to strengthen his case, he refers to the heroic figures in British labour history and the campaign for democratic and civil liberties. John Lilburne, Wat Tyler, Thomas Hardy, John Wycliffe and Keir Hardie may all be used at a moment's notice to buttress his case based upon a heroic view of the past.

As an added bonus, Tony Benn is the man who gave us Concorde when the 'suits' at the Treasury were trying to pull the plug on the project. I went to see him speaking at East Finchley where, to my surprise, the meeting was sold out. It took all the cunning of my fifty years to sneak in through a side entrance. There still exists a hunger among people to be told what is right in the world and how to achieve it.

Sixty years earlier, his great moral predecessor, George Lansbury, had the same effect as men and women gathered round to stroke his coat and place their hand upon his shoulder, motivated by a combination of awe and affection. There is a sense in which Benn and Lansbury are the template of how politicians should be; towering in their integrity, modest in their accomplishments, inspiring in their passion and, above all, identifying with the needs of ordinary people.

It is difficult to think of any political figure in the past forty years who fits this description. Perhaps it is a feature of the development of society and democracy in the first half of the twentieth century that it threw up the likes of Bevan, Cripps, Lansbury and Benn.

We have now entered a new age in which administrative skill and political acceptability is more important than moral inspiration. Hence, even on the other side of the divide, there are no figures to compare with Enoch Powell, Alan Clark, Keith Joseph and, of course, The Lady herself. At least she had a vision even if it was one that not everyone was in agreement with.

It is likely the selection process for choosing prospective MPs for both main parties eliminates potentially interesting maverick candidates. The temptation to select a dull but worthy candidate who will be approved by central office means that the backbenches are full of very bland men and women who will only be remembered by their families when they retire or lose the next election.

What has happened to the likes of Gerald Nabarro, Julian Amery, Waldron Smithers, Robert Boothby and Anthony Meyer? Is it of any significance that by far the two most interesting MPs in the massed ranks of the New Model Labour Party are the distinctly elderly mavericks – Dennis Skinner and Tam Dalyell? If we needed just one example of what we are missing, the late Sir John Stokes was ideal. He was a man who enlivened our lives with his bizarre, and at times repellent, views. To quote from his obituary: "He saw a Britain rife with fornication and homosexuality, and peopled with drug addicts, drunken divorcees, foul-mouthed alcoholics and priests with beards."

Stokes identified the 1970s as a particularly damaging decade epitomised by what seemed to be endless rounds of industrial discontent and strike action at British Leyland. His solution was both novel and disarming: the shooting of a few strike ringleaders, 'Petain-style'.

This was a man who, when the Jewish Leon Brittan was Secretary of State at Trade and Industry, suggested he should be replaced by a 'red-blooded, red-faced Englishman, preferably from the landed interests'. Perhaps his finest moment came when he predicted the acquittal of Clive Ponting, charged with breaches of the Official Secrets Act concerning the sinking of the Belgrano, on the grounds that 'some of the jurors were not wearing ties'.

It is easy to poke fun at such an eccentric figure or to take sour-faced offence at some of his less than politically correct views but that is to miss the point. Stokes became the embodiment of the diversity of views that are now missing from our political ruling class. We do not have to agree with Stokes in order to be able to enjoy him.

It is equally acceptable for a left-wing labour eccentric like Tam Dalyell to pronounce views of a similar degree of eccentricity on the ground that they entertain and break us out of the mould of sourpuss politics dominated by a personality cult of the mundane. Did you know, for example, that Tony Blair is surrounded by and under the influence of a Jewish cabal? Provided we do not take such froth too seriously it does little harm and adds to the increasingly small stock of life's harmless (or fairly harmless) pleasures.

It may be seen as a point of some significance that the mavericks on the right of British politics have, on the whole, been reprehensible but entertaining characters.

F.E. Smith, later the Earl of Birkenhead, was between 1906 and his death in 1930 an equal part of the dynamic triumvirate that included Lloyd George and Winston Churchill. He was a brilliant, instinctive politician endowed with a razor-sharp wit and a powerful legal mind who in 1919 became the youngest Lord Chancellor for two hundred years. FE, as he was known to his friends, and Winston Churchill stood out as exotic birds of paradise amongst the dowdy house sparrows of the 1920s' Conservative Party. Smith's weakness was what the *Dictionary of National Biography* rather coyly called 'a fondness for gaiety'. In short he drank himself into an early grave while pursuing a grand lifestyle, running up huge debts, being blackmailed by the notorious Maundy Gregory and pursuing, with great success, his daughter's twenty six year old friend. He even paid a younger man to marry her in order to provide cover for their affair. He died of cirrhosis of the liver at the age of 58.

Enoch Powell continues to intrigue. Having become the youngest professor in the British Empire after the war, he carved out a reputation as the cleverest man in the House of Commons and a monetarist before Mrs Thatcher. All that promise was brought to an end by his spectacular act of self-immolation in 1968. The contrary nature of the man was illustrated by his advice to Conservative supporters in 1974 to vote Labour in the coming general election on the grounds that Labour was committed to pulling Britain out of Europe. Perhaps this was not so surprising. Although he was one of the half dozen most important and influential British politicians of the second half of the twentieth century, his greatest wish was that he had died in combat during the Second World War.

Alan Clark was a highly-respected military historian who, when he entered politics became, or rather continued to be, a serial philanderer with dubious views on race and the working classes. During the 1998 World Cup in France he praised the very violent English football supporters who had been chanting 'I'd rather be Paki than a Turk' in anticipation of the England/Turkey game. He complimented them as 'a splendid example of the English martial spirit'. On the other hand, he was very kind to animals and a very unlikely vegetarian in a party that enjoys red meat. It was always somehow inevitable that he would be more remembered for his brilliant and witty diaries than for any political achievements.

These three Tory mavericks may have been heavyweight intellectuals but it is difficult to argue that they had the moral authority of what some might see as their left-wing equivalents – George Lansbury, Stafford Cripps and Tony Benn.

I recently attended a speech by Tony Blair. It was dull but competent. He spoke about Private Finance Initiative and the need for war with Iraq. At best, he was rewarded with tepid applause from the audience but he was completely lacking in what George Bush Senior once termed 'the vision thing'.

Having been uninspired, I reflected on where the charismatic and brilliant politicians had gone. Even looking back to the Labour government of the 1960s, no more than a generation and a half ago, it is like watching a brilliantly-gifted Brazilian football side up against England at their worst. Harold Wilson was a wily midfield captain; Michael Foot and Tony Benn proved a solid left side to the defence with Anthony Crosland and Jim Callaghan shoring up the right hand side while Roy Jenkins was an effective stopper at centre half. Dennis Healey was a useful, if not quite Premier League, goalkeeper while Dick Crossman and Barbara Castle were always a threat up front even if they refused to pass the ball to each other. George Brown would be one of those stridently abusive defenders always shouting at the goalkeeper, fortifying himself with brandy at half-time, and throwing a tantrum on being substituted. I am afraid the only role I could find for Shirley Williams would be distributing the half-time oranges.

Given the wealth of talent it is difficult to understand why they failed to win any silverware. But who in the present cabinet would get into the line up?

I suppose Tony Blair might get in as a versatile sweeper type and Gordon Brown would be one of those big old-fashioned centre forwards (Nat Lofthouse or Bobby Smith perhaps) who would bulldoze his way towards goal, flattening defenders en-route. Straw, Blunkett, Darling and Hewitt would not make it to the substitutes bench. Being charitable I might let Margaret Beckett bring on the half-time oranges and a case could be made that Claire Short would be a useful, pugnacious and fiery left-sided midfielder although it is very doubtful that she would last the full ninety minutes. Peter Hain would be one of those eccentric but skilful midfielders whom the English game mistrusts. And I can imagine Charles Clarke as a big burly fullback in the traditional mould rising up to head the old style brown leather football on a wet and gloomy November afternoon, with the lace mark glowing red on his forehead.

*

Less than seven hundred thousand of us in a population of sixty million are members of a political party and most of us are profoundly ignorant of the political process to the extent that a micro-celebrity in a poorly-written soap opera is better known than virtually all of the cabinet. Our worst failure, however, is that we have allowed politicians to become a separate caste who have become immune to the scorn and ridicule heaped upon them. This has been compounded by a sense of powerlessness in which we shrug our shoulders and effectively admit 'That's the way it is, what can we do about it?'

In any properly empowered civic society, ordinary people would demand accountability. The proper response to the various Labour and Conservative scandals of the 1990s should have been direct action by constituents outraged at the breach of trust by those they sent to the Palace of Westminster to represent them. It is a pleasant thought to imagine a crowd of militant constituents marching into the Commons, scragging their unworthy MP and publicly debagging him before placing him in a pillory outside, let us say, the Queen Elizabeth Conference Centre where the public could heap abuse and worse on him. I say 'him' without hesitation. Although women comprise twenty per cent of all MPs, I cannot think of a scandal worthy of the name that involved women even though Edwina Currie has done her best to create one.

There is no easy solution to the problem of politicians becoming a separate caste. We are told that politicians in Sweden, that bastion of liberal democracy, do not have bodyguards, that they use public transport and can be seen pushing trolleys around supermarkets. Anna Lindh, the Foreign Minister, was often seen sitting on the floor of a packed commuter train reading papers of state while travelling out to the Stockholm suburbs. We applaud the principle because there is something slightly nauseating about seeing government ministers being ferried around in government limousines at the taxpayers' expense.

Unfortunately, the reality is that Anna Lindh was stabbed to death in a Stockholm department store while Jack Straw remains safe in his ministerial Jaguar. In 1986, Olaf Palme, the Swedish Prime Minister was gunned down while walking through the streets of Stockholm without a bodyguard. In 2002 the right-wing Dutch politician Pim Fortuyn was murdered in a car park in the city of Hilversum while without the protection of bodyguards.

America adopts the opposite principle. When George Bush came to visit Tony Blair he was protected at any one time by 5,500 police officers. While visiting the Prime Minister's Sedgefield constituency, 800 police officers ensured there were no unpleasant surprises during Mr Bush's visit to the local pub for a pint of alcohol-free lager. There is no such thing as a free lunch. There is always a price to be paid.

The consequence of politicians' failure is that voters either sit at home watching television or they divert their political animus into other channels. This may take the form of voting for the BNP in Burnley or, more healthily, it takes the form of an anti-establishment, populist, Poujadist disdain for the established political system.

We see this clearly in the case of the Angry Cobbler of Durham, a cause célèbre that has erupted in the corrupt and venal Labour barony of the North East. This is the land of the one party state, the embodiment of Acton's aphorism that 'power corrupts and absolute power corrupts absolutely'.

Anyone with a memory of the 1970s and the corruption trials of T.Dan Smith and John Poulson that exposed the mire of Labour politics in the North East will have some understanding of the current situation.

The problems began in 1998 when the Labour council on 'safety grounds' painted double-yellow lines outside the 150-year-old city centre cobblers business owned by Tony Martin. This troublesome individual is not to be confused with that other Tony Martin, hero of the popular press, who did to burglars what this Tony Martin would like to do to the members of Durham Council.

Mr Martin claims the yellow lines were painted for political reasons – to steer customers towards the council-owned Prince Bishops shopping centre. For the past five years, he has exacted his protracted revenge by waging a populist campaign against the council. The front window of the Angry Cobbler's shop has become a Beijing-style political notice-board highlighting the corruption, racism and venality of various council officials and councillors.

I have visited Mr Martin's several times and can testify to both the popularity of his window display and its entertainment value. I was particularly impressed by the solicitor's letters that take pride of place in the display, threatening him (using public money of course) with legal action as he exposes what is effectively a Tammany Hall on the River Wear. His scatter gun technique means that even the Liberal Democrat leader is a subject of his venom although a petition in the corner of the window demanding a referendum on a European constitution gives an insight into the right-wing populism of his politics.

Accompanying my brother, as he dropped a pair of shoes in to be repaired, Mr Martin informed us that he had run out of soles. Perhaps this political campaigning business is going to this head though he was prepared to sell us a copy of his book, unoriginally entitled, *Cobblers To The Council*.

However, his one-man campaign is producing results. A senior council official has been arrested by the fraud squad, the council's recreations services chief has been dismissed after the discovery of a video showing him having sex with four different women, and various councillors have now been suspended as a result of dubious land deals.

Outside Mr Martin's shop in Claypath, I asked various onlookers two simple questions: "Do you admire Mr Martin?" and "Do you vote in local council elections?" The answers were unanimously, with one exception to the latter question, 'Yes' and 'No'. Clearly, the Angry Cobbler has punctured a vein of dissatisfaction with the political system that says little for conventional politicians.

There is a second example of what we might term 'outsider politics from the North East'. In 1996, Detective Superintendent Ray Mallon, head of the Middlesbrough CID, was dubbed Robocop by the press for promoting an American-style policy of Zero Tolerance. He promised to resign if crime in his 'patch' did not fall by 20 per cent over 18 months. DS Mallon achieved his objective but found himself suspended and then finally forced into resignation because of the alleged irregularities in his policing methods. Defenders of Robocop argue that he was undermined by the resentful jealousy of his superiors: his detractors argue that he turned a blind eye to corrupt and unlawful practices within his squad.

There is something hopeless about the police. My motorcycle was stolen from outside my house. A week later I received six identical letters from the police all offering me counselling and asking if I 'want to join a victim support group'. There was no mention of recovering my property or apprehending the criminals.

Six months later the same motorcycle was stolen again. The following week I was walking my dogs in the local woods when I saw a boy aged about sixteen riding it along a bridleway. I challenged him and informed him politely that I was going to apprehend him, rather pompously announcing that he was under citizen's arrest.

I held the young man lightly by the arm at which point he burst into tears shouting that it was 'not ******* fair.' I then called the police and informed them I had found my bike and caught the thief.

After ten minutes, my young criminal had gathered himself sufficiently to realise I could not hold him and broke away from my grip. He ran into the woods shouting that I was a '******* ****' and that he would '******* do me'.

The reality was that I was so apprehensive about the possibility of ending up in court, having used what might be deemed as excessive force, that I felt obliged to let the young felon go. In any properly morally-ordered society, of course, I should have been free to set my dogs on him and then run him over several times with my motorcycle.

An hour and a half later the police had still not materialised so I resignedly pushed the bike home in the darkness followed by two disconsolate dogs. As I was pushing the bike along Camlet Way, an expensive if rather plutocratically vulgar housing development to the west of Barnet, a large Toyota Land Cruiser pulled up beside me and a very attractive and expensively-groomed black woman asked if I needed assistance. Sitting next to her was a well known Arsenal footballer.

I immediately began recounting, in a semi-hysterical fashion, my incident in the woods. As I reached the bit about placing the youth under citizen's arrest she said abruptly, "I must go. I'm in a hurry." Then she sped off.

Three and a half hours after making my initial call to the police, I was reporting what had happened in the police station. The desk sergeant confirmed that my call was still 'live' and was waiting to be 'actioned'. Worthy of note is the fact that this occurred in the week before the Metropolitan Police deployed 5,000 officers to protect the President of another country who has never paid a penny in tax to Her Majesty.

In contrast, I pay many thousands of pounds each year in income tax and I endure successive increases in my council tax, part of which will go, I am told, to improving London policing. Yet I am not able to summon the assistance of a single police officer when I have apprehended a criminal in the course of committing a crime.

The police, unfortunately, are the victims of a culture. Symptomatic of this is their depressing habit of painting inane slogans on the side of patrol cars. The Royal Parks Police are 'Making the Parks Safe for Londoners'; The River Police are 'Making the River Thames Safe for Londoners'; the Metropolitan Police are 'Working For a Safer London'. What do we think they are doing? Making London a safe and fruitful environment for terrorists and rapists?

I would not have been surprised when I made my call for urgent assistance to be told, "Sorry, the officers are engaged in painting a new slogan on their patrol car. Do you need any counselling?"

The following day I rang the police station on a routine matter relating to the theft. I think I was put through to a call centre in Cambodia. I only wanted to give the VIN number of the bike.

"What do you consider your ethnic origin to be?"

"Nordic," I replied. I was tempted to say Aryan or Teutonic but I figured that was a bit risky.

It would appear that DS Mallon was a police officer cut from a different cloth. I am confident that, if I had phoned him after having grasped my felon in the woods, he would have been over right away, truncheon at the ready. The charges brought against him were not proven although he pleaded guilty to minor irregularities in order to be able to resign from the force.

He then stood for office as the first executive-style Mayor for Middlesbrough. He won, roundly beating the official Labour candidate. Clearly the people of Middlesbrough liked the high profile Mr Mallon. In contrast the voters in his previous 'patch' in Hartlepool, ten miles to the north, elected as their first executive mayor a monkey in the form of the football club's mascot.

Since his election, Mr Mallon's stock has risen although the price to be paid is a visible increase in the power of the state. His 70-strong force of community wardens, nicknamed 'Robocop's Army', aided by anti-social behaviour officers, drug action workers and rapid response squads, have contributed to reduce overall crime by 18 per cent in a year. Street offences and burglaries have been cut by 40 per cent. The month after being elected, he insisted that all expenses claims by councillors be backed up by receipts. The amount claimed fell by forty per cent.

A friend's parents, who live in Middlesbrough, complained recently about a refrigerator that had been dumped in the street at the end of their front path. It had been there for nearly a week when they made their complaint to Mr Mallon's department. An hour later, Mr Mallon, the highly-paid chief executive of Middlesbrough, appeared personally and helped to carry the fridge away. Politicians never do that sort of thing.

Anyone used to dealing with a traditional local authority will know that, several weeks after making numerous phone calls, two men in a van will eventually appear. They will stare at the offending object for ten minutes, grimace, purse their lips and will eventually drive off to have a cup of tea. About two weeks later, two more men will arrive and will place a sticker on the object with words to the effect of 'Council Aware'. Then the object will remain in the road for several more weeks before it is finally removed. If the 'removal' service has been contracted out, then it is safe to add several more weeks to this sequence.

Other Middlesbrough residents ringing to make a complaint have been surprised to find Mr Mallon himself answering the phone. Opinion appears to be divided over their new high-profile Mayor. Those who have suffered on the crime-ridden estates of Whinnybank and Grove Hill tend to think that he is marvellous. Those on the progressive side of politics who sleep soundly in their beds in Marton and Acklam disapprove of his authoritarian populism and fret at night about their civil liberties. They worry that they are rearing a low-rent Mussolini on the Tees.

The voters of Middlesbrough will know when Mr Mallon's administration is starting to fail. They will receive through their letterbox, as I do in the borough of Barnet, a glossy and expensive publication telling them how marvellously he is doing while the litter is blowing down the street.

I receive, courtesy of Ken Livingstone, Mayor of London, a *free* newspaper called 'The Londoner' parading Ken's achievements. I have two points to make on this matter. Firstly, the newspaper is not *free* – it has been paid for by the long-suffering London council taxpayers. Secondly, improvements and successes have to be self-evident otherwise they are not worth boasting about.

The moral of the experiences of the Angry Cobbler and Ray Mallon is that there is life outside the party system; that people can be re-engaged in the democratic political process but that there needs to be a willingness to defy convention. The problem is the style of politics. It is personal, it is populist, it hints at authoritarianism, and it threatens existing party structures.

Is it enough to say that people who were excluded from conventional politics now feel part of the process? The same question might be asked about the way Hitler mobilised apolitical Germans in the 1930s. To justify it on the grounds of civic involvement never seems quite reason enough.

It would be entirely wrong to say I am a big fan of my local authority, Barnet, despite the fact that they have been awarded 'Beacon status' – whatever that means.

My most recent experience concerned the subsidence in the road opposite my house. My neighbour and I made (between us) fifteen phone calls to the council over a four week period. Eventually a subcontractor's lorry turned up and demonstrated an innovative and interesting road mending technique. Without getting out of the lorry, a workman on the back shovelled tarmac from the flatbed into the hole. The lorry was then driven backwards and forwards over the tarmac leaving an ugly black lump in the road before driving off. Needless to say the hole reappeared a few weeks later. I can't help feeling that, had I lived in Middlesbrough, Mr Mallon himself would have been repairing the hole and doing it properly.

We occasionally need to remind ourselves about a subject (sometimes slightly-pompously) called social contract theory. Governments are formed as a result of receiving the consent of the people and each of us give up a small part of our liberty in order to be governed well. If government fails, then that consent is withdrawn and the government can be thrown out.

This rather Lockean view (after John Locke, the eighteenth century political theorist of liberalism) begins to fall down when we are faced with a lack of political choice. Given that all three main parties are now firmly camped in the middle ground of politics, it is not surprising people feel rendered powerless by the process.

*

I find myself interested in a detached way in the politics of the extremes. Whether it is of the left or the right these politicians occupy a different universe from those politicians who seek to represent us. I am particularly interested in those who are renegades from the Fourth International. They are worthy of analysis.

Founded in 1938 by Leon Trotsky, the Fourth International, possibly more than any other intellectual movement in history, generated massive amounts of energy for a negligible political impact. By the 1950s it was hopelessly divided. On one side were the Pabloists, (followers of Michel Pablo, 1911-96, leader of the Fourth International) who for Trotsky purists were hopeless apologists for Stalin, while on the other side were the followers of Ernest Mandel.

Mandel possessed, in abundance, that supreme characteristic of far left intellectuals: an impressively powerful intellect but no capacity to recognise that he was flogging a dead horse.

There has also been a tendency on the far left to write in a way that is absolutely meaningless to 99.9 per cent of the population. I quote from a recent essay by Terry Eagleton, the Marxist academic, Professor of Cultural Theory at the University of Manchester (whose salary is paid by the taxpayer) in the Bulletin of the Marx Memorial Library:

> "If the working class for Marxism has a special role, it's neither because it's especially miserable nor necessarily numerous but because it is, in the Freudian sense, 'symptomatic' – that which represents contradiction, that which like the boundary of a field, by being both in and out – 'ex time', as Jacques Lacan has it – manifests something of the dual; or contradictory logic of the system as a whole. If it's in some sense a 'totaliser' of that system, it's because it represents the contradictions of the regime as a whole, which is to say the way it escapes any harmonious totalisation."

Help!!

The general philosophy of the ideological left has been that it is better to be ideologically pure than to be politically effective. I have the distinction of having fallen asleep during a meeting organised by the Brighton Socialist Workers Party that Mandel was running at the University of Sussex in 1978. Worse, my snoring actually disrupted the meeting.

My excuse for attending was the carnal ambitions that I entertained towards the SWP's female membership secretary. I have no idea what excuse any other attendees may have had but I have to report I was sadly unsuccessful. I was though denounced as a 'contemptible bourgeois apologist' for my pains. I am not exactly sure why this was but I suspect it was either because of my snoring or because I suggested that a spot of carnal recreation might be more interesting than listening to Mr Mandel.

As a footnote, it is worth recording just how male-dominated the revolutionary far left has been. I have just finished reading Bill Hunter's *Life and Times of a Revolutionary*. A rough calculation indicates that, during the four hundred pages, he makes reference to about two thousand two hundred male names while making less than thirty female references. In the Trotskyist far left, it really is the role of women to make the tea and bring in the sandwiches. In that sense it is uncannily like the Sunday afternoon cricket side that I used to play for.

The only revolutionary Trotskyist figure I had any time for was the late Gerry Healy, the veteran leader of the Workers Revolutionary Party. In 1985 he forced himself upon the attention of the tabloid press through his sexual proclivities towards the younger female members of the party. They were informed it was their revolutionary duty to entertain (in a bed) their elderly leader as part of their initiation into Trotskyist theory.

For the News of the World it became a matter of 'Reds in the Bed' rather than 'Reds under the Bed'. As a left-wing journalist wryly remarked at the time, "History is made in the class struggle and not in bed."

The whole organisation made my Sunday afternoon cricket club look socially progressive. Healy was charged by the WRP that he had established 'entirely non-communist and bureaucratic relations inside the party'. This, of course, gives us an entirely new construction of the word bureaucratic but the far left do have a way with words. I am afraid Healy ended his days as a Trotskyist without a party.

The nadir of Trotskyism was surely reached when the Revolutionary Workers Party (never to be confused with the Workers Revolutionary Party) gave up the class struggle and alienation, and focussed on UFO visitations instead. Their 'Chariot of the Gods' type of argument was that aliens in their UFOs were clearly an advanced civilisation. Any advanced civilisation will, of course, choose a socialist method of organisation therefore UFOs were the emissaries of intergalactic socialism. For the RWP it was not so much a case of Socialism in One Country as Socialism in One Galaxy. Other flat-earthers of the revolutionary left have even managed to muster sufficient humour to mock the RWP.

It is essential to be optimistic if you are a member of the far left. This was demonstrated to Terry Eagleton when he attended a Socialist Workers Party meeting in 2003.

There has never been a time in the past one hundred and fifty years when the left has been weaker but one comrade rose to announce that 'there have never been so many revolutionary chances as at present'. Sometimes it is necessary to distinguish between cheerful optimism and blind self-delusion.

The attitude of some Pioneers was not that far removed from American Libertarian individualists like Henry David Thoreau and Lysander Spooner and there is a reasonable parallel here. For three hundred years, Europeans made the hazardous journey across the Atlantic in order to forge a new life for themselves, free from the political, social and religious constraints of the old Europe. As the Eastern Seaboard filled up, so those who sought a different way of life took to the wilderness. Famously, Thoreau took to the woods in Massachusetts and lived at Walden Pond. The result of his libertarian meditations was *Walden* written in 1854. In it he argues that the individual has the right to detach himself from society and that the government should be able to exert no authority over such an individual. This is a declaration of the sovereignty that lies in all of our hearts. Above all, they desired freedom to live free from the restraints of others, subscribing only to the Rousseauesque notion that freedom was 'obedience to a law that one prescribes to oneself'.

It is possible that the natural desire to be freed from government control can transmute into hostility to government itself as a conspiracy against the individual. The sinister logical conclusion of this position is demonstrated by the extreme right-wing libertarian militias of Montana and Wyoming who reject all government authority. They believe that the whole of federal government is a Jewish conspiracy and that the right to carry a gun is a symbol of individual freedom. It was on this sort of basis that Timothy McVeigh felt justified in planting a bomb that killed 168 people in the federal building in Oklahoma City. The desire for freedom can lead to the most perverted and unfree of actions.

Chapter 12: Heroes and Villains

Readers have you ever seen a fight?
If not you have a pleasure to come.
William Hazlitt.

I cannot tell you why I acted as I did.
*Mike Tyson, after biting a chunk out of Evander Holyfield's
ear during their 1997 heavyweight clash.*

Boxing has often dominated my thoughts and sometimes I even dreamt about it. Only in the last few years have I begun to wean myself off this hopeless addiction. I reached my low point on the night I dreamt of Jack Johnson.

The last tube from the West End finished at Golders Green. I therefore began the long walk home in a mildly intoxicated condition along the route of the Northern Line towards High Barnet. Passing through Whetstone, a mile from my house, I came to the Black Bull pub and stopped, for a moment, to look at a small outhouse on the south side of the pub.

More than ninety years earlier, this building had been the training gym for Jack Johnson – arguably the greatest of all heavyweight boxers and the first black champion. He was a mysterious and enigmatic figure who was at the centre of the most disgraceful episode ever to disfigure professional sport.

At the time he was fighting, the heavyweight championship was the sole preserve of white fighters like John L. Sullivan who, twenty years previously, had pronounced, "I have never fought a nigger and never will."

Black fighters were consigned to fighting each other while the heavyweight championship was always contested by white fighters. Two of the outstanding black heavyweights of the period, Sam Langford and Harry Wills, fought each other twenty-three times in an interminable series of bouts across the American continent. Today they would be hugely-wealthy, globally-known sportsmen. Ninety years ago they were consigned to a brutal sporting ghetto.

Johnson, through the sheer genius of his talent and a mountainous self-belief, broke through this barrier. He took the title from the brave, but hopelessly outclassed, Tommy Burns at Rushscutter's Bay, Sydney in 1908 having first pursued him half way round the world.

This sparked the search for the 'Great White Hope'.

The novelist, Jack London, called for the restoration of the pride of the Caucasian race in order to wipe 'the golden smile' from Johnson's face. Challengers came forward and were beaten with almost contemptuous ease.

For the moment, white boxers had to satisfy themselves with contesting something called the White Heavyweight Championship of the World. In 1910, the old white champion, Jim Jeffries, lumbered into the ring in the name of restoring racial honour. The previously formidable Jeffries was cruelly humiliated at Reno, Nevada in a fight that attracted the attention of the world.

The contest can claim to be the world's first global sporting event and possibly the most significant moment in the development of modern sport. As the news of Jeffries' defeat came through on the cables just hours after the event, an eager public in England queued for the first editions of newspapers carrying reports of the great event.

The first great black sports star had been born and, at its highest level, sport had become a global commodity. Johnson's victory triggered a series of race riots across America that led to eleven deaths and two lynchings. Johnson, because of his race, his athletic genius, his arrogance, and his fondness for white women, was a hated and reviled figure. Official America was determined to crush him. In 1912 he was prosecuted under the Mann Act for transporting a white woman across state lines for 'immoral purposes'. Sentenced to a term of imprisonment, Johnson fled to Europe and made Paris his base for the three remaining years he reigned as World Heavyweight Champion.

From Paris he came to Whetstone and to his residency at the Black Bull in order to prepare for a fight with the British champion, Bombardier Billy Wells – a fight that never took place.

And so, in some very minor and strange way, our paths crossed although he died eight years before I was born. I wondered what Johnson, who hailed from Galveston on the sub-tropical Texan coast, would have made of the quiet little Hertfordshire village on the fringes of London.

Trudging through the night with an overfull bladder, I relieved myself against the wall of what had been his training gym and wondered if, in some way, his shade might be beckoning to me.

That night I dreamt of Jack. The hooded black basilisk, in the robe of a Chinese emperor, was beckoning to me and pointing out something that, no matter how hard I tried, I could not understand. In the morning I awoke and, for a while, I was convinced I had seen him the night before as I stood silent in the darkness. Only later, in the bright light of a midday sun, did I realise it was all the fault of an overwrought imagination.

After three years of exile, Johnson was homesick for America. According to his autobiography, he cut a deal with the authorities that, in return for throwing a fight and restoring the championship to the white race, the charges against him would be dropped.

Johnson duly obliged.

In 1915, in a match against Jess Willard at the Oriental Park race track in Havana, Johnson stayed down in the 26th round, shielded his eyes from the sun, and allowed himself to be counted out so that honour was restored to the white race. Critics said he was out of condition and ran out of gas against a bigger, stronger opponent in the blazing Cuban sun. It is part of his persona that he took the mystery of what really happened to the grave.

Given the quality of his previous record, and the fact that he continued to fight into his sixties against good quality opponents, it seems unlikely that Johnson would lose legitimately to a fighter as inconsistent, and at times mediocre, as Willard. Johnson was never allowed to fight for the championship again and, for another twenty years, neither would any others of his race until the rise of a much more respectable and deferential black fighter, Joe Louis, who outwardly at least, was prepared to abide by the white man's rules.

My association with the noble art was reinforced by its prominence in our games lessons that were always an entertaining trial. Boxing was an occasional choice for the sports master – vital, he would tell us, to develop those manly qualities of self-defence so necessary to the martial spirit of an Englishman. When he learnt that one boy was attending a Judo class, he began telling us about 'sneaky Jap tactics', somehow holding Judo responsible for the attack on Pearl Harbour.

There never appeared to be much strategy involved when he was teaching pugilistic skills. At the start of the lesson, several large tea chests, full of old boxing gloves without laces, would be dragged out into the gym. We would then be told to choose a partner based on relative sizes. I always ended up with a large, blubbery, slow-moving boy called Davis.

We would then be put through our paces – "left jab, right cross, back on your heels, guard high, parry blow, double up, double up" – and so it went on. For the last five minutes we would be told, "You may now strike your opponent at will". This was the signal for a mayhem of flying leather during which the physically adept would unmercifully batter those who were less gifted with shouts of "Get up, you poof!" every time someone fell to the ground with blood streaming from his nose. Being a stylist I managed to avoid most of Davis' flailing efforts while getting in a few satisfying digs that only served to enrage him further.

My friend's school on the other side of town was definitely a more advanced institution. They not only had a proper boxing ring with ropes and an apron, but they had also refined and elevated the practice of forcing boys involved in playground scraps to resolve their differences in a manly fashion at the end of the day.

Walking past the school, I usually knew when there was a bout on by the number of bicycles in the bike shed and the shouts coming from the gym building. It was my habit to steal in and observe the small terrified boys with their white pipe-cleaner arms attempting to settle their bout with some semblance of dignity while not enduring too much physical pain now that the lunchtime spasm of anger had abated.

Given that the protagonists were often of different sizes, it was as even-handed as the United Nations refereeing a war between the USA and Vietnam and then pronouncing it a fair contest. This was simply a 1960s version of the medieval practice of trial by combat. The bouts were made worse by the senior mistress, who looked like a squat, compact English bulldog, pacing around the edges of the ring shouting, "Make him bleed, boy! Make him bleed!" I was never clear which boy she was referring to but I suspect either would have done.

My own boxing career came to an abrupt end when I met 'the Animal' at Berry Boys' Boxing Club. The coach would say to me, "You punch like an eight-year-old girl but you're a good stylist." On that basis he put me in for a preliminary bout with the 'Animal', aka Terry, who had at least one extra chromosome. I should have realised his nickname did not signify junior membership of the RSPCA. The giveaway was the hair tufts on top of his broad muscular shoulders.

My stylistic excellence protected me for about twelve seconds. In the thirteenth, a roundhouse haymaker flattened me.

"But I'm a stylist," I protested.

"Get up, you poof!" he replied.

I did. Then he punched me on the nose. This sent me into a windmill-style flailing fury before an overhand right, delivered straight to my forehead, pole-axed me. I could have beaten the count but I reasoned, "What's the point?"

This, broadly speaking, has continued to be my philosophy for the past thirty-five years.

Boxing is a vice that, if picked up early, is difficult to shake off and, for that, I blame Terry Downes. In 1961 we were visiting my great aunt in Paddington. She lived in one of those gloomy mid-Victorian terraced houses that always smelled of linoleum, mothballs and furniture polish. In my moments of extended boredom, I would wander into the tiny back garden and stare at her massive whalebone corset hanging on the clothes line.

One day we escaped for a stroll – even my father could take no more tinned salmon sandwiches and Battenberg cake. As we walked along Praed Street I saw a crowd in the distance. The traffic had stopped and a motorcade was being mobbed by well-wishers. Standing in the back of an open-top car was Terry Downes who had just beaten Paul Pender for the world middleweight championship. I can even remember the car. It was a pink and white Vauxhall Cresta with tailfins; Luton's homage to late-fifties American styling.

Tough looking men with broken noses were shaking his hand and slapping him on the back, saying, "Good on ya, Tel."

I wondered what it must be like to receive such adulation and this incident raised in me a pinprick of awareness of the existence of the noble art.

Two years later, at the age of eleven, I was sitting in Sid's waiting for a haircut while reading a well-thumbed copy of The Ring magazine. Sid was an expert on child rearing. A boy a few years younger than me was remonstrating with his mother about the number 2 cut Sid had given him. Sid had only one style so there were no cuts numbered one or three. Just number two.

"Give him a crack, love," was Sid's advice.

The sharp slap the boy immediately received showed that Sid's word was valued and not to be taken lightly.

The Ring Magazine carried an account of the narrow points victory of a prominent new talent, Cassius Clay, against an overblown light heavyweight called Doug Jones. With his lightning speed and brash boastful predictions, Clay was soon the talk of the schoolyard, at least within my boxing-mad fraternity.

Nearly a year later he fought Sonny Liston for the world title. I confidently predicted that Liston would win. My certainty was based on having seen him twice crush Floyd Patterson, a thoroughly decent heavyweight champion, within a round.

The previous year the Americans had launched Telstar which, for the first time. allowed live television broadcasts of heavyweight championship fights to be beamed across the Atlantic. I knew then what Old Joe in Grove Avenue must have felt like thirty years before when he listened to Tommy Farr versus Joe Louis on his crystal set.

My PE teacher disagreed with my pre-fight verdict that Liston would win so I bet him two shillings. As the entire world knows, Clay won in seven rounds and humiliated the previously-indestructible Liston. To my surprise, I was confronted by the PE teacher at the start of school on the Monday demanding his two shillings. I had assumed he would be too embarrassed to take my week's pocket money but no such embarrassment was felt. When I explained that my money was at home, he said, "You mind you bring it tomorrow or I'll get the slipper out."

On the whole, it seemed good value handing over my pocket money and not getting a beating.

During those early Telstar years, my father woke us at three in the morning to watch the world heavyweight championship fights. Sitting in the front room in our dressing gowns, sipping a cup of Horlicks, we marvelled at the genius of Muhammad Ali's (Clay had now changed his name) athleticism and towering courage.

In hindsight, it may seem odd.

"Yes, your Honour, he came into our bedrooms in the middle of the night and made us watch films of large black men hitting each other."

At the time, it was a window into another world just a tantalising distance away.

The following year I saw Sonny Liston in the flesh although he never actually fought in Britain. Fortunately for all our heavyweights, his only visit to Britain was to watch a highly promising East End heavyweight, Billy Walker, training at Blue House Farm on the fringes of Basildon.

The place was packed with the press and I marvelled at the size and power of the man as he punched a speedball for the benefit of the photographers. I wanted to go up to him and say, "I hope you beat that loudmouth Clay. Button his lip for good." But I didn't.

A month later, he lost in the rematch at Lewiston, Maine in the most mysterious fight of the century. The biggest, toughest, and most fearsome heavyweight of the past fifty years was knocked out in the first round by an innocuous, almost invisible punch that left him struggling on the canvas with mayhem all around him. The image of that fight is seared across my memory like a shaft of ragged lightning. Ali is standing over his fallen opponent in a frozen moment of black and white photography screaming at the 'ugly old bear' to get up and fight.

After that humiliation, Liston began the long slide into oblivion and a drug-induced death in Las Vegas while Ali went onto become the most famous person on the planet.

Many years later, I stood in Brixton as Muhammad Ali's motorcade passed down Coldharbour Lane. Despite the ravages of Parkinson's Disease he looked as if he was the Emperor of the World. For a moment, the intervening years slid away and in my mind's eye I saw his majestic performance against Cleveland 'Cat' Williams at the Houston Astrodome when he was as close to unbeatable as any boxer in the history of the brutal business.

I remembered the most dramatic night in the history of sport when, as an ageing ex-champion, he defeated the supposedly unbeatable George Foreman on a hot African night in Kinshasa. We marvelled at his athleticism, at his lightning speed (although there were signs that he was slowing), at his daring and above all at his reckless courage. But deep in my heart I knew the years had taken their toll and that this was no longer the dazzling athlete who had been so unjustly deprived of his title.

Then I blinked and again I was standing in Brixton amongst a frantic, ecstatic crowd come to see the king. I am not embarrassed to admit that there were tears rolling down my cheeks as the great man rolled past. I fancy that, for just one moment, his eyes met those of the tall white Englishman standing among a crowd of black faces.

It is one of the many tragedies of recent American history that bodily infirmity has robbed black Americans of the inspirational political and moral leader they so desperately need.

The following year, I stood in a crowd, again in Brixton, no more than two hundred yards from where I had seen Muhammad Ali. This time they were transfixed by the aura of violence and sullen menace that surrounded the dangerous Mike Tyson. I felt none of the frisson of greatness that I felt during my fleeting glimpse of Muhammad Ali. The contrast between the two men encapsulated the difference between the 1960s and the 1990s. The optimism of the 60s was matched by the generosity of Ali's spirit and his mercurial genius: the crass materialism and violence of the 90s seemed to suit the dark, violent and at times squalid nature of Tyson's persona. It is tempting to say that boxing gets the champions it deserves but in the case of Ali it got far more than it deserved.

Fighters exert a certain primeval fascination that no other sportsman or personality can elicit. Even those repelled by boxing often admit an attraction to the idea of one lone individual pitting himself against another. No other breed of sportsman casts himself into the outer darkness for the purpose of destroying another individual.

A few years ago I was coming out of the West Ham ground, Upton Park, when I noticed Frank Bruno hurrying away. He was wearing a long coat with the collar turned up and it was clear he did not wish to be recognised.

"Frank, Frank," the cry went up. A moment later he was surrounded by a crowd of well-wishers asking for his autograph on their match day programmes. Frank good-naturedly obliged, standing in the middle of Green Street with the traffic halted in both directions. The curious thing was that drivers at the front of the queue who could see the cause of the obstruction was Frank Bruno signing autographs did not seem to be concerned. After all, what better reason can there be for blocking the Queen's Highway?

The irate bibbing of horns came from those who were further away and did not understand there was legitimate reason for the hold up. Eventually the police came and respectfully asked Frank and the crowd if they could move on to the pavement. It was exactly the way I felt as a child when we had our daily football matches in the street. There are times when the road is too good a place for drivers to spoil it with their cars.

"God Bless. God Bless," Bruno shouted as he hurried away on the other side of Green Street, his collar turned up against the cold night air and the stares of passers-by.

To hear that good old Frank is suffering from mental problems is more distressing than it would be if it was a sportsman from any other area of athletic endeavour. We know that in some way boxing must be the culprit because of the cruel loneliness it thrusts upon competitors at the highest level.

*

There is something intriguing about East and West Ham. It is a community in a state of flux making the late transition from respectable Victorian-terraced white working class to advanced multicultural status. The old and the new can be seen in Robin's pie shop in East Ham High Street. A substantial majority of the people traversing up and down the High Street are Asian. Inside the pie shop, the customers are white and elderly, the last of the 'Alf Garnett' types. And there is me.

The shop is a last refuge for a disappearing generation: the pies, the mash, the liquor sauce, and the jellied eels are a homage to a lost way of life. An old lady is sitting close to me, enjoying a bowl of stewed eels. Her face is pinched and thin. I ask her if she has lived here long.

"All my life," she replies.

"Has it changed much?" I ask.

Her expression says it all. Its verbal equivalent would be, "What the **** do you think?"

I am not very good at this vox pop interviewing.

In Stondon Walk, on the Barking Road a few hundred yards to the east of Upton Park, there is an attractive social housing development formerly part of the GLC and now owned by the Borough of Newham. At the front of the development is a series of works of filigree; metal cut into relief and illuminated from behind, created by the artist Stephen Peart. On a chill winter evening it is very attractive. There is a Kathleen Raine poem, the words cut out and shimmering from the bright light to the rear.

> The very leaves of the acacia tree are London
> London tap-water fills out the fuchsia buds in the back

garden
Blackbirds pull London worms out of the sour soil,
The woodlice, centipedes, eat London, the wasps even.
London air, through stomata of myriad leaves
And a million lungs of London breathes.

I contrast the fierce intellectual mysticism and piety of Raine's verse with the crude attempt at defining a Newham Borough Council aesthetic. The poem is vaguely appropriate in that Kathleen Raine was born nearly a century ago in Ilford, five miles to the east which was then as much a part of Essex as Southend still is. Now it is part of the amorphous swirl of suburban east London. My friend, who has been buying a bag of chips, catches up with me.

"What you looking at?"

I gesture and stare at the poem while eating over-salted vinegar astringent chips and ask, "Who is Kathleen Raine?"

"**** knows!" comes the reply from my West Ham-supporting friend.

I am ambivalent about this flimsy municipal attempt at defining a culture courtesy of the council taxpayer. It nestles among the competing Sky dishes and sits uneasily with the peeling 'Residents Only Parking' and 'No Ball Games' signs.

*

On the whole, during the past thirty years, we have lost interest in boxing as it has become consigned to the pay per view satellite channels. These arrangements may have made multi-millionaires of a small number of fighters but it also means that twenty world champions could walk down the middle of Oxford Street and would not be recognised. They have lost their Henry Cooper-style folk hero status.

My early interest in the noble art was reinforced by my fascination for that hangover from an earlier era – the boxing booth. Each year a circus arrived in town and erected its big top in a field close to the town centre on a site that is now occupied by a SavaCentre. Next to the big top was a smaller tent that contained a boxing booth.

Whenever I catch that characteristic male odour of bitter beer and under arm sweat, I am taken back to that seedy little booth. Each evening, while the circus was putting on a show, the booth did a brisk trade of its own. Inside, it was brightly lit by unshaded acetylene lights that revealed a fog of cigarette smoke and a small elevated square boxing ring in which, with considerable ceremony, the booth champion was introduced – 'Stripped to the Waist' Smith. He slipped off his towelling robe to reveal a solid physique that had slightly run to fat. Impressively, he was wearing the off-white canvas breeches of a nineteenth century bare-knuckle prize-fighter rather than the trunks of a modern boxer. He bore a close resemblance to the actor, Philip Madoc.

The ringmaster announced that a ten-pound prize awaited anyone who could last more than a round with the booth champion. I stood at the back peering through the standing crowd in a state of apprehension, my pulse racing, waiting to see who would be brave enough to volunteer. There was always a succession of pasty young men with the occasional middle-aged gallant waiting to try. They were taken behind a curtain and fitted with gloves. I assume they were also told to lie down after a few blows. When they emerged, they were stripped to their pale and flabby waists, and looked completely unfit for the task. Under the fierce lights, their apprehension was clear. Egged on by friends and usually full of beer, the realisation dawned quickly that the man in front of them was likely to inflict a great degree of pain.

The booth fighter moved around the ring with surprising grace but he always gave his opponents a minute or so to allow them some self-respect. It was little encouragement to other hopefuls in the crowd if the challengers were consistently flattened after a few seconds.

After a minute or so of ineffective pawing, a few crisp thudding punches soon put the challenger down. I often wondered how much it hurt but, having been on the receiving end a few times at Berry Boys' Club, I knew all about the thudding, stunned sensation when a hard punch hit home.

I only remember one opponent who put up a significant fight at the booth. A large burly, bearded middle-aged man with a sweeping round house blow knocked the booth champion off his feet. His wife screamed out, her voice carrying clear across the tent, "Kill him, Roy! Kill him!"

A look of panic crossed the face of the ringmaster. It was not part of the business plan to give away the ten pound prize money.

The champion came back with a solid blow to the face that left his opponent's nose spurting blood. The ring master stepped in to save the bearded man from further punishment provoking much booing and cat-calling from the beery audience, including myself.

All the boxing booths have now gone. The last one, based in Newcastle, packed up in 1995. It was not lack of demand or punters wanting to try their luck, it was just that the demands of our increasingly litigious society meant they could no longer get insurance cover or a medical practitioner to be present for all fights.

Human nature does not change. Witness the rise of the clandestine sport of total fighting, the unlicensed matches that take place far away from the controls of the British Boxing Board. In the summer of 1966, a few weeks after England won the World Cup, I went down to Pitsea Marshes with a friend. We had heard there was to be a fight between the gypsy champion and a bargee from the local fleet anchored in Pitsea Creek – a small, still tributary of the Thames. Beyond the railway line and going onto the marshes there was a sense of stepping away from civilisation.

The gypsy encampment was a semi-permanent affair – a mess of feral dogs, derelict vehicles and dilapidated caravans that looked if they were the broken down rejects from one of the sites that dot the Essex coast line. We were given encouragement by the size of the crowd and the numbers made us bold. We had heard the stories about gypsies stealing children and putting spells on young girls. This was a nomadic England of the margins.

Neither the gypsies nor the bargees, those who plied their craft along the Thames and its tributaries, were likely to fit into a central government plan for organising a new town. Their mere existence was an act of rebellion.

Standing in a crowd of men with flat caps, dirty neckerchiefs, lurcher dogs and sharp little terriers, I was in a very different England from that of the glossy Home Counties colour supplements, the prosperous suburbs of our great cities or even the new town just a few miles away. This was an England of the displaced, those who refused to conform to the demands of an increasingly powerful state.

The pall of personal defeat and the odour of blood hung in the air. There were poachers, lamping men, social security claimants, people who existed on the edges, men who were prepared to organise dog fights and badger baiting and, of course, those who were prepared to stand on the wet marshland to watch Trickerman Lee, the gypsy champion, race to a thudding victory over the stout bargee, the pride of the Thames.

I did not see the fight – the crowd was too dense – but we hung about the edges and afterwards I saw the bargee spitting blood from his mouth and pulling out a white tooth. This was a throwback to the nineteenth century prize ring.

Twenty years later, I sat in a friend's darkened living room watching a hand-held video recording of a fight that took place in a pub car park in Worksop, Nottinghamshire, between the late Bartley Gorman, King of the Gypsies, and a miner from one of the local pits. My friend had bought the clandestine tape during a lunchtime drinking session at a pub in Bounds Green, North London. The picture quality was poor but it was enough to get a sense of what was happening.

The fight was nasty, brutish and short. It was settled by Mr Gorman's speciality – a short hard bull-hammer punch to the Adam's apple that left the ex-collier rolling in the gravel of the car park floor gasping for breath. It was not an edifying spectacle. I left the darkened room with its Carlsberg Special Brew cans strewn across the floor feeling in some way diminished. I did not feel I had used the limited number of minutes and hours that I had been granted to their best effect.

When I learned more about Mr Gorman, I could not bring myself to condemn the Gypsy King and his brutal achievements. There was a curious, quiet, introspective nobility about the man. A sense that he felt detached from what he was doing but was nevertheless compelled to compete by virtue of his God-given excellence.

He was not doing it for vast sums of money or to become a national celebrity and appear on television chat shows. He was fighting because of his heritage and the sense that it was his destiny to be the best bare-knuckle fighter in all of England, following the tradition set by his uncle, his grandfather, and his great grandfather. Bartley Gorman was subject to a melancholy notion of continuity that drove him to pursue this most violent means of validating individual worth.

Perhaps there was a natural attraction between Basildon and boxing. In 1987 I witnessed Terry Marsh, the Fighting Fireman from Basildon, win the World IBF light welterweight title from the American, Joe Manley. We shouted ourselves hoarse in a marquee pitched in the car park of the Festival Hall. The atmosphere was hot, frantic and hysterical: just right for boxing. Punters at boxing matches are different from any other sport. I never see their type at football matches, dog racing, or even at the most disreputable National Hunt courses. In fact, they are types of individuals I never seem to come across in any other aspect of my life. The sort whose gaze I am reluctant to meet, who I consciously skirt around, take extra care not to bump into, and deliberately walk away from if the opportunity presents itself. I could label them 'Psychotics from Chigwell' but they could come from anywhere within that quadrant that starts at Aldgate and fans out fifty miles into Essex and eastern Hertfordshire.

It was eerie standing in that marquee on that overheated night knowing this was where I rambled and wandered in my carefree childhood, hunting snakes and stealing birds' eggs.

*

For the Pioneers, this interest in boxing was a disturbing new development, particularly when I boasted that a friend's father had taken me to the Wembley Pool to watch Brian Curvis fight Dave Charnley for the British Welterweight championship. This was the same man who, when Sugar Ray Robinson – probably the greatest pound for pound boxer in the history of the sport – visited England in the early 1960s, took us to wait outside a restaurant in Knightsbridge for an entire afternoon on the strength of a rumour that the great man was inside. It was a fruitless few hours but I enjoyed sitting with my friend on the front bench seat of his father's Ford Consul as he stared at the restaurant exit.

On that day, I learned something of the nature of obsession. These were halcyon days for motorists in that we could park outside an expensive restaurant in the heart of fashionable London with no fear of a parking ticket or a clamper van. The next year the hated and reviled Ernest Marples introduced parking meters and traffic wardens and the war against the motorist, that still rages today, began in earnest.

*

Boxing followed me around as a child. In the August of 1968, I went on a day trip to Brighton on what proved to be my last Pioneer outing. The trip can be easily dated as it was the same day the Soviet tanks rolled into Czechoslovakia. In hindsight, I suppose this event must have been one of the final nails in the coffin of any of the Pioneers who still kept faith with the old Communist spirit, Soviet-style.

We travelled in four cars, which in itself was proof that the Pioneer spirit was in decline. The Pioneers had looked upon mass car ownership with suspicion and many, like my father, had regularly cycled to

Brighton in their youth. But that day we raced down the A23 in a cavalcade of motorcars.

Bowling across the South Downs in our Austin Proletariat, without the benefit of seat belts, heating, or an electric starter motor – the engine was hand cranked – the world seemed a simpler and safer place. When we parked at the seafront, I was keen to go off by myself. After all, I was sixteen and I was particularly anxious not to be associated with the Hammer and Sickle flag that would be planted on the beach next to the grand sandcastle. It was not that they were pro-Soviet but more that there was no other flag designed to indicate their political leanings. It would, of course, have been a spectacularly inappropriate way to make such a gesture on Brighton beach.

I wandered off in the direction of the West Pier and saw the old pug from a distance. He ran a sweet and rock shop at the pier entrance. In case his past profession was not evident from his cauliflower ear and broken nose, the walls of his shop were covered with framed prints of ancient boxing matches.

I asked tentatively, "Is that you?" pointing to the first picture.

"I was king of the world then, sonny, known in every household in the land."

I did not know his name but he told me he had been born in Whitechapel in 1909, turned professional at fifteen and had the first of his seventy-five fights in America at the age of seventeen before becoming world lightweight champion. He talked to me for more than an hour but I was still reluctant to ask him his name. I later learned he was Jack 'Kid' Berg, one of the long line of great Jewish boxers who literally fought their way out of poverty in Britain and America in the first half of the last century. There are no Jewish fighters today. On the whole, people of that race have discovered there are less painful ways to make a living.

A sort of crisis was reached when I was walking back home clutching the *Old Holborn Book of Boxing*. The wife of one of the Pioneers who was a friend of my father's engaged me in conversation. She was different from most of the other Pioneers because she had been to University and spoke with a cultured accent. Like her architect husband, she had made a conscious decision to move with the Pioneers.

"You do know, Magnus, that boxing is exploitative, don't you?"

"Is it?" I replied lamely, desperately trying to think of the right response.

"It is poor working class men fighting each other for the edification of others due to the poverty of their circumstances."

"Is it?" I said again. What else could I say in the face of such erudition?

"My favourite fighter is Muhammad Ali," I announced, at last able to string a sentence together. For the previous two years I had been a Clay convert having dumped the old ogre Liston.

"Why is that?" Mrs Nixon replied.

I wanted to say, "Because I admire his grace, power and dazzling athleticism." but instead I forced myself to say, "Because he is fighting for the oppressed of the world, he is fighting for the dignity of the black race, and he is fighting for the Vietnamese." I wasn't sure about this last point but it sounded vaguely right and I knew that Ali had conscientiously refused to go to war in Vietnam.

That shut Mrs Nixon up.

I then added, for good measure, "He is the new Paul Robeson."

You might have expected me to think that Paul Robeson was a former black heavyweight champion but I had sat through enough dreary Paul Robeson songs to know that his brand of solemn deep bass protest was a particular favourite. Does anyone listen to him now? On a lighter note, we also used to listen to Nat King Cole who had a connection with the Civil Rights movement and was therefore approved of.

I was on the cusp of developing political consciousness and Mrs Nixon had fallen right into my trap. She could hardly criticise a man who was fighting on behalf of the poor and the oppressed, who was a symbol of the struggle for black dignity in the face of white oppression and, of course, who had the fastest fists in town.

To my feminist nation of anti-boxing friends, I have presented a moral dilemma. Which is more morally reprehensible of the following? To go to a conventional boxing match where two fairly evenly-matched opponents will, under close medical supervision, attempt to beat each other up while remaining within the Queensbury rules. Once in every two and a half thousand bouts there results a fairly serious injury to one of the contestants. Once in every eleven thousand bouts there is a fatality. No matter what the level of supervision, the irreducible core of the sport is to inflict hurt on your opponent and strike him down.

The alternative is to go foxy boxing as I did recently in Epping under the misapprehension that it was a sporting occasion. It turned out to be an Essex sort of thing. Heavily made up young women, wearing tight spangled shorts put on outsize boxing gloves, more resembling pillows than the real thing, and stage a mock fight with an opponent during the course of which they contrive for their tops to fall off. Although it is deeply exploitative, I am not aware of any injuries or fatalities occurring during a bout of foxy boxing except among the audience where choleric, drunken, red-faced men shout themselves stupid.

It is a dilemma, is it not? In both varieties of the sport the contestants take part of their own free will and the spectators are not coerced into attending. In a free and open society you may argue that such activity is allowable although we may individually disapprove.

Boxing as a sport has been eclipsed in the national consciousness and the decline has been slow but remorseless. The key moments were probably the terrible brain injures inflicted on Michael Watson and Gerald McClellan in their respective fights against Chris Eubank and Nigel Benn. It is probably not unreasonable to argue that the savagery demonstrated, particularly in the Benn–McClellan fight, has no place in a legitimate sport particularly when it is broadcast on terrestrial television. If it is broadcast on Sky then it is probably more suited to its audience.

Forty years ago such fighters as Henry Cooper, Brian London, Terry Downes and Howard Winstone were household names, as well known as any top league footballer. Today, with the exception of one or two heavyweights whose publicity usually exceeds their talent, this is no longer true. As a consequence, boxing has retreated into the ghetto of satellite broadcasting and the wee small hours of Channel 5's consistently underrated 'Fight of the Week'. The result has been a peculiar inversion. Forty years ago boxers were not well paid but they were part of our national consciousness and almost universally recognised. Today our top boxers are very well paid but a parade of all our national weight division champions down a suburban high street would not elicit a flicker of recognition from anyone beyond the most hardened of fight fans.

Boxing has had a bad press over the years although the Fight Club factor has led to a surge in interest in so-called white collar boxing. Here a paunchy solicitor in early middle age will attempt to batter an equally out of condition accountant in the name of satisfying some basic primeval instinct and getting back in touch with their vestigial manhood that 'soft living' has deprived them of. We do of course wish them every success in trying to inflict damage upon each other; the more the better in my view.

*

In the area where I live, I generally see only two types of young people after eight o'clock in the evening. The first are the crowds of round-shouldered young men and women wearing obligatory Nike hoodies as they gather outside Sainsbury's. They throw fireworks, shout at motorists, shout at me, drink White Lightning cider, steal supermarket trolleys and, by about nine o'clock, are usually attracting the attentions of two police officers.

The other young people are the small groups of broad-shouldered young men who move purposefully to and from Finchley Boxing Club two hundred yards down the road from my house. Each week approximately one hundred and forty boys between the ages of twelve and sixteen are instructed in the rudiments of the noble art by volunteer trainers.

Needless to say, their application for National Lottery funding has been rejected yet, during fifteen years of passing the Club in the evening, I have never seen a police car there. As my old anarchist acquaintance Albert Meltzer explained in his autobiography: "I found that boxing and socialism went hand in hand." His coach was Johnny Hicks, Marxist and professional boxer, and he also said, "I found that boys who might otherwise have drifted into street gangs never did after taking boxing lessons."

Chapter 13: Hanging out with the Woodcraft Folk

Span the world with friendship.
Motto of the Woodcraft Folk.

Membership of the Woodcraft Folk was an optional diversion for those of a left-wing disposition. As a member I went on weekend camps either to Loughton near Epping Forest or to Castle Headingham in North Essex. At either venue George Orwell's basket-weaving, sandal-wearing, nut-eating, carrot juice-drinking, yoghurt-consuming cranks had their day. In the 1960s, yoghurt was seen as an exotic, if not downright subversive, confection – a sort of bizarre junket gone wrong.

Where the Scouts stood for King, God and Country and saluting the flag with a very straight-laced censorious morality, the Woodcraft folk were decidedly off-centre, espousing a vague pantheism and a resistance to conformity and convention. Based upon the educational theories of Rousseau's *Emile*, the Woodcraft Folk adopted Indian names, (we had not yet been told that the original inhabitants of the Americas should be referred to as native peoples) sang folk songs, immersed themselves in basket weaving and sandal making, rejected formal education and attempted to pretend that the past two hundred years of industrialisation had not happened.

There was the attractive possibility of being able to adopt an Indian name. I was intensely disappointed that my suggestion of Running Bear was rejected in favour of Prairie Marmot which did not have quite the same ring to it. As a result I began to form the conviction that this was not an organisation for me.

The activities of the Woodcraft Folk in the 40 years before 1967 probably influenced the hippy revolution of the late 1960s though I have to admit that I cannot recall any offers of 'free love' or cannabis cigarettes.

In the evenings, a few of the Woodcraft Folk who were early members of the Campaign for Nuclear Disarmament would discuss that year's march to Aldermaston walking behind such luminaries as Bertrand

Russell and Michael Foot, though the advanced age of the latter meant he only walked the last symbolic stage of the march.

Around 1966 I was taken to see Bertrand Russell, the grandson of Radical Jack, who was speaking at Caxton Hall in London. It seems quite extraordinary that, in the twentieth century, I actually saw someone who was born in 1872. Russell was then well into his 80s and was entering a cranky phase, the prerogative of famous old men. He was campaigning virtually single-handed it seemed, against nuclear weapons, American imperialism and the Vietnam War. Unfortunately, I remember very little beyond a wizened old man crouching at the front, leaning on a stick and nodding to what seemed to be a music that only he could hear. In a roundabout sort of way he was 'an old man in a hurry'.

Returning to my loose association with the Woodcraft Folk and the Scouts, I was in the embarrassing position of being in organisations that were the polar opposites of each other although the Woodcraft Folk were more defined by what they were against rather than what they were for. I even briefly joined the Methodist-inspired Life Boys but did not follow through to the Boys' Brigade because their meetings clashed with those of the Woodcraft Folk. I have always been a rapid joiner and a rapid leaver of organisations.

Being of a shallow and rather superficial nature I abandoned the Life Boys prematurely because I had developed a youthful crush on Julie Christie who, in her pre-Dr Zhivago days, was starring in a BBC science fiction serial, *A for Andromeda*. Unfortunately, it was broadcast on the same evenings as Life Boys' meetings.

Despite this exception, my commitment to finding means of entertainment outside the home reflected a distinct lack of television and Playstations. If the truth of my duplicity had been known, I would have been drummed out of one or the other, epaulettes torn away; Prairie Marmot no longer.

I imagine that many of the more *driven* members of the Woodcraft Folk would these days find themselves in the further reaches of some of the more extreme environmental movements. A cautionary reminder of the vagueness of its principles comes from the fact that its German counterpart, Wandervogel, was absorbed by the Hitler Youth in 1935. Perhaps this shouldn't come as a surprise for always lurking somewhere beneath the surface of the Woodcraft Folk was the idea of protecting kith and kin. In hindsight, I have to acknowledge it had a very northern

European, Teutonic feel about it.

Before the war, a few of the Pioneers had been members of the Kibbo Kift Kindred, a 1920s youth and political movement that was the predecessor of the Woodcraft Folk before the split of 1925. These people were about fifteen years older than my parents and were in their early fifties when I knew them. Born around 1910, their earliest childhood years had been scarred by memories of the Great War. To an extent the Kibbo Kift was a reaction to that experience. They exhibited a fierce pantheism and a determination to revert to a pre-industrial way of life that was a cross between an imagined version of the early Saxon tribes and North American native peoples.

John Hargrave, their founder, was a renegade from the wholesomeness of the early Scout movement with its addiction to the British Empire, the monarchy and saluting the Union Jack. Hargrave was also a visionary who had been one of Baden Powell's original scouts and had developed natural healing powers later in life. The purpose of the Kibbo Kift was to reconnect people with the natural world; to re-establish the connection that the soft living of the twentieth century had destroyed. From the movement, a body of young men and women would emerge, fit in mind, body and spirit, who would lead a decadent and directionless society back to health and happiness under the leadership of White Fox (Hargrave). The principles of the movement smacked of fascism but at that time it seemed harmless.

In the late 1920s, the Kibbo Kift developed into a more overtly political movement when Hargrave adopted the Social Credit ideas of Major C.H. Douglas. This was an attempt to solve the flaws of capitalism without going down either the socialist road or the path that was to be trodden by Oswald Mosley's New Party. Douglas was convinced that the problem with capitalism was a lack of purchasing power that created mass poverty within an affluent society due to a defect in the pricing system. This was caused by a shortage of money in circulation because the bankers treated money as a commodity to be bought and sold.

Douglas argued that money should be regarded as the National Credit and that it should be allowed to increase as the real wealth of the nation increased. The crucial point was that this proportion of the nation's wealth should not be regarded as the property of any individual or group but should be owned and shared by all society as it represented the fruits of the collective inherited knowledge and wisdom. Douglas called this 'the increment of association'. He also recognised that the technological revolution that was gathering pace in the inter-war years would create mass unemployment. This was to be welcomed since it would liberate mankind from the drudgery of industrial labour and each person would be paid an increment of the nation's credit. This was the Wages of the Machine.

These two closely-related ideas became known as Social Credit. For the Kibbo Kift leadership they represented the way that mankind was to break back into the natural world while the drudgery of work was performed by machines.

By 1931, the Kibbo Kift was committing itself publicly to breaking the power of unrestrained capitalism and the institution of Parliament in its quest for the new life. Significantly, no more than ten months previously, Oswald Mosley had formed his New Party that failed to appeal to the electorate. As a result, a year later, he formed the British Union of Fascists inspired by Mussolini's success in Italy.

In the early 1930s it seemed to many that capitalism had failed and that people were floundering around looking for new ideas. By 1932, the Saxon-inspired uniform of the Kibbo Kift was abandoned in favour of a paramilitary green shirt uniform combined with fascist-style marching accompanied by drums and banners. They were seeking the publicity that was denied to them by a largely uninterested press. They did not have the equivalent of Rothermere's *Daily Mail* that promoted the British Union of Fascists. Instead the Greenshirts showed their sympathies by joining hunger marches organised by the ILP and the Unemployed Workers Movement.

The anthem of the Greenshirts *Wake Now the Dead* gives us an insight into what they believed.

> Wake now the Dead!
> The Living Dead who stand
> Waiting for the Call
> That will echo through the land!
> Green Shirts advance!
> The steadfast and the strong
> Rally to the ranks
> As the Hosts march on!

Apart from liking exclamation marks, the author, White Fox, is telling us that the dead are those whose spirits have been enervated by modern living. The antidote to this state of torpor is the invigorating nature of collective action in the natural world. The vaguely socialistic position of the movement is revealed in the final coda.

> Wake now the dead!
> By numbers held in thrall:
> On this fruitful Earth
> There is Earth-wealth for all!

In 1935, the Greenshirt Movement completed the transformation of the Kibbo Kift by renaming itself as the Social Credit Party of Great Britain. This was the equivalent of the Boy Scouts declaring that they could see the way forward and that they wanted to run the country. The high point for the Social Credit party was gaining four thousand votes in a Leeds constituency in the General Election of 1935. This proved to be a false dawn.

The 1936 Public Order Act banned the wearing of political uniforms and was designed to deal with the threat of Mosley's Blackshirt Fascists. It also dealt a significant blow to Hargrave's Greenshirts.

With the outbreak of war in 1939, the youthful membership of the Social Credit Party was spread with the British armed forces around the world. By 1945, the impetus of the movement was lost and the promise of a 'New Jerusalem' under a paternalistic Labour Government undercut the Kibbo Kift vision.

The Social Credit Party was dissolved in 1951 but, for those who experienced the whole evolutionary cycle since the Kibbo Kift was formed in South London in 1920, it remained a life-affirming experience.

As far as historians are concerned the Kibbo Kift have vanished into the undergrowth of the inter-war years. I recently read three weighty and learned histories of the period totalling more than two thousand pages. They did not contain a single reference to the Kibbo Kift, the Greenshirts, the Social Credit Movement, John Hargrave, Major C.H. Douglas, Leslie Paul or the Woodcraft Folk. An argument that is sometimes difficult to avoid is that history is whatever historians choose it to be.

Those who wanted to pursue a vigorous form of outdoor life freed from the political baggage of the Kibbo Kift/Greenshirts/Social Credit Party could join the socialistic but apolitical Woodcraft Folk or, if they were sufficiently desperate, the Scouts.

Some in the Kibbo Kift were disturbed and frustrated by the autocratic leadership of John Hargrave, a sort of left side mystical version of Baden Powell. They were also suspicious of the Social Credit ideas he was starting to espouse. In 1924 a group of representatives from the Co-operative Lodges of South London met at Bradenham Farm, in Buckinghamshire and initiated the split away from the Kibbo Kift that lead to the founding of the Woodcraft Folk.

The mock Anglo Saxon philosophy can be seen in such phrases as 'The Headman, KK has blackspotted Eric C. Peake, Wanderwolf of Eppingthing'. The language of Althings, Wappentakes, Kindred, Kinsfolk, The Headman and Moots indicates a very conscious rejection of the modern.

Under the leadership of Leslie Paul, the Woodcraft Folk adopted a programme of vigorous outdoor education focussing on physical fitness, dietary improvement (preferably vegetarian) and dancing (savage and folk), all with the aim of achieving racial improvement. Curiously, all members were told 'it is the duty of Woodcraft Folk to assist the revival of folk dancing'. This partially explains why a major feature of my life in primary school was performing *The Cumberland Reel* and *Marie's Wedding* to a very low standard. We were somehow persuaded that it was good for us but, in these days of league tables and constant assessment, this now seems very odd.

The Folk very self-consciously offered an alternative to wage slavery in order to 'save youngsters from the toils of mammon'. There was no 1960s equivalent of learning relevant computer skills for us. Instead, we practised flint chipping, fire drilling, spear making and the use of bows and arrows to be followed by 'savage dancing' to the rhythms of the tom-tom. The Folk had also acquired the 1920s German obsession with sun worship, hence the secondary tests for full Woodcraft Folk membership included 'to be sunburnt to the waist and over the limbs' as they put it. Modern skin specialists would be wincing in horror but the aim of this programme was 'to free the young spirit from the complexes and reversions produced by the hideousness of industrialism'.

As a consequence, my memory is of running through the woods wearing an I-Spy Indian head dress while trying to wipe out any piece of hapless wildlife that strayed across my path. With this aim in mind, I once took an air rifle with me (we all owned them in those carefree days) to a group meeting. Encouraged by fellow Greensticks, I took pot shots at birds.

Little Wolf had an extremely pained look on his face as he gently prised the gun from my grasp and indicated the severity of my transgression. It was equivalent to sliding a few coins out of the collection plate as it was passed round the Holy Cross Church where we decamped each Sunday before chasing down to the corner shop to buy fruit salad and blackjack chews.

My relationship with Little Wolf never recovered from the day he showed me his collection of blown wild birds' eggs. The extent of it was, I imagine, a partial explanation of the decline in the wild bird population on a scale that would now earn the owner five years in prison. As I picked up the case, the bottom hinged open and a lifetime's collection of rare birds eggs filched from nests in the remotest parts of the country smashed to the ground.

Simultaneous membership of the Scouts was a difficult issue and brought forth moderate parental disapproval. My father, while clearly a supporter of all manner of wholesome outdoor activities was always suspicious of the vaguely paramilitary ethos of the Scouts. I was asked questions like, "And do you salute the Union Jack?" or "Do you sing God Save the Queen?" in the tones that a social worker investigating a sensitive case of child abuse might adopt. Even at the age of twelve I found it bizarre saluting the Union Jack and I would cross my fingers as we rendered *God Save the Queen* with some gusto.

I think that I must have been born this way. When I was aged seven my entire primary school lined up along Whitmore Way, the main road running through the town. A plastic Union Jack was thrust into my hand, and I was told to wave at the rather insouciant gentleman in the back of a large Rolls Royce. Barely into the idea of conscious childhood, I thought to myself, 'what is the point?' I later discovered that the insouciant gentleman was the Duke of Edinburgh on a day excursion to see the New Town plebs.

The Scoutmaster was a slightly plump, pasty-faced man with a thin moustache. His habit of combing the hair of younger boys as they sat on his knee did not seem at all odd at the time. We just thought that he was being kind but, in these more world-weary times, it seems rather sinister.

A few days before my very last Scout meeting, Enoch Powell made his

'Rivers of Blood' speech. The Scoutmaster told us 'that man has been sent to save us'. Save us from what? I had no idea then but now I understand. He was going to save us from black people.

I met Enoch Powell many years later and I was immediately surprised by how small he was. The wide-eyed, unblinking, wax-like homunculus carried around the room with him a rather forbidding air and a large black briefcase. Being short on small talk, I asked him if he ever regretted the speech. His answer was a peremptory "No" and his expression indicated very firmly that this former Professor of Greek, and by reputation the cleverest man in British politics, had no wish to discuss the incident that had destroyed his career with a complete stranger. I was hoping he would whisper something melodramatic like, "This country is in great danger but Arthur will arise." But he didn't.

I felt an instinctive sympathy as he stood alone in the crowd; a tiny figure clutching a shiny black briefcase. He may have been a racist but his philosophy was a universe away from the poisonous crudity of many who supported him. He was an instinctive English nationalist who was simply too intellectual, honest and refined for the brutish business of politics.

Lord Hailsham falls into the category of politicians of undoubted brilliance who did not possess the sureness of touch necessary to rise to the very top of the 'greasy pole'. I observed this brilliant but flawed politician as he presided over the Observer Mace Inter-School Debating Competition. He was about eighty-five years old but he was perfectly lucid albeit somewhat eccentric in manner. Occasionally, as the debate proceeded, he would bang his stick on the ground and utter a strange harrumphing sound that seemed to bear no relationship to the proceedings at the front. At the end the contestants were treated to a charming and witty speech that was full of backhanded compliments to their abilities.

In a previous incarnation as Quentin Hogg, he had stood as the Pro-Chamberlain candidate at the famous 1938 Oxford by-election. In a triumphant moment – certainly for Chamberlain and possibly also for Hitler – he was returned to the House of Commons. As a child I was exposed to the contrast between the old and new Tories when in 1965 he challenged for the Conservative leadership. Hogg represented an already old fashioned style of Toryism while the victor, Edward Heath, was more suited to the meritocratic vision of the 1960s. As Alf Garnett used to put it: 'That 'ogg, 'e should be Prime Minister.' He was, of course, second choice to Enoch. However, Mr Powell discovered that he was not to be the great leader to take the party forward after the resignation of the aristocratic Alec Douglas-Home. Her time was to come a decade later.

*

Some time around 1964, a group of Pioneers went on a day trip to Southend ten miles to the east of Basildon at the point where the Thames becomes part of the North Sea. Staring at the cards in a newsagent's window, an advertisement for bedsits caught my eye. Printed across the bottom was the phrase 'No Coloureds'. I had never seen the phrase before and I asked my father to explain. At the time I was not enraged but then this was a period when we accepted a casual, endemic, low-key racism as being a fact of life. Perhaps I was unduly sensitive to the rights of property owners to let their rooms to whom they wanted.

Ten years later I went into a pub in Earlsdon, Coventry and failed to register that I was the only white person in the bar.

"You're in the curry bar, mate," the barman helpfully told me. "Whites on the other side."

I scurried through to the saloon bar and ordered my pint of mild and bitter without thinking any more of the matter. In fact, much of what we did was reprehensible though we did not recognise it as racist. Any activity that involved choosing was settled by the crude doggerel 'Eeny, meany, miney, mo, catch a nigger by his toe. If he hollers let him go - eeny, meany miney mo'. An attitude shift of seismic proportions was evident when it was gently suggested to us that we should substitute the 'one potato, two potato' sequence instead as a less offensive way of choosing. It was somehow never as viciously satisfying.

We knew of no other way. My headmaster, when introducing a new biology teacher from Tanzania, told us, "She is no ordinary wog. She is a cultured woman; a Parsee from a good family." I suppose he thought of himself as liberal and enlightened in that he could discriminate between 'ordinary wogs' and those who were more cultivated.

When Rajiv joined us from Sri Lanka, we were instructed to call him Roger presumably on the assumption that we would find Rajiv too complicated. The sad fact was that Rajiv had been institutionalised by these attitudes. When, at the mature age of eighteen, I tried to call him Rajiv he very firmly told me his name was Roger.

His father, a doctor at Billericay Hospital, had been almost pathetically anglicised. When his application for membership of a local golf club was rejected on the grounds that he was 'coloured' (to use that odious 1960s word) he derived a perverse pride from the fact such a good club would not accept the likes of him as a member.

All of this happened in spite of the 1968 Race Relations Act, which in theory made such overt and crude discrimination illegal. This was an era in which race was becoming the issue of domestic politics. The 1948 British Nationality Act had conferred, almost Roman-style, the right of any member of the British Empire and Commonwealth to settle in Britain. In the 1964 election, the Conservative candidate at Smethwick in the West Midlands had campaigned under the slogan 'If you want a nigger for a neighbour vote Labour'. To support their candidate, local Conservatives released a bizarre version of the Irving Berlin classic renamed *I'm dreaming of a white Smethwick*; a good tune but a shame about the words.

Twenty-five years ago I taught a boy from a well-known right-wing nationalist family. He was a nice boy, always polite and attentive, with his big black boots and shaved head. We got on fairly well but then I was white. His older brother was a high profile figure in a number of extreme right-wing racist groups who achieved some notoriety for organising violence at Anti-Nazi League meetings. Both Steve and Charlie Sargent have featured with some regularity in the press for their court appearances while trying to put some moral fibre into the British people. Typical of their view of national decline is the state of the Church of England which Charlie told the journalist Nick Ryan is 'now is so full of poofs and every sort of scum, what can you expect?'

The end of the road came for both of them in 1998 when older brother, Charlie Sargent, was sentenced to life imprisonment at Chelmsford Crown Court for murdering a fellow member of Combat 18, the violent neo-Nazi group, at a flat in Harlow.

The Sargent brothers, with their links to the violent white power music scene, football hooliganism and the Protestant paramilitaries in Northern Ireland were the originators of the bizarre and forlorn attempt to establish a Aryan Homeland in the Chelmsford–Harlow area of mid-Essex. From their fastness the pure Aryan community could launch a war of intimidation and violence against minority communities. Like Basildon, these towns were the swollen recipients of the white working class London diaspora. For the moment, Essex was cast as God's own country – white, and as England ought to be.

But perhaps things have changed. I sometimes spot Steve in the pubs of New Barnet. Rather than projecting himself as a disciple of the coming race war, these days I see him as the softly-spoken and thoughtful child I taught a quarter of a century ago.

The turbulence of the racial politics of the late 1960s expressed itself in a series of visits to the town by various fascist 'flat earthers' who had broken away from the British Union of Fascists. In the 1930s, Oswald Mosley had made his best stab at becoming a British Hitler or at least its Mussolini but the British people, with their customary caution, put their trust in the likes of Stanley Baldwin and Neville Chamberlain instead.

The BUF had been a substantial organisation during the 1930s but most of its leading members, including Mosley, were interned during the war. The remnants then spent the twenty years after 1945 engaged in a bitter internecine struggle for control of a tiny and increasingly extreme kingdom. Their fervour was fed in the 1950s by the mass of New Commonwealth immigration, particularly from the West Indies. The ambivalent attitudes of some Pioneers reflected their own lack of a clear ideology and a general confusion over matters of race and nation at a time when the perceptions of political correctness had not blunted what people instinctively felt.

It was clearly felt that Hitler had been evil and that Nazism was a pernicious doctrine. Many of the Pioneers had risked life and limb fighting Nazism during the Second World War. Some Germans in the 1920s and 30s had felt an attraction towards the National Socialist aspects of Nazism with its ideas of blood and soil, and the primacy of the volk without being rabidly anti-Semitic. In a similar way, it was still possible to find otherwise sensible people, Pioneers, who cautiously suggested that Hitler had been good for Germany until he went off the rails in 1939.

The mass murder of the Jews was almost a non-issue; a matter that did not impinge upon our consciousness or judgment. For twenty-five years after the War, it was a matter that was hidden away. It was only in the period following the mid-1970s, when what is sometimes unpleasantly called the 'Holocaust Industry' had cranked up into full gear that our awareness of all that had happened became complete. When I came across a copy of Lord Russell's *Scourge of the Swastika* (no relation to

Bertrand Russell) on the bookshelves it was prised from my grasp like a particularly filthy piece of pornography. For the previous thirty years the issue had been so intensely painful and traumatic that it had been hidden away. Of course we knew of the terrible names like Auschwitz and Birkenau but the suffering was abstract and unquantifiable.

When Adolf Eichmann was hanged in Israel for the murder of hundreds of thousands of Hungarian Jews, my father, a man who staunchly opposed the death penalty suddenly expressed strong approval.

The issue of race was always hovering in the background. Definitely beyond the pale was Mr Bradshaw who lived four doors away and was a member of the League of Empire Loyalists. Run by the ex-BUF propagandist, A.K. Chesterton, (cousin of G.K. Chesterton), the League campaigned not only for the preservation of the British Empire but also for the maintenance of Britain as a great power and a sort of reactionary die-hard conservatism that has now largely disappeared.

The collapse at Suez in 1956, the slow withdrawal from colonial rule in Africa, and the subservience to America were all issues that fired Mr Bradshaw, and the retired colonels, genteel Cheltenham ladies and right-wing Catholic priests who seemed to make up the rest of its membership. I remember Mr Bradshaw celebrating when a particularly odious British fascist, Martin Webster, assaulted the leader of the newly-independent Kenya, Jomo Kenyatta, on the grounds that he looked like an escaped gorilla. Webster was later imprisoned for the assault. These were people who went round chanting, "Lassie for the dogs, Kit-e-Kat for the wogs" while they gave each other the PJ – Perish Judah – signal. It was not very sophisticated. Later Mr Bradshaw justified the Apartheid system in South Africa on the grounds that 'the blacks are only just down from the trees'. A change of the past thirty years is that it is now very rare to hear such crude, virulent racist comments uttered publicly.

I recently bought an oil painting at an auction. While I was waiting for it to be wrapped, the auctioneer, a stout Lancastrian from Lytham St Annes, felt sufficiently sure of my views that I was treated to a string of racist jokes that would have made Bernard Manning look like a liberal multiculturalist. They were the sort of crude jokes I had not heard since my childhood but it did not stop me from buying the pictures.

His jokes usually began with lines like "What's brown and lives in

Birmingham?" My response was "Tell me another. Go on, tell me another." Finally he got fed up with me. "Do you want the bloody picture or not?"

His assistant was a Pakistani student from Karachi studying for an MA at London University. "Hey, Gunga Din, wrap the man's picture up. Chop-chop, you're not in Calcutta now. Look at those teeth. Go give us a flash. Bet you could even sell those in Bombay."

The student duly obliged revealing a flashing set of white teeth that contrasted with his dark skin. He reminded me of the performing Sambo charity box that used to be located on Southend Pier. By putting a penny into the black boy's hand, he raised it to his mouth and swallowed the coin.

The measure of the auctioneer was that he offered to knock another twenty pounds off the cost of the picture if my 'lovely wife would give me a kiss'. There was a little initial squeamishness but in my view twenty pounds is not a sum to be scoffed at. It was a pure Bernard Manning quality moment.

I suspect that Mr Bradshaw, if he is still alive, still harbours such sentiments but he has probably learned to keep them to himself or he has moved to Lytham St Annes.

As late as the 1960s there was still a powerful 'kith and kin' argument; the belief that white Britons had a semi-sacred duty to spread their racial stock around the world. This was the era of the White Australia policy, the Ten Pound Assisted Passage Scheme, and the belief that immigration to the white dominions represented a legitimate safety valve for the British working class. When Ian Smith and his white cronies in Southern Rhodesia illegally declared independence from Britain in 1965 in preference to facing black majority rule, their actions were justified on the grounds that he was protecting his kith and kin.

The last time I heard of Mr Bradshaw (about 1968) he was talking of emigrating to South Africa because the 'Jew lovers' were in charge in Britain and it was 'all up for honest white folk' like him.

"Them blackies have got the upper hand now," he whispered conspiratorially to me. "You mark my words."

In 1962, the fascists came to Basildon in the form of Colin Jordan and John Bean. To understand this, it is necessary to be aware that post-war British fascism was hopelessly split between those like Colin Jordan, who wished to promote a world-wide Nazi movement and those like

John Bean, who wanted to create a distinctive English national socialism. They had been part of Oswald Mosley's post-war Union movement that was essentially the remnants of the old BUF. In addition, there was a residue of those who were simply old-fashioned anti-Semites who believed in the protocol of the Elders of Zion but had little interest in Nazism. There were also old-fashioned die-hard Conservatives who loathed the One Nation policies of the 1950s and 60s and there were of course those who simply disliked black people but who carried no ideological baggage.

The 1950s and 60s saw the endless splitting and reforming of a variety of extremist right-wing groups. By 1960 the White Defence League and the National Labour Party had merged to form the British National Party with its emphasis on northern European racial purity and a demand for compulsory repatriation of all non-white immigrants. In 1962 the National Socialist Movement split away from the BNP as it was keen to promote a much more overtly Nazi party. These people were more significant than a mere lunatic fringe and in early 1962 the two groups held rival meetings in Basildon. They used the old Radion cinema in Laindon at the western end of the town.

The National Socialist Movement meeting made little impression. Colin Jordan explained the threat from the Jewish conspiracy and demanded their elimination. I was not there but I was told that the audience sat in stony silence. It would appear the demand for Britain to become part of a worldwide Nazi movement held little appeal in Basildon.

I did, however, attend the second meeting addressed by John Bean a few weeks later. At best there was muted enthusiasm because here the focus was on 'coloured' immigration emphasising not the creation of a mongrel race and the dangers of miscegenation but the overloading of the National Health Service, wages being undercut by cheap unskilled labour and housing shortages that would be created. He told us what was happening to various areas of inner-London where the white stock was being driven out by 'the coloureds'. He even threw in – Enoch Powell-style – the occasional allusion to little old ladies being driven from their homes by the 'coloured hordes'.

It was not very sophisticated but it hit home with some of the audience, particularly those who recognised and knew the areas Bean was referring to. These were the old London heartlands from which many of them had originated; areas where they still had family and often visited.

Mr Bradshaw was sitting a few rows in front of me in his belted raincoat, still wearing his bicycle clips. Every time Bean made a strong point, Bradshaw turned round to the rest of the audience and announced, "He's got a point there you know."

Eventually someone from the back shouted, "Shut up, you ponce, Bradshaw. We all know what you like."

That shut him up for the rest of the meeting.

It was out of this whirl of minor groups that the National Front was formed in 1967. At this time John Tyndall was the deputy leader of the National Socialist Movement. In the mid- and late-1960s, the NSM was an openly violent organisation. Its paramilitary wing, Spearhead, acknowledged the spiritual leadership of Adolf Hitler and promised a final reckoning with world-wide Jewry.

Having served three jail terms for racial incitement Tyndall is still around as a front man for the BNP although these days he makes party political broadcasts set against the white cliffs of Dover emphasising the problems of the countryside rather than engaging in Hitler worship. He was expelled from the BNP in 1999 and then subsequently readmitted as he had developed the habit of using Spearhead, the magazine that he owns and edits, as a platform for attacking BNP leader Nick Griffin.

Fourteen years after my first encounter with the National Socialist Movement and John Tyndall, I was on a walking holiday with some friends during a late Easter in the Wye Valley. As we tramped along a footpath deep in the Gloucestershire countryside a grand Palladian house came into view at the front of which was a flagpole. From about 200 yards away I saw a number of figures moving around purposefully. As we approached it became apparent that the flag fluttering on the pole was the Nazi Swastika and that the figures were wearing a variety of Nazi-style uniforms.

At first I thought a film was being shot. The absence of camera crews and the stony hostile stares that we attracted disabused me. One of our party was black. Further down the track I heard the chug of a military motorcycle slowly pulling an open sidecar. Sitting inside dressed in full brown shirt uniform, sat the passenger, an eerily disconcerting Hitler look alike. My cheery "Good morning" was greeted with complete indifference.

As we walked further down the path into the woods the chilling roar of

"Seig Heil, Seig Heil" drifted in the wind. Someone later pointed out that the day of our encounter, April 20th, was Adolf Hitler's birthday.

Chapter 14: The Great Wen

You'll reach this city always.
Don't hope to get away:
For you there is no ship,
no road anywhere.
C.P. Cavafy.

Arthur Machen, that great and neglected mystical writer, claimed in his story 'N' that from certain vantage points in Stoke Newington it is possible to see another land. I too have stood in those same positions and seen another land. It is called Hackney.

I never fail to be impressed by the power of coincidence. Having completed this brief reference to Arthur Machen, I went for a short stroll in Whitby, that most atmospheric of English towns on the northeast coast. I stopped at a seafront pub, the New Angel Hotel, for a pint of bitter. As I left the pub half an hour later I noticed a small plate on the wall: it informed me that Arthur Machen had lived there during the First World War.

In true Machen-style, it is possible to stand in Bunhill Fields cemetery just to the north of the City and catch glimpses of another London, the fabric of which has been thrice crushed during the last sixty years. What the Luftwaffe failed to destroy during the war, rapacious property developers and the municipal vandals of the various inner-London Boroughs have finished off.

My paternal grandfather, who was born in 1886 and lived in a cold water tenement called Verulam Buildings at the southern end of Grays Inn Road, bore witness. He was late-Victorian and he remembered the city as it was before the turn of the century. I often walked with him as he pointed out what he saw as the wonders of the city. It would be a lie to claim that I remember all the things he told me: alas, I was more interested in the prospect of a visit to the Lyons Corner House at the western end of the Strand.

My only specific memory of our perambulations was attending the

Remembrance Day parade in 1961 and seeing a group of Boer War veterans wearing their bright red jackets as they marched proudly past. Old men with their chests puffed out. With a few more years on his shoulders, my grandfather might have fought alongside them but, instead, he was saved for a much more sombre and deadly struggle that lay a decade and half away.

Forty years later, I attended the 2001 Remembrance Day parade and was standing at the base of the Clive Steps close to the Cenotaph when three young people, in their early twenties I imagine, unfurled a banner calling for an end to sanctions against Iraq that were killing innocent children. They stood in peaceful silence but within a minute four police officers arrived, tore down the banner, snapped the poles and roughly pushed the demonstrators away just as the motor cavalcade of the royal family came past. It was all part of the pretence of loyal and happy subjects.

I took some photographs of the incident. When the police shouted at me to stop, I slipped away into the crowd. The right to protest peacefully in this country has sharp limits. When it suits them, the police treat it with contempt. We live much closer to an authoritarian police state than ninety-nine per cent of the population realise.

This became very apparent to many people after the Chinese leader, Zhao Ziyang, visited Britain in 2000. A group of about two hundred people protested against China's human rights record and against the illegal occupation of Tibet. Even though the demonstration was peaceful and lawful, the police tore down the banners and bundled away many of the protesters, fearful of giving offence to the leader of the largest country in the world which, potentially, might be a huge trading partner. It can only be assumed the police acted in this way on the instructions of the government.

At the inquiry afterwards, the Metropolitan Police Commissioner, Sir Paul Condon, admitted the police had been wrong, said sorry and everything was once again all right. But it wasn't alright for those peaceful demonstrators who had no redress for the fact that Britain had, temporarily at least, become a police state.

On one of my Sunday wanderings with my grandfather, we stopped in Bunhill Fields at the grave of William Blake, the visionary poet and engraver. I remember very little about the reason for stopping but I do recall it was a misty autumn day with thin sunshine illuminating the ancient moss-covered slabs. Perhaps there was an instinctive awareness that Blake understood the world like no other.

> To see a World in a grain of sand,
> And Heaven in a wild flower,
> Hold infinity in the palm of your hand
> And eternity in an hour.

A few weeks ago I returned. His gravestone is still decorated with ribbons from modern devotees although it is one hundred and seventy years since he died. I believe that only Blake and Karl Marx still inspire such a degree of devotion.

In the distant past, I thrilled to *The Tiger* in an English lesson and the observation from my English teacher that Blake, the son of a hosier and a working man, was a poet for the ordinary person. I think she was trying to make a contrast with rough contemporaries like Wordsworth, Coleridge and Shelley who were clearly not for ordinary folk.

Nearby stands the grave of Thomas Hardy, cobbler and political radical, who found his final resting place after the tribulations of his last few years.

I have occasionally walked past Marx's bust in Highgate Cemetery and seen the floral tributes laid upon the marble plinth accompanied by intimate notes of affection as if he was a favourite uncle who used to bounce children on his knee. I have never seen anyone place them there, or remove them, although I accept that it does not happen in a magical way. Before the collapse of East European communism, I observed, on my Sunday wanderings, the delegations of Eastern European diplomats and spies who would come down from the forbidding blocks of flats on Highgate West Hill to lay their wreaths. It was not so much a 'thanks for communism Karl'-type ceremony as a 'thanks for the privileged position that your system gave me'.

Each year on March 14th at 2:32 p.m. – the exact moment of his death – there is a graveside oration attended by a group of enthusiasts. Somewhat elderly, hangdog, and probably unemployable, they cluster in the rain. They are the sort of people who might run an otter sanctuary, be involved in a vintage car run or perhaps keep bees. By insisting on conducting the ceremony at the moment of his death they exclude most of those engaged in gainful employment.

In 2003, the oration was on The Engagement of Karl Marx. Not being a

Marxist, I thought it was going to be about his engagement to his wife-to-be, Jenny; showing the man's human side. In fact, to my disappointment, it was about his engagement with the ideas of his time. I don't disagree with the Frederick Engels observation written shortly after Karl's death that 'mankind is shorter by a head, and the most remarkable head of our time'.

Blake and Marx were both visionaries about the human condition. Blake mourned our loss of innocence and the way that modernity corrupted our lives; Marx lamented the chains that tied and enslaved us. And, of course, they had very different prescriptions for salvation.

Living among the Pioneers, there was a very specific moment when I realised Blake's importance to some of them. I would go as far as to say that he was a guiding light because he showed through example that ordinary men and, I suppose, women could possess an extraordinary imagination and have a rich inner life. It was not necessary to have gone to public school and attended Oxford or Cambridge Universities to have a unique talent.

I had a friend called Paul McGovern who lived with his parents on the Lee Chapel estate. The McGovern family had come down from Newcastle to live in Basildon and were therefore quite untypical of the town. Mrs McGovern was a large, formidable woman who regularly offered me homemade oatcakes and, through her expression, defied me to say they were not delicious.

Mr McGovern was a thin, dark, solemn, quiet, if not silent, man, who flitted in and out of the rooms as if he were not quite part of the household. I realise now, but did not know then, that he had a severe drink problem. Between them, Mr and Mrs McGovern looked like of one those saucy McGill seaside postcards with the fat dominating wife and the thin husband looking wistfully at the pretty buxom girl cycling past, her dress flapping suggestively in the breeze.

Mr McGovern worked at the York Shipley factory assembling refrigeration units. The work must have been soul destroying and demeaning for a man of his extraordinary imagination. I knew Mr McGovern painted and I had occasionally seen his pictures being mounted in the kitchen. I regularly expressed my admiration for his work.

One day when his wife was out, he silently beckoned me into his studio. In most houses of that design it was a middle television room between the kitchen and the front room, without any form of natural light. Mr McGovern had fitted ceiling spotlights that illuminated the paintings mounted in a crowded fashion on the walls. They were extraordinary, a combination of Hieronymous Bosch and those 1950s poster artists who produced advertising billboards for cheap science fiction films like *Night of the Living Dead* and *It Came from Outer Space*.

The paintings were of other worlds. I can remember vividly a scene from a distant planet looking out into space as the light of the sun broke through from behind a cratered moon, all set against the black of the distant universe. For the first time in my life, through his brush strokes the infinite and mysterious nature of the cosmos was clearly suggested to me.

Along one wall he had a series of cosmic scenes as he imagined them; the surfaces of the solar system's planets. I was particularly struck by the green icy vastness of Neptune. Other paintings were of worlds that lay beyond ours; one picture was crowded with strange creatures, hobgoblins, wraith-like spectres and anthropomorphic rat creatures. It was entitled *The Other World That God Created*.

Today such images are common, found on the lurid covers of cheap fantasy and science fiction stories but at the time they were a revelation. I wanted to talk about his work but I did not have the language to engage him in discussion and, in any case, I do not think that he would have responded.

I never visited Mr McGovern's studio again but I became intensely aware that his rich inner life probably made the job at York Shipley bearable. When I came home from University at the end of my second year, I heard that Mr McGovern had died. It was a small tragedy that, although his talent was to some extent realised, it was not acknowledged because of the narrowness of his circumstances.

*

I continue my walk up the City Road for a mile or so to The Angel tube station. A plaque tells me that on this spot stood the tavern Thomas Paine used when he was in London. I hurry away, walking eastwards along the Euston Road, until I come to number 137 where William Lovett, that great figure in the history of Chartism and working class emancipation, lived and finally died in 1877 after a lifetime of strenuous labour.

In a curious coincidence, like Thomas Hardy, who was born fifty years earlier, Lovett's father also drowned at sea and never saw his newborn son. Also like Hardy, Lovett campaigned peacefully for political rights for working men and found himself persecuted and jailed by the fearful authorities. In 1836, Lovett founded the London Working Men's Association and agitated for the six political demands that crystallised into the mass political movement, Chartism, that for a dozen years terrified the early Victorian political establishment.

Lovett the cabinet maker, Thomas Hardy the cobbler, and Francis Place the radical tailor of Charing Cross Road, represented that powerful tradition of skilled, self-educated, intellectually-curious artisans who were increasingly demanding a say in running the political system. Lovett's reward was both rich and meagre. Toward the end of his life, living in poverty on the Euston Road, he wrote pathetically: 'Few persons have worked hard or laboured more earnestly than I have for the betterment of his fellow man; but somehow I was never destined to make money.'

There was to be no wealthy benefactor to ease him through his declining years in the fashion of Thomas Hardy yet, within eight years of his death in 1877, the 'respectable' working class had gained the vote and the Chartists' demands that had so frightened Queen Victoria and the Duke of Wellington had been met.

William Lovett is buried close to Karl Marx in Highgate cemetery. Although they both devoted their lives to the betterment of the working class, it is difficult to imagine any meeting of minds. Given they were such close contemporaries in Victorian London I am curious about the extent to which their paths crossed. Karl would have had nothing but contempt for such a solid citizen and would have branded him a petty bourgeois. Lovett did not even qualify for that most damning of Marxist criticisms, being labelled a revisionist.

The site on the Euston Road is now occupied by a rather bland 1960s office block with a branch of Britannia Building Society at ground level. Lovett would certainly have approved of the principle of mutuality if not the vast salaries that the Britannia directors lavish upon themselves.

*

One hundred and fifty years later, the Pioneers were still maintaining the same tradition of self-improvement. The main change was that, by the mid-twentieth century, as a result of the 1902 Education Act, society had sufficiently opened up that able young working class men were able to find a position in which they could express their abilities. From the 1880s onwards, working class men like John Burns and Jimmy Thomas and, occasionally, working class women like Ellen Wilkinson were finding their way into cabinet.

An abiding memory of my childhood is of talking to clever and talented working class men and women whose lives had been stunted by lack of educational opportunity. Instead they had found other ways of expressing themselves, through mechanics' institutes, the Workers Educational Association, or simply by devouring the contents of the local library.

Political contemporaries such as Nye Bevan, the former coal miner, had risen through the trade union movement to become the most inspiring politician of his generation in the fifteen years after the war. They could look to Herbert Morrison, elementary school pupil and fourteen-year-old errand boy who rose to become foreign secretary and Labour Deputy Prime Minister in the post-war Attlee government.

George Lansbury, the 'John Bull' of Poplar, pacifist, teetotaller and Christian who went to prison in 1921 for refusing to levy a rate on the poor, held a very particular place in their affections. He was that rarity, an MP who actually lived and worked amongst the people he represented. His house in Bow Road was a centre of local activity from where literally thousands of East Enders received his personal advice and support.

In a sense, the contrast between Lansbury and his contemporary, Ramsey MacDonald, symbolises the divide within the Labour movement. Once MacDonald became Prime Minister, and a part of the political establishment, he went native and lived in a degree of executive, almost regal splendour that Lords Roseberry and Salisbury, grand hereditary peers who both became Prime Minister, would have recognised. In contrast, Lansbury, despite being leader of the Labour Party, retained a degree of humility and a sense that he was the servant of the people he represented.

The choice in the 1930s for Labour between the saintly Lansbury and the pragmatism of Macdonald summarises the dilemma. It depends how individuals want to be remembered but it is difficult to find either a contemporary or a historian who has a good word for Macdonald. The two minority governments he led were both failures that damaged the Labour Party and the Labour movement. He triggered a split in the party that only the trauma of the Second World War ended.

In contrast, Lansbury remains a revered figure even amongst the people born after he died. He never had to grapple though with the problems of being a minority Prime Minister at a time of extreme economic crisis. Perhaps the moral is to avoid the top job and stick to being kind to people. For the same reason, it would have been disastrous for Tony Benn's reputation if he had defeated Dennis Healey for the deputy leadership of the Labour Party in 1981.

I recently visited the Lansbury Estate in Poplar and stood outside the house where my great aunt lived until her death in 1963. It was a warm summer evening and a number of young people were hanging about in a harmless sort of fashion. I asked a few of them, in my normal guileless manner, if they knew why it was named the Lansbury Estate or who Lansbury was. Not one of them knew but, as several of them did not speak English, it was not entirely surprising. Why should they know of a dead white politician from another age and another culture? Perhaps David Blunkett should make one part of the new citizenship qualification for asylum seekers a test to ensure the applicant has a thorough knowledge of George Lansbury.

Perhaps it is not an issue in the way that I see it. The moral is the folly of naming anywhere after anyone, given the shallowness of our public memory. With a very small number of exceptions, we are all forgotten very quickly no matter how notable we were in life. There was a time when I passed down Rhodes Avenue each day on my way to work but it now seems rather pointless that I should be reminded with such regularity of one of the fallen heroes of the British Empire.

The contemporaries of the younger Pioneers were that generation of the Labour Party who came to maturity in the 1950s and were central to the Labour government of the 1960s. George Brown, after being educated at a south London elementary school, rose through the Transport and General Workers Union to become Labour's Foreign Secretary and was also, in the 1960s, a potential leader as well as being a destructive influence on the right of the party. Jim Callaghan rose through the same route, elementary school and then the Civil Service union on his way to becoming Labour Prime Minister. Harold Wilson, the clever grammar school boy from a modest background who won a place at Oxford and, through a mixture of cleverness, guile and luck (the premature death of Hugh Gaitskell in 1963), became Labour leader and

Prime Minister.

*

I now turn right on the Euston Road between St Pancras and Euston Station and proceed along Chalton Street. Before either station was built, this area was on the very fringes of London with wheat fields waving in the distance.

For most of his working life the philosophic radical, William Godwin, lived at number 99, no more than a few hundred yards from the new British Library. Godwin would have appreciated the proximity as he was one of the first writers to use the papers of the old British Library when writing his monumental *History of the Commonwealth*. If William Godwin had been born in 1950 he would probably now be a professor of Moral Philosophy at one of our ancient universities and we would see him with irritating regularity on one of those late night, intellectual talking heads discussion programmes. He was a one-man university who married the godmother of the feminist movement, Mary Wollstonecraft, and fathered Mary Shelley, the precocious author of Frankenstein. He was also father-in-law to Percy Shelley, the radical poet. Dinner conversations must have been somewhat precious.

The unusual nature of his relationship with Mary Wollstonecraft can be illustrated by their mutually-convenient domestic arrangements. Godwin moved out of the house in Chalton Street and moved into the Polygon building twenty doors away on the pretext that 'too much intimacy would render their relationship wearisome'. His rationalist habits were pushed to the extreme when, as Mary Wollstonecraft lay dying, Godwin asked her how she was.

She replied, "In heaven."

His response was calm. "You mean, my dear, that your physical sensations are somewhat easier."

Godwin established himself as the most original and prolific intellect of his day. Inspired by Tom Paine, he was a philosophical anarchist who read the *Rights of Man* in manuscript form. From that moment, he truly saw the light as he made the transition from protestant divine to an anarchist who believed in human perfectibility and questioned the need for both government and laws.

"Perfectibility is one of the most unequivocal characteristics of the human race," he told his readers.

It was probably no coincidence that he wrote his *Principles of Political Justice* in 1793, two years after Paine published the *Rights of Man*. In addition, Godwin was a successful novelist as well as a printer and bookseller. However, he spent his business life limping from one financial crisis to another. He was also without a conscience and would borrow from anyone who would lend him money. Even the amoral and quite conscience-free Percy Shelley was appalled by his father-in-law's shameless borrowing. Literary and intellectual London in the first decades of the nineteenth century learnt to dread the soft knock on the door which presaged a profound intellectual discussion followed by a request for funds.

Unlike the radical Francis Place who was one of the main victims of his borrowing, Godwin seemed unable to combine a life of high intellectual endeavour with the business of making enough money to sustain himself and his family.

When he died in 1836 he was buried along with Mary Wollstonecraft at the Old St Pancras Churchyard. The arrival of the railway destroyed the churchyard and, in 1851, his remains, and those of his wife Mary and his daughter Mary Shelley were reburied in Bournemouth. Most people go to Bournemouth before they die but I suppose it might be considered typical of Godwin's contrary nature that he went after his death.

St Pancras Church still remains although it is blighted by the constant traffic thundering along the Euston Road. Godwin's stamping grounds are remarkably extant although the pleasant character of the area was destroyed by the arrival of the railways in the 1840s which also helped to create the notorious Somerstown slum. Today the area is mixed social housing of a 'not unattractive' nature.

The Polygon has gone but a Mary Wollstonecraft House has been erected within the last few years on the site of 99 Chalton Road. It seems rather churlish that her equally distinguished husband is unacknowledged but Godwin's name has been expunged from local legend. I see the hand of Camden Council's Women's Unit at work.

I recently visited Godwin's birthplace at Wisbech, in the flat Cambridgeshire fenlands just south of the Wash. The town is not obviously proud of him. There is a William Godwin Primary School and a Godwin Way but no more. I was hoping to find the William Godwin Free House overlooking the old market square or the Godwin Arms, imposing and inviting. It would seem to be inappropriate that such a private, intense and introspective character should have an alehouse – a house of good cheer – named after him. However, he was not the 'hail-fellow well met' type, preferring instead to conduct his philosophical explorations in the solitude of his rooms in Somerstown.

I conjure up in my mind's eye an image of the thin, spindly Godwin hurrying away from Wisbech to London via Norwich and Stowmarket. It is, though, a pleasing coincidence that four years after Godwin's death, Octavia Hill, the pioneering housing reformer and co-founder of the National Trust, was also born in Wisbech. Upon sober reflection it is probable that, for all Godwin's mastery and great abilities, it was actually Octavia Hill, Wisbech's most distinguished progeny, who has had the most beneficial influence on mankind.

I now plunge south along Tottenham Court Road which must be the ugliest thoroughfare in London although New Oxford Street offers fierce competition for the title. Passing a large and garish lap dancing club, it is difficult not to feel that a profound degradation of the spirit has occurred in these few square yards of London. I stand outside for a moment, peering in at the lissom young women in the foyer and the glowering shaven-headed bouncers. I am wearing oversized waterproof trousers, holding a crash helmet in my hand, with my hair plastered down from the rain and I have an enamel Lenin badge on my motorcycle jacket – a piece of revolutionary chic rather than proof of any political commitment.

"Oi, you! Clear off!" says one of the bouncers standing in front of me like a block of flats. Obviously, I am not the sort of person they are looking for: I might bring them into disrepute.

Turning right into Oxford Street it is easy to forget that what has become an emporium of tat was once an historic thoroughfare. At the far eastern end, at number 449, once stood William Morris' shop where the hangings, drapery, murals, furniture jewellery, tiles, and embroidery that so entranced late-Victorian progressive taste, were purveyed. On this exact spot now stands the grim Centre Point building, symbol of the plight of the homeless and the irresponsibility of corporate wealth.

On the opposite side of the road once stood the Boar and Castle Inn where the unstable but dynamic Chartist leader, Feargus O'Connor, stayed in the early 1820s. In 1842 he was the leading force behind the Oxford Street March that attempted to stop troops marching up Tottenham Court Road to Euston Station where they were to be deployed against the Northern Chartists. Six years later he led another march along

Oxford Street before he addressed a crowd that was sustained by sandwiches filled with Chartist pork, sliced from pigs that were reared on the Chartist farm in Rickmansworth, Hertfordshire.

At the far western end, close to where Marble Arch now stands, number 20 was the home and shop of Thomas Spence the revolutionary bookseller. Here he was arrested for selling the revolutionary pamphlet *The World Turned Upside Down*, a conscious and inflammatory reference to the revolutionary doctrines of the Diggers and Levellers one hundred and seventy years previously. Yet Spence was not such a dangerous individual. He simply believed passionately that each person should have the right to a rich and fulfilled life. He proposed that all land should be held in common by the parish which should lease the land out with the income providing public amenities such as free schooling, cultural activities and a public library within which would be contained 'all the best books in the world'.

Once again, we come across the notion that literature has the power to uplift and enrich peoples' lives. The site of Spence's shop, the place where he died in 1814, is now an open-fronted shop selling cheap bags and sports gear.

Hurrying along the crowded pavement I reflect that William Blake must have walked this street ten thousand times. He was born in Golden Square, a few hundred yards to the south, and attended Pars Drawing School on the Strand.

His first business was at 23 Green Street, Leicester Fields (now Leicester Square) – a reminder that two hundred years ago the countryside intruded into the centre of London. A later residence and business at 28 Poland Street, running south of Oxford Street, has been obliterated by a 1960s office block. The house he died in, 17 South Molton Street, is now a nails and waxing establishment. It would have tested even Blake's visionary powers to predict that the place where he produced some of his most memorable engravings would later become a refuge for women wishing to have their hairs torn from their legs, underarms and upper lips. Like Marx, Blake was a revolutionary but the machinations of his plots took place within his extraordinary inner life.

Walking south down Dean Street, in the middle of Soho, we come to the former home of Horne Tooke, one of the co-defendants in the Thomas Hardy treason trial. By a pleasing coincidence, he lived four houses along from the place where my great, great uncle, Carl Magnus, worked as a silversmith in the 1860s. Tooke was no revolutionary but the Pitt government could not see that. From a prosperous background, he was one of those old-fashioned pre-socialist radicals who represented the London tradesman against the privileges of the aristocracy rather than favouring the emancipation of the masses. His hospitality and his house on Wimbledon Common were legendary. He is buried at Ealing where the gravestone bears the inscription 'happy and contented' after his name and dates.

Further along Dean Street, we pass numbers 28 and 64, two of Karl Marx's London residences where he lived in what cannot even be described as genteel poverty. At number 28 he succeeded in impregnating the housekeeper, Helene Demuth. Given the nature of the two shabby rooms they occupied, there was not too much house to keep. Their illegitimate child, Freddie, was adopted by a working class East London family. When he died in 1929, aged seventy-seven years, he was still oblivious to the identity of his real father. During his lifetime, Freddie Demuth was a founder of Hackney Labour Party and a trade union stalwart so it may be argued that his commitment to socialism was genetic.

Number 64 Dean Street is now a discreet private dining club, I assume for individuals of sufficient wealth, celebrity and public profile that they do not wish to be pestered by the likes of me.

Outside slumped against the railings is a young African man holding out a polystyrene cup begging for change. For a moment I catch the gaze of his soft African eyes – I think he is Somali or Ethiopian. I turn away feeling slightly ashamed and I am confronted by a man of east-European origin who asks me if I want 'a laydee'. With a rush of embarrassment I decline the offer. The 'laydee' in question is standing at the other end of the railings. She looks no more than fourteen or fifteen.

Further along the road, a young white man wrapped in a dirty sleeping bag is slumped in the doorway of a tobacconist's shop. What went wrong? His mother must have loved him once; there must have been a time in his life when he had hope but now it is reduced to this. Why do people beg on the streets of London? The London of my childhood was beggar-free although I am sure the historians would point out that London has always been at the centre of the mendicants' art and that, somehow, I have drawn a veil over its existence during my early years.

We understand the existence of beggardom in Elizabethan and

Victorian times. The compression of wealth and privilege amidst a sea of poverty and ignorance was always likely to result in the poor demanding their share of the wealth of the rich in one way or another. Now it seems that the poor are back.

The first thing I have learned is not to be afraid of them. I have developed a habit of talking to the *Big Issue* sellers in the places I frequent. Very rarely do I find that they do not want to talk. They become so used to the crowds sweeping past them with no more than a flicker of hurried guilt that even my conversation is accepted.

Sometimes I sit down on the pavement beside Charlie and his dog, Fleet. I really know nothing more about him. I watch the people rushing by. A few of them catch my eye and then turn away because, just for one moment, I am the symbol of what might be. Charlie and I never discuss anything profound and I always pull back from the question that I really want to ask, "How did it all come to this?"

It seems to be so intrusive and personal and piercing to the heart of his existence. I am very aware of the phrase that my mother always used: 'There, but for the grace of God, go I.' It helps that I usually take a tin of dog food for the docile creature on the end of a piece of rope. I always buy a copy of the *Big Issue* and offer to buy Charlie some coffee and a hamburger from McDonalds, fifty yards down the road. Perhaps it is a way of expiating my conscience but more often it is the need for humility and a simple reminder of the random, capricious nature of fortune as she bestows her favours.

On a summer trip to Scotland I was chatting with a group of Tennants Extra drinkers on the benches beside the river in Inverness. The police came and took my name. It seems that in Scotland one is considered to be behaving suspiciously by showing a little civility to those who have slipped over the precipice.

It was with a palpable sense of shock that I came cross my first London beggar in the early 1980s outside Euston Station. I blamed Mrs Thatcher at the time for something I had previously associated with Dublin, Istanbul and Naples. Now beggars are everywhere: dark, inscrutable Romanian gypsy women on the underground clutching pathetic young children as they move from carriage to carriage; hopeless alcoholics on the Embankment; crackheads in Vauxhall; failed asylum seekers who congregate each night at Centrepoint, and the squeegee merchants with buckets full of dirty water on virtually every major road junction.

It reflects that world in which we live: the movement of peoples; the disintegration of family networks; the growth of drug and alcohol abuse; the decline of the welfare state; the loss of self-respect, and the breaking of old taboos that inhibited people from accosting complete strangers in public and asking them for money.

I can barely bring myself to ask a stranger in the street for the time so it is almost impossible to imagine how many levels of degradation I would have to pass through before I could routinely ask strangers for money. I am reminded of the lines from Philip Larkin's poem, *The Whitsun weddings*.

> And none
> Thought of the others they would never meet
> Or how their lives would all contain this hour.
> I thought of London spread out in the sun,
> Its postal districts packed like squares of wheat.

He tells us that, for every hour we spend in this city with its 'twenty thousand streets under the sky', millions of people we do not know and cannot comprehend are going about their lives within the 'squares of wheat' whether it is as beggars, prostitutes, bankers or simply those who have been bankrupted by life.

I press my face up against the small windows of the private dining club at Number 64 and gaze at the rather plutocratic diners. It calls to mind the scene at the end of Orwell's *Animal Farm* where the animals are looking in through the windows of the farmhouse as the pigs and humans congratulate themselves on their mutual prosperity. It is the coarseness of the juxtaposition between those who lie on the pavement outside and the sleekly prosperous on the inside that is so depressing when we are seven years into a socialist government. Was it ever thus?

For those of a beery socialist disposition, it is possible, in the space of an hour or so, to visit three of the pubs in the centre of Soho where Marx felt so at home. He was always at his best when delivering his political lessons in public houses. The pubs in question are the Dog and Duck in Bateman Street, the French House in Dean Street and the Red Lion in Great Windmill Street.

In the Dog and Duck I look around for Madonna. I've read in a magazine that it is her local where she pops in for a pint of Timothy Taylor's Landlord Bitter wearing dark glasses and an old tracksuit.

"Mine's a pint, Madge," I think I will say to her, but she stands me up.

Marx's addiction to bitter beer and porter is a reminder of just how human he was. For those of an even beerier and more socialistic disposition it is possible to follow, at least partially, the pub crawl Marx undertook along Tottenham Court Road in 1851 in the company of Edgar Bauer and Karl Liebknecht.

Their watering holes included the Blue Posts (demolished as recently as 1998), the Horseshoe (demolished in 1983), the Rising Sun (which still remains), the Black Horse, the Fox and Hounds, the White Hart, the Apollo, the Mortimer Arms (which also remains), the Italian (now renamed the Jack Horner), the Talbot, the King's Head, the New Inn (now known as Ye Olde Surgeon), the Plasterers Arms, The Mortimer Arms (at which I recently enjoyed a pint of Courage best), the Roebuck (now strangely known as The Court), the Northumberland Arms, The Bull's Head, the Rose and Crown and the Southampton Arms.

Karl was not the sort of man who indulged in halves so in order to emulate his feat you would need to drink nineteen pints. This, in my view, would take interest in the old man a little too far and would reveal an unhealthy, even morbid, disposition. Perhaps he sat out a few of the rounds.

A stroll down Tottenham Court Road indicates that only six pubs remain from the nineteen that it boasted one hundred and fifty years ago. Most of them are buried under the modern development of electrical retail shops at the southern end of the road. This is actually a good survival rate: less than a fifth of the pubs listed in the inner London trade directories of the mid-nineteenth century have survived.

Continuing down Oxford Street to Marble Arch and then a few hundred yards up the Edgware Road, I reach Cato Street. Here, in a barn on the rural west side of London in 1822, Arthur Thistlewood and his desperate co-conspirators planned to assassinate the cabinet, take over the Tower of London and Mansion House, and declare a provisional government with Thistlewood as Prime Minister and the cobbler, John Ings, as Home Secretary. (There is definitely something about cobblers.)

It was a mad venture that never had any chance of success. Thistlewood and four of his co-conspirators were hanged outside Newgate prison. Their heads were then removed and put on public display. In a moment of grisly gallows humour, the executioner, his hands slippery with blood, dropped one of the heads to which the crowd roared, "Ah, butterfingers." But their mood soon changed. Towards the end of the gruesome proceedings, they made a serious attempt to castrate the masked executioner before troops could intervene.

The only uplifting aspect of the whole miserable escapade is that Thistlewood, having been led on and then betrayed by government spies, died defiantly as he declaimed, "Albion is still in the chains of slavery. I quit it without regret. My only sorrow is that the soil should be a theatre for slaves, for cowards, for despots."

One hundred and eighty years later these words are only marginally less true. The chains may have changed but the cowards and despots remain and are the same type. Thistlewood showed a fine sense of the occasion right up to the end. When John Ings began a noisy rendition of *Death or Liberty*, Thistlewood quietly responded, "Be quiet, Ings. We can die without all this noise."

Little of London has survived from the early nineteenth century. The charitable would say London constantly renews itself as it sloughs the skin of its past. I would say that it cares little for its own preservation.

White Street in Moorfields, where Thistlewood was arrested, is now covered by a canyon of green glass and stainless steel. Castle Street, little more than an alley off Oxford Street where Thomas Spence died, is now covered by Selfridges while Chandos Street in Covent Garden, where John Thelwall, the third defendant in the Thomas Hardy trial, lived at number 42, disappeared as a result of inter-war LCC development.

And what has happened to all the pubs and taverns where the Regency radicals hatched their plots over clay pipes and pints of porter? It seems quite possible that none of the working class movements of the past two hundred and fifty years would have happened but for the public houses where groups of like-minded and similarly-aggrieved men could meet, discuss and plan how they would right the world.

The Cock in Grafton Street, The George in East Harding Street, the Fleece in Windmill Street, the Green Dragon in Fore Street, The Cecil in St Martins Lane, the Swan in New Street, and the Mulberry Tree in Moorfields; all were notorious as radical pubs between 1780 and 1850. A two hour walk around the city and its environs shows they are all now gone.

A similar fate has befallen the pubs frequented by the London Chartists; the Windsor Castle in Holborn, the Lord Denman in Great Suffolk Street and the Black Jack in Portsmouth Street. It is hard to imagine the serious, sober and abstemious William Lovett comfortable in such a milieu of republican toasts, socialist speechifying and costermonger banter.

And what are the modern equivalents? Would there be a wild anarchist meeting plotting international revolution in a Café Rouge or one of those modern, antiseptic, style-ridden bars. I suppose it would be possible to plot in one of those Wetherspoon pubs except they would put yet another sign up saying: 'No Dogs. No Swearing. No Music. No Socialist Wild Talk'.

Though I was removed from London in my early childhood to live in eastern Essex, I was always aware of a voice – the voice of London that was calling me back. I knew that when the opportunity presented itself I would return. There is always a sense that London was calling me whether I lived in Ireland, the north of England, Basildon or Europe. The same insistent voice always fills my head. I leave from time to time though I know it is necessary to hasten my return. But the relationship is not clean. There is something corrupt about it. As the Greek poet, C.P. Cavafy, put it:

> You will not find new lands, not find another sea.
> The city will follow you. You'll wander down
> these very streets, age in these same quarters of the town,
> among the same houses, finally turn grey.
> You'll reach this city always. Don't hope to get away:
> For you there is no ship, no road anywhere.

Chapter 15: Something Warmer, Sir?

Surely this sex business isn't worth all this damned fuss.
T.E. Lawrence on reading D.H. Lawrence's Lady Chatterley's Lover.

Everything is good as it comes from the hand of the Author of things: everything degenerates in the hands of man.
Jean Jacques Rousseau. From Emile.

The London Chartist movement consisted of early democrats who wanted the vote and an element of fairness in the political system. For fifteen years in the very early Victorian period, they spread apprehension and at times terror as a result of their very reasonable demands. They used public meetings, newspapers, campaigns and petitions to articulate their moderate and sensible views.

From a twenty-first century perspective, the desire for universal male suffrage, payment for MPs, equal electoral districts and the secret ballot does not look that subversive. The reactions of Peel, Russell and Palmerston – all prime ministers at various times in the mid-nineteenth century – suggest that the way we form and articulate our views makes us all prisoners of our time.

It is more instructive to look at the actions of the political establishment of the day to see the unfairness that our ancestors suffered. Upon hearing the news that, as a last gasp tactic, the Chartists were going to hold a final rally on Kennington Common, the reaction of the near-hysterical government was to bundle the relatively youthful Queen Victoria to Osborne House on the Isle of Wight. The rather ancient Duke of Wellington, having seen off the French in an earlier life, volunteered himself to organise the defence of London.

Kennington Common, on the south side of the Thames, had been the site where, a hundred years previously, many of the 1745 Scottish rebels had been hung, drawn and quartered. Now it is the site of the Oval cricket ground and Kennington Park but then it was the chosen venue for many

London families who assembled on the common, as much for a day out as to precipitate an English Revolution.

The Thompson side of my family (the family of Elizabeth Thompson, wife of my Swedish great-grandfather, Henrik) had some peripheral involvement in the Chartists. My great, great grandfather, John Thompson, owned a market garden in Walthamstow and a house in Spitalfields. He was not part of the sunken destitute mass that the political authorities so greatly feared but, according to the pocket book that he kept, the Kennington Common meeting was a day in which ordinary people could show the government and the Prime Minster, Lord John Russell, that they were part of the country as well. John Thompson was amongst the crowd.

The meeting turned out to be something of a damp squib despite the terror of the government. The crowd of perhaps 50,000 (the estimates ranged from 15,000 to 500,000) listened to the old Physical Force firebrand, Feargus O'Connor, before the moderate Chartist leaders made the decision not to cross the bridges to the north bank of the Thames which would probably have provoked military action.

By then, many of the crowd were more interested in the side shows, the stilt walkers, the jugglers and the fire eaters than in any obvious political action. So, while the continental revolutions of 1848 ended in a hail of gunfire with bodies lying across the barricades, this moderate would-be revolution was ended by a brief rain shower.

The London Trade Directory for 1846 lists John Thompson of St James Street as a Trade Wholesaler. He was part of an emerging class of moderately prosperous superior artisans who were starting to shape London life. It would seem unlikely that he would support any revolutionary movement given that he had a considerable stake in society – a stake that was becoming progressively larger. But it does seem reasonable that, as someone whose star was rising and who perhaps even aspired to join the middle class, he felt entitled to some small piece of influence in the way that the country was governed. The fact that two of his daughters, Annie and May, ran a dame school in Hoe Street, Walthamstow in the 1860s indicates a degree of social advancement and at least a modest level of education.

John Thompson's other three children all pursued routine working class occupations. William was a plumber in the Balls Pond Road, Edward was a grocer in Wych Street (just off the Strand) and Frederick was a foreman bricklayer who, in 1861, was recorded as working on Joseph Bazalgette's great scheme to provide a sewerage system for London. It seems likely that Frederick laid his share of the three hundred and eighteen million bricks that were used to lay the fourteen thousand miles of sewers that relieved London of the haunting spectre of cholera which had caused many early deaths during the previous fifty years.

John Thompson's children secured respectable occupations for themselves, placing them either at the artisan end of the working class or on the fringes of the lower middle class. They had failed though to burst through into the bourgeois prosperity that John Thompson's advances in the 1830s and 40s had suggested might be possible. The effort of the Thompson clan trying to pull themselves clear of the sunken London mass was too great.

The grandchildren of John Thompson, according to the recently released 1901 census, were recorded as resident in Clerkenwell, Farringdon, Bethnal Green and Poplar and were clearly an authentic part of the London proletariat at the turn of the century. They had failed to move out to the new suburbs or to the more prosperous parts of inner London and their addresses indicate the sort of terraces and tenements that were to be the subject of mass demolition schemes over the next fifty years.

John Thompson may have been the coming man in the 1840s but the inheritance he bequeathed to his children was 'hard times'. It is a small indication that Victorian society was both dynamic and offered a significant degree of social mobility but it was very unforgiving to those who slipped back into the abyss.

There has been a tendency, at least amongst the more general historians of the nineteenth century to dismiss Chartism as a failure, even to deride it because of the possibly fraudulent nature of the petitions. When I was taught O-level history more than thirty years ago, the fact that Mr Punch, Queen Victoria and the Duke of Wellington had signed in support of the Charter meant that the entire movement could be dismissed as a piece of working class nonsense. But this is hardly the point. Within the lifetime of the younger Chartists, five of their six demands had been met and the sixth, annual parliaments, has still not been achieved on grounds of practicality rather than principle.

The fact that the popular Liberalism of the mid-Victorian period came to monopolise the political attentions of the working class does not mean that Chartism failed. It is the broader nature of the movement that is often overlooked. The way it allowed those who were marginalised by the dominant political classes to feel they had a voice. Chartism tapped into a powerful auto-didactic, self-improving tradition that allowed ordinary people to enrich their lives outside the methods approved by the ruling elite.

According to conventional historians, the Chartist movement was finished by 1848. The London Peoples' Paper (one of the many short-lived radical newspapers that emerged as Chartism fragmented into its constituent parts) informed its readers in June 1852 that later that month a dog show at the Caxton Hall was to be judged by Mr Ernest Jones, the great leader of the late-flowering of Chartism 'for all men whose sympathies lie with the aims of the Peoples Charter'.

Karl Marx despaired of the English working class because they had an obsession with gardening and walking their dogs rather than fermenting proletarian revolution. It never seemed to occur to him that it was possible to do both.

The Pioneers had a very similar idea. They used a school hall to hold a pet show. True to the egalitarian spirit, there were no winners or losers but all entries were given either a green or a purple rosette with no explanation as to the distinction between the two.

I remember an argument between a man with a white boxer who was awarded a purple rosette and another entrant with an Alsatian who got a green rosette. The nub of the argument was which of them owned the superior animal and much bad feeling was generated by the failure to clearly indicate winners and losers.

*

I am very aware that what I am writing is full of names of men and women who have, to use a famous phrase, been 'hidden from history'. I recently combed through almost nine thousand names that are listed in the London Trade Directory for 1846. Women are notable by their absence – less than two hundred are listed and most of those mentioned were tavern keepers. We need to look much harder if we are to find women anarchists, radical political activists and autodidacts but they are there. There are processes, both conscious and unconscious, that hide them away.

To take an example: both Laurie Lee (through *Cider With Rosie*) and

Flora Thompson (through *Lark Rise to Candleford*) record with stark, elegiac beauty the style of life in the English countryside in the first decades of the twentieth century. Both are powerful writers yet it is Lee's work that is included in every GCSE syllabus. It has been made for television and is eulogised for the evocation of a way of life that has gone. Flora Thompson remains a far more marginal figure in terms of cultural relevance despite the beauty of her writing.

My great-great-great aunt Annie was active in the Chartist movement particularly in the 1850s when it was in its political nadir and the impulse to improve the lives of ordinary people had been transmuted into other forms of action. As a member of the Leyton Methodist Mutual Improvement Association she actively organised poetry readings, dramatic productions and lectures on popular science. In 1868 she records going to listen to the great naturalist and teacher, Thomas Huxley, though it is unclear if the great man condescended to visit their humble mutual improvement association in Leyton.

I have some of her letters, written to her sister and mother, expressing her great hopes for the future. Although membership of the mutual improvement association was open to both sexes, there was a tendency to regard the presence of women as necessary to make the tea. Running the dame school in Walthamstow seems to have been an extension of these activities.

There may be some significance in the fact that Annie never married. She may have been educated or, at least, intellectually emancipated beyond her class but this fact may have served to make her less attractive to a prospective suitor from her own class. Whilst the pursuit of education and cultural enlightenment was an acceptable activity for men, attitudes towards women were far more ambiguous.

Like Felix Holt the Radical, there was a tendency to regard women as a distraction from more esoteric and uplifting pursuits. In some ways, being self-educated and running a dame school would have made Annie an unattractive proposition to a working man looking for someone who was a skilled domestic homemaker. Nor did Annie have the family pedigree (her father being a nurseryman) to vault clear into the middle class marriage stakes. Perhaps she simply felt content to be who she was: that great rarity in the second half of the nineteenth century – a financially independent working woman.

*

One should feel pride at the indefatigable determination of Chartists and their families to create rich and meaningful lives for themselves in the most unpromising of circumstances. With tea meetings, Chartist dances and bible classes that focused on the scriptures as the fount of democracy, their lives were enriched and given dignity. Chartist women's groups were formed in some northern towns where women were encouraged, for the first time, to become involved in the political struggle. These were uplifting experiences for tens of thousands of the poorest people in Britain, particularly in the north of England where the more intimate nature of community meant that people were often bound more closely together.

While the artisan class dominated London Chartism, the north of England membership was cut from an altogether coarser cloth. In small, often remote communities intelligent, but uneducated, men and women took advantage of the Chartist day and the Sunday schools that sprang up in the late 1840s and 1850s. As Julian Harney, one of the earliest English Marxists put it, the Red Republican working people needed 'the Charter and something more – the ability and the means to enrich their lives'.

Regrettably, I have not been able to find any account of the activities that took place within the Chartist Reading Rooms in Fig Tree Lane, Sheffield but it is a fair guess there were bible classes, public readings of the Northern Star newspaper for the illiterate, and readings from Shakespeare, Robbie Burns and John Milton.

John Bunyan's *Pilgrims Progress* remained a staple of the devout and humble who nevertheless railed against the injustice of the manmade world. It was inevitable that there would be several heavily-used copies of Thomas Paine's *The Rights of Man* and perhaps William Cobbett's *Rural Rides*. The walls would be covered in banners from past campaigns, teas would be held, heroes would be commemorated, old comrades would be welcomed back and collections would be made for impoverished Chartist families. Lectures would be given on popular history and current issues such as the slavery debate in the United States and how to pursue their own just demands.

It would not do to be too starry eyed though. The Fig Tree Lane reading rooms were at the centre of the 1840 rising. After a series of secret meetings, Samuel Holberry, a leading physical force Chartist, led a group of Sheffield Chartists in a desperate attempt to take over the city. Betrayed by a pub landlord who overheard a secret conversation, Holberry was imprisoned for four years.

Meanwhile those at Fig Tree Lane reverted to their moderate self-improving activities. Perhaps, as did so many other groups at this time, they would have organised a day visit to the 1851 Great Exhibition at the Crystal Palace in Hyde Park using the newly-opened Sheffield to Kings Cross railway. Here, just three years after the meeting on Kennington Common, they might have reflected that society now seemed far more stable and content than it had in the violent and hungry decades that had preceded it.

William Gladstone would have approved. Only fifty years earlier the government had been terrified of the prospect of ordinary men arming themselves with knowledge out of fear that they would bring the whole edifice crashing down. By 1851, the position had been reversed. Education was encouraged as a means of exorcising the viciousness that lurked in a dormant state within the working class character. It would encourage those great Victorian virtues, thrift, sobriety and prudence.

In the days before an all-enveloping welfare state emerged, to develop such a support network of ties and obligations within a community was essential.

The Fig Tree Lane Reading Rooms are now gone, demolished some time in the first decade of the twentieth century. In their place now stands a rather forlorn parade of shops, including the obligatory video rental store. Two of the remaining shops are boarded up. We may have become much richer as a country but in some other ways we are very much poorer.

*

Not that everyone was quite so wholesome. John Thompson's own brothers, Arthur and William, were involved in the production of 'books indicative of a depraved appetite'.

Arthur and William are listed in the 1851 census as resident at number 82 Newcastle Street at the southern end where it joined the Strand and the western end of Holywell Street.

Holywell Street: the name elicits a little shudder, a spasm of anticipation and surprise. There is a frisson of expectation as I scan the census sheets for I know of the reputation of Holywell Street. I look for the listed occupations of Arthur and William. Arthur is given as a printer and his younger brother William is a compositor. It all fits quite neatly.

Holywell Street had a reputation as the filthiest and lewdest street in London, the epicentre of that Babylon of human desperation and suffering. From this vortex poured forth a terrible poison that contemporaries claimed was responsible for infecting the whole of London with depravity.

The area has now gone, destroyed in a Baron Haussman-style scheme that resulted in the construction of Aldwych and Kingsway at the start of the twentieth century. All moral and upright Londoners greeted the destruction of the warren of ancient and low streets with relief. It had become a sordid anachronism in the heart of what had become the greatest city in the world.

With the City of London to the east, the ever more fashionable and prosperous West End to the west, the Royal Courts of Justice being constructed to the north and Kings College to the south, Holywell Street and the Dickensian warren of shabby alleys that surrounded it were a relic from an earlier London that had not yet become the great imperial capital. It is possible today to walk the exact line of the street from St Mary's in the Strand to St Clements Danes and to be aware that one is tracing over the adumbra of an ancient and ghost-ridden thoroughfare.

Picture if you will for one moment, a mid-Victorian gentleman of some evident prosperity, traversing carefully the ancient thoroughfare. He moves cautiously from building to building among the crumbling shop fronts, lopsided gables and overhanging eaves. Dressed in his dark frock coat, light grey trousers, complete with top hat and cane, he lingers in front of the dingy print shops and dealers in antiquarian books. He is evidently a man of solitude, occasionally glancing around him at the flower girls, child hawkers, rag pickers, costermongers, knife grinders, washer women and tradesmen who rush past. They are oblivious, for they are occupying separate worlds that just happen to inhabit the same space.

The gentleman stops for a moment outside a shop that has a case of books at the front. He picks up a book and carefully scrutinises the title page. It is probably an ancient Latin text or perhaps a work of ecclesiastical history or jurisprudence. Then he enters the dimly-lit shop and asks if he can speak to the proprietor. He waits for a moment until the proprietor appears and asks him if he has anything for the discerning gentleman customer. Perhaps he is after that early Victorian favourite, *The Lustful Turk*, or Rosa Fielding's *A Victim of Lust*.

If the scene is set a little later in the century, it may be *Randiana* that has caught the attentions of our connoisseur or the *Amatory Experiences of a Surgeon*, the elegant nineteenth century equivalent the *Confessions of a Taxi Driver*. Offered the classical writings of Petronius or the seventeenth-century meanderings of Lord Rochester, our gentleman asks if he can be supplied with something 'warmer'. He is then shown the latest collection of 'stereoscopic gems' newly arrived from Paris that, in reality, have been produced in a backstreet photographic studio less than a mile from Holywell Street, probably in one of the courtyards close to Drury Lane.

But no, our gentleman is after something a little more elegant and tasteful. A particular favourite is the writings of the impoverished army officer Edward Sellon. In such minor classics as *The Adventures of a Schoolboy* and *Phoebe Kissagen* Sellon invented his own discreet and tasteful 'pornotopia' for the educated and cultured gentleman, modelled loosely on a classical prose style and the conventions of formal literature. If our gentleman's tastes are a little less refined then he may be enlivened by the lengthily titled *The New Lady's Tickler*, or the *Adventures of Lady Lovesport* and the *Audacious Harry*.

It would appear that being a more than averagely-talented author within the genre brought little happiness or prosperity to Edward Sellon. In the spring of 1866, while staying at Webbs Hotel, Piccadilly, he blew his brains out.

Our gentleman has now made his choice. He pays his guinea and then hurries away to feast on the pleasures of the written word. Meanwhile in the remote backrooms and garrets of Holywell Street, Arthur and William Thompson continue to man the secret presses to meet the demand for this new form of entertainment that has increasingly become a feature of Victorian life.

Caution would have been their watchword. Ever vigilant, the Society for the Suppression of Vice – 'those who croak for the safety of Christian England' – sent representatives to the Holywell Street area, ever eager to be shocked and outraged. Having been suitably offended, they would rush out and find a member of the Metropolitan Police who, assuming he was not in the pay of the pornographers, as many of them were, would arrest and charge the offender.

For this, significant manpower was necessary. In one raid in 1851, 882 books, 870 prints and 110 catalogues were carted away. For aiding and abetting such a notorious figure as William Dugdale, Arthur and William could expect at least two years' hard labour in Pentonville or Clerkenwell Prisons.

They did not realise it themselves, but the Thompson brothers were involved in the democratisation of pornography in the mid-nineteenth century as technology and demand turned it into a mass leisure activity. For those who search for evidence of a decline in literacy in modern times they might well compare the demands of reading *Flossie: A Venus of Fifteen* from the mid-nineteenth century with staring at the contents of the modern *Asian Babes*, *Sweet Black Cherries* or the equally top-shelf *Down and Dirty*. The former demands a degree of literacy and a sensitivity to literary genre; the latter merely requires strong nerves and a significant level of gynaecological knowledge.

Pornographers may be too strong a description of the occupation of my great, great grandfather's brothers. But, almost certainly, they were involved in the production of what were termed 'low books'. Holywell Street, in its own desolate way, was occupied either by secondhand clothes and furniture shops, or print shops.

As the nineteenth century progressed, it was the 'down at heel' bookshops for the discerning gentleman that caught the eye. If we are to believe some of the lurid press reports of the 1850s, it was also increasingly catering for the less discriminating customers who were keen to obtain their thrills for just a few shillings. Pornography, while it was the preserve of a small monied and educated elite, could be safely ignored. Once it became available to the masses, then it was a danger to public morality and had to be dealt with.

Newcastle Street would have been a natural place of residence for anyone working at one of the discreet printing presses behind the crumbling facades in Holywell Street. There is nothing particularly surprising about the nature of the street and the area from the 1840s onwards. Improvements in the technology of cheap printing had made mass book ownership possible if the demand was there. Before an age of mass literacy, there may have been a market for highbrow novels and the less demanding fare of popular novelists such as Mrs Henry Wood. There was also, however, an emerging demand for something more salacious.

During the first two decades of the nineteenth century, a radical anti-government press had emerged, fuelled by popular resentment against oppressive government policies. By the 1820s, much of the discontent and political radicalism had faded but the presses remained, as did the skilled printers, compositors and bookbinders. It was not a huge step to move from printing radical political literature to printing radical or at least prurient sexual material. After all it was only another way of shocking the early nineteenth century political establishment. Whether it was the production of *The Poor Man's Guardian* or *The Pearl* – that wordy mid-nineteenth century equivalent of a modern 'lads' mag' – both indicated a disengagement from society, a rejection of conventional mores and a realisation of self that, in many ways, we are more likely to associate with the second half of the twentieth century.

In the 1960s, radical politics went hand in hand with what was quaintly called 'free love'. In the 1840s, the radical impulse was transforming itself into something similar.

For the discerning customer, Holywell Street offered *The Wedding Night* or *Battles of Venus*, *The Man of Pleasures*, *Private Companion* and *Gems for Gentlemen*. These rude but probably harmless publications comprised the basic trade of the shabby run-down Holywell Street shops with their sad and decayed fronts and dusty cobwebbed interiors. Into this milieu came the technicians, the printers, the compositors, the bookbinders, and the photographers who insinuated themselves into the ancient and dilapidated buildings of the area.

By the 1850s, Holywell Street commanded a reputation that placed it at the very heart of the corrupting trade. I do not know the precise role of William and Arthur Thompson but their proximity casts a cloud of suspicion over their activities. It is possible they were involved in the legal book trade that centred on Chancery Lane but why live so close to that sink, Holywell Street, if the nature of the work did not demand it?

In response to the 'vile trade', a morally-outraged mid-Victorian government passed the Obscene Publications Act. This gave any half-educated police officer the power to initiate proceedings for obscenity whether it was Leonardo's *Virgin on the Rocks* or Paul Pry, a mid-Victorian favourite that sat on the ever-shifting boundary between the obscene and the merely scurrilous and distasteful.

The 1861 census indicates that Arthur and William Thompson still pursued their trades in the vicinity as a printer and a bookbinder

(William's occupation had now changed from compositor). The brothers had moved a few hundred yards to the eastern end of Wych Street, which was parallel to Holywell Street and only slightly less notorious as part of the capital's sexual subculture.

Again this suggests they were working locally, quite possibly for that prince of mid-Victorian pornographers, William Dugdale, whose premises over the years were at a number of addresses in Holywell Street and in neighbouring Wych Street. Having been involved on the periphery of the 1822 Cato Street conspiracy to blow up the cabinet, Dugdale became the living embodiment of the political radical who then embraced the sexual revolution. Sex and politics have never been that far apart.

As early as the mid-1830s, Dugdale was responsible for publishing an expurgated edition of John Cleland's *Memoirs of a Woman of Pleasure* otherwise known as *Fanny Hill*. He had discovered his niche in life and, more than thirty years later, found himself once again on trial at the Old Bailey. In the 1850s, Dugdale was prosecuted and imprisoned on several occasions for supplying the pornographic needs of much of mid-Victorian London. For such a persistent and committed offender, it was perhaps appropriate that Dugdale died in 1868 in the Clerkenwell House of Correction while serving his final sentence for contravening the Obscene Publications Act.

There is something pathetic in the fact that Dugdale was so persistently incapable of pursuing an alternative trade despite numerous court appearances and custodial sentences. I suspect that, in Dugdale's case, as De Sade put it, "Happiness does not consist in enjoyment, but rather in the destruction of the barriers that have been erected against desire."

It may be significant that, in the 1871 Census, the first after Dugdale's death and after Holywell Street had lost some its notoriety, Arthur and William, by now aged fifty-five and fifty-eight respectively, are to be found in Viaduct Buildings in Charterhouse, Saffron Hill – just to the north of the City a mile and a half distant from Holywell Street but still conveniently placed to be involved in the production of law books. There is no reference to them in the 1881 or the 1891 census suggesting they had died or, far less likely, moved away from London.

In June 1903, Holywell Street was demolished.

Chapter 16: My Great Grandfather and Karl Marx

The beginning of wisdom is knowing who you are. Draw
near and listen.
Swahili proverb.

Consider your origins: you were not made to live as brutes
but to follow virtue and knowledge.
Dante

Ethical socialism is a peculiarly English concept. A few years ago I was
in the old Reading Room of the British Museum when I spotted the
distinguished and elderly historian, Eric Hobsbawm. He was taking
round what I imagined to be a small group of elderly central-European
intellectuals. Perhaps he was showing them the seat that Karl Marx
habitually used.

Hobsbawm has never taught me but I do know people who have been
taught by him and I have attended several public lectures at Birkbeck
College. I know him to be a cultivated, humane and highly intelligent
individual. It is therefore all the more surprising that, for the past sixty
years, he has been the most intellectually-distinguished champion of
communism or scientific socialism in British academic life.

Given that history tells us this has been a miserable failure causing
untold human suffering, I am at a loss to explain why Hobsbawm should
hold this view. With the range of his understanding and his empathy with
ordinary people, he would have been a natural candidate to join the
distinguished ethical socialist tradition that exists in Britain.

Unfortunately, high intelligence is no guarantee of sound judgment. In
fact, it is more likely to be an impediment. This was illustrated when, in
1980, Mr Hobsbawm compared the state of Britain under Mrs Thatcher
to that of Germany after the Allied bombing of 1945. He seemed to miss
the point that Mrs Thatcher and her government had been democratically
elected and had a mandate to pursue their chosen policies even if some of
us disagreed with them. That is the nature of our form of representative

democracy and I am at a loss to explain such delusions; or rather I was at a loss. What I did not realise was that Eric Hobsbawm is not British. He is an Austrian who fled to Britain with his family in the 1930s to escape Nazi persecution.

His intellectual world is that of Mittel Europa, the world of Liebknecht, Kautsky and Bernstein and that generation of revisionist Marxists. If he had grown up in Oxford rather than Vienna then his inspiration would probably have come from William Morris, George Lansbury and Robert Blatchford. None of us can escape what we are.

This is not to claim that mainland Europe had not produced ethical socialists. France spawned Pierre Leroux (the mystical Christian Socialist), Charles Fourier (the inspiration for Robert Owen) and the utopian communists, Victor Considerant and Etienne Cabet. These figures, although significant, were peripheral to the development of mainstream French socialism in a way that the likes of William Morris and Keir Hardie never were in Britain.

An earlier but equally distinguished historian, Richard Tawney, famously claimed that 'the Labour Party owes more to Methodism than to Marx'. The Marxists claimed to have uncovered immutable iron laws of history that meant the triumph of socialism was inevitable via revolution and the dictatorship of the proletariat. Such phrases as historical materialism and the constancy of the dialectic were alien to the British tradition. British socialists on the whole have been unimpressed beyond a small and excitable minority.

For a Christian socialist like Tawney, the failures of capitalism were not due to any immutable laws. They were result of the absence of moral ideals that led to an unchecked acquisitiveness, material inequality and an unfair society. The solution was to apply Christian principles to both politics and the ordering of society. The vision of Tawney and his generation has been both humanistic and Christian.

From the 1860s onwards it became increasingly common to equate the central principles of socialism with Christianity. The Guild of St Matthew, founded in 1877 by the radical clergyman, Stewart Headlam, argued that universal brotherhood, human equality, the belief that we are all equal in the eyes of God, and the biblical disapproval of personal wealth, meant that all good Christians must accept socialist principles. Not surprisingly, the Bishop of London disapproved of his Old Etonian cleric and sacked him despite the devoted following he inspired amongst the poor of Bethnal Green.

*

My Swedish great grandfather, Henrik, along with his younger brother, Carl Magnus, emigrated to this country from Sweden in 1860. En route, while on their journeyman travels, they lived in Berlin and St Petersburg where it would appear Carl Magnus picked up some bad habits.

Henrik, once in London, naturalised sufficiently and successfully to be awarded a medal at the Crystal Palace in 1865 for being 'An Industrious member of the Working Class, Third Class'. His reward for being an industrious member of the working class (Third Class) was to die alone in St Pancras Workhouse and be buried in a pauper's grave alongside what is now the North Circular Road close to East Finchley. Today the spot is covered by a briar patch in one of the extensive unmaintained sections of the cemetery. It is inexpressibly sad that the long journey from rural northern Sweden, via Berlin and St Petersburg, ended with him lying for all eternity next to the roaring traffic of the North Circular Road.

Carl Magnus lived and worked as a silversmith in Old Compton Street and neighbouring Dean Street in London's Soho district before migrating to the north of Oxford Street close to the Middlesex hospital. He achieved brief notoriety when he was arrested and tried for criminal damage as a result of Black Monday – the Sack of the West End in 1886.

It is difficult to know Carl Magnus' role beyond the evidence of the trial papers. It would appear he was one of a group of unemployed who marched through the West End protesting against government indifference to unemployment. The rally had been organised by the early English Marxist, H.M. Hyndman, and the fiery young socialist, John Burns, later to be Liberal cabinet minister. Whether Carl Magnus was a member of Hyndman's SDF (Britain's first Marxist Party) is unclear and will remain so as membership records no longer exist but it is near certain he was an active sympathiser.

A letter I have received from the Stockholm Archive office indicates that Carl Magnus was either expelled from St Petersburg in 1865 or at any rate felt obliged to leave because of his political activities. Tsarist Russia in the mid-nineteenth century was a very unforgiving environment. He then came to London and joined his older brother

Henrik as one of the ever-swelling band of European political exiles.

The circumstances of Carl Magnus' fall from grace are reasonably clear. Starting at Trafalgar Square, the group of unemployed workers marched up Pall Mall in the direction of Hyde Park. The police, exhibiting their usual incompetence, became confused and were waiting in the Mall.

Passing the various gentlemen's clubs, the unemployed were jeered at by the rich and privileged members. At this stage, Carl Magnus was accused of throwing a stone through the windows of the Carlton Club. There followed a certain amount of modest destruction of club windows, shop fronts and gentlemen's carriages before the police realised they were in the wrong place. The general line of the press was that this was the work of foreign agitators, anarchists and socialists as no right-thinking English workmen would throw stones at the windows of the clubs of his social superiors.

Carl Magnus, being a foreigner with a suspicious name, was sentenced to two years of hard labour in Pentonville.

*

In the summer of 2002, I went on an anthropological expedition to observe the participants in the Save the Countryside March or at least those parts of the countryside that they have not crushed under the outsize wheels of their four-wheel-drive vehicles. I can report that the natives were good-natured, rather raucous and overbearing, unpleasantly overconfident and rather plummy in their use of language.

I stood in Pall Mall opposite where I imagine Carl Magnus was arrested. The members of the various gentlemen's clubs, mainly the Carlton and Pratts, were out front identifying with their country cousins in a sinister exhibition of class solidarity.

I have long found the use of the word 'gentlemen' in this particular context to be an irritating oxymoron. Most of the members looked like spivs, bloated capitalists, die-hard Tories, corpulent ex-navy types, bloodshot generals, members of criminal gangs and pornography barons with a bit of spare cash. If the marchers looked posh and prosperous, which most of them did, then they were sponsored for temporary membership, signed in and treated to a sumptuous breakfast. If they looked as though they were an agricultural labourer or a hunt worker, i.e. a bona-fide country person, then they were simply allowed to pass by.

Most of these people were simply displaced suburbanites in green Wellingtons probably with a Joanna Trollope novel on the back shelf of the four wheel drive.

A novelist once wrote that the past is 'another country' to which I would also add 'the English upper-middle classes'. My general conclusion at the end of the afternoon was that there can be no other good reason for standing outside the Carlton Club than to throw stones through the windows.

There is minor symmetry to all of this. Carl Magnus was the brother of my great grandfather who was my father's father. My father's mother's father, i.e. his maternal grandfather, one Henry Green, was in 1886 a police constable – warrant number 72286 – in the Metropolitan Police serving in S Division, Hampstead. The Metropolitan Police records held at Kew show that, on the day of the riot, Henry Green was assigned to 'special duties elsewhere in the Metropolis'.

It is not too difficult to surmise what those special duties were. It is even possible that Henry Green was the officer who arrested Carl Magnus although this would be stretching the point a little too far.

At the time, Carl Magnus was forty-two and Henry Green, who had only just escaped the rural confines of Gloucestershire living at Awre on the banks of the Severn, was just twenty-six. The distressingly complete Metropolitan police records, MEPO 7 54, indicate that in 1892 he was dismissed from the force 'suspected of improperly retaining the sum of 4s 11d overpaid him with his pay; absent from duty and Division without leave, not yet returned and considered unfit for the police force. Dismissed without pay'. Victorian England could be a harsh place.

Perhaps the distance between him and Carl Magnus was not so great and probably, by 1888, they would have met when his daughter married Carl Magnus's nephew – my grandfather.

For a working class man to be denied one of the few jobs in late-Victorian Britain that guaranteed a regular, if modest, wage would have been a devastating blow made all the more severe by the loss of his police house in Well Walk, Hampstead. To walk down this little pathway of discreet pedestrianised privilege is to be reminded of just how ghettoised London wealth has become compared to the robust and varied community who lived there more than one hundred and twenty years ago.

The little police house has now gone and the site is covered by Wells

House, a particularly grotesque 1930s London County Council block of flats that has an Eastern European 'suburbs of Warsaw' feel about it.

After abandoning his leafy north London purlieu, Henry Green recovered to the extent of marrying, and fathering a daughter – my maternal grandmother. Successive censuses reveal him as a labourer in a steelworks, a sixpence-a-day dock worker in London's East End and finally, employment as a railway track worker at Neath, in South Wales.

*

Never underestimate the power of coincidence. When Sir Anthony Eden, the most patrician, intellectual and cultured of prime ministers, sailed away from England in the January of 1957 on the RMS Rangitata bound for New Zealand in the wake of the Suez debacle, his cabin steward was the sixteen-year-old John Prescott. If the working class boy from Hull, who had left his secondary modern school at the age of fifteen, had told Eden that, forty years later, he would be deputy prime minister himself it would have been dismissed, politely but firmly, as the most outlandish fantasy. Eden had a lofty concern for the welfare of the working classes but this did not extend to allowing them into positions of power and influence.

On a similar level of coincidence I was talking recently to the mother of a good friend. She told me that Brian, her older brother (he was really a half brother and was twenty-three years older than her), was a corporal and a mechanic in the newly-formed Royal Flying Corps during the First World War. His commanding officer was the youthful, but already dashing, Sir Oswald Mosley.

Being apolitical, Brian was not one of those who fought against Mosley's fascists in mid-1930s London but in his last year of service with the Military Police in 1943, he found himself assigned to special duties. His job, with three other members of the military, was to accompany Sir Oswald on the short journey from Brixton prison to Holloway where he was to continue his enforced incarceration. There he was to be permanently reunited with his wife, Diana, who was also one of the famous Mitford sisters.

Brian, for a moment, thought that Britain's aspirant Mussolini had recognised him. No words were exchanged between the lofty Mosley and his working class captor although Brian did say that Lady Mosley was charming and had a charisma about her that the shrunken and emaciated Sir Oswald lacked.

*

My great, great uncle, Carl Magnus, had one son who was christened Wilhelm at St Peters in Saffron Hill in 1890. I have to assume that this was not out of any particular affection for Kaiser Bill although it could be argued that Wilhelm did his bit for the German war effort by becoming a conscientious objector and refusing to be conscripted. This was because he espoused the cause of international socialism. He believed the conflagration that began in 1914 was a war within capitalism in which the working classes of both sides were going to be used as cannon fodder to prop up a corrupt and unfair system. Even at this distance that does not seem an unreasonable analysis.

Wilhelm spent fifteen months in York prison, a dangerous and brutalising experience for all conscientious objectors. He narrowly avoided being transported to France where, at the military camp at Etaples, he would have come under military law. Refusal to fight then would have meant death in front of a firing squad. Fortunately for Wilhelm and more than two hundred other conscientious objectors, the architect of the plan, Lord Kitchener, went down with HMS Hampshire off the Orkneys in 1916.

Not surprisingly, Wilhelm changed his name to Will Elton after the war and rose to become a senior official in the Transport and General Workers Union as well as a key ally to Ernest Bevin, the TGWU leader in the 1920s. In 1930, Danish Will (I have no idea why it was not Swedish Will), as he had become known, was elected Mayor of Bermondsey and became something of a local celebrity although it is difficult to know what rancour and bitterness was felt over his refusal to fight in the war. He died in 1935 as a result of fracturing his skull when he fell from the ladder while changing a light bulb. The coroner was unable to say whether Will had received an electric shock or whether he had suffered some sort of seizure.

*

My great grandfather, Henrik, knew Karl Marx. Karl was born in 1818 and began his London exile in 1849 while Henrik was born in 1834 and began his exile in 1860.

The Berlin of the 1850s was hardly a place to tolerate political dissent and a socialist agitator such as my great grandfather would have found life uncongenial in the Prussian police state of Friedrich William IV with its network of informers, censors and police spies.

My grandfather, Frank, was born in 1886 when Henrik was 51. To become a father past the age of average life expectancy probably reflected the extreme instability of Henrik's life as a roving European exile. In genetic terms, I was probably born forty years too late.

After Henrik's late attempt at parenthood, the efforts of his son, Frank, were delayed by the outbreak of the Great War and the fact that he did not return from the Mesopotamia Mandate until 1921. His son, William (my father), was in turn caught up in the Second World War, which delayed his courtship plans. If normal generation trends had been in place, I should have been born round about 1914 which would have made me eligible for service in the Second World War.

My grandfather, Frank, recalled with pride, that his father Henrik was a fierce socialist and a friend of Marx. He had brought his socialism with him from Germany which meant he was never going to be part of a rather cosy British Labour movement that was traditionally suspicious of continental political influences.

Frank's great grandfather, Lars Granath, had been a paid mercenary in Blucher's Prussian Army that fought at Waterloo in 1815. One of Lars' three sons, Olaf, emigrated to America in the 1870s, quite late on in life, and settled in the state that is now called Minnesota. He became part of the Swedish mid-western farming community. His great granddaughter, Tiffany Granath, recently became Playboy's Playmate of the Month and has her own website called Babeworld. This, I suppose, is one version of the American Dream: that the progeny of a gloomy early nineteenth century rural Lutheran should disport herself naked across the centrefold pages of an adult magazine to the lustful delight of millions of Americans and make herself rich in the process. (For aficionados and scholars of family history, this Playmate is my fifth cousin once removed.)

As part of the revolutionary socialist diaspora, Henrik would have come within Karl's orbit though it is unlikely there would have been any sympathetic meeting of minds between an impecunious bookbinder cum leather worker and an impecunious peripatetic intellectual of a revolutionary disposition.

Henrik was a habitué of the Scandinavian Anarchist Club in Rathbone Street which sits in the small triangle formed by Oxford Street and

Tottenham Court Road. A few hundred yards away, in the area around Middlesex Hospital, he would have mixed with anarchists from among the one thousand Germans who, the Evening News proclaimed, comprised a colony in that area. Within this milieu Henrik would have been part of the polyglot and conspiratorial world of Italian nationalists, Jewish anarchists, Irish brick workers, Polish and Hungarian exiles, and German socialists. Factional disputes over relatively minor matters, quite impenetrable to outsiders, were the bane of such inward looking communities that were forever plotting to overthrow a hated foreign tyrant or to challenge the authority of the police.

Henrik was also a drinking man, a fact that may have been the main reason why he ended up alone in the workhouse. Of the four addresses I have for him, three are in rooms above or attached to a public house. In 1861 he was living above the Crown Tavern at 64 Clerkenwell Close. For a while, Marx lived less than one hundred yards away in Clerkenwell Green. In 1871, Henrik was living above the Red Lion in Great Windmill Street, which was also the meeting place for the German Workers Education Society, a group of central European émigré socialists who included Karl Marx among their number.

Henrik's younger brother, Carl Magnus, is listed in the 1901 census as a tenant in the Cleveland Residences, a grim redbrick tenement that still stands opposite the Middlesex Hospital in Cleveland Street. Two hundred yards away, at number 6 Windmill Street was the Autonomie anarchist club frequented mainly by German and Scandinavian exiles. The name says it all. Henrik and Carl Magnus were part of that diverse and broad group of foreign malcontents who regarded anarchists and communists as part of the same broad tradition and slipped with some ease between the two beliefs.

For those who were not deeply ideological, the riven, bitter and dramatic debates between Marx and Bakunin on the role of the state in post-revolutionary society must have seemed both obtuse and obscure. For most of the revolutionary diaspora it was enough to rail at the unfairness of the system and the tyranny of government and to enjoy the company of like-minded revolutionaries amidst the smoke, beer, laughter, coarse schnapps and good fellowship that such clubs provided. It was easy to agree with Bakunin when he proclaimed that 'social solidarity is the first human law; freedom is the second'. It is the way such sentiments manifested themselves in practical action that gave cause for concern.

The activities of these desperate and dangerous people did not elude the police. In 1892 the Autonomie was raided thanks to the bomb-making activities of a number of its members. The intention was to blow up the Russian Tsar but the result was that one of its members, Auguste Coulon, was expelled from Autonomie for celebrating the bizarre revolutionary act of blowing up a cow in Belgium while others received lengthy prison sentences. Two years later, the police were once again interested when a club member, Martin Bourdin, travelled to Greenwich with a home-made bomb intending to test its effectiveness. Unfortunately for him, he blew himself up in a mighty explosion but the discovery of an Autonomie membership card in a jacket pocket brought more than just a curious visit from the police.

These events were observed by the Polish novelist, Joseph Conrad, resulting in the publication in 1907 of *The Secret Agent* with its reminder that it would be foolish to take a sentimental view of such activities. Beneath the romantic rosy aura of late nineteenth century anarchism, lurked the real life equivalents of Conrad's characters – Verloc, Ossipon and Mr Vladimir. Their cynicism, indolence, moral bankruptcy and above all sheer desperation embodied the hopelessness of the exiles' plight. There may have been a peaceful mutualist strand to nineteenth century anarchism but it somehow never found its way into the hearts of those whose inspiration was the 'sacred violence' of Michael Bakunin.

Today the area bears no trace of its anarchist past. The traces have been well and truly kicked over: Whitfield Street, Percy Street, Charlotte Street, Mortimer Street and Rathbone Street, which at the start of the last century housed several thousand families whose members were sympathetic to the principles of anarchism, have now become part of London's pavement café society. There are no blue plaques and not even a chic little bar or restaurant named Autonomie or The International.

What happened to the progeny of the five thousand or so anarchists (if the Evening News is to be believed) who lived in that warren of streets in the area known as Fitzrovia? The numbers of descendants of this group of foreign exiles must now number at least fifty thousand. The answer is that they were assimilated and dispersed. The anarchist beliefs of their great, great grandparents did not pass down the generations.

The sense of outrage that exiled Italians, Poles, Russians and Germans felt against their oppressive native governments was simply not present in England to the necessary degree. This, combined with Britain's more moderate political culture, meant that any sense of outrage at the unfairness of British society was always more likely to be channelled in the direction of conventional socialism.

Prosperity, and a simple lack of urgency in our concern for what we see around us have served to brush over the traces of the past. We have forgotten where we came from but, I would argue, this is simply a symptom of the human condition.

In the late 1970s, I knew the late Albert Meltzer, the leading British anarchist of the post-war period. The mother of a good friend, Mary Wilson, had been a friend of Meltzer since the early 1950s. Mary was only a part-time anarchist. She had a very nice house in Princedale Road, Notting Hill, where she lived peacefully during the week but she was right behind the cause of smashing capitalism at weekends.

An earlier neighbour of Mary's, a contemporary of her parents, was Arnold Leese, the ghastly fascist leader who was sufficiently anti-Semitic to accuse Oswald Mosley of being a Jew lover. He claimed to be prone to spontaneous vomiting if he was near a Jew.

Meltzer was a rather forbidding character but I discovered that the way into his confidence was through boxing. He had been a boxer in his youth and, whilst at school in Edmonton, had argued against the Labour candidate, Edith Summerskill, for the 1935 General Election. For the rest of her political life, Dr Summerskill was primarily known for her vocal opposition to the noble art despite the fact that she later became Home Secretary. Meltzer later repeated the argument with Emma Goldman, who was to anarchism what Muhammad Ali is to boxing – beyond comparison.

Albert was surprised by my embarrassing profusion of boxing knowledge as I was able to discuss the relative merits of Bruce Woodcock, Don Cockell, Len Harvey, Eric Boon and Arthur Danaher. We commonly mourned the fate of the tragic and doomed Glaswegian drunkard and world champion, Benny Lynch. In fact, we discussed all the great British fighters from the 1930s and 40s although Meltzer had particular admiration for the Americans, Rocky Marciano and Tony Zale.

Despite my lack of obvious interest in anarchism, Albert took me around the area of Fitzrovia pointing out the pubs where the various anarchist factions met. Surprisingly, most of them still remain: the

Cambridge, the One Tun and the Northumberland Arms on Goodge Street; the Fitzroy Tavern in Windmill Street; the Wheatsheaf in Rathbone Place and the Bricklayers Arms in Gresse Street. He also pointed out the Malatesta Anarchist club that he had helped to found in Percy Street in the 1950s. Given his rather forbidding personality and his reputation for intolerance and sectarianism, I was surprised that he was prepared to turn what, in some ways, had been his life's work into a tourist trail.

I was not so much interested in anarchism itself. I was more curious why a person of such obvious ability, determination and courage should devote the sixty years of his active political life to something that, in my opinion at least, is as rational as arguing that the earth is flat.

By a curious coincidence, I later taught in the school where Albert had once been a pupil – the scene of his dispute with Edith Summerskill. The punishment book has been preserved as a curiosity of a more vigorous past and I noted that one Albert Meltzer received three strokes of the cane from the headmaster in 1933 for the heinous offence of 'muttering at a master'.

What was he muttering? "Mankind will only be free when the last headmaster has been strangled with the guts of the last teacher." (After Bakunin.) Could this incident have set him on the road to anarchy or was it a journey that he had already embarked upon before the painful intervention of his headmaster? Obviously, any young anarchist worth his salt would have nothing but contempt for the rigidity and rules of school life. Indeed, Albert recorded in his autobiography that school taught him nothing beyond the desire to be free and the need to fight injustice and privilege.

There is little point in undertaking a pub crawl in the area as all reference to their extreme activities has been obliterated. However, that did not stop me raising a silent glass in the Wheatsheaf in recognition, not so much of the validity of their beliefs but to acknowledge their sheer bravery, persistence and optimism in founding a new life for themselves in a foreign country far from home.

*

Henrik, my great grandfather, had lived for four years as a bookbinder in Berlin in the mid-1850s where he had learned to speak German – a language that always came more naturally to him than English. By 1881 he was living in Farringdon Buildings, a cold water tenement just north of the City of London and notorious as the haunt of foreign anarchists and other disreputables. Here, he was a friend and neighbour of Johann Most, ten years younger than him, a fellow bookbinder and, at various times, a desperate anarchist who was imprisoned for incitement after publishing instructions on how to make explosives. They were part of the London of the Bessarabians and the Odessians, the rival gangs of Russian youth who focussed their activities in the area around Saffron Hill.

An examination of the 1881 census for more than three hundred dwellings in the Farringdon and Viaduct buildings reveals a substantial proportion of people whose country of birth was Russia. Having escaped the extreme repression of the Tsarist system, they were carving a criminal future for themselves in the relative freedom of the East End. Henrik and Johann would have blended into this environment simply as European exiles.

During the mid-1980s, I was involved in the Charles Booth project examining and cataloguing the papers of the great Victorian social reformer who in forensic detail listed those who were living in the area of Spitalfields. To my surprise I came across a Henrik Granath, occupation jewel case maker (in census returns and marriage and birth certificates he is listed as variously a bookbinder and a jewel case maker) living in the Old Nicholl in 1886. This was the most feared and notorious of all London slums; the scene of Arthur Morrison's fictional *Jago*.

Morrison is an early example of the East End boy making good by a variety of ingenious means and then moving out to his Essex nirvana. Born in Poplar in a street that is now covered by that symbol of hesitant post-war East End regeneration, the Lansbury Estate, the whole of Morrison's life is shrouded in mystery. This was particularly true of his early life up until about the age of thirty when we find him established as a successful journalist.

In 1896 he became a nationally known figure with *A Child of the Jago* followed by *To London Town* and the *Hole in the Wall*. Each novel is written through the eyes of a child corrupted by the taint of the East End. In *To London Town* the lead character, Johnny May, is born in the purity of Essex but moves to the corruption of the East End where his travails begin. Essex is ever present in Morrison's writings as a place of escape and of purification.

In between this East End trilogy Morrison wrote *Cunning Murrell*, an Essex regional novel, a story of mid-nineteenth century witchcraft set in the area around Hadleigh Castle where the Thames starts to open out into the North Sea.

It was not Morrison's writings that made him rich however. During the 1890s he developed an interest in Japanese art and prints and, as a result, turned himself into one of the country's leading authorities. The East End was a prosperous hunting ground for this new interest. Armed with his knowledge of Japanese art, Morrison purchased prints from sailors returning from far eastern voyages and from the immigrants who were arriving in an increasingly cosmopolitan docklands area.

After twenty years assiduous collecting, Morrison was an acknowledged authority. In 1913, tired of journalism, he sold part of his large and valuable collection to the British Museum and retired to a grand house in High Beech, Essex. Here he continued his studies and his speculative dealing in oriental works of art. A mysterious and reclusive figure, he was deliberately misleading about both his origins and his life. Morrison remains an intriguing individual; an East End scholar and aesthete yet also a man of sound commercial instincts and, one might say, an Essex wide boy with an unerring eye for the main chance.

In Morrison's *Jago* life was hard. Each day gangs of young toughs would issue forth from the Old Nichol ready for shoplifting, burglary and street robbery, secure in the knowledge that the police would not dare enter their fortress.

Ever helpful, Booth provides a colour-coded map. The black of the Old Nichol indicates that this area was inhabited by the 'lowest class, most vicious, semi-criminal'. At least I can draw some comfort from the fact that Henrik was only classified as a semi-criminal although, in reality, I suspect he was just poor.

Three years later in 1889 the newly-formed London County Council demolished the Old Nichol in a fit of reforming zeal, convinced that better housing would make better people. In its place, they built the Boundary Estate, Britain's first municipal social housing project. Henrik was possibly beyond redemption because he is not mentioned in the list of tenants that was drawn up in 1890 for the new tenements. When any massive slum demolition and renewal project was launched, there was no attempt to consult or re-house the displaced. The six thousand or so people who lived in Old Nichol, including Henrik, were simply absorbed into the fabric of the modern Babylon.

The slums were demolished with a relentless thoroughness and the homeless decamped, many of them to live on the streets around Shadwell and the Ratcliffe Highway in the depths of East London. If they survived, and were so inclined, then they might find themselves re-housed in the new LCC estate.

The Boundary Estate today has an eerie desolate presence, as if the ghosts of the past have never quite gone away. Sitting outside in the warm stillness of a summer evening, it is difficult to imagine it as the site of a vast mass of seething humanity, most of whom were only one step away from the workhouse.

Henrik never returned. His last known address before his death in the workhouse was number 82 Clerkenwell Green. Perhaps he had been able to use contacts from his earlier stay in the area. Foreign exile, political sympathies and drinking habits would have drawn Karl and Henrik into each other's orbit. Marx was always hard up and had no compunction in scrounging drinks from friends and acquaintances or indeed any poor, honest working man. I can imagine him sidling up to Henrik, perhaps in the Red Lion in Soho or the Museum Tavern in Bloomsbury after a hard day's work on Das Kapital. If they had been for an evening stroll, they might even have finished up in The Flask at Highgate.

"Hey, Henrik, buy me a pint will you? I'm a bit short of funds today. It's hard work studying the contradictions of the dialectic."

"Sod off will you? What do you think I am? A communist?"

"Henrik, don't forget what I told you."

"What is that, Karl?"

"From each according to his ability to each according to his needs."

"Not in this pub mate."

Karl would not have minded. He had all the sensitivity of a blundering rhinoceros and would simply have turned to another of his habitual drinking companions, perhaps Wilhelm Liebknecht or Edgar Baeur, in order to slake his thirst.

He argued with, chewed up, and spat out almost every European philosophical intellectual of the mid-nineteenth century. Perhaps the only people he did not fall out with were the Romantic poet, Heinrich Heine, the recipient of his admiration in the early days, and his life-long acolyte and disciple, Frederick Engels. The rest – the anti-Hegelian philosopher Ludwig Feurbach, Bruno Bauer, his early companion at

Berlin University, Max Stirner the anarchic Young Hegelian and Michael Bakunin, the great anarchist leader – were dragged into his orbit, intellectually coshed and discarded by the wayside. I hope Henrik was never too close.

Marx, along with his great dollop of genius, dragged around with him a black cloud of bad luck. His wife Jenny's suffering in the cause of her husband is legendary and, of his six children, four pre-deceased him and the other two committed suicide.

After Karl's death, Laura Marx and her husband decided there was nothing left to live for and entered into a successful suicide pact in the same year Henrik, tired after a lifetime of hard labour, died in St Pancras workhouse.

Marx's other surviving daughter, Eleanor, entered into a suicide pact with her unreliable lover, Edward Aveling. Clearly, she had inherited Karl's lack of judgment. Having swallowed a lethal dose of prussic acid, Eleanor expired while Aveling changed his mind, and slipped out of the house to abscond with the young actress he had secretly married the previous year.

Aveling was one of those individuals about whom it is difficult to be unfair. He was expelled from every organisation that he joined, usually for seducing the members' wives and daughters or running off with the petty cash. On some occasions it was both.

A sentimental portrait of him can be found as Dubedat in George Bernard Shaw's *The Doctor's Dilemma*. Perhaps it was because Shaw recognised a fellow Irish adventurer.

The great tragedy of Eleanor Marx's life was that she ever met Aveling in the first place given that her destiny was to carry on the work of her father. It was as if nature and fortune had given Karl such a supernatural force of vitality, originality and intellect that there was not enough left for his children.

To examine the fate of children in Victorian England is to be reminded that tragedy and grief were ever present in peoples' lives. With much larger families, and only a rudimentary understanding of the causes of diseases and cures, the average family could expect to lose more than one child but the Marx case is extreme.

Henrik enjoyed a fecund span of twenty-four years with two different women which resulted in eleven children. Three of these died before the age of five and only three survived beyond the age of thirty-five. Of the remaining eight, Robert died at Spion Kop in the Boer War when he was only eighteen, Frederick died of septicaemia aged nineteen having cut himself working in the kitchens of the Savoy Hotel, while May suffered a seizure at twenty-eight when she was alone at home in Plaistow.

Daughter Florence (and the rest of her family) died in 1923 – in the course of one year, she and her husband and three children all died from tuberculosis. They were all living in the same small terraced house in Balham.

Son Henry died at the battle of the Somme in 1916 while Charles, for reasons unknown, became a rural labourer in North Allerton, Yorkshire. He died from heart failure at the age of forty.

Of all eleven children, only three had children of their own. Florence's line came to an end in the sad house in Balham while my grandfather, Frank, and his older sister, Minnie, had two children each. I suspect this pattern of death and grief was not untypical of the late nineteenth and early twentieth century.

Perhaps, on the whole, Karl did not have it too bad.

Chapter 17: On the Relationship between Wallpaper, Cycling and Socialism

The Gospel of Socialism. Socialism is not simply about politics …..it offers a better way of life.
Robert Blatchford.

The tragedy of British socialism in the twentieth century is that it has increasingly been defined by economic objectives. Once the Labour Party had developed a stranglehold on socialism, the route to the New Jerusalem was that of providing decent housing, ensuring that citizens had reasonable provision for their old age, a very modest redistribution of wealth, and ensuring that everyone was entitled to a set of false teeth.

When Herbert Morrison, the Labour deputy leader of the 1940s, announced that, 'Socialism is what the Labour Party does' it was clear there was little room for alternative visions.

These traditional collectivist objectives are both laudable and understandable yet there has been a singular failure to acknowledge that these things alone cannot truly enrich our lives. Parliamentary socialism has failed to recognise the importance of the aesthetic and the spiritual. It has ignored the need for fellowship and community. Ethical socialism has found itself caught in a pincer movement.

On the left flank, Karl Marx and his legions of scientific socialists dismissed the utopians as being unscientific sentimentalists. Marx would have snorted with derision at those who talked and dreamed of creating a better world but who failed to embrace his vision of alienation, surplus value, and the dictatorship of the proletariat. They were, to put it simply, not scientific.

On the right flank were the dreary parliamentary socialists who thought that, with the introduction of clean water supplies and a warm house, the spiritual needs of mankind would be satisfied.

When Ramsey MacDonald, the first Labour Prime Minister, remarked to Philip Snowden, his abrasive Chancellor of the Exchequer, that he was 'tired of socialist dreamers' he was summing up a long-standing tension within the British labour movement.

The conflict was epitomised by the sourness that existed between those two giants of the British Labour Party in the 1940s – Ernest Bevin and Nye Bevan. When Bevin, the pragmatic, blunt-speaking, right-wing, former trade union leader, heard someone remark that Nye Bevan, the darling of the left, was his own worst enemy, he quickly replied "Not while I'm alive, 'e ain't." He had no time for the moral visions of the idealistic left. It was Bevan who warned that the vision was in danger of dying when socialism became confused with the distribution of material plenty.

"This so-called affluent society is an ugly society still," he told a Labour Party Conference more than forty years ago "It is a vulgar society. It is a meretricious society. It is a society in which the priorities have gone all wrong."

Bevan went on to tell an unwilling British public of the need for passion and moral judgment in the creation of a socialist society. "I know that the right kind of leader for the Labour Party is a desiccated calculating machine who must not, in any way, permit himself to be swayed by indignation. If he sees suffering he must not, in any way, permit himself to be swayed by indignation. If he sees suffering, privation or injustice he must not allow it to move him for that would be evidence of the lack of proper education and of the absence of self-control. He must speak in calm and objective accents and talk about a dying child in the same way as he would talk about the pieces inside an internal combustion engine."

Bevan may, or he may not, have been talking about the Labour leader, the emotionless (at least in Bevan's view) Wykehamist, Hugh Gaitskell.

Although he died forty years ago Bevan would recognise the position in which we find ourselves today. We live in the land of plenty. OECD figures indicate that we are the fifth richest country in the world yet we are regularly told that poverty stalks the land.

The European Union claims that a higher proportion of the British population lives in poverty than in any other EU state. Just what sort of poverty are they referring to when families who own a car, live in a warm dry house, have access to free medical care, own a television and video, and dress in new, good quality clothes are classified as being poor?

Poverty is, of course, a moveable feast – or rather famine. It has to be measured relative to the society around it. Thus Portugal, a fellow EU state with less than half the UK's gross domestic product, is classified as less poor than Britain despite a much more obvious lack of material plenty. I am confident Bevan would say that the poverty many families in Britain suffer is a poverty of spirit, a poverty of aspiration, a poverty of self-respect, of community and empathy with their fellow citizens.

The irony is that the lack of these qualities is quite possibly produced by the surfeit of material plenty that has dulled our senses to other needs in our lives. To put it even more starkly, the grotesque materialism that all governments have striven to promote in the name of the national good since 1945 has all but obliterated the idea that we have other needs – love, fellowship, fulfilment, intellectual challenge, aesthetic expression – that all have to be met in order that we may be fully realised as human beings.

Whether the British people or the Labour Party were interested in the nature of the just and enriching society is another matter. It is not in the nature of politicians to devote themselves to meeting our desires for beauty and fellowship. Harold Macmillan, the altogether decent and avuncular Conservative Prime Minister, had just told the nation in 1959 that they 'had never had it so good' as the people took delivery of cars, washing machines and televisions in the new affluent society. It seems that a hair shirt vision of a morally-improving society is unlikely to have had wide appeal.

But Bevan's words still have a resonance today in a society that is vastly more materialistic and wealthy than it was forty years ago. They are peculiarly appropriate to Tony Blair whose vision of the advancement of society is the diametric opposite to that of Aneurin Bevan.

A Bristol University study conducted in 2003 showed that in the United Kingdom, men under forty-five are now twice as likely to commit suicide as they were in 1950. The most vulnerable group is aged between 25 and 34. Parallel changes have been seen in France, Norway, New Zealand and Australia. During the same period, average living standards have almost trebled. In the Bristol University report, the critical factors are clear. For young men, life is less secure than it was. Divorce, drug abuse, living a single life, unemployment, low wages and low self-esteem have all served to undermine young men's sense of security and self-respect.

The countries with the highest suicide rates – Japan, for example –are those where the pressure to succeed, in material terms, is greatest. Increasing suicide rates are also a feature of countries where the social fabric of the nation is in a state of advanced disintegration. American men in their twenties are now four times more likely to attempt suicide than they were thirty years ago.

Interestingly, the suicide rate for women under forty-five has remained stable during the same period. The Bristol report suggests this is because their preferred method of suicide – overdosing with pills – has become less effective as the toxicity level of modern drugs has fallen. They are less competent at killing themselves.

It would appear that while governments, both non-socialist and socialist, can provide us with clean water and material plenty it is beyond the scope of their powers to make us happy. It may be that our ability to purchase cheap DVD players and cars at European prices creates the illusion of happiness.

Governments can compel us to pay our taxes and observe the speed limits but they cannot compel us to care for our neighbours, value our communities, or see the worth of fellowship. Increasingly, governments realise this, hence the emphasis on communitarian values, neighbourhood watch schemes, and a realisation that governments have a limited capacity to solve our problems. It would appear that the route to happiness is something governments cannot map out for us. We have to find our own way.

Governments however, do the 'governed' a disservice by promoting the notion that affluence alone will solve all our problems. It is true that the basic material needs have to be met but, beyond that, we have been fed with the cruel illusion that everything would be fine if only we could win the National Lottery. Over the past fifteen years there has been a wealth of evidence about the impact a large windfall has on levels of happiness. The first reaction is one of elation followed quickly by contentment. However within a year, the effect has worn off and the majority of people are less happy than they were before their win.

Psychologists identify the most critical factor in determining our happiness quotient as the quality of our relationships with family and close friends.

When I was at University I had a garrulous and chirpy cleaning lady called Vera who could, in another context, have been one of those minor characters in Crossroads. To her credit she spent more time gossiping with the students than working. Her cleaning duties appeared to consist of redistributing the dirt. One day she did not appear and we later learned she had won a hundred and twenty thousand pounds on the football pools.

In those days that kind of money was enough to buy four luxury houses so she moved out of her council house in Canley and bought a large executive house on Tile Hill. Three months later, she was back cleaning our rooms still wearing her floral print housecoat and a hairnet but arriving each day in a gleaming black Jaguar. The reason for this strange behaviour? Tile Hill was full of snobs and none of them spoke to her. She missed her old neighbours and she missed dispensing her pearls of worldly wisdom to callow students like myself. Affluence may have brought her a degree of comfort and the thrill of driving her Jaguar down the A46 but it had not made her happy.

*

The ancient battle lines in the history of socialism are between those who wish to morally uplift society and those who simply want to provide clean water and free health care. Even the father of scientific socialism, Karl Marx, recognised the need for spirituality and job satisfaction. Without these we are alienated from both society and from our true selves. In this condition our existence degenerates into the fetishism of money and possessions. In these impoverished circumstances, according to Marx, we turn in on ourselves because, even when capitalism or for that matter democratic socialism has given us material plenty it has also created a false consciousness that prevents us from being truly happy.

It is an awkward analysis because, even when an individual believes him or herself to be deliriously happy and emotionally and spiritually fulfilled, the sourpuss Marxists would dismiss all this as an illusion. They would tell us we are in the prison of our consciousness created by our enslavement to capital.

It is instructive to contrast Marx's prescription for happiness and fulfilment with the loving misery that he inflicted upon his wife and children. The entire married lives of Karl and Jenny, and their various living children, were spent one step ahead of the bailiffs, refusing to answer the door to irate tradesmen demanding payment, and slipping shamefacedly into the pawn shop with the children's school clothes and the wedding gift cutlery under their arms.

*

In the second half of the nineteenth century, William Morris came closer than any other socialist writer or practitioner to expressing the idea that mankind has a driving need for both fellowship and aesthetic expression and that the two are linked. As he explicitly observed, "Fellowship is heaven and lack of fellowship is hell."

I drive regularly into the London Borough of Waltham Forest. Within the last year or so the Labour Council has erected, at considerable expense, signs informing visitors to this part of north east London that the Borough, or to be more precise Walthamstow, is the birthplace of William Morris. It is ironic that an artist and designer who dedicated his life to creating objects and designs of great beauty is celebrated by what is surely the ugliest of the London Boroughs. Anyone from Enfield, Hackney, Haringey, Harrow and Hillingdon will probably testify that the competition is very intense. I am looking forward to the signs declaring that 'You are now entering William Morris Country'.

The more distant we become from Morris, the more omniscient and influential he seems. For the apolitical Habitat-frequenting classes, he designed attractive wallpaper; for the romantically inclined he was a considerable poet and pivotal figure within the Pre-Raphaelite movement. More significantly, he offered a vision of socialism that had a human perspective.

My grandfather, Frank, worked for the Co-op at their wallpaper manufacturing plant in Wandsworth. He was not a designer but he tended the machines and was a craftsman in his own right. In 1910 he went to work at the William Morris factory at Merton Abbey near Wimbledon. Each day he cycled the four mile journey from Colliers Wood and back again in the evenings. He did not know Morris, who died in 1896, and I cannot even claim that he transferred his labour for either political or aesthetic reasons, despite the fact that he was a lifelong socialist of the abrasive kind. It may simply have been that the three pounds a week the Morris factory paid was more attractive than the two pounds and fifteen shillings the Co-op paid.

Events, however, were to force his hand. In 1930 Sandersons took over the printing of William Morris wallpapers and the factory at Merton Abbey closed. So he returned to the Co-op, this time as a painter and decorator. Changing public tastes, particularly amongst the newly-emerging suburban middle classes, militated against the Morris vision of rustic design. By the 1930s, a pastiche of art deco was the order of the day for the aspirant middle class while, for the lower end of the market, distemper and embossed wallpaper were in the ascendant.

Despite Morris's privileged upbringing – Marlborough and Oxford – there can be no doubting his sincerity. The irony is that when he sublimely announced, "Have nothing in your house that you do not know to be useful or believe to be beautiful" it was only the moneyed middle classes who were listening and that remains broadly true today. The murals, the furniture, the metal and glassware, the cloth hanging screens and wallpaper inevitably appealed to a middle class audience. This was partly because their expense hinted at exclusivity and partly because the elementary education offered to the mass of the population as a result of the 1870 Act placed little emphasis on the appreciation of things that were beautiful and well made. Despite the universal nature of Morris's message, and his earnest desire to make the aesthetically beautiful available to the masses, his impact upon the lives of ordinary people was minimal.

Juxtaposed beside his design and aesthetic skills was his fierce and pure commitment to a form of socialism a mile removed from that of both Marx and the Labour Party. He was a man from the prosperous upper middle class who would stand outside the law courts on the Strand shouting, "Justice Twopence." The justice that he sold for so much less than that dispensed inside the courts was the newspaper of the Social Democratic Federation, Britain's first Marxist party. Yet he had nothing in common with either Marx or the autocratic Henry Hyndman who founded the SDF.

Like some current members of the Labour cabinet, Hyndman could see no incompatibility between living a patrician, almost imperial, lifestyle and being a socialist. Two such explosive temperaments were incompatible and in 1884 Morris left the SDF and formed the Socialist League.

The writings of Morris give us a unique take on how British socialism was developing in the days of its infancy. Morris had little faith in the parliamentary process and was completely out of sympathy with any talk about the scientific inevitability of revolution. He was concerned with the quality of peoples' lives, what he called 'the art of living' following

John Ruskin's belief that 'There is no wealth but life'. From this springs Morris's reputation as a Luddite; someone who wanted to turn the clock back to the Middle Ages and forget that the industrial revolution ever happened. It was a reputation that was never justified. He just wanted machines to be the servant not the master. He feared the abject slavery of the working man to the machine that characterised the industrial revolution in Britain.

His most important work, *News from Nowhere*, painted a picture of a British Utopia. He projected forward sixty years to 1952, to a society where there was no government, no prisons, no law and no buying and selling; a time in which people lived in perfect harmony with each other as all avarice, greed and aggression had been bred out of them. It all sounded very dull though there was a touch of whimsy in his vision of a Trafalgar Square full of apricot trees and, of course, a powerful symbolism that the Houses of Parliament were used for storing horse dung. Like all visions of the future, the Morris version was wildly inaccurate but that did not really matter.

There is no real evidence that Morris thought any of this would happen but he was saying that it was possible to do things differently from the way they were done at present.

It would be fair to say that Morris's vision had more in common with the anarchism of Michael Bakunin and Peter Kropotkin than it had with any mainstream socialism. In the twentieth century it is possible to find echoes of Morris in the writings of Murray Bookchin. In a sense though, the exact details of belief are irrelevant. What Morris implants in our consciousness is the idea, the belief that a better society is possible and that we are not just condemned to retreading the old visions. Within this new society there is a recognition that our humanity is determined by our environment and that socialism does not have to involve dehumanising scientific theory, state planning, Five Year Plans and grim council estates.

It is possible to walk out of Sanderson's clutching a roll of William Morris wallpaper and still be completely ignorant of his political message. But then it would not be possible to enjoy the wallpaper because Morris saw art and life and politics and aesthetic understanding as part of an indivisible whole. It would simply be just another pretty wall covering. Morris had nothing but contempt for those who appreciated art but who 'showed absurd ignorance of the very elements of economics'.

Perhaps Sandersons should insist that all purchasers of William Morris wallpaper must produce proof that they have read *News from Nowhere*, *A Dream of John Ball* and the magnificent Kelmscott Press edition of *Chaucer*. If not, they should be sent packing with a roll of anaglypta or directions to the nearest B & Q.

*

There is something very socialistic about riding a bicycle although a Conservative-voting cyclist friend does not agree with me and just cannot see the point I am trying to make. The bicycle is an invention of genius, possibly the greatest invention of all. It is accessible and affordable to ninety per cent of the world's population under the age of seventy. In contrast with the car, which is accessible to only twenty per cent of the world's population, it is the embodiment of something for nothing. Bicycles are also very egalitarian in that, give or take a few gears they are all of broadly the same design.

Before China discovered capitalism, one of the great sights in the world was to walk in the Beijing rush-hour and witness the occasional car, usually carrying a puffed-up Communist Party dignitary, surrounded by thousands of identical cyclists wearing their dark blue Mao suits. A sure sign of the fall from socialist grace of the Peoples' Republic (if at any time during the past thirty years it has ever been in that position) is the 2003 news that Shanghai – the Mecca of rampant, authoritarian capitalism – is to ban the humble bicycle from its large roads in order to make room for the dramatically increasing number of cars.

Since joining the World Trade Organisation, Chinese car imports have leapt by sixty per cent so, clearly, it is now time to get rid of those irritating cyclists. Once hailed by Chairman Mao as the perfect form of proletarian transport, China's six hundred million bicycles are now in danger of becoming victims of the capitalist boom. They are viewed as an embarrassing relic of a misguided past. The irony is that while the advanced capitalist economies are struggling to control the motor car and encouraging the use of bicycles, the opposite principle applies in communist China.

It is still possible to witness the motor car in the ascendant in that liberal progressive would-be utopia, Holland. There the car drivers (who are mostly cyclists as well) are, on the whole, good-humouredly resigned to their fate of being pushed around by the bicycle.

On my last visit to Holland, I witnessed the wonderfully uplifting sight of about twenty people who were confined to wheelchairs being propelled along in strange devices that were bicycles at the back and wheelchairs at the front. The occupants looked happy but, at the same time, terrified. Behind them a mass of other cyclists rode tandems, tricycles and recumbents (a fast low bike that is pedalled from virtually a horizontal position). A few rode autocycles (bicycles with small petrol engines fixed into the rear wheel) while there was also an impressive four-seater machine that was essentially a four-wheeled tricycle.

The whole magnificent spectacle struck me as a fighting gesture against the tyranny of the motorcar. My enquiries revealed that the cyclists were volunteers who took out those who were housebound as part of their national service. I particularly enjoyed the way they controlled and dominated the road daring any car drivers to come near them. The figures illustrate the difference between the two countries. In Holland one and a quarter million people cycle to work each day representing a quarter of the working population. In Britain just one person in four hundred cycles to work.

Unfortunately, cars, which provide a fairly inefficient means of personal transport, also carry with them layers of meaning related to status, self-image and levels of sexual adequacy.

"What car do you drive?"

"I drive a Sexual Substitute 2000 because, alas, I only have a very small penis."

It was not always thus. Before the rise of what Mrs Thatcher called 'our great motor car economy' the humble bicycle was a staple form of transport. One of the abiding memories from my childhood was seeing the Ford plant and the Marconi and Ilford factories disgorging thousands of workers on bicycles as the 'end of shift' klaxon sounded. Now the cycle lanes leading away from the industrial estates are empty and strewn with bags of fly-tipped rubbish, broken branches and pieces of disintegrated lorry tyre. To venture onto the road on a bicycle is now a fearful, death-defying experience where the odds against not being knocked into a ditch by a spotty youth driving a small Peugeot or a sporty BMW 3 series are not attractive.

Several times a year, I am spat at by car drivers or their passengers for no other reason than I am a cyclist. I recently cycled past the spot in Tottenham where a middle-aged cyclist was shot and critically wounded by a motorist. His crime was to hold the car up at a traffic light. This is obviously symptomatic of a much broader problem. It would appear that, for some motorists, having a gun in the glove compartment is akin to having a functional spare wheel and a jack.

I had my own rather less terminally violent encounter with road rage very recently. I was sauntering along the A1081 on a motorcycle approaching the huge M25 roundabout at South Mimms. A driver pulled up beside me at the entrance to the roundabout and accused me of impeding his progress, although he did not use those exact words. I replied very calmly that the key to good driving was to be relaxed.

"You ******* tosser!" he shouted through the open window.

I then suggested in a jovial fashion that if he undertook a course in anger management it might help him with his driving.

"You ******* smartarse!" he screamed and made to get out of the car grasping what appeared to be a hammer.

At this stage I decided my attempts to be helpful were not appreciated and slipped away between the cars ahead leaving my friend wrestling with his inner rage and shouting incoherently.

There is a deep-seated fear of people being different. I own an electric bicycle and a splendid invention it is. Some of the time I attract curious stares and even the occasional admiring comment. However for the most part I attract jeers and shouts from groups of local youths, cigarette packets thrown from passing cars and, on one occasion, a half brick hurled out of a car window. I can only assume that the passenger in the car had been driven around the streets for some time before finding a suitable target, and that happened to be my back. I haven't been able to think what other reason someone might have for keeping a house brick in the foot well of the car.

Fortunately, it is not always like this. On a late night expedition to Sainsbury's I tied my electric bicycle to the railings at the front of the shop. The usual crew of hooded youth were hanging around at the front playing with the trolleys and smoking. As I was removing the numerous locks that I use to secure the bike, a small group of them approached me and asked what manner of machine it was. I spent the next fifteen minutes explaining how it worked, going into some of the technical details concerning the motor, the battery, the torque sensors and the trip computer. And very appreciative and thoughtful they were.

The vast majority of young people are very pleasant once their attention has been engaged. This is particularly true if they are sober and by themselves or in very small groups. It is when they are fuelled up with Jack Frost White Cider, and in large groups, that they become uniformly beastly. I like to think that, through our little conversation, this group were shown that it is possible to be different. A bicycle invites intimacy.

On another occasion, again while chaining my bicycle to the railings outside Sainsbury's, I was approached by an old man who began recounting the cycling adventures of his youth. I was particularly impressed by his feat of cycling from London to Falmouth in thirty-six hours non-stop. He was now ninety-two but he had given up cycling at the age of fifty when he purchased a secondhand car. Twenty years later at the age of seventy he had attempted to return to cycling.

"I was frightened out of my ******* wits, ******* car drivers don't give a **** about any other ****** on the roads," he told me.

Despite the limitations of his vocabulary, I knew exactly what he meant and I concurred with his sentiments.

There is a close association between cycling and genius. Albert Einstein, when he was not revolutionising our understanding of the world, spent much time on his bicycle. Indeed, the Theory of Relativity came to him while he was pedalling along at night. He noticed that the moving beam of his cycle lamp always travelled at the same speed whether he was accelerating quickly or coming to a halt and the theory that light from a moving source has the same velocity as light from a stationary source was born.

Einstein famously observed, "I thought of it while riding my bicycle."

The tough guy and macho novelist, Ernest Hemingway, loved cycling as did Pablo Picasso who regularly included its imagery in his art. The French philosopher, Jean Paul Sartre, adored cycling up hills but was so indifferent to cycling on the flat that it was not unknown for him to end up in the ditch. There is a part of the brain whose capacities are only released when we are cycling ... or so I believe.

The links between cycling and socialism are mainly due to a happy coincidence. In 1892, the Raleigh safety cycle, the first modern bicycle, was invented. In the following year, the Independent Labour Party was founded in Bradford. Two years before this the Manchester socialist journalist, Robert Blatchford, founded the Clarion newspaper with the intention of spreading the gospel of socialism. Under the slogan 'instructive without being dry, and amusing without being vulgar' Blatchford, in a jolly, non-theoretical way, sought to convert the masses to socialism.

It is no exaggeration to say that, for every convert Marx and Engels made, Blatchford made a hundred. His book *Merrie England* became the bible of British Socialism by emphasising fellowship, fairness, helping each other and good times. With sales of two million it is, outside the Soviet Union and China, the best selling book ever written about socialism.

Blatchford and the Clarion attempted to provide, in the years up to 1914 and in the decade after the First World War, a socialist lifestyle aimed particularly at young people. To this end he set up the Clarion Scouts, Clarion Glee Clubs, Clarion Field Clubs, a Clarion Football League and the National Clarion Cycling Club.

I am often asked how people entertained themselves before we capitulated to the television. The answer is here. They were inventive, they enjoyed each other's company, they became involved in their communities and they constantly sought new ways to wring a little more pleasure out of life. Clarion horse-drawn vans toured the country setting up in small towns and on village greens, selling copies of Merrie England, the Clarion bible, and trying to convert the British population to the joys of the socialist life. It was no coincidence that many of the Clarion Cycling Clubs founded in the 1890s grew out of ward branches of the Independent Labour Party.

Although vague about the exact nature of the socialist state and how it would be achieved beyond having fun, Blatchford stands out, along with William Morris, in the decades before the First World War, as a beacon in the campaign for a humane and humorous vision of socialism.

The Clarion Cycling Clubs intrigue and have survived, in name at least, up to the present day. It is almost impossible to exaggerate what a social revolution cycling created in the 1890s. For the first time in history, it was possible for young men and women who could afford a bicycle to escape the cramped confines of industrial inner cities and to explore the beauty of the English countryside. Some people living in the dark industrial depths of the great conurbations had never seen the countryside before.

H.G. Wells in his 1896 novel *The Wheels of Chance* captures perfectly the mood of the cycling revolution as clerks and shop assistants of south London discovered a whole new world in the unspoilt Kent and Surrey lanes. For the next fifteen years or so, cyclists had the roads to themselves. Then, along came the motorcar and the long drawn out campaign to displace the humble bicycle.

As a recent history of the Clarion Cycling clubs put it rather primly, 'the Clarion Cyclist is a Socialist utilising his cycle for the combined purpose of pleasure and propaganda'. In many ways it was a project of genius. Cycling offered young urban workers an escape from the long hours and bleak inner city landscape while socialism offered a faith, a reason for fraternity and a vision of a better life.

By 1914, the Clarion network had spread all over the country with weekend rides, holiday tours and Clarion Club houses in the country, and on the coast, that pre-dated the formation of the Youth Hostels Association. My father was both a Clarion and a YHA member. In the 1930s he thought nothing of cycling from Mitcham to Brighton and back in a day. This was a round trip of more than a hundred hilly miles broken by a bracing dip in the sea at Brighton.

The great days of Clarion were those up to 1914. After the war, the steady growth of the motorcar and other forms of leisure began to slowly chip away at membership although many Clarion riders took part in the inter-war International Workers Olympiads. After the Second World War, the cycling and racing continued but the rise of the motorcycle and then the advent of something approaching universal car ownership saw a sharp decline in numbers in the 1960s and 70s.

By this time the socialist purpose that had shone so brightly in the 1890s had all but disappeared. In the mid 1990s a number of Clarion Clubs celebrated their centenary and still continued to offer a wonderful facility of fresh air, convivial company, good exercise and the embodiment of the idea that 'Fellowship is Life' for cyclists of all political outlooks. There is a sense of fraternity amongst even the most apolitical of cyclists. You don't have to be socialist to enjoy cycling but it helps. Spinning along the country lanes of Hertfordshire on a Sunday morning with Barnet Wheelers it is just possible to imagine what it must have been like with those early Clarion Clubs.

For the Socialist Pioneers, cycling and cycles had an almost semi-sacred mystique. Some of them were former Clarion Club members and (in at least one case) the father of a Pioneer had been a

Clarion member in the 1890s. As I have observed, there is something very egalitarian and fraternal about cycling. Even the bikes were near identical, usually BSAs or Raleighs with Sturmey Archer 3-speed gears and the occasional 4-speed bike for those who wanted to be a bit different. To the best of my knowledge, those who had four speeds were never accused of deviationism or sectarianism or revisionism or any of those strange crimes that have bedevilled those who uphold a particular vision of socialist purity. When one of our number turned up on a Viking bicycle sporting 5-speed Campagnola derailleur gears I can remember experiencing the indignation of the conformist that the unwritten code was being breached.

On Sundays, we would sometimes cycle down the A13 to Coalhouse Fort at Tilbury overlooking the Thames, searching for the spot where Sir Walter Raleigh, in a moment of legendary gallantry, laid down his cloak for Queen Elizabeth. Each time the spot had moved. If we were feeling a little more adventurous we took the ferry across to Gravesend and visited the grave of Pocahontas. I do not think there was a particular affinity with her it just gave a purpose to the ride.

At weekends, we often cycled to Epping Forest spending the Saturday night at Loughton Youth Hostel. Today it has become *Birds of a Feather* country and is inhabited by an abrasive Essex type, the sort that would have brought despair to Aneurin Bevan.

For a bit of variety, we sometimes cycled north to Maldon, Colchester or Castle Headingham on the Essex–Suffolk border. Climbing the hills was straightforward as we were taught to zigzag across the full width of the road in order to reduce the gradient. Such a tactic would now lead to an abrupt end to the holiday.

During the long summer holidays we went on two and three week cycling tours across southern England and the names of the hostels sit very clearly in the memory. On our very first Pioneer tour we stayed the night at Crockham Hill Hostel in Kent in a barn-like dormitory. We spent the night listening to the farting, whistling and snoring of more than forty tired cyclists.

To list all the hostels we stayed at is to list the component parts of that swathe of England south of London that has been destroyed by the motorcar. In Kent and Surrey we stayed at Kemsing, Tanners Hatch, Ewhurst Green, Holmbury St Mary, Hindhead and Chaldon. The M25 has now cut a car-blasted corridor through our former happy cycling grounds. The hostels at Chaldon, Ewhurst Green, Kemsing, Tanners Hatch and Crockham Hill all lay within the malignant path of the motorway and are now all gone, being only a reminder of a gentler past age. They were the core traditional hostels of the youth hostel movement when it was established in this country in 1932. It is difficult to argue that the construction of the M25 has increased the sum of human happiness but it is very easy to argue that it has added to our misery and woes. Perhaps I am just a victim of the Blue Remembered Hills syndrome; the useless and corrosive desire for what has passed and cannot be recovered.

For those unfamiliar with A.E. Houseman's famous lines:

> Into my heart and air that kills
> From yon far country blows;
> What are those blue remembered hills,
> What spires, what farms are those?
>
> That is the land of lost content,
> I see it shining plain,
> The happy highways where I went
> And cannot come again.

The youth hostels were austere and spartan with a set of immutable rules that were enforced rigidly: no smoking, no alcohol, lights out at ten-thirty and, above all, hostellers must arrive on bicycle or by foot. The one exception to this was Winchester hostel where some hostellers arrived by canoe as the building was a converted mill house. In the evenings we allowed ourselves to be lowered in a harness into the foaming millstream as it rushed through our washroom.

The rules were strict but they were to be obeyed. I witnessed a pair of hapless Italian hostellers who were ejected from Salisbury Youth Hostel. Their luggage was literally thrown out onto the gravel front by the warden who wore sandals and lederhosen that exposed his big white legs. Their crime? They had arrived in their Fiat motorcar and were wearing fashionable leather sneakers and modish Italian clothes. Most unforgivably of all they had made a feeble attempt to pretend they were bona-fide hostellers by hiding their red Fiat around the corner, claiming to have walked while carrying their huge smart suitcases. With sunglasses perched on top of their heads, and packets of cigarettes in the breast pockets of their crisply-ironed shirts, our zealous hostel warden was quickly onto them.

This was only twenty years after the end of the war and I expect the warden had fought at El Alamein. With all the righteousness of Christ expelling the moneylenders from the temple he told them they were not welcome at an English Youth Hostel. After expelling these loathsome continental scrimshankers with their fancy shoes and filtered cigarettes, the warden looked at me with an air of weary resignation about all the wickedness in the world and said, "An Englishman would not have done that."

I am embarrassed to admit that I agreed with him. Thank God for red-blooded, red-faced Englishmen. I have occasionally reflected on what those Italian visitors must have thought of English hospitality.

We spent our evenings preparing food in the member's kitchen and playing with sets of battered board games in the common room. There was, of course, no television and in the morning we all had to perform a simple cleaning or tidying task in the spirit of fraternity and co-operation. Mine was nearly always sweeping a heap of dirt in the dormitory under a mattress or rug.

My most uncomfortable memory is not the smell of boiled cabbage in the member's kitchen, or the cold showers, but the iron bunks stacked two and sometime three high that swayed perilously every time one of the occupants moved. This is in no way intended to belittle the Youth Hostel movement. It gave a unique opportunity to hundreds of thousands of people, young and old, to explore England in a way that would have been impossible for their grandparents.

The term 'youth hostel' now seems to be inappropriate. I have stayed in a few of the hostels that still remain over the past couple of years and I am struck by the absence of youth or, indeed, anyone under thirty. Most of the customers seem to be men in battered early middle-age. They have the hangdog look of public sector employees.

I remain grateful to the YHA for a unique education. I just wish the thin mattresses had not been so lumpy, the hairy blankets had not been so itchy, the wardens had been a little less self-righteous, and that, as I grew older, I had not been forced to climb back in through the windows so many times after I spent harmless evenings in local pubs and found myself caught out by the ten-thirty lock up.

*

Some of the Pioneers, particularly those who were members of the Young Communist League, often went to Woodlands, the communist holiday camp situated on the North Downs close to Dorking. They camped in the woods, re-enacted Indian pow-wows (as they imagined them to be), danced around blazing camp-fires in the darkness and addressed each other as Little Beaver and Brown Owl.

At the start of the long summer break, several Pioneer families went hop picking on a farm near Chilham in Kent. Even then we were acutely socially conscious. It was, on the whole, the poorer families – those for whom a week at Butlins was a distant fantasy – who took part in this annual working class pilgrimage. The usual travel options were either to get a train from London Bridge or, more commonly, to travel down in an open-backed lorry that collected families from Whitechapel High Street. Once in the hop fields, they stayed in huts provided by that great rarity – a socialistically-inclined farmer.

This must have been virtually the last throw of that East End tradition – most popular during the inter-war years – of families decamping to the countryside for the summer just to pick hops. In 1931 during his tramping phase, George Orwell stayed among the hop pickers of Mereworth and graphically recorded both the hardships and the camaraderie of the life.

I have never really been taken in by those working class fantasies of the 'we were happy but poor' variety. One night spent in a rickety Nissen hut, urinating into a galvanised bucket, and eating two-day old Irish stew from a vast communal saucepan was enough to convince me that the attraction lies in the memory rather than the experience at the time.

By the mid 1960s, the hop industry was in decline. Rising levels of affluence meant that hop pickers could spend some of the summer in Brighton, Margate, Clacton and perhaps even the south of Spain, in preference to stripping their hands raw in the fields of Kent. But, for many of the older generation it was still a happy reminder of the camaraderie and sense of community that life in the old East End engendered.

*

If the Labour Party had not hijacked the development of British socialism then an alternative evolutionary tale might have been told of a life-affirming political belief at the core of which was cycling.

I would love to see Tony Blair, John Prescott and the New Labour cabinet get out of their black ministerial Rovers and Jaguars and cycle between Downing Street and the House of Commons. It would give them a more human quality.

In 1994 I asked Peter Bottomley, who was then junior transport minister, why it was impossible to leave a bicycle anywhere safe within a mile radius of the House of Commons. Why was it, I asked, that every set of government railings contained a dire warning about chained bicycles being cut away and destroyed? His reply, given in all seriousness with the gravitas of a parliamentary answer, was that terrorists might try to pack the crossbars with high explosive. I did not have the heart to point out the thousands of cars in local parking bays from where explosions a thousand times more deadly could be triggered.

I would be curious to read an analysis of why one western European Liberal democracy, Holland, seems so at home with the bicycle as an alternative means of transport while another, Britain, just wants to drive bicycles off the road and into the ditches. Before I am told it is because Holland is flat, I can dismiss this as a false theory. The flatness encourages those raking North Sea winds, which in turn means that cycling much of the time in Holland is hard work. Cycling across the Amstel Meer Polder against a typical north-westerly is like undertaking a long, indeed never ending, one-in-ten hill climb.

So is there a relationship between the most liberal drugs laws in Europe, the lowest rate of teenage pregnancies, a state-regulated system of prostitution, liberal attitudes towards homosexuality, same sex marriages and the highest per head use of bicycles anywhere in the world? Some would vehemently dismiss my theory and I suppose the Daily Mail – champion of the motorcar and the motorist – would argue that cycling encourages homosexuality, underage sex, drug taking and prostitution.

It seems the British instinctively distrust and dislike cyclists. Read any motoring magazine and you will come across articles about Lycra-clad thugs and the pointlessness of bicycle lanes.

The motorcar is the diametric opposite of the bicycle. It offers an all-enveloping, comforting security and is a cosy little personal world. It is a symbol of the atomisation of society and a metaphor for our sense of alienation from our fellow man and for the increasingly ruthless competition we are engaged in. It is the embodiment of the autonomous, egocentric individual and the rootlessness and disengagement that increasingly characterises our society.

We do things in cars that we would not dream of doing as pedestrians. We shout and swear and gesticulate at our fellow citizens and, if they've really asked for it, we assault them with a hammer, a car jack or any other handy implement. In short, the car dehumanises us. When was the last time someone stopped to help when you had a puncture or your car broke down? My bicycle chain flew off recently and jammed between the frame and the chain wheel. Within five minutes two young men on mountain bikes had stopped to offer me assistance.

A similar camaraderie exists between motorcyclists. While waiting at red traffic lights I chat with my fellow riders about such arcane topics as disc fade, chain drive versus shaft drive and whether it is worth having a Scott Oiler fitted and, of course, the deficiencies of car drivers.

Last summer I was riding up the M11 on a small and underpowered motorcycle to see an air display at RAF Duxford. I was struggling to maintain 65 mph with car drivers sweeping past, often perilously close. It was as though I had a sign on my back saying 'Please Overtake Me Dangerously'.

After a while, I was aware that the traffic was suddenly giving me a much wider berth then I realised why. In my mirror I could see a large cluster of about twenty high-powered motorcycles. They sat on my shoulder for the next twenty miles forcing the traffic wider.

We all pulled into the car park at Duxford and the leader of the group who was riding a Honda Pan European told me they could see that I was struggling and had decided to give me some assistance. It is difficult to imagine a group of drivers in a fleet of Porsches and BMWs trying to help a fellow motorist who was labouring up the motorway in a Reliant Robin.

On a recent ride up the M1 on my trusty Honda CB 750, I was caught in an exceptionally heavy downpour and pulled in for shelter under one of the motorway bridges near to Newport Pagnell. What a pleasant time I had chatting with three fellow motorcyclists about, you've guessed it, Scott Oilers and the advantages of shaft drive, all while smoking Drum roll-ups in true biker style.

Increasingly, I am driven to adopting a more aggressive attitude towards motorists. I am particularly incensed when they pull out in front of me while they are talking on a mobile phone. They seem to assume that I will stop for them so that their conversation is not interrupted by the need to concentrate on their driving or exercise any knowledge of road craft. Depending on what sort of bike I am riding, I do not. Instead I ram them. A few words of cautionary advice on the subject of ramming cars. Firstly, make sure you have a robust bike. A mountain bike will do but my favourite is my Dutch roadster with extra thick wheels. It also helps if you weigh about two hundred pounds and can therefore proceed with a fair momentum.

Secondly, aim for the middle of the front door as they buckle in a very satisfying manner. Thirdly, do not ram anyone with tattoos or if they look as if they might have a gun in the glove compartment. Unfortunately, this only leaves you with about ten per cent of the motoring population to aim for.

Fourthly, if they have one of those pathetic fish symbols stuck on their back window, do not assume they are a Christian or that they will, if they are, act in a Christian manner. The very process of driving a car can turn even the most devout Christian into a mad axe man and I can illustrate this very clearly.

Close to where I live is a church where the worshipers regularly park on the pavement to save having to walk at least one hundred yards to the church. They have absolutely no thoughts for the blind person tapping along the pavement with his stick. The police, in frustration, recently issued a number of parking tickets. If these Christians formerly believed Christ being nailed to the cross was an injustice, it was nothing compared to the injustice of being issued with tickets for parking on the pavement.

The fifth, and final tip, is to insist on having their insurance details. After all, they pulled out in front of you so it was entirely their fault.

I am not irresponsibly advocating that anyone deliberately accelerates into a car but I do feel it is reasonable to demonstrate that bicycle brakes are not as efficient as those of a car and that motorists should not make assumptions about how soon a cyclist can pull up, particularly if the motorist is distracted by talking into a mobile phone. (Incidentally, the most satisfying car to ram is a Honda Civic. Its door panels are like tissue paper)

*

What is the great political issue of our time that makes the citizens of this country burn with indignation at the wickedness of the world? Is it the terrible things that Israelis and Palestinians do to each other? Is it the crippling levels of third world debt? Is it the fact that every minute of every day someone dies of gunshot wounds somewhere in the world? Is it the holocaust of Aids in sub-Saharan Africa that has Mondeo man out on the streets?

No, it is none of these things. It's much more important: it is speed cameras and wheel clamps. We now have a new popular hero in Axle Grinder Man, who in the dead of night, dressed in a blue cat suit and gold boots 'liberates' clamped cars. As a result, he has become the hero of the motoring middle classes. Captain Gatso, as head of Motorists Against Detection, now stalks the land during the hours of darkness decapitating speed cameras - seven hundred to date, it is claimed.

It would be as meaningful, and as morally dubious, to form Muggers Against Detection or Burglars Against Detection. Nearly two hundred years ago, Captain Swing rode the land under the cover of night burning down the homes, barns and hayricks of rich landowners on behalf of the downtrodden and poverty-stricken farm labourers. As the new factories of the industrial revolution emerged, Ned Ludd led the machine breakers on behalf of those who feared that the old ways were changing forever. In 1880s Ireland, Captain Moonlight championed the cause of the Irish peasant farmers in their nocturnal Land War against the British occupiers.

The grand principle of the individual struggling against an overbearing and tyrannical government has been reduced to taking a chainsaw to speed cameras so that we can behave in a dangerous and anti-social fashion without fear of state retribution. Today, we lack a grand cause so we just fixate on the motor car instead. We need to get out of the habit of selectively judging individual laws and feeling that we should somehow be exempt. There is something about the motor car that renders us less than human and deprives us of any moral sense.

Now here is a curious point. I often ride in London on a scooter when I lack either the energy to cycle or the physical strength to wrestle with five hundred pounds of motorcycle. Yet there is no obvious sense of camaraderie amongst scooter riders. At traffic lights they studiously ignore each other. The reason is that scooter riders are simply displaced motorists who, even when they are on two wheels, bring with them all of the angst and alienation that characterises car drivers. They have simply swapped four wheels for two in the hope of speeding up their journey rather than engaging in any conscious rejection of what the motorcar stands for. Thus, as a general rule, they are as miserable and selfish as car drivers.

In 1993, John Major appointed the High Court Judge, Sir Richard Scott, to investigate Britain's shabby dealings in the Arms to Iraq affair. A number of broadsheet newspapers reported that senior civil servants distrusted Sir Richard. The reason? He cycled to the inquiry each day and took his bicycle inside the inquiry building.

Declining the offer of the black ministerial Rover was disturbingly non-conformist. During the late 1980s and early 1990s, Sir George Younger, in his role as a government minister, was the subject of regular press reports because of his odd habit of cycling in London. Predictably, as the holder of that honours peculiarity – a hereditary knighthood – he earned the sobriquet 'the bicycling baronet'. Yet there was something appealing about this gentle and courteous man, the only one who wore his bicycle clips in a government full of Thatcherite thugs. It was like Bambi innocently grazing amidst a pack of wolves.

Sir George wasn't alone. Consider for one moment why Quentin Hogg (later to be Lord Hailsham) failed to become the Conservative Prime Minister after the resignation of Harold Macmillan in 1963. Does anyone seriously consider that Sir Alec Douglas Home was a more effective political leader? Was not R.A. Butler well past his 'sell by' date to the extent of being in a state of semi-dotage.

I suspect that the Magic Circle of Tory Grandees who were presiding over the process of who would emerge as the next Tory leader viewed Mr Hogg with some suspicion thanks to his well-publicised habit of riding an ancient boneshaker bicycle around central London. Clearly the Magic Circle was in danger of elevating a closet socialist.

In those far off days, the Conservative Party did nothing as democratically vulgar as electing their leader. And, it would seem that with the recent elevation of Michael Howard they are reverting to their old habits. Proper Conservative politicians, of course, travelled by car. Preferably something like a Rover 90 or a Humber Hawk or maybe even a Super Snipe. I asked Boris Johnson, the fluffy MP for Henley, editor of the Spectator, and court jester to the Conservative Party, whether his habit of cycling and letting it be known publicly that he nurtured such a vice would limit his progress in politics. The shrug of the shoulders and the rolling of eyes indicated it was either a very stupid question on my part or it was something that did not overly concern him. Given the hopeless state of the Conservative Party, I suspect the latter.

It is heartening to see such an eminent Conservative figure advancing the cause of socialism and individual freedom. There is something dangerous and subversive to good order about cycling. There are powerful forces at work in society that pressurise us to become motorists to make us the drones of the great motorcar economy. Getting on a bicycle is a blow for the freedom of the individual against the oppressive nature of the capitalist state in all its manifestations. When did you last see an advertisement for a particular make of cycle or a cycling product?

As an activity, cycling exists below the horizon of avaricious capitalism and the parasitic advertising industry. As Ivan Illich, the radical educational philosopher and deschooler, whimsically put it: "Socialism will only come riding on a bicycle."

I agree, though I wouldn't have liked to be the one who told Joe Stalin or Leonid Brezhnev, the last effective leader of the world's most powerful socialist republic. At the time of his death he was hoarding a fleet of more than one hundred luxury cars in a secret car park below the Kremlin. No wonder he could not concentrate on governing the Soviet Union. The reality was that in his world outlook, he was nothing more than a used car dealer who got lucky. The word 'socialism' had somehow passed him by apart from using it as a means to amass a vast collection of expensive foreign cars.

Chapter 18: The Frailty of Memory

> I have come to believe that the
> whole world is an enigma, a harmless
> enigma that is made terrible by our own
> mad attempt to interpret it as though it
> has an underlying truth.
> *Umberto Eco. Foucault's Pendulum.*

> I have sworn upon the altar of God eternal hostility against
> every form of tyranny over the mind of man.
> *Thomas Jefferson, third President of the United States of America.*

Basildon – a town of perhaps thirty thousand people – had been built but it had no doctors. When our portly, middle-aged, jovial representative of the NHS did eventually arrive, he was treated like royalty. Yet he had no notion of patients as 'customers with rights' nor was he in any way a part of the town. He and his awful wife lived in one of those large five-bedroomed council houses specifically not designed for Ford production line workers.

There was no appointments system. We just went along and queued and waited, sometimes all morning in the barn-like waiting room that resembled a village hall. When someone suggested the possibility of an appointments system, he was immediately removed from the patient list and told to go elsewhere. A major problem as there was no other doctor in the town. I later learned he had eventually found another doctor in Thurrock, about five miles away.

The doctor's wife was a dragon, a brisk, all-weather, 'walking with a Labrador' type. To prevent us malingerers wasting her husband's valuable time she conducted a pre-examination in the waiting room. In full earshot of up to one hundred people, the weather-beaten harridan would shout, "Come on, what's wrong with you?"

"I'd rather speak to the doctor, if you don't mind," some very deferential patients would reply.

"I do mind, what's wrong with you?" Mrs Dragon would retort.

The embarrassed, whispered response would usually elicit one of three decisions. Firstly, she might write a prescription and then disappear into the consulting room for the doctor to sign it. Her lack of any obvious medical training was never an impediment.

Secondly, there might be a reluctant, almost surly, "Alright, you can see the Dr." Or thirdly, the dreaded words, "There is nothing wrong with you. Go home!"

It was only after the arrival of Dr Chowdhury, who has a local school named after him and who introduced the revolutionary idea of appointment times, that the original old medical curmudgeon was forced to change his awful ways. Unfortunately our Doctor had trained and worked in the old pre-1948 health service with its notions of General Practitioners as independent fee-paying professionals who could pick and choose who they treated. Before 1948, most of the medical profession were treating the wealthy elderly in Bournemouth. To be regarded as an employee of the state was seen as an affront to professional dignity.

Today the medical profession is so busy posing as the defender of the National Health Service it has conveniently forgotten it fought tooth and nail against its creation in 1948. It was something to do with having that too clever by half working class Welshman who had left school at fourteen to work down the pit telling them what to do. Nye Bevan never meant it to happen that way but, for most of its existence, users of the NHS have been considered as cap in hand supplicants, despite the fact that by the sweat of their brow they have paid for the service.

Over the past forty or so years there has been some loss of status amongst the medical profession occasioned not so much by a variety of medical scandals but more by the rise of a consumerist attitude towards medicine that endows patients with rights and doctors with obligations that would have been inconceivable forty years ago.

Probably the fears of the BMA in 1948, that a system of state-run medicine would reduce the medical profession to just another branch of the consumer culture, were justified but it has taken the best part of half a century for this to come about. The exaltation of the demigod of choice, and an uncritical welfarism that has encouraged an attitude that 'every demand should be met', has inevitably led to a lowering of the medical profession in public esteem. The change of attitudes has been reflected in our popular television programmes.

In the 1960s we were treated to *Dr Finlay's Casebook* in which Doctors Finlay and Cameron commanded universal respect for their professionalism, judgment, position, integrity and their stern moral outlook on life from their Presbyterian fastness. In all likelihood they were never involved in a ménage à trois with Janet, their housekeeper. "Will ye noo have anoother scone, docta?"

For those who sought something glossier, Dr Kildare gave us a transatlantic model of handsome clean-cut integrity. Today we have *Casualty* in which doctors have it off with nurses in medical stock cupboards and are clearly as flawed and stupid as the rest of us.

*

Going to the dentist in Basildon was, in one way, a better experience than going to the doctor's as there were no queues. In every other way it was a much worse experience.

The notorious Dr Mengele of Auschwitz infamy had not fled to Brazil after all. He had set up as a dentist in Basildon New Town. Well, that was my theory. At this time dentists were little more than tooth pullers and, as late as 1948, only 40 per cent of dentists had any form of academic training. I am confident my dentist was not amongst the privileged 40 per cent.

Despite the fact that Novocain injections had been around since the 1860s, Mr Cameron refused to give them on principle.

"What do you want one of them for?" he would say. "They are for girls. Are you a girl or a boy? Stop wriggling!" he would command as he drilled into my sensitive teeth. It was a low-key version of the terrible dental torture scene in *Marathon Man* as our hero was tormented in the chair by the elderly Nazi dentist. Finally I shot out of the chair, clamped my hand over my mouth, and, dodging the embrace of the nurse, escaped from the surgery.

Although I never visited a dentist for twelve years after that experience, every tooth in my head has now been filled. Dentists in the 1960s and 70s would fill a tooth as soon as look at it.

"Why take the chance?" he would cry as the drill bit churned out healthy tooth.

It all harks back to an earlier philosophy that when you reached a certain stage in life, usually early middle age, you would go to the dentist and have every tooth removed in preparation for dentures. This suggested it saved a lot of mucking about and unnecessary visits. I still remember my great aunt going to have 'a new kitchen sink put in' as my great uncle cheerfully put it.

In the 1950s, the practice was to go for what had been called 'half crown extraction' rather than the wholesale and indiscriminate removal of an entire set of teeth on the grounds of convenience. Since that time I have regarded, with a particular horror, the sight of dentures soaking in a glass of foaming Steradent. Today, I regularly go to the dentist's surgery with its soothing tropical fish tanks, unending reels of the Simpsons, the sound of a whale song, and my female dentist (I gave up on male dentists after Mr Cameron) earnestly requesting me to tap the side of my seat at the slightest twinge of pain while I imploringly eye her bosoms through the clingy white surgical top.

*

There is one incident I experienced with the Pioneers that I have no means of explaining. It often comes back to me in the darkness and, nearly thirty years later, I still feel perplexed and no nearer a rational explanation.

The Pioneers had little interest in sport and recreation so my occasional visits to the bowling alley were frowned upon as a distraction from the serious business of life. The exceptions were walking and cycling which, for wholesome socialist reasons, were encouraged. Walking in particular was seen as an uncorrupting and even noble activity that embodied the right of the free-born Englishman to walk where he pleased, and when he pleased in the land of Albion, irrespective of fences, private property rights, 'Keep Out' signs or class-traitorous gamekeepers and bailiffs.

One of the Pioneers claimed to be part of the mass trespass on Kinder Scout in 1932 but I was never quite convinced. In those days of localised activity, the reason for a working man from Tottenham to be in a remote part of Derbyshire seemed somewhat unclear and I have long been suspicious of those who claim to have participated in the great events in an anonymous, unrecorded fashion. Whether it was to trespass on Kinder Scout, fight the fascists at the Battle of Cable Street, walk with the Jarrow Hunger Marchers, or even just to stand outside Buckingham Palace on VE day in 1945, there usually seems to be an element of fantasy wish fulfilment involved. It reflects a desire to be validated through participating in the making of history.

In the context of the lost culture of the Young Communist League Walking Club, his claims do seem more credible. Rambling as it came to be known, although the name does imply a degree of aimless wandering, became a political cause in the 1930s. The conflicts between left-wing walkers and landowners became a symbol of the struggle of the dispossessed against unearned privilege.

It was about this time that I first heard the Weavers' version of the Woody Guthrie song *This Land is our Land* that became an anthem for ordinary people against those who 'bag and barn up the treasures of the earth from others'. In my imagination, we strode along proclaiming England to be our land although the reality is that thirty-five years later in the twenty first century there are still massive areas of the United Kingdom that are barred to its citizens.

Just as cycling had been the agency for spreading socialism in the decades before the First World War, so the vigorous outdoor life, as embodied by walking, was the equivalent for the inter-war years. Some of the Pioneers were the last remnants of that outdoor walking culture that gave physical focus to their political views. The craze was such that, when the Southern Railway advertised a South Down Moonlit walk in 1937, at most fifty customers were expected. They were overwhelmed when fourteen hundred keen hikers turned up.

It is difficult for us to over-emphasise the liberation that the walking craze offered, particularly to the young. We were regaled with stories of the great pedestrians with the implicit assumption that travelling by foot gave us a degree of moral superiority. Our examples were Samuel Taylor Coleridge walking the thirty-five mile round journey from Nether Stowey to Bristol to renew his library books, William and Dorothy Wordsworth walking the two hundred and fifty miles from Rydal Mount to London, and the redoubtable Captain Robert Barclay who walked one thousand miles in one thousand hours for a wager of one thousand guineas.

On a more modest scale, late nineteenth century inner-London suburbs such as Ladbroke Grove, Camden Town and even Mr Pooter's Holloway were built with the assumption that the residents would walk into the City and the West End. Walking is a natural, if rather slow, human condition that took us four million years to develop. We are now in the process of deliberately crippling ourselves.

*

It happened in the summer of 1966. I cannot be sure of the exact date but the Rolling Stones had just thrown the nation into a state of moral outrage by singing *Let's Spend the Night Together* although there was a cleaned-up version for the easily distressed – *Let's Spend Some Time Together*. We climbed the hill that is now home to Basildon Municipal golf course. Then it was a piece of rough farmland looking out in the direction of the Thames. It was late evening and, as we approached the ridge, the daylight was beginning to fade. Before us stretched the flatlands of the Thames estuary with the oil refineries at Coryton and Stanford-le-Hope glowing in the semi-darkness.

Staring through the gloaming, I could see the tiny marshland village of Fobbing no more than a mile away. Thirty years ago, the road to the village was empty, flanked by silent marshland. Today it is an American-style mixture of individual properties built in what I can only call 'the South Essex vernacular'. I doubt if Pevsner or for that matter Jonathan Meades would approve.

More than six hundred years previously, the Peasants Revolt began when the villagers refused to pay an unjust tax and cut off the heads of the King's tax collectors – a story I was told in hushed, reverent terms by one of the old Pioneers every time we ascended the hill.

Unjust taxes was a theme that most Pioneers warmed to. Not only did the people have no influence on how much was levied, just as crucially they had no say in how it was spent. Whether it was to develop the H-Bomb, to pay for the Polaris programme, to oppress the peoples under colonial rule or to subsidise a German royal family, ordinary people were never consulted. They felt a deep empathy with the Fobbing rebels and I came to the broad conclusion that a perfectly satisfactory way of getting back at the rich was to cut off their heads and walk around with them on poles.

From the vantage point of the early twenty-first century, it is just possible to imagine how the rebels felt. From their world of church privilege, King and court, hierarchy, brutality, illiteracy, feudal obligation and the denial of self, it is possible to see the peasant leaders – Jack Straw, Wat Tyler, John Wrawe and John Ball – starting to peer dimly into the future in search of a vision of the just society. Their demands were about realisation of the individual, an end to serfdom and bondage, the end of labour services, the dispossession of the church landowners, the division of land among the common people and the creation of a popular monarchy as opposed to a feudal monarchy.

At the heart of their demands was the idea that the peasants, their leaders, and many others in late medieval society were struggling towards the ideal that freedom is the natural condition into which we are born and that to deny that freedom is to deny both God's will and the human condition. Whether they were looking backwards to the Waldensians, forward to the Lollards, or sideways to the Albigenses, the Fobbing peasants were part of that broader Western European movement that was trying to create for themselves fuller and more realised lives out of the slow disintegration of a Catholic feudal society. They were daring to be different in the most profound meaning of the term.

In this sense the Pioneers were amongst their many lineal descendants and, on that warm summer evening, it was possible to understand how intelligent and profound individuals had, hundreds of years before, in the tiny village across the marshes, struck their blow for the freedom of all, even if it was expressed in the most brutal of terms.

Unfortunately Castlepoint, the local authority, have chosen to rename the area 'The Wat Tyler Country Park'. This of course does violence to the fact that Tyler was actually from Dartford in Kent and had little to do with the Essex rebels.

In the far distance we could see the twinkling lights on the Isles of Sheppey and Grain – remote parts of Kent despite their close proximity to London. There were seven of us and I was the only child. We sat and watched the darkness fall next to the old farmhouse that had long been abandoned but which held an overwhelming fascination for me. For years an old woman had lived alone there until the house was compulsorily purchased to make way for the golf course. She probably never did any harm to anybody but she reached a point in her life when she found herself standing in the way of progress and she could do nothing to fight against it. When you are twelve it is difficult to feel empathy for the plight of others particularly when old age is such an unimaginable distance away.

Even now, I am slightly embarrassed to admit why we were up on that hill overlooking the Thames estuary but it was the result of an incident that had occurred a few weeks earlier. I quote now, as far as my memory will permit, the description that was given to me. In particular, I was struck by the sincerity of Helen Knighton and her husband as they told me what had happened in hushed sombre tones.

"We were standing on the hill enjoying the cool night air. The estuary glowed with the yellow of the burning oil flares when my husband said, 'What's that over there?' I turned to the west. I find it difficult to describe what I saw and sometimes I think it was just a dream. About half a mile in front of us and at a height of no more than a few hundred feet a large airborne craft was moving slowly in the west to east direction of the Thames. It was wedge-shaped and glowed a dullish purple and green as it glided silently in the direction of the North Sea. Behind at a distance of perhaps two hundred feet trailed two intensely bright lights. It passed in font of us like a great dark cloud full of omens of what was to come. This incident occurred just a few days after the Warminster UFO sightings and perhaps the matter had been on our minds. No one uttered a word until Lilith Jones said, 'They have come for us.' There was no response.

"Lilith had a history of mental illness and killed herself about twelve years later. She was found in her kitchen with a plastic bag over her head.

"The craft disappeared into the darkness of the east and I imagined that I felt a buzzing around me of static electricity and I felt a dragging sensation on my skin. My face and hands were sore afterwards. It was hurriedly agreed we should say nothing of the incident for fear of ridicule. Despite this, I have told a number of people over the years but I do not think anyone has ever believed me.

"The Pioneers were deeply impressed by this strange, dark incident and, for the next few nights, Lilith and her husband climbed to the top of the hill at dusk in the hope of a repeat performance.

"I only lived about a quarter of a mile away from Lilith and sometimes at night I saw her scurrying alone in the direction of the hill. She passed me without a word, because she knew that I knew she was either going to or coming from the place where we had been up on the ridge. There she waited in the darkness.

"Although she never spoke again to me about the matter, it was clear what she was looking for. Her husband was suffering from Parkinson's disease and I think she had formed the idea in her mind that somehow her husband could be cured by bathing him in starlight. To this end, she believed it could be captured in a condensed form. It never happened and he died about five years later.

"After Lilith's suicide it became clear that her mind had turned completely. Amongst her notes and writings on the matter was a detailed diagram of a machine comprised of a series of complex mirrors and lenses that could capture starlight and then bathe the sufferer in what she presumed would be a purple light. I did not see that picture but I was told the figure being bathed in light was recognisably that of her husband and that the machine had been meticulously and beautifully drawn.

"For many years, I climbed the hill in the darkness and sat on the ridge watching the flares and lights from the oil refineries. I had no expectation or desire to see the craft again but, so deep was my contemplation of the matter, I found myself imagining the stately progress of the great illuminated ship along the Thames estuary. So intense had become my thoughts on the matter, that I was driven to conclude the entire incident was something that lay in the domain of my imagination. Somehow, I believe those others had collectively willed the ship, or rather its image, into existence."

These are, as best I can remember, the words Helen Knighton told me when I came home from university in 1974. I can offer no rational explanation for what they had seen, nor can I vouch for its accuracy.

For many years I stood on the same ridge at night and saw nothing. Shortly afterwards the land was turned into a golf course and, although it remained open grassland, it had somehow lost its magical quality.

A few years later it became my habit to take my post-hippy friends to sit on the ridge smoking Camel Cigarettes and gazing at the twinkling lights.

"Hey Magnus why do you always bring us up here?" they asked.

"Because," I would say, smiling to myself, "you never know what might happen."

It never did though.

A close encounter on the ridge of the fourteenth fairway never seemed a likely possibility. It has now become the haunt of the Pringle-wearing, golf-club-wielding classes and is all the worse for it.

As a result of this incident, I read extensively on the matter of UFO sightings. Although I have seen one above the skies of southern Hertfordshire I am convinced the dozen or so Pioneers who were up on the ridge that night suffered a collective neurosis in which they transferred their intense desire for a socialist utopia into an actual vision – the glowing embodiment of their desires for a better life.

*

Thirty years later, during the 1998 World Cup, I was accosted by an old man in Basildon Town Centre as I was walking past the Mother and Child statue. The fountain was not working. It never does; a symbol of municipal failure. The old man grabbed me by my arm and stared wordlessly at me in a wild-eyed way. A recipient of Care in the Community, I thought. He reminded me of the Ancient Mariner.

> By thy long grey beard and glittering eye,
> Now wherefore stopp'st thou me?

For one moment the old man spoke. "I have something to tell you," he said, and then he turned away.

It was not, after all, to be a raging tale of being becalmed in the middle of a great ocean. At the time I was mentally blank but later I reflected that he was perhaps one of the older Pioneers who had been on the hilltop that night. Or perhaps it all just lay in my fanciful imagination. For a moment though, I was disturbed by him, my equilibrium was shaken.

> I fear thee ancient Mariner!
> I fear thy skinny hand.

I could not rid myself of the image of the old seafarer, the salty dog of the horse latitudes.

> I pass like night, from land to land;
> I have strange power of speech;
> That moment that his face I see,
> I know the man that must hear me:
> To him my tale I teach.

Could it be the old man? I asked myself. Could the sight have so crazed him that he was never right in the head until, thirty years later he recognised me and took my arm because he had something to say and then found there were no words.

I followed him for a few minutes curious to see if he took someone else's arm in order to tell his tale. He wandered up towards the market moving slowly through the crowd. I turned to look in a shop window for a moment and then he was gone ... as if he had never been there.

> He prayeth best, who loveth best

All things both great and small:
For the dear God who loveth us,
He made and loveth all.

My favourite local eccentric was Jones the Terrier Man. He owned a tyre depot out on Wash Road, on the fringes of the town. He lived on several acres of rough land in one of the old houses that had existed before the new town was built.

Jones was an enthusiastic dog breeder and it was his ambition to breed a new sort of terrier able to exist in the watery flat lands that are a feature of that part of Essex. The rivers Blackwater, Mersea and Crouch have created tongues of remote, inhospitable land jutting out into the North Sea that comprises mainly saltwater marsh and little brackish creeks. The marshes were alive with rats and coypu. A quick, hardy dog with terrier instincts and the ability to cope with wet conditions was needed to catch them in such desolate places.

The concrete yard at the back of Jones' house was covered with a dozen or so metal pens that contained the fruits of his labours. His basic stock was a Manchester Terrier, a smallish, smooth-coated black and tan ratting dog that he crossed with a Bedlington Terrier to produce what looked like a black and tan whippet with a linty rough coat. The trouble with Terrier Jones was that he did not have sufficient security to control the bitches when they were in heat. The result was that some of his breeding was random.

Having produced a Manchester/Bedlington cross, he now sought to give the dog both some substance and some wet-ground ability by crossing it with a Poodle /Staffordshire Bull-Terrier cross. The result was an odd-looking dog that was neither terrier nor waterdog and had no aptitude for either vocation. Jones now crossed this dog with a Welsh Terrier and whilst this produced a dog with terrier instincts it seemed to be no better than a Welsh or a Manchester in producing a dog for wet ground with some retrieving ability.

It was at this stage that I got to know him and he confessed that he had been at it for fifteen years and was not making any obvious progress. But he was not to be put off and once said to me, "Someday I'll get it right, you know. Some day you'll see the Essex Water Terrier."

The by-product was that many local families paid £2 to Mr Jones for a terrier-type dog of doubtful provenance.

For the Pioneers, the value of a dog was undeniable if it could be seen as part of a proletarian lifestyle. While lap dogs were frowned upon, a lurcher, a whippet, or an all-purpose ratting dog was an animal to be prized – a true proletarian terrier. I remember all this because, in my wanderings during the holidays, I used to cut across country to Wash Road with my copy of the *Observers Book of Dogs* and, as he was an affable old man, I quizzed him on his search for the Essex Terrier. I flicked through the pages and he pointed out the dogs to me.

"An Airedale?"

"No, too big."

"A whippet?"

"No, too thin."

"A beagle?"

"No, too noisy."

"A bull terrier?"

"No, too stupid."

And so we went through the book until he paused for a moment to rub his white stubbled chin and say, "Yes, that might do the trick, it might just work." At one point I suggested that he use a Lakeland Terrier because one had just won the 'best of show' at Crufts.

This will help the reader date this episode as 'Stingray of Derrybach' was the Lakeland Terrier who won the prize at Crufts in 1967.

"Don't want one of them fancy show dogs," Jones said. "I want a working dog for a working man."

All was in vain for he died shortly afterwards surrounded by thirty dogs in metal pens. Some were taken away, probably to be put down, but many escaped and became feral – part of the packs that wandered the estates beyond the reach of the local authority. Today in Basildon, so I have been told, there are many terrier-type dogs of doubtful origin that are undoubtedly descended from the dogs that Jones the terrier man bred in the mid-1960s.

*

There was one incident in my childhood that first alerted me to the unfairness of life, the potential helplessness of the individual, and the despotic nature of all governments. The former mainly rural nature of the area was reflected in the fact that a number of farms had been swallowed up by the new town. Their names are remembered in some of the street names such as Blue House, Fairhouse and Boytons. In the early days,

Basildon was still surrounded by farms but as the town grew so the demand for land increased. In 1959, Ford decided it wanted to build its main tractor plant next to the town in order to tap the pool of unskilled and semi-skilled low wage labour. The major hindrance was Jolly Farm which lay on the site Ford wanted to use.

The Jollys were an old Basildon family. The father, whose name I never knew, but I shall call him Septimus, claimed the Jollys had been on the land since Elizabethan times and held a copyhold title to the land in perpetuity.

I imagine they had probably been there since the Norman Conquest, poaching and thieving and scouring the land. I sat next to Peter Jolly in primary school.

With the connivance of the Development Corporation, Ford engineered the compulsory purchase of the farm. There was an instinctive sympathy for the Jollys amongst the Pioneers but there was also the feeling that they were standing in the way of progress.

"You can't hold up the future," my overweight pipe-smoking neighbour said in his smug self-satisfied way, safe and secure in his little council house.

Some of the Pioneer children were now leaving school at the age of fifteen and sixteen and the families knew the tractor plant would provide good employment opportunities with the prospects of an apprenticeship and becoming a skilled worker so sympathy for the underdog sat uneasily with the reality of jobs and houses. When the day came, it was the starkest illustration of how the state can steamroller the individual in the name of the ideal of the collective good. Those less charitable, like me, would say it was for the sole good of Ford Motor Company.

Nevertheless, the compulsory purchase went through and 28 days later the siege of Jolly farm began. We were kept at a distance on the pretext of safety and there may have been something in this as the farmhouse was bristling with shotguns. I suspect the real reason was that to allow too close a view of proceedings would allow us to see at first hand the terrible injustice that was being inflicted upon this ancient family.

A few times, I crept round to the other side of the farm with a pair of old Second World War field glasses to see what was happening. The police, with uncharacteristic efficiency, had thrown a coil of barbed wire across a field one hundred yards away from the farmhouse.

The Jollys put up a noble resistance. They had a large water butt, sacks of apples and crates of Spam and baked beans for sustenance but they were no match for the forces of the state. After more than three weeks they were led away to be re-housed in a council pullet cage on the other side of town. For their two-acre farm they were given only £2,200, probably no more than a fifth of its true market value.

For a family of sturdy yeoman descent who prided themselves on their independence, this was a humiliating end. To find themselves the unwilling recipients of the welfare state with the compensation of an unskilled job in the Ford tractor factory after having been the backbone of England, was unbearable. These people were the descendants of those who had drawn their longbows at Crecy and Agincourt.

Septimus Jolly died within two years of losing the farm. He was just past forty. I have no idea what happened to the rest of them. Reduced, I imagine, to being the supplicants of an over-mighty state. Effectively, the Ford Motor Company, the Development Corporation, the police and the judiciary murdered them and their way of life in the name of progress.

*

Throughout my childhood, Winston Churchill had been a slumbering somnolent figure of revered memory who towered over British politics. And then he died. I was exposed to two sharply conflicting points of view.

My headmaster, who had served in the Royal Navy during the war, told us from behind the lectern at school assembly that he was a great man who had served the nation at the moment of its greatest crisis.

My grandfather, a solid, committed Labour man, told me that he was the enemy of the working class and that he 'was not worth the dust on my shoes'.

I later learned they were talking about two different Churchills. My grandfather voted in every single election between 1906 and 1966 except that of 1918 when he was stuck in Alexandria at the end of the War and could not register to vote.

My grandfather and the Labour Party ran parallel lives. For him there had been no other sweetheart. Like most working class men of his generation, he resisted the siren voices of the dying Liberal Party. The Labour movement, with its close relations with the Transport and General Workers Union, its Co-op savings club and funeral plan, together with the Daily Herald newspaper, created the framework of his life based upon class solidarity and implacable hostility towards Conservatism. His hero was Ernest Bevin, the pugnacious head of the TGWU. It must have been a trying moment when Bevin joined the coalition government of the Second World War under the premiership of Churchill.

The Labour Party and my grandfather came to maturity together. He was married in 1918, the year Sidney Webb wrote the constitution that created the modern Labour Party.

Grandfather Frank's marriage vows may have come from the Book of Common Prayer but of equal significance to him were words of Clause 4: 'To secure for the workers by hand or by brain the full fruits of their industry and the most equitable distribution thereof that may be possible, upon the basis of the Common Ownership, the Means of Production, and the best obtainable system of popular administration and control of each industry and service'.

This commitment was his sort of socialism. Frank and the Labour Party conducted a lengthy courtship that culminated in the formation of the first Labour government of 1924. For him Churchill was the embodiment of undeserved aristocratic privilege – the Home Secretary responsible for the brutal violence against the Tonypandy strikers in 1909 and the hammer of the unions in the General Strike of 1926.

For all of my grandfather's hostility he still took me to the Cenotaph parade in 1962 on the promise that we would see the great man. He was not there. Perhaps it was the infirmity of his years or perhaps we had just missed him but the next time I heard his name was the announcement of his death. My father asked if I wanted to go and view the lying in state at Westminster Abbey but I preferred to play football with my friends.

*

It is curious how Tonypandy keeps cropping up. Tommy Farr, the old boxer who fought the great Joe Louis was from Tonypandy. When, a few years ago, I met Lord George Thomas of Tonypandy, the old Speaker of the House of Commons, I sensed he did not wish to be asked the usual questions about the squalid business of politics. Instead I asked him the obvious, indeed necessary, questions. Did he know Tommy Farr? Had he seen him fight? How good had he been? Was he robbed against Joe Louis? And how would he have stood up to the likes of Mike Tyson?

His answers were "Yes, many times."; "Outstandingly quick and strong."; "No, he lost on points." and "He would not have been quite big enough to match modern heavyweights like Tyson."

For a moment I wished I could have gone back thirty years to that little Plotlands house in Grove Avenue and told Old Joe what I had heard from someone who had been a good friend of Tommy Farr. I glowed when Lord George told me it was a pleasure to meet someone who knew his boxing. For the only time in my life I felt that here was someone who deserved his title as opposed to all those ne'er-do-wells, scrimshankers and charlatans who frequent the House of Lords.

For my headmaster, a man thirty years younger than my grandfather, there were no such memories. His view was one of pure and unadulterated worship of Churchill who had stood alone as a voice of sanity in the 1930s. When Britain was alone in 1940, he rallied the nation with his grand rhetoric.

For the Pioneers, the wartime Churchill was of their generation. Despite that fact that they had never voted for him, and that he represented a class, and an England, to which they were bitterly opposed, they still held him in deep reverence. When he died, it was as if a slice of their lives departed with him.

I came to the conclusion that it was possible for my headmaster and my grandfather to both be right and that Churchill could be many things to many people. The day of his funeral, we were given the day off school, I suppose with the intention that we watched the proceedings on television. With an appropriate lack of reverence, I went with a group of friends and, on a freezing February day, we played a football tournament on the Holy Cross Recreation Ground, despite the attempts of the groundsman to make us pay our respects. He claimed to have been at El Alamein but over the years I had become wary of the military claims of my elders. Most of them had been young men during the Second World War and felt the need to embellish their role.

He would tell us pathetic jokes about Italian wartime cowardice.

"What's the shortest book in the world?"

"I don't know."

"The Italian book of war heroes."

He would roar with laughter, despite probably having told the same joke a thousand times before.

"Why are all Italian soldiers issued with plimsolls?"

"I don't know."

"So they can run away."

I am sure that, if he had been there, he would have had respect for any man caught in that hellish battle. I suspect that organising the NAAFI dances at the army depot in Rhyll was probably the limit of his military experience. Running around on the playing field, we were completely oblivious to the funeral barge as it made its way down the Thames on that foggy day.

The following week the Rolling Stones went to number one in the charts. I was struck by the contrast between the old and the new, the frivolous and the solemn and, clichéd as it may sound, the sacred and the profane.

Churchill bridged an age. He was a minister when my grandfather voted in the 1906 election and he was Prime Minister nearly fifty years later when I was born. While my grandfather despised Churchill for his anti-socialist activities, Meredith Evans, one of the Pioneers despised him for his hostility to Gandhi and the cause of Indian independence. Just as the ruling class oppressed ordinary people so, by extension, did it oppress the peoples of other countries? Churchill was the bitter foe of Gandhi and I wondered, later in life, how he could have shown the foresight and wisdom to oppose Hitler and Nazism in the 1930s and yet be convinced that Britain could permanently deny independence to India.

Amongst a few of the more aware and internationalist Pioneers it was almost obligatory to support the likes of Kwame Nkrumah, Jomo Kenyatta and Julius Nyrerre in the belief that their struggle was our struggle. We were all the enemies of British upper-middle class and aristocratic privilege. As the Pioneers struggled to make a decent life for themselves against an unjust society through the principles of self-help, self-improvement and mutuality, so the putative leaders of the colonial peoples of the third world were struggling against their European overlords. Whether it was the British ruling class at home, or the British ruling class in the colonies, the mentality was the same – the oppression of subject peoples. Anti-colonialism was still a live issue in the 1960s.

We should never underestimate the influence of family and background. This point was brought home to me when I was hanging out with a group of rough lads who, with good reason, met with my mother's disapproval.

One evening we were loitering next to the Plough and Tractor pub smoking thin, spindly Players Number 10 cigarettes. My main interest was trying to get back some money I had lent to Tony. He was not interested and, when I pressed the matter, his response was, "Do you want to make something of it?"

Almost the moment he said it, there was a tremendous shattering noise of plate glass. Another boy, Terry (my old friend aka Animal), had thrown a brick through the window of a shoe repair and leather goods shop. Before I could react, he stepped inside the window and helped himself to some purses and a leather handbag. They ran away down the street laughing.

I walked away in the opposite direction and thought of the poor man who would find his shop wrecked and his livelihood damaged in the morning. He had done nothing to deserve such treatment. He may even have been a Pioneer, and he was almost certainly an honest working man trying to make a living. The offence was made worse by the fact that the man was a cobbler, the sturdiest of independent occupations.

I found myself troubled by my conscience for several weeks after the incident although it was inconceivable that I could have gone to the police about it. Was I some sort of teenage tearaway? Why did we have so little idea of right and wrong? Was I simply the product of what Marx called environment determining consciousness?

As youngsters, we did not make political distinctions. I played indiscriminately with all sorts of children. One boy called Tony sticks in my mind. He was not one of the Pioneer children but he was a playmate although I never really liked him because he was a bully and large for his age. In the early summer of 1960, he disappeared and was never seen again. I am afraid I gave his disappearance little thought at the time. There were continual police searches until finally there was a tacit acceptance that he would not be seen again.

The mystery was never solved to the satisfaction of the police although it has been to mine. About a mile from where we lived was a large area of woodland known as Rectory Wood where we sometimes went to play. A group of us would go deep into the woods, climb the trees and make a rope swing from the branches.

One day, a gang of about ten of us were playing when Tony arrived. He immediately announced that he was going to form a new gang and that he was to be the leader. He would also decide which of us could join. He also told us that, as members of his gang, we would be known by names that were the reverse of our Christian names, as we called them in those God-fearing days. Thus I was to be known as Sungam and my friends Geoff and Tim were to be Ffeog and Mit.

I quite liked the idea. I was to be Sungam the Mighty or Sungam the Brave or Sungam the Invincible. They all had a Norse Teutonic feel to them that I found attractive. Our new self-appointed leader now turned to a thin red-headed girl called Nimrod. After some hesitation and accompanying facial contortions he announced that she would be known as Dormin.

"But I don't want to be," Nimrod protested.

At this stage I just cannot tell if what happened was a dream or if it was reality. Because it happened more than forty years ago, it seems as if there is no real distinction between the two. Tony continued to tell us who was in the gang and who was not but we were no longer interested in him because, from deep in the woods, a buzzing sound caught our attention. The buzzing became a rumble that in turn became the sound of marching feet.

We stood rooted to the spot in a state of abject and pitiful terror. The bushes and undergrowth were waving and shaking and with a horrible, almost incomprehensible, speed a troop of the most terrible creatures emerged and marched straight towards Tony. I can only describe them as being from one of those middle-European fairy tales featuring a creature called a hobgoblin.

They were perhaps three and a half feet tall, thick set and powerful and wearing green smocks and leggings bound by criss-crossing lengths of tape. Their faces were quite inhuman but they did not resemble any sort of animal. They had red eyes and a pig's snout that concealed thin white delicate fangs.

Tony screamed but there was no point. Ignoring us completely, the hobgoblins hauled him above their heads and ran back through the forest while making a gleeful, buzzing, chanting sound that signified they had their victim. Tony shrieked and shouted in the most pitiful way. We heard his cries as he was carried deep into the forest until his screams trailed away into silence.

We said nothing of the incident to each other and went our separate ways home. For the first few months after the disappearance there was a great fuss as the police made their increasingly forlorn inquires. We maintained our silence except for Nimrod who went to the police station on her little pink fairy cycle with a doll in the front basket and told them that the trolls in the woods had taken Tony away. The Police chuckled and laughed and patted her on the head.

Many years later while walking my dog I came across an old gnarled tree that I had never seen before but which was still familiar. I knew instantly that Tony had been taken inside the tree and that, if I dug down between the roots, then I should find his bones. For a while I considered telling the police. I underwent a long crisis in which I did not really know whether I had dreamt the incident. For twenty years, I told myself over and over again that it was a dream.

Then it went away and I thought very little about it until a few months ago when I dreamed of the incident once again and heard Tony's screams trailing away through the forest. It had such an effect on me that I visited the National Newspaper Library at Colindale and spent a day going through the microfiche newspapers looking for some reference. I could not find any copies of the local paper but I will return at some stage because I feel I should take the police to the tree.

I know the incident must have been a particularly intense dream but I have never been able to convince myself beyond doubt of this fact. At the time of the incident, I was just on that cusp between the fantasy world of early childhood and the dawning of life's realities. I have told myself many times that what I experienced was a powerful nightmare but somehow, over the past forty or so years, I have convinced myself it was real. The problem is that I cannot quite banish the belief that I saw hobgoblins in the woods and that they carried Tony away. There are limits to the powers of rational explanation.

The woods have now gone. In their place is a large Brookside-style housing estate.

Chapter 19: My Part in the Collapse of Socialism

Comrades; we must abolish the cult of the individual once and for all…..
Nikita Khrushchev; General Secretary of the Communist Party of the Soviet Union 1953-64.

Margaret Thatcher liked to claim that she was responsible for the end of socialism in Britain and the collapse of communism abroad. This may be an oversimplification of history but I would like to lay claim to having had a minor role in the process myself.

It is axiomatic to the principles of political science that all forms of government are a trade-off between individual liberty and personal security. An old fashioned liberal will say, "Give me a little of your liberty and I will provide with a modest degree of security." A socialist will say, "Give me a lot of your liberty and I will provide you with enough security to compensate for your loss. In fact, you will experience a new form of liberty that security brings with it."

The purpose of government, therefore, is trying to strike an acceptable balance between liberty and security. The problem for socialism, particularly in its Marxist forms, is that it has tended to get the balance wrong by taking a very large amount of liberty while only providing modest security.

Take, for example, the nominally-communist China of 2004. Liberty in this socialist republic is allowed in only the most modest portions. It is therefore all the more puzzling to find that 79 per cent of the population are excluded from the state system of health care and are forced to rely upon a fee for commodity service that the majority of the population cannot afford. This partially explains the inability of the Chinese authorities to contain the spread of the SARS virus in 2002.

In contrast, Singapore, which is a decidedly non-socialist authoritarian state, has a system of socialised medicine that enabled it to effectively control the virus. This, however, sits uncomfortably with its addiction to flogging its citizens and the occasional foreigner for matters as trivial as traffic offences and visa overstays. Each week on Tuesdays and Fridays it inflicts this punishment on about seventy of its male residents. For good measure, it also has the unpleasant distinction of executing nearly three times as many citizens per head of population than any other country. Yet Singapore regards itself as part of the free world.

The contract between the individual and state is tilted decidedly in favour of the state although the compensation offered to the average Singaporean is a degree of security that, with the exception of Japan, the rest of Asia can only envy.

Our major problem is actually defining what socialism is. Is it as simple as being a form of collectivism in which the independent decisions of the individual are replaced by the collective decisions of the state? Does a government-directed collectivist approach to social problems simply merit the title socialism? Is it enough to assume the increasingly ubiquitous New Labour position that, while they may not be a socialist party (sigh of relief from Millbank Tower), they promote socialist values? This is a deft and interesting sleight of hand but it is very unsatisfying.

So what has socialism given us? Most importantly it has made common currency of the idea that everyone has a right to a decent and fulfilled life in which their talents are being realised. In contrast, the more individualist liberalism has imbued us with the progressive realisation of a free, equal and secular society and has given shape to the basic institutions of modern civilisation that we take for granted – the nation state, the free market economy, and the principle of representative democratic government. In varying degrees all western political parties now accept these ideas.

When socialism has adapted to these principles it has been relatively successful. Its great failures have come when it has rejected, as inappropriate and tiresome, the notion of the liberty of the individual. The smaller failures of socialism have mainly been a result of ignoring some of the more pressing realities of a free market economy.

Take, for example, the demise of the old Triumph Motorcycle company in the mid-1970s under pressure from a more technologically-advanced Japanese motorcycle industry. With Tony Benn as Secretary of State for Trade and Industry, substantial amounts of taxpayers money were used to turn this into the Meriden Workers Co-operative producing the (frankly redundant) 750cc Bonneville.

Reading the 1976 editions of the magazine *Workers and Industry* it sounds like a Stakhanovite feel-good session courtesy of Tass: 'All the cynics and the quacks who foresaw a speedy collapse of the Meriden Motorcycle Co-operative have been reduced to an embarrassed silence.'

I wanted Meriden to work but I did not want to buy a Bonneville. Instead, I bought a Honda CB750 because, although slightly heavier, it was a better bike in every way. There was no room for sentimentality. The foreign competition was too strong and the 'cynics and quacks' were proved right. Twelve million pounds of taxpayers' money disappeared and the free market had its way. Only in a Soviet-style command economy offering one make of motorcycle, could Meriden have survived.

This is the position that the Ural Dnepr enjoyed in the USSR for decades before the collapse of communism, insulated against anything as unreasonable as customer demand or the possibility of choosing another motorcycle.

Triumph did not die because of a capitalist conspiracy. It died because it was producing a product that not enough people were prepared to buy. Happily, the Triumph name lives on at Hinckley, twenty miles to the east of Meriden. In 1983, John Bloor, a wealthy property developer with no history in the motorcycle industry, bought the Triumph name, invested £76 million and is now producing, courtesy of a sensible and restrained capitalist enterprise, some of the best motorcycles ever made.

*

Socialism has given us the National Health Service, a great blessing despite its many problems. It has helped to create a consensus that the welfare state, for all its deficiencies, is necessary and beneficial. It has been the midwife to the idea of a national minimum wage that all citizens are entitled to receive and that it is unacceptable for some to be excluded from society.

It has also given to the world the square steering wheel of the Austin Allegro, a social security system that consumes more than forty per cent of all government expenditure and a forty per cent rate of income tax for those who are on slightly more than average income. Most worryingly, it has given us a vast and apparently irreducible number of civil servants, equal opportunities managers and general apparatchiks of an over-centralised state whose jobs have been created on the assumption that our lives were intolerable before their appointment.

For instance, in education in schools we now have a situation where the inspectors (Her Majesty's Inspectorate) inspect the Inspectors (OFSTED) who inspect the inspectors (those who are employed by the local authority) who inspect the school's resident inspector (the headteacher). The Tsar of all the Russias would have been proud of such a system.

Unfortunately, socialism always encourages an indiscriminate and excessive use of state power. It has given us China's devastating one child policy complete with rampant female infanticide, gender selective abortions, and a mass of young Chinese men who have little prospect of finding a partner in life. They were murdered or aborted by the state a quarter of a century ago.

To the west, China's semi-Asiatic cousin, Russia, has visited upon its citizens some of the worst atrocities of the twentieth century in the name of socialism. The list is so appalling as to form a litany of the capacity of mankind for cruelty.

1918 saw the Red Terror launched by Lenin against those who disapproved of Bolshevik Communism. This was followed by Stalin's liquidation of the kulaks, the slightly more prosperous peasant farmers, for being unsocialistic. At least six million lives were lost. Simultaneously, in 1932-33, Stalin engineered a man-made famine that killed twelve million people at a time when Russia was exporting food abroad to pay for western machinery.

The grim irony was that it was in the Ukraine – 'the bread basket of the Soviet Union' – that the casualties were the highest. The west then found itself mesmerised by the show trials of the mid-1930s, driven on by Stalin's ruthless megalomania and conducted in the name of furthering socialist purity. A similar list of horrors could be recounted for China during the later part of Mao Zedong's rule.

The surprising fact is that it took so many people so long to realise that Marxist totalitarian socialism was not the key to mankind's future. As late as 1950, a key Cold War text, *The God That Failed*, was published against the background of the Soviet takeover of Eastern Europe and the now widespread knowledge of the mass murder of ordinary Russians in the gulags of the East. Here a disparate group of western intellectuals, including Andre Gide, Stephen Spender and Arthur Koestler, jettisoned their long held beliefs in the expectation of applause for their moral honesty.

Why wait so long when it was obvious to all in the West, from at the latest the early 1930s, that appalling cruelties were being visited upon the population of the world's only communist state? For many western intellectual communist sympathisers, it was not until the Soviet invasion of Hungary in 1956 that the true nature of communism, Soviet-style, became apparent. The reality was that the global left was in deep crisis the moment Stalin came to power but, to a generation of European leftist intellectuals, this was not apparent.

The experiences of the following twenty-five years were used by the enemies of socialism to discredit the whole left agenda despite the fact that some of the most telling critiques of what was happening in the Communist world came from within the left. There are some, mainly Marxists, who believe the Soviet Bloc was artfully ensnared and lured to its destruction by a deliberately ruinous, western-engineered arms race. This is to underestimate the vanity, the myopia and the sheer capacity for self-delusion of the world's communist leaders in the post-war decades.

In the 1960s, socialism was given new momentum under the banner of what was broadly called the New Left. It rejected both Soviet-style state socialism and also the increasingly deradicalised western social democracy embodied by the British Labour Party. Instead, the New Left drew from anarchism and the idea of personal autonomy; existentialism with its notion that individuals should not be bound by the rules of society and a brand of humanistic Marxism that recognised the dehumanising nature of capitalism. It was central to the New Left that it rejected conventional society.

This reflected disillusionment with a 'conservative' working class as the agent of revolution and a commitment to self-realisation that fuelled the social upheavals of the 1960s and early 70s. Faced with conventional pipe-smoking Labour politicians, trade union officials clutching copies of the union rule book, and the Stalinist residue in the western European communist parties, it was always unlikely that the ideas of the New Left were going to have any influence beyond a small, radicalised, youthful and educated minority.

The impulse that was given to socialism under the cloak of the New Left ideology of the 1960s became too diverse for consistent leftist ideas to be sustained. Increasingly, the political-economic core of socialism became diverted into lifestyle issues that, via their radicalism, have acquired a socialist tinge. The sort of people who sixty or seventy years ago would have driven mainstream socialism forward now find themselves drawn to issues such as black activism, gay rights, environmentalism and feminism.

The reality is that for individuals of a socialist disposition there is little choice of where to go. They can join the Labour Party and be profoundly dissatisfied or they might choose to join the Socialist Workers Party and stand outside W.H. Smith on the High Street selling the *Socialist Worker* and be asked questions like "Are you one of those socialist shirkers?"

Alternatively you can just ask yourself 'What's the point?' and go to play golf.

The difference between the failings of socialism in Britain and the human disasters visited upon the USSR and China is the existence of the principles of democracy and representative government. Whatever we may think of the defects of our political system, it contains sufficient restraints (just about) that when socialism fails the consequence is little greater than being forced to deal with an inefficient state-owned industry as opposed to embarking upon mass genocide.

Yet history continues to repeat itself in all sorts of strange and perverse ways. The Communists vigorously contested the Russian elections of 2003. Among their candidates were at least thirty individuals who are hugely wealthy 'millionaires for Marx' representing a political party that now claims to be 'business friendly'. One of their leading spokesmen, Alexei Kondaurov, explained that the Communists are now for 'more social justice ... based on good economics'. Sounds like New Labour to me.

Sadly, for the Russian Communist Party, the people were not convinced the leopard had changed its spots and with just 12 per cent of the vote they secured a miserable 53 seats in the Duma. The party leader, Gennady Zyuganov, condemned the election as a fraudulent and shameful farce inspired by the undemocratic forces that Mr Putin had at his command. He then denounced the United Russia Party as wanting a 'police state'.

Both claims are quite breathtaking. I am reminded of the reaction of Mr Zyuganov's predecessor, Vladimir Lenin, when he lost the 1918 elections for the Constituent Assembly. With his feet upon the table and cleaning his fingernails with a knife, Lenin ordered the Red Guard to clear the Assembly building at gunpoint and had the doors secured with a padlock and chain. It was more than eighty years before Russia had another democratic election.

So is it entirely clear that socialism has failed? It depends, of course, on what we mean by socialism. The Soviet-style planned economies have been an unqualified disaster. The Peoples' Republic of China is no more than a hollow pretence of a socialist state. Western European social democracy has, through the process of moderating and taming capitalism, assisted in the process of delivering ever-increasing living standards to us. Yet we have not achieved the transformation that the early socialists dreamed of. We do not live in that milk and honey utopia the likes of William Morris and Robert Blatchford believed to be within our reach.

Instead we live in a social democracy in which gun crime and drug use are soaring; we have to build new prisons because the old ones are full; child poverty stalks the land; divorce rates spiral; the rich are becoming very rich and old people die alone in unheated houses.

Life for the masses, as they throng to their local Ikea or Costco warehouse, is tolerable. We do, however, enjoy a material plenty that has been beyond the grasp of all previous generations. For many people this is enough and for others it is not. Most of us do not wander up the aisles of Asda pondering the nature of the just society. I have to confess that sometimes I do. I accept capitalism as the least flawed of a number of political systems but, for it to work, we have to assume a modicum of human generosity otherwise its 'every man for himself' ethos will lead to our destruction.

Thus our present system works on the notion of greed moderated with good sense, hard work rewarded, and a general overall benevolence to the rest of mankind. Provided that a sufficient number of people are able to muster a sufficient amount of benevolence then the system will limp on in a generally tolerable way although those who are least advantaged by the system will find it least tolerable. My concern is that we are increasingly unable to summon sufficient generosity of spirit that it can be made to work for the benefit of all.

For those who are on the post-Marxist left, as opposed to individuals like me who just have a gadfly interest, these are depressing times. There is a feeling on the left that they have won the argument about the nature of the world, exploitation and the destructive nature of capitalism but that they have lost the war. Capitalism in the past thirty years has proved to be very strong and very seductive although it does little to address the great problems that face the world. The seventy per cent of the world's population who live below the poverty line do not benefit from such a system yet it dangles in front of them the prospect of riches. It acts like a global version of the National Lottery.

Governments and peoples in the developing world wait breathlessly to see if the application of capitalist principles and globalisation will bring them the big lottery prize. Maybe it will, maybe it won't, it is impossible to predict.

In many ways, a more rational choice would be to support some form of democratic socialist organisation that is committed to social justice and greater economic equality rather than simply becoming a sweat shop adjunct of the west. To witness the queues of people waiting to buy their lottery tickets at my local W.H. Smith on a Saturday, is to be reminded that rational behaviour is at a low premium when the prospect of instant wealth floats into view.

In no sense is socialism bankrupt of ideas. There has been plenty of fresh thinking taking place on the left by individuals such as John Rawls and John Roemer particularly concerning the issues of personal liberty and the role of the free market in a socialist economy. The problem is that nobody is listening.

I had an experience in the late 1970s that convinced me socialism lives on in our hearts. We have a deep unarticulated desire to live in a state of socialist harmony but, when we are confronted with the practical reality, we recoil away from it. In 1976 I was offered the chance to live rent-free in a rather grand mansion flat just off the Finchley Road, North London in the outer environs of very fashionable and expensive Hampstead. Twenty-five years ago, most of these flats were inhabited by elegant elderly women clutching small dogs. They reeked of decaying and slightly distressed gentility.

At the time I was studying to be a solicitor at the College of Law and the offer seemed to solve some of my problems. I can date the event precisely because the leader of the Liberal Party, Jeremy Thorpe, had just resigned as party leader because of a homosexual affair with a former male model. Mr Thorpe had a rather grand house in Lancaster Gate close to the College of Law. Each day it was under media siege. This was the start of the process that drove him out of politics. The price of my rent-free existence was that I should undertake a little tidying and cleaning and more relevantly become the administrative secretary for what became known as the Amersham Commune.

Amersham, that prosperous piece of Buckinghamshire pleasantness, was the final staging post on life's journey for the Welsh mystical writer, Arthur Machen, who I seem to follow around. Ladbroke Grove, Camden Town, Stoke Newington, St John's Wood, and Whitby in North Yorkshire were all Machen halts where I have stumbled across traces of him.

My benefactor, Paul, was from a minor branch of a titled family and possessed significant private wealth and a disposition that attracted him to the idea of experimenting in alternative modes of living. Paul also had an interest in the ladies and, three or four times a week, would arrive back at the flat with different women, some of whom consented to stay the night. I should explain that in this grand flat were four bedrooms. Paul had the largest and I had the second largest. The smallest room was Paul's study while the third bedroom, that was always kept locked, was what he described to me as his 'Chamber of Love'.

The true nature of my benefactor became apparent one night when I was alone in the flat. The telephone rang. It was Paul and he was in the process of undertaking an assignation in love.

"Magnus," he said, "I would like you to get me a telephone number that is in an address book in the Chamber of Love. There is a spare key tied behind the gas meter."

I dutifully obeyed and came back to the phone clutching the black book. I then gave him the phone number of the poor unfortunate young woman whose company he was seeking.

"Magnus," he added ominously, "I would be most displeased if you were to read the contents of the book."

Needless to say I spent the next two hours perusing the small black bound volume secure in the knowledge that Paul was pursuing his carnal ambitions down in Belgravia. I even went to the local newsagent and had several pages photocopied. To summarise, he was a sex addict and a pervert and, quite possibly, a multiple schizophrenic. The Chamber of Love was a small room with black walls containing a large water bed, a considerable number of sex toys, an impressive collection of unwholesome magazines and some very unpleasant photographs of my landlord in what was referred to as an 'undraped' posture. More disturbingly, the black book revealed that Paul had multiple personas and that he spent his waking hours pursuing young women through sex contact magazines pretending to be everybody from the Duke of Buckingham to the local dustman.

I also had a copy of the key made. I was slightly alarmed to read that he lived in a luxury flat in fashionable Hampstead with his 'manservant, Magnus'. All of this cast an entirely new light on our relationship.

It is appropriate to add at this stage that, having considerable private wealth, Paul had purchased a large ex-children's home in Amersham, Buckinghamshire that he was in the process of refurbishing.

Now that I had the key to the Chamber of Love, I investigated its contents more thoroughly and discovered that Paul was advertising in Danish contact magazines for sex holidays in Britain where customers would have the opportunity to stay at both a luxurious London residence where they would be 'tended to by my manservant, Magnus' and at a country house in Buckinghamshire. I was less than keen on this arrangement.

It was Paul's habit to disappear for days, sometimes for weeks at a time without telling me where he was. One day I returned from the College of Law to find four Danish men outside the door of the flat. They explained that they had paid money to Paul for a holiday and were expecting a cooked breakfast in the morning. On the pretext of finding some documents, I slipped into the flat and attempted to close the door. The frustrated Danes were having none of it and attempted to barge their way in. Fortunately the narrowness of the corridor in the mansion flat meant that I could get plenty of purchase on the front door by placing my back against the wall, using my legs to force the door closed. I then phoned the police and complained that some intruders had got into the block.

With the failure of the sex tourism enterprise, largely due to my efforts, Paul decided he was going to set up a commune using the Buckinghamshire country house. Over the next few months, I placed a number of advertisements in a variety of left-wing journals, principally the New Statesmen, and prepared an information pack for prospective communards.

I was staggered at just how many people were interested. There were a small number of single professionals but most of the applicants were couples with young children who were tired of the claustrophobia of the nuclear family and the semi-detached lifestyle. The principle was simple. The house was to be divided into a number of private apartments but approximately half the house was to be devoted to communal living. There were to be no private televisions but there would be a television room, a snooker room, a library, a small indoor swimming pool and a large kitchen and dining facility.

The flats themselves would have no more than a kitchenette as there was a commitment to dining communally, a rota for the communal preparation of food (inevitably vegetarian although meat was to be allowed in the individual kitchenettes), a commitment to growing much of their own food in the extensive grounds, and an agreement to holding a weekly meeting to discuss communal issues.

At this stage there was much arcane discussion about the use of a talking stick. A series of meetings were held at the Hampstead flat that I observed and minuted. I was struck by both the innocence of those who wished to join and their sense of expectation that a new life awaited them. The first question asked was, "Will we be allowed to have tomato ketchup?" It was at that moment I began to have doubts about the whole enterprise.

Paul always kept the meetings very well lubricated with cheap Bulgarian red wine. I was particularly bemused by a woman who came along from the flat below ours. She was a Professor of English Literature at Westfield College on Kidderpore Avenue. Tall and rather narrow, she was a 22-carat bluestocking but not unattractive in a mannish sort of way.

I was still at the stage in my intellectual development where I had only just consented to reading female novelists so my attitude to Professor Jones was summed up in Dr Johnson's observation upon hearing that James Boswell had been to see a woman preacher. "Sir, a woman's preaching is like a dog's walking on its hind legs. It is not done well; but you are surprised to find it done at all."

Professor Jones had been laying into the wine. She suddenly blurted out to me, "How old do you think I am?" Now I was new to this game but experienced enough to err on the side of caution. She looked about fifty-five so I graciously suggested that she was in her mid-forties.

"I'm thirty-nine, actually," the drunken sot snapped at me before tottering off in the direction of the leader of the enterprise.

After a series of meetings, and the lengthy and expensive involvement of a firm of solicitors, agreements were drawn up and the process of converting the old children's home began in earnest. It was at this stage that my involvement began to lessen. I had a series of disagreements with

Paul that ended with me exercising my long-neglected boxing skills and being summarily dismissed from my position.

At the same time, Paul had become obsessed with a very attractive young woman called Lavinia who lived in the top floor flat. He had managed to persuade her to pose for a series of rather compromising photographs in the belief that he was a professional photographer of some renown. On the last occasion I went into the flat, I found Paul drunk and insensible on the floor of the living room. Occasionally, he roused himself to shout out that he loved Lavinia. The walls of the room were literally covered with several hundred photographs of the woman in question. When Paul lapsed into a complete stupor on the living room floor I gave him a firm tap in the head with my foot on my way out. As I left the building I noticed his Citroen 2CV car had been involved in an accident and must have been a write off. I assumed that this was not unconnected with his condition upstairs.

Several years later I heard the commune had collapsed. I suspect it was destroyed by the weight of expectation that was placed upon it. The idea that it was going to provide the panacea to the unhappiness in peoples' lives was a sure recipe for failure. What the communards did not realise was that they remained the same people they had always been, but in different circumstances. They brought to their Buckinghamshire Shangri-La all their obsessions and problems, and expected them to be solved. They were not. All the old neuroses and unhappiness were still there whether they were living in a semi in Pinner or at nirvana in the Buckinghamshire countryside.

There were arguments about just how socialistic the enterprise should be. Should people contribute on a flat rate irrespective of earnings or should it be proportionate according to income? How many communal meals could they miss before they were deemed to be unsocialistic? The commune comprised just over fifty people and, although in such a number of individuals there is a chance they would each find people they were genuinely simpatico with, there was also a good chance they would not. The ideal of a socialistic communal style of living is rather different from the reality. To find that someone has failed to replace the toilet roll, avoided their shift on the cleaning rota, insists on watching the vivisection programme on BBC2 when you want to watch Coronation Street, and snores so loudly that the walls may as well not exist is very disillusioning.

Here in microcosm were the reasons why socialism will always struggle to succeed. There lies within all of us a battlefield. On the one side is the desire to express ourselves as autonomous realised individuals; on the other is that instinctive self-preserving desire, nurtured and formed at the very birth of our existence as a species, for love, fraternity and an overwhelming sense of belonging.

> No man is an Island, entire of itself; every man is a piece of the Continent, a part of the main; any man's death diminishes me, because I am involved in mankind; And therefore never send for whom the bell tolls; it tolls for thee. *John Donne.*

The End

Acknowledgments

Although an author writes a book that is mostly based on his or her own thoughts, other people are inevitably involved in one way or another. I wish to acknowledge the help of all those people who contributed directly or indirectly to my book.

First and foremost, I must thank my wife, **Jenny**, for putting up with the trials of my attempt to write something original.

Julie Kitchener provided advice that I took very seriously. Her son **Sam**, provided me with thoughtful criticism and strong lager.

Annie Crombie showed me the way forward at an early stage.

Terry Lewis supported me during my low moments, my brother **Dave Granath** advised on car and motorcycle matters while my friends put up with the tedium of my obsession.

I must also acknowledge all the clever young people I have been fortunate enough to teach over the years.

Finally, my thanks to **Mike Carver** for rescuing the manuscript.

*

I am sure there are still many shortcomings in this book but they are entirely my own.

About the author

Magnus Granath (known to some as Andrew) lived in Basildon for twenty years. He now resides in North London in a large crumbling Victorian house with his wife, three children, and two Irish Terriers.

A teacher by profession, for the past fifteen years Magnus has been head of History and Politics at a large North London School.

His first book to be published makes full use of his historical and political academic knowledge but is written in such a way that it can be enjoyed by anybody who ever wonders what is wrong with the country we live in.

When he is not working, Magnus actively pursues his hobby – cycling. This may be the unpowered variety, electrically assisted or you may see him riding a powered version from his personal collection of motorcycles.

Contact: magnuscgranath@hotmail.com